Cultivating Success
in Uganda

EASTERN AFRICAN STUDIES

Cultivating Success in Uganda

Kigezi Farmers
& Colonial Policies

GRACE CARSWELL

Lecturer in Geography, Sussex University

The British Institute in Eastern Africa
in association with

James Currey
OXFORD

Fountain Publishers
KAMPALA

Ohio University Press
ATHENS, OH

The British Institute in Eastern Africa
10 Carlton House Terrace
London SW2Y 5AH
& P.O. Box 30710, 00100 GPO, Nairobi

in association with

James Currey Ltd   Fountain Publishers Ltd   Ohio University Press
73 Botley Road   P.O. Box 488   19 Circle Drive
Oxford, OX2 0BS   Kampala   The Ridges, Athens, Ohio 45701

1 2 3 4 5 11 10 09 08 07

British Library Cataloguing in Publication Data
Carswell, Grace
Cultivating success in Uganda : Kigezi farmers & colonial policies. - (Eastern
African studies)
1. Agriculture and state - Uganda - Kigezi
I. Title II. British Institute in Eastern Africa
338.1'86761

ISBN 978-1-84701-601-0   (James Currey Paper)
ISBN 978-1-84701-600-3   (James Currey Cloth)
ISBN 10 0-8214-1779-7   (Ohio University Press Cloth)
ISBN 13 978-0-8214-1779-9   (Ohio University Press Cloth)
ISBN 10 0-8214-1780-0   (Ohio University Press Paper)
ISBN 13 978-0-8214-1780-5   (Ohio University Press Paper)
ISBN 978-9970-02-682-1   (Fountain Publishers Ltd)

**Library of Congress Cataloging-in-Publication Data
is available on request**

Typeset in 10/11pt Baskerville
by the British Institute in Eastern Africa
Printed and bound in Malaysia

Contents

Contents

List of Maps, Photographs, Figures, Tables, Boxes & Case Studies

Maps

Photographs

List of Maps, Photographs, Figures, Tables, Boxes & Case Studies

Figures

Tables

Boxes

Case Studies

Abbreviations

AAO	Assistant Agricultural Officer
ADC	Assistant District Commissioner
ALG	African Local Government
AO	Agricultural Officer
CMS	Church Missionary Society
CO	Colonial Office
DAO	District Agricultural Officer
DC	District Commissioner
DfID	Department for International Development
DFO	District Forestry Officer
DMO	District Medical Officer
DoAAR	Department of Agriculture Annual Reports
DVO	District Veterinary Officer
EARC	East African Royal Commission
ENA	Entebbe National Archives
FO	Field Officer
KDA	Kigezi District Archives
KDA DC	Kigezi District Archives, District Commissioner's Office
KDA DoA	Kigezi District Archives, Department of Agriculture
KDAR	Kigezi District Annual Reports
LC	Local Council
LegCo	Legislative Council
LTPP	Land Tenure Pilot Project
NAC	Native Anglican Church
NRM	National Resistance Movement
PAO	Provincial Agricultural Officer
PC	Provincial Commissioner
PCWP	Provincial Commissioner, Western Province
PRO	Public Record Office, Kew, London
RC	Roman Catholic
RH	Rhodes House
SAO	Senior Agricultural Officer
TOL	Temporary Occupation Licence
WDD	Water Development Department
WP	Western Province
WPAR	Western Province Annual Reports

Glossary

In Rukiga 'ki' is pronounced 'chi' and for this reason references are frequently made in correspondence, memoranda and reports to the 'Chiga'. In addition, 'l' and 'r' are sometimes used interchangeably. Thus, in quotes the spelling is used as written, otherwise the most commonly used spelling (for example, Kalengyere) is used. Some of the words listed here are actually Luganda words, used for administrative purposes all over the country.

bakopi	peasants
baraza	public meeting
bazungu	Europeans or white people (plural)
boda boda	transport (bicycle or motorbike)
bukungu	sub-parish (plural)
bulo	millet
butongole	sub-parish (plural) (alterative for *bukungu*)
gombolola	sub-county
kuzetera	'seen as'
lukiko	government
luwalo	labour obligations to colonial state
matoke	plantain
miluka	parish (plural)
mitala	small area, used for survey purposes (plural)
mtama	sorghum
mtwale saza	chief of Bufumbira
mukungu	sub-parish (singular)
muluka	parish (singular)
mutala	small area, used for survey purposes (singular)
mutongole	sub-parish (singular) (alterative for *bukungu*)
muzungu	European or white person (singular)
okukwu encuro	working for food
okutendera	working in lieu of brideprice payment
okwatira	working for someone else
okwehereka	cultivating for self
omuryango	lineage
omwehereko	a man's own land (not allocated to his wives)
oruganda	clan
Plani ensya	New Plan
saza	county
waragi	local spirit
wimbi	millet

Acknowledgements

Many different people have helped in the writing of this book, in many different ways, and I am happy to have the chance to thank them here. I have received intellectual support, advice, practical assistance, research support and generous hospitality, and am indebted to many people. The time that friends and colleagues as well as complete strangers have given, and the enthusiasm and interest shown by them, has been enormously appreciated.

David Anderson, in particular, has provided constant encouragement and immense enthusiasm for my work at all stages. Bill Adams, Richard Black, Geert De Neve, James Fairhead, Alan Lester and Kim Lindblade have all provided intellectual support and critical comments at different times. The comments of the anonymous referee proved to be extremely valuable, and helped shape the book. Others who provided suggestions or comments on drafts include William Beinart, Henry Bernstein, Joanne Bosworth, James Katalikawe, Lynn Khadiagala, JoAnn McGregor, Michael Twaddle and Richard Vokes. Hazel Lintott and Evelyn Dodds, both in the Department of Geography at the University of Sussex, provided help with the production of maps and photographs. To all these people I am extremely grateful.

In the UK the staff at the PRO and Rhodes House were particularly helpful, as were the staff of the CMS offices in London and the librarian staff of the Special Collections at the University of Birmingham. Personal papers and photographs of John Purseglove were used with the kind permission of his widow Phyllis and son Jeremy. G.B. Masefield, J.C.D. Lawrance and Phyllis Purseglove were generous in giving me their time to talk about their experiences in Kabale.

In Uganda the staff of the History Department, Makerere University did all they could to assist me, and particular thanks are due to Godfrey Asiimwe. In Kampala I received advice and support from Dr Kamuhangire. The assistance of Mr Wani and Mr Ongom at the Entebbe National Archives and the librarian staff at Makerere Institute of Social Research is gratefully acknowledged. At the Kabale District Offices the Assistant District Executive Secretary, Mr Okiroro, and the District Agricultural Officer (DAO), Sunday Mutabazi, kindly allowed me access to the attics, storerooms, and long forgotten cupboards of the offices. With the kind assistance of David Kaberega, Bernard Rutandikire and especially Mr Katanyeta these revealed more than anyone could have hoped. Others in the Kabale District offices who have been most helpful include Mr Katehagwa, James Mwisigye,

Acknowledgements

Nyakairu Cox Apuuli, Mr Tukwasibwe and Paulo Sabiiti, while Sam Nkundiye of Kabale's Museum helped with the relocation of photographs. Johnson Turyamwijuka, Simon Waswa Barugabare and Andrew Kato Barugabare helped with the mammoth task of sorting the piles of chaotic files that made up the Kigezi District Archives. The assistance and support of the staff of CARE International, Kabale, and in particular Kim Lindblade and Jackson Mutebi is gratefully acknowledged.

Research assistance in the field was ably and enthusiastically provided by Alison Batuta, Andrew Kato Barugabare and Rhiannon Stephens, as well as by Annette Babigumba and Johnson Turyamwijuka. Others who took me up and down Kabale's hills, introducing me to their friends and families, include Bedan, Mr Baraba, Semu Kamuchana, and Hilda Tibaribaasa. It was through them that I met the elderly men and women of Kabale who provided so many valuable insights into this study, and to whom I am most grateful. Without them this book could not have been written.

In Kabirizi I received generous hospitality from Father Gitani Batanyenda, while Esau Kyokuzaarwa, Edward Baryayanga, Lydia Atuyambe, Nelson Bazarwa and Bruce Natakunda welcomed me into their lives. In Muyebe Mr and Mrs Otunga, Efuransi Batuta, Prossie Nsiima and Alison Batuta opened their doors to me, offering not just a home, but friendship as well. In Kampala Angello and Joan, and Kate and Adam, offered me kind hospitality and as much sun-dried fruit as I could eat. In Kabale Els, Kim, Vanessa, Karen and Phil were both generous hosts and good friends - they were always there to encourage me when that was needed, and to take my mind off the task when that was appropriate. I am extremely grateful to all these people for making my time in the field so enjoyable.

I have received generous financial support from a number of sources. Fieldwork was conducted with grants from the British Academy (1995), the Rockefeller Foundation (1996, with Kim Lindblade, J.K. Tumahairwe, C. Nkwiine and D. Bwamiki), the British Institute of Eastern Africa (2000), and the Leverhulme Foundation (2002). Permission to carry out the research was granted by the Uganda Council for Science and Technology. I would like to thank the British Institute of Eastern Africa, Nairobi, (particularly Justin Willis, Paul Lane, Shane Doyle and Andrew Burton) not just for their financial support, but also their practical assistance, and for 'lending' me Rhiannon Stevens, who proved to be an incredibly able and enthusiastic research assistant. She made the 2000 fieldtrip particularly enjoyable and productive.

Earlier versions of some of the material in Chapters 2, 3 and 6 have appeared in *Geographical Journal* (2002, 168(2): 130-40), *Journal of Agrarian Change* (2003, 3(4): 521-551) and W. Beinart and J. McGregor, *Social History and African Environments* (James Currey, Oxford, 2003). I thank Blackwell and James Currey for granting permission to use this material.

It was through my parents that my interest in Uganda was first generated. Their support has been continuous, and I am enormously grateful to them. But my largest debt is to Geert, who has helped in so many different ways, but mainly simply by being Geert. All mistakes remain, of course, my own.

In memory of Alice

One

Introduction

This book is about Kigezi, a district in south-western Uganda that has proved itself, in many ways, to be an area of exceptionality. In contrast to many other parts of the colonial world, this district failed to adopt cash crops; soil conservation practices were successfully adopted; and the area had a remarkably developed and individualised land market from the early colonial period. It is also an area that has successfully and sustainably maintained agricultural production in the face of increasing population pressure. This book is about the nature of colonial policy, the relation between policy and practice, and the endurance and evolution of agro-ecological practices ir the context of a changing economic and political order. It explores a numb᾿ of different colonial policies that were implemented with differing resu᾿ and the reactions of the people of Kigezi to these policies. It de᾿ transformations in agricultural practices during the twentieth century examines their changing policy and social context.

Development today is ever more focused on results. The Mille Development Goals provide a 'bold new set of targets': poverty re is now at the top of the development agenda, and throughout t᾿ there has been a growing emphasis on results.[1] Focusing on r outcomes[2] (rather than on inputs such as expenditure) raise about how these are evaluated and about 'success' in develop and practice.[3] What is success? What makes a successful project? How is success measured, and by whom? In this bc differing notions of 'success' – what it was to claim ᾿ implementation of policy in the colonial period, which in tu᾿ for contemporary development policy. While there is a ᶠ on policy processes,[4] and it is clear that policy intentior as policy outcomes, little attention has been paid to the 'success'. Mosse's book is a notable exception which r᾿ in the context of contemporary development. He ex᾿ between international development policy and pr᾿

1

on 'participatory approaches' that were prominent in the 1990s, and is concerned with *how* 'success' is socially produced or constructed. Mosse argues that different key actors in the development process may have limited control over events and practices, but they do have control over the *interpretation* of events.[5] In this book I examine how people responded to colonial policies, and how colonialists presented policies – as successes or failures – making the book an innovative discussion of the history of this 'packaging' of success. While the approach is historical, I engage with debates that are current in other disciplines. For example, debates in anthropology and development studies about the nature of 'success', modernisation and contemporary development policy; debates in history about colonial policy and practice; and debates in geography about the environment and natural resource management.

Colonialism, development and the environment

The idea of development as economic growth and 'modernisation' was largely unquestioned throughout the colonial period. Up to the Second World War this was to be achieved through *laissez-faire*, while in the post war period there was a move towards planned development, with the state being given an increased role. British colonial policy aimed to raise the living standards of people in the colonies, make the resources of the colonies available to the wider world, and Britain in particular, and to provide a market for British manufactured goods. The modernising project that was colonialism sought to transform tradition-bound, subsistence societies into modern market-based economies, involved in the cultivation and export of cash crops. Monetarisation, commercialisation, wage labour, the development of land markets, the provision of education and improved infrastructure were all a part of this process. The twin concerns (of social welfare and broader economic development, associated with Lugard's *Dual Mandate*)[6] set colonial governments on a particular development path. In practice this meant that Departments of Agriculture, for example, were seen as 'revenue raising' departments, which, by promoting cash crops, aimed to maximise the wealth of people and the revenues of the colonial governments.[7] The postwar period saw an increased desire to develop the colonies and an increased readiness to spend money and resources doing so. Much larger than previous commitments, the Colonial Development and Welfare Act of 1945 aimed to encourage British colonies to plan development as a whole, rather than piecemeal schemes. There was thus a move towards increasing intervention by the state, and long-term planning of development. This period also saw the 'second colonial occupation'[8] with an intensification of government activity throughout British Africa, and an expansion in the capacity of administrators to get involved in development. Into the 1950s the belief in a path of development through modernisation continued, with high levels of state involvement.

Thus throughout the British colonial period 'modernisation' served as a 'backdrop' to the agricultural policies that were to follow: cash cropping (and thus engaging in the market), more 'rational' systems of agriculture (technical, scientific, productive and sustainable), individualised land tenure and so on. Colonial aims were 'modern' systems of agriculture, that engaged with 'modern' markets (for crops, land, etc.) and these were contrasted with 'traditional' (read inefficient) systems of agriculture and tenure.

Kigezi, a district in Uganda, serves as a case study through which to examine colonial policy, and responses to that policy. Kigezi has experienced some very different trajectories from those that are often assumed in the colonial world. This introduction explains how some of these trajectories are usually conceived, and how the case of Kigezi proves to be an exception. These modernising policies did not, however, always succeed, and when policies did 'succeed' it may have been as much to do with how success was being defined, as anything else. Furthermore, traditional systems were not always inefficient: they sometimes already incorporated the very things that the policies aimed to introduce. I argue that both the agricultural system and the land tenure system were vibrant and evolving in particular ways.

Like other British colonies, Uganda was under pressure to be financially self-sufficient, and therefore the production of cash crops was encouraged.[9] From the early 1920s, having ruled out the promotion of a substantial planter economy, Uganda's colonial administration focused on increasing the acreage of cotton and coffee grown by Africans.[10] Across much of the colonial world cash crops were successfully introduced by colonial powers, and adopted by farmers. In contrast to many other colonial examples, the farmers of Kigezi failed to adopt cash crops. But I argue that what Kigezi farmers failed to do was to adopt *colonial* cash crops: they were in fact already producing cash crops – food crops – for sale on regional markets. The study also shows that what was important to colonialists was their failure to maintain control over the *marketing* of cash crops (illustrated by both the cases of tobacco and food crops which were largely outside the control of colonial marketing). The production of cash crops – i.e. crops for sale – did not simply 'fail', but rather failed according to the definitions set by colonialists. For Bakiga farmers there was no failure, and they continued to produce crops for sale on a vibrant, regional market.

Part of the 'modernisation' thinking that ran through colonial development policy was the perceived need to transform and 'modernise' African agriculture, with agricultural development focusing on the spread and growth of cash crop production. But there was more to colonial agricultural policy than this, and from the 1930s agricultural policies began to reflect heightened concerns about the environment, and these concerns gave rise to a range of policies and schemes, in which science and technology had a central role to play.

Concerns about the environment have a long history.[11] Grove has argued that the history of environmental concern 'has its origins in the non-European tropics ...largely in the context of the history of colonialism and European expansion'. He has explored the rise of environmental consciousness in the

3

island colonies of Britain and France from the eighteenth century, and the influence of missionaries and religion on the evolution of the environmental discourse in nineteenth-century southern Africa.[12] No single writer has been more influential in African environmental policy thinking than Malthus,[13] and increasing African populations heightened concerns about the environment in the early part of the twentieth century. Neo-Malthusian concerns about the effects of increasing population have re-emerged regularly in the colonial and post-colonial eras, with arguments being made that population growth rates are such that it will be impossible to maintain adequate food supplies, and environmental decline will inevitably result. In the early 1970s writers such as Ehrlich and Ehrlich re-ignited the familiar debates, and neo-Malthusianism is still present today in debates about environment and development.[14] More immediate triggers for heightened concerns about the environment in the colonial period include the 1930s American Dustbowl, and the effects of the Depression, particularly on settlers.[15] Concerns about sustainability (although the language of 'sustainability' was obviously not used at this time) were seen across colonial Africa and there are several studies of areas where such concerns played a major influence in the formulation of agricultural policy.[16]

Central to the policies that arose out of these concerns was a belief in the power of science and technology. In John Mackenzie's words, natural sciences were 'inextricably entwined' with imperialism, and science was central to ideas about colonial environmental management. The belief that science could 'unlock ... redemptive and regenerative forces on a vast scale' emerged from the scientific endeavour and evangelicalism of the nineteenth century.[17] As a writer in 1928 wrote, 'only western science was capable of unlocking minerals and agriculture, thereby transforming the stagnation of the most backward of continents.'[18] Reference to an international scientific community was used to 'legitimate' conservation, and this allowed the colonial state to use 'the righteous language of conservation.'[19] As Beinart has noted, 'the social darwinist attitudes in which science came to be embedded made it difficult for outsiders to accept that local practice was also a form of science – the result of extensive experimentation in specific environments.... technical wisdom and African practice tended to become separated [and] Africans were constructed as unscientific overexploiters of grazing, trees and of land.'[20]

The importance of science and scientists to colonial development was stressed in a number of colonial publications, such as Worthington's 1938 *Science in Africa* Report, while the aptly labelled 'second colonial occupation' stressed the importance of scientists to colonial government.[21] Colonial agricultural officers saw themselves, in Masefield's words, as 'missionaries of science bringing hope and prospects of progress to underprivileged peoples'.[22] The colonial state's belief in the superiority of Western knowledge, its 'tendency to take the technological high-ground' and the 'arrogance of rationalising science' had profound implications for colonial agricultural policy.[23] Plans for development through 'betterment', and technical solutions to environmental problems were conceived.[24] When choices were being made about which technologies to use, imported, western technologies, based on engineering (rather than indigenous methods or biological or agronomic methods) were always favoured. As Fiona Mackenzie has noted, this choice partly reflected the 'pervasive influence' of America's Department of Agriculture's Soil Conservation Service, a department that was created to deal with the Dust Bowl.[25] I argue that this 'technicalisation' of problems has contributed to their depoliticisation, as well as to the legitimation or justification of further interventions. Science played a central role in the 'articulation of colonial discourses,' and this central role of science in ideas about environmental management and development has continued to this day.[26]

But, of course, there were more fundamental reasons why colonial states argued that they should be intervening in African agriculture, and these were political. Such reasons were particularly strong in settler states, where they helped to justify the allocation of agricultural land to settler farmers. As Beinart has shown for southern Africa and Fiona Mackenzie for Kenya, the construction of a discourse about poor African agricultural methods was politically expedient, helping to legitimise state involvement in African agriculture.[27] In Ranger's words, the conservation ideology was 'convenient' and land evictions could be 'justified in terms of conservation rather than segregation'.[28] As Mackenzie has so eloquently stated, the 'discourse of environmentalism [was] useful ...for recasting the political quest of the racial division of land as a problem amenable to a technical solution'.[29] Top-down, technical solutions were offered, to a problem that was one of 'too many people, ignorant of scientific farming'.[30]

It was in settlers' interests to characterise peasant methods as both inefficient and destructive – for example, Grogan, a settler in Kenya, described them in 1933 as 'parasites on the land'. Others presenting evidence at the Kenya Land Commission 1932–34 spoke of the 'carelessness' of cultivation, and 'haphazard method' of planting crops.[31] In the 1930s and 1940s both settlers and officials in southern Africa commonly described African agricultural methods as 'careless and dangerous to the environment'. Thus laying 'blame' became an important element in the colonial debate about environmental regulation.[32] At the same time African knowledges were 'silenced', and external knowledges, methods and technologies were privileged. As Fiona Mackenzie has noted, 'an environmental discourse, which involved the introduction of universal solutions to the resolution of widely diverse problems, and silenced African knowledges, became part and parcel of a reconstruction of relations of power ... in colonial Africa.'[33]

The dismissal of African agricultural methods, the privileging of Western environmental knowledge, and the use of technological solutions legitimated colonial policies of land alienation in settler states. But non-settler states – such as Uganda – were also influenced by such thinking, and the particular debates that I explore here are those around agricultural practices and over-population. Schemes that arose out of concerns about the environment were put forward as the 'virtuous face of colonialism'; they were presented as 'development and improvement' aiming to intensify or 'improve' agricultural production, solve problems of overcrowding, drought, or food shortage.[34]

While this environmental discourse took hold, it would be a mistake to suggest that there were no 'counter voices'. While most settlers (as would be expected) and colonial officials regarded African agricultural methods as wasteful and environmentally degrading, there were some colonial officials who took a different view, and saw the benefits of African agricultural systems, what Beinart dubbed a 'significant sprinkling of sensitive scientists'.[35] Well-known examples of colonial officials adopting what Richards has called a 'counter-colonial ecology' include John Ford and William Allan.[36] But some lower-level administrators also took a 'counter' view. In Uganda, for example, McCombe, a DAO in the early 1940s, noted: 'There is often much in the indigenous methods of cultivation which it is a mistake to ignore and to assume that the actual tillage and planting methods are easily capable of improvement.'[37] In Kenya, Mackenzie observed that 'those with closer (i.e. more local) administrative experience tended to express great sympathy for local needs, both with respect to land claims and to local agricultural expertise, than those at higher levels of the bureaucracy.'[38] The recent work of Tilley also suggests that, particularly in the interwar years, some aspects of colonial science could be sensitive to local knowledge. Some colonial scientists, such as Worthington, advocated the wisdom of local approaches, recognising the need for sensitivity to African knowledge.[39]

Concerns about the soil justified intervention in African agriculture, and across colonial Africa (in both settler and non-settler states) soil conservation schemes or policies were implemented from the 1930s through to the 1950s. Responses to these schemes were largely, but not exclusively, negative and most studies that have explored African responses to the schemes have done so in the context of colonial resistance and the growth of nationalism.[40] Few studies examine the methods used by the colonial state to ensure their implementation, and even fewer investigate the fortunes of these policies in environmental, agricultural or technical terms.[41] In this book I consider the environmental discourse that was used to justify intervention in the district of Kigezi, the policies that arose out of this discourse, the process of implementation and the reception given to the policies by Kigezi's people.[42] Here again Kigezi was exceptional, as, in contrast to many other colonial examples, the colonial soil conservation policies were successfully adopted. Once more this was not a simple story of 'success': rather many of these policies were in fact adaptations of existing practices, and it suited colonial officials to present them as new, so that they could say they had been successfully implemented. Similarly, a resettlement scheme was 'successful', but this was partly related to existing migratory practices. I also argue, by drawing comparisons with similar conservation policies across Eastern Africa, that part of the reason that Kigezi's policies were 'presented' as successful was because they were successful in political or social terms: they did not lead to resistance or unrest.

One area of 'modernisation' that was central to development in the latter part of the colonial period was in relation to land tenure. The East African Royal Commission (EARC) of 1955 argued that efficient mixed farming was impossible under traditional systems of land tenure, and so there should be a move towards properly demarcated smallholdings, individualisation of land ownership, mobility in the transfer of land and encouragement of progressive farmers.[43] This represented a shift in colonial policy, as until the Second World War colonial officials had generally sought to maintain African societies as socially and economically undifferentiated. From the postwar period official policy began to favour 'progressive' Africans, seeing the need to encourage a 'select group' who were seen to make better use of opportunities offered, and who would act as catalysts for development. Increased differentiation was thus recognised as a possible outcome of policy, and in some areas of policy was to be positively encouraged. [44] The focus on the individualisation of tenure that the EARC brought about, and interest in the Evolutionary Theory of Land Tenure, continue to be influential amongst policy makers today. The ETLT argues that as land becomes more scarce, people demand greater tenure security: private property rights in land emerge and evolve towards greater individualisation and formalisation, and ultimately there is a 'pressing demand' for legally protected land titles.[45]

The EARC and attention to individualisation of land tenure led to a number of policies of land reform in Kigezi, which are explored in Chapter 5. Here I will show that Kigezi's land reform policies had a mixed reception. The Land Tenure Pilot Project that was implemented in the north of the district was a 'success' in that titles were indeed issued. But this was unsurprising, as the area selected was chosen because it would be easier to implement here. Furthermore, it was not a success in that few of the titles were taken up by people and actually used. The broader aim of promoting titles more generally also failed in Kigezi. This was in large part because Kigezi's land tenure system was already highly individualised. In the face of a changing socio-political system and population pressure it had evolved to allow for exchanges of land, and a vibrant land market already existed by the time that titles were introduced. This is not to suggest that social networks were not important – they were, especially for in-migrants to an area – and they were used in association with institutional arrangements through which people got access to land and other resources in return for, for example, labour.

The colonial policy of land consolidation failed completely, despite propaganda and all efforts to offer incentives. The study shows that this was because, while to the colonial mind consolidated plots might be more rational and modern, for Bakiga farmers scattered plots suited the agro-ecological environment. Some land was enclosed, but because it happened separately from consolidation it was viewed by colonial officials as a failure. Swamp reclamation occurred, in that swamps were reclaimed, but much of the reclaimed land was not distributed equitably to people living on the edge of the swamps. Here, policy changed during the time that it was being implemented, and there was a shift towards encouraging progressive farmers, which meant that giving 'economic' sized plots became official policy – so in this sense it was a success. All these land policies had unintended consequences, specifically around chiefly authority over land.

Beinart has noted a move in recent Africanist writings 'away from narratives of … victimhood', while recent literature has drawn attention to agency of Africans in relation to their environment. These approaches, showing the positive roles that Africans can and do play in environmental management, and inverting colonial stereotypes which saw Africans as environmentally destructive have begun, in Beinart's words, to assume the status of a 'new paradigm'.[46] For example, the ground-breaking study by Tiffen *et al.* of Machakos, Kenya, presents a positive picture of African agricultural systems, and African agency.[47] Here colonial officials tried to implement soil conservation policies from the 1930s, but these had to be abandoned due to strong opposition by the local population. What is so significant about this case study is that in the post-colonial era the productivity of the area has increased as people have decided to invest (with both labour and capital) in their agriculture, doing many of the things that they have refused to do when instructed to in the colonial era. This case also makes an anti-Malthusian argument, that increased population density actually induces positive changes which offset the decrease in the land available.[48] The Machakos case is one of a number of studies that suggest that positive land use changes can be, and have been, associated with increasing population densities, and that global correlations between population growth and environmental degradation cannot be extended to a local level.[49] The case of Kigezi shows that, against all widely held beliefs, the people of Kigezi have successfully and sustainably managed their agricultural system. It is argued that they have managed to maintain production and simultaneously avoid serious environmental degradation, so that degradation has not reached the proportions envisaged.

Similarly, the much-cited work by Fairhead and Leach in West Africa has shown that forest cover increased in the savannah region as a direct result of population growth. Rather than being blamed for destroying their forests, West African farmers should be credited for 'enriching or stably managing their landscapes', having 'experienced, and being partially responsible for, increased woody cover over their lifetimes'.[50] Beinart has observed that this study has 'rapidly achieved paradigmatic status in the literature', while Carruthers has declared that this work has 'transformed African environmental history'.[51] Other work – such as the studies in *The Lie of the Land* – similarly challenge environmental orthodoxies, as well as showing how contemporary development practice may be founded on these 'received wisdoms'. While the environmental narrative of the colonial period justified colonial state intervention and centralised planning, it also 'laid the ground for much more recent action'.[52] These 'received wisdoms' have continued to have the effect of promoting external intervention in the control and use of natural resources, with negative consequences for local people. Work such as this has not, however, been without its critiques. Bernstein and Woodhouse criticise the Leach and Mearns' collection for the absence of analysis of processes of commoditisation and social differentiation. Similarly, Murton's research shows how the Tiffen *et al.* study of Machakos paid insufficient attention to processes of increased differentiation.[53] Engaging with these debates, I show how in Kigezi agricultural changes that occurred were not happening homogenously. Rather, different people followed different environmental practices, for different reasons. Some of the changes have been associated with increased differentiation, and there has also been a shift to cash-based exchanges, from earlier non-cash-based institutional arrangements. This shift, which could simply be viewed as increased diversification, means that there have been changes to the ways that people can access resources such as land and labour. Some of these changes, I argue, have had positive effects on broader aspects of livelihoods, such as well-being and self-esteem.

This study of Kigezi in the twentieth century sheds light on the way that 'success' and 'failure' have been evaluated in the colonial period, something that continues to be relevant for contemporary development policy. In Mosse's analysis, project success was not just a matter of measurement of achievement and empirical evidence – of yield increases, trees planted, etc. – success was a matter of definition, a question of meaning, of sustaining a particular interpretation of events through the categorisations and causal connections established by the policy model. And while this model was not empirically falsifiable, it was replaceable. And, indeed, when UK aid policy changed in 1997, so the project became, by definition, a failure.[54]

The evidence from Kigezi shows that success can be measured in many different ways, which are worth highlighting briefly. First there is the achievement of the planned outcomes in the physical sense. Thus, for example, a soil conservation project may define success in terms of the mileage of terraces constructed, resettlement schemes measured the number of people resettled, while land reform projects measured the numbers of land titles adjudicated. Then there is success in socio-political terms: that is, whether or not people accepted the project and whether there was acquiescence or at least an absence of resistance to the schemes, such that the scheme was considered to be a success. Another measure of success might be successful expenditure – that is, whether project funds had been successfully disbursed. Individual colonial administrators might measure success in terms of what a project did for their own personal careers: did the project help them take the next step up their career ladder? None of these measures has anything to say about the technical success of the measures – that is, whether, for example, the terraces that were built actually prevented soil erosion. Nor, more broadly, do they say anything about whether their construction improved the livelihoods of the people that they were supposed to benefit. Furthermore, while the intended outcomes of a development projects may be assessed and considered to be a success or failure, rarely are the unintended outcomes evaluated.[55] To locate these debates in the particular setting of Kigezi, Uganda, I will now introduce the district.

Introduction to the district

Kigezi is a densely populated highland area of intensive agricultural production, surrounded by thinly populated lowlands. Here land, rather than labour, is a limiting factor of production and land shortage has been perceived to be a problem for many years. This section will introduce the district, providing some agro-ecological, demographic and socio-economic information. Kigezi is located in south-western Uganda bordering Rwanda and Congo (see Map 1.1) and covers an area of approximately 2,000 square miles. The district of Kigezi no longer exists formally, having been divided in 1974, and further subdivided subsequently, [56] but the south-western part of Uganda is still commonly referred to as Kigezi.

Much of the focus of this book is on present-day Kabale district, around Kabale town, in the south-eastern part of Kigezi. It lies at an altitude of between 1500m and 2759m above sea level. Temperatures range between 9°C and 23°C. The mean annual rainfall is 1000mm, it is bimodal with peaks in March–April and October–November, and precipitation is usually gentle and evenly distributed. See Figures 1.1 and 1.2.

The district is made up of undulating hills with steep slopes. About nine per cent (183 sq miles) of the district's area was once occupied by papyrus swamps, although most have been drained during the last 50 years and are now cultivated or used for pasture. The soils of Kigezi are derived from the Karagwe-Ankolean series and are largely deep red loam soils. [57]

Kigezi has experienced an extremely long history of human settlement, with palaeoecological research providing evidence of 'prolonged human occupation and in particular agriculture' over the past 2500 years. [58] Southern Kigezi is particularly densely populated, as a result of both in-migration over a sustained period and high natural increase. See Figure 1.3.

While statistics produced by early censuses must be treated with some caution, being extrapolations of very small surveys, Figure 1.3 does suggest substantial increases in population. In addition to natural increase, there were also high rates of in-migration from Rwanda. Rwanda's famine of 1928–9 (*Rwakayihura*) caused some 100,000 people (or nearly seven per cent of Rwanda's population) to move to Uganda and the Belgian Congo, while the 1943 famine (*Ruzagujura*) also caused many to move away. [59] Population density in the area is high, and was calculated at 290 persons/km² in 2002 for Kabale district. As a result of the dense population, small acreages of land are available for farming and the system of inheritance has resulted in fragmentation of land holdings and widely scattered plots. [60]

Kabale district is populated largely by Bakiga, a non-stratified society. This is in contrast to surrounding areas (such as Kisoro and Rwanda to the south and west, and Rukungiri and Ankole to the east) which are populated by societies in which there is a distinction between cattle-keepers (Tutsi and

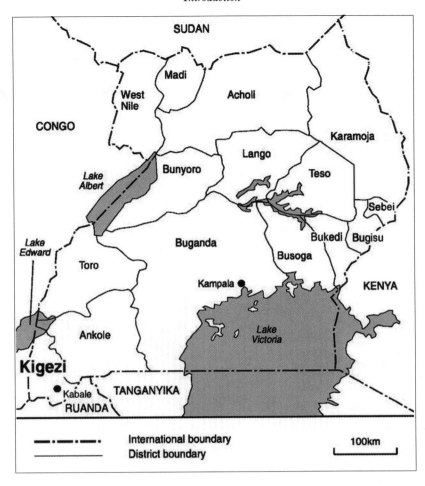

Map 1.1 *Uganda, showing colonial district boundaries and location of Kigezi District*

Figure 1.1 *Monthly average rainfall, 1942–2001*[61]

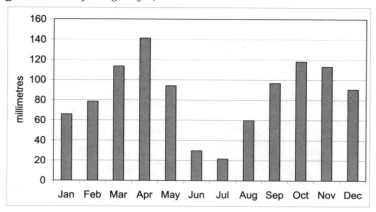

Figure 1.2 *Total rainfall, 1942–2001*

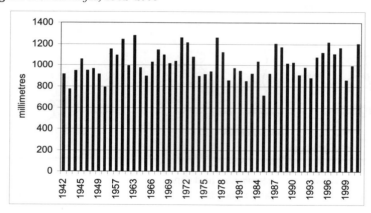

Bahima respectively) and agriculturalists (Hutu and Bairu) (see Map 1.1). The anthropologist, May Edel, who lived in Kigezi in the early 1930s, described Bakiga society as patrilineal, polysegmentary with exogamous clans (*oruganda*), further subdivided into lineages (*omuryango*) – the members of a lineage being descended from a common ancestor. But, as Bosworth, an anthropologist writing more recently, has noted, 'given the dynamic nature of Kiga ethnicity and residence during the nineteenth century, it is unlikely that any "snapshot" portrait could effectively capture the totality of Kigezi society during the pre-colonial period.'[62] The clan should not, therefore, be seen as a static descent group, as individuals could be incorporated into the clan or lineage through marriage, patronage and blood brotherhood. For each of these the movement of people was important, and migration has played a significant role socially, economically and politically in the history of this area.

12

Figure 1.3 *Population statistics for Kigezi District*[63]

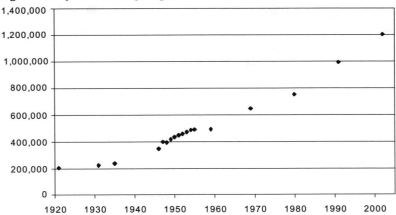

The degree of political unity, and the systems of authority in place in pre-colonial Kigezi have been a matter of some debate amongst historians and anthropologists. Most sources agree with Edel, who undertook a detailed study of Bakiga in the 1930s, and who argued there were no individuals or groups of individuals with authority over others. Bakiga were an 'independent one-class peasant people' who were not united, had no tribal organisation and no formal authority beyond that exercised by the father over his household.[64] At a higher level (such as the lineage) respected elders might become leaders of opinion whose advice was sought to settle disputes, etc., but they had no formal powers to enforce their decisions. Colonial authorities, finding no system of authority that they could recognise and incorporate into their administration, did what they did elsewhere in Uganda and appointed Baganda Agents as administrators. Civil administration was established in 1911 (after the Anglo-German-Belgian Boundary Commission of 1911 had settled the different colonial claims to the area).[65] Kigezi was divided for administrative purposes into counties (*sazas*), sub-counties (*gombolola*), parishes (*miluka*: pl; *muluka*: sing) and sub-parishes (*mukungu* or *mutongole*) (see Map 1.2). With chiefs appointed at each level, a hierarchy of authority was established. Initially Baganda agents were used at *saza* and *gombolola* levels. But from 1922 the use of Baganda agents was phased out, and by 1930 three *saza* chiefs and all the lower chiefs were indigenous to the area.[66]

Chiefs (with the exception of the lowest rank) were salaried employees of the Administration. They were given both executive and judicial powers, and supervised tax collection and public works, as well as working in the courts.[67] The colonial administration 'worked through the Chiefs entirely,' and chiefs were given substantial power over, for example, methods of cultivation, bride wealth and famine reserves.[68] Courts were established from 1916 at *gombolola* level with the *gombolola* chief hearing disputes, which could then be referred up to the *saza* court. District officials reviewed cases

13

Map 1.2 *Kigezi District, showing* saza *boundaries and physical features*

on tour, and appeals were made to the District Court, but the 'native courts' dealt with by far the majority of cases and they could punish through imprisonment, corporal punishments and fines. Chiefs were thus placed in an extraordinarily powerful position. As Baxter has noted, *mukunga* chiefs had to see that members of their sub-parish paid their taxes, followed all agricultural and veterinary regulations, did their communal labour, etc., using a combination of 'exhortation and ... prosecution. ... They have to achieve a nice balance between not incurring the hatred of their neighbours by excessive keenness and not losing their jobs by incurring the wrath of their superiors.'[69]

Thus for the first time men could be appointed with power over non-family members, and over people from different clans and lineages. From the mid-1940s changes were introduced handing over some of the chiefs' powers to councils of both chiefs and elected members, the latter eventually forming the majority. In some cases chiefs succeeded in continuing to dominate their councils, and it could still be said in the mid-1950s that 'chiefs, in their various capacities, are judges, legislators and executives'. But from the mid-1950s the power of the chiefs changed more significantly: chiefs were the minority on all councils from 1956 and at the same time the process of separating the judiciary from executive began to take place.[70] Kigezi also had high levels of European administrative personnel throughout much of the colonial period with a substantial District Team consisting of the District Commissioner (DC), Assistant District Commissioner (ADC), District Agricultural Officer (DAO), District Veterinary Officer (DVO) and District Medical Officer (DMO).

Uganda's colonial administrators viewed Kigezi as peripheral in a number of ways. Geographically Kigezi was some distance from the centre (of both administration and economic activity), economically Kigezi was never a major producer of colonial-encouraged cash crops for export, and Kigezi was politically peripheral, with no system of chieftainship for the colonial powers to engage with. Nonetheless, Kigezi was quickly incorporated into the Uganda administration through, for example, tax collection and compulsory labour obligations. Poll tax collections began from 1915 and anyone who failed to pay their tax was employed on government work the following year.[71] Tax books (one for each wife) recorded all land and livestock held.[72] *Luwalo* labour obligations began in 1912 and initially involved each adult male working for 10 days, later increased to 30 days. From 1924 certain groups could commute their *luwalo* by paying in cash, but initially few people had the cash to be able to do so. From 1935 commutation was widened so that anyone who had the cash (and had already paid their poll tax) could pay their *luwalo* obligation.[73] Cash payment for both poll tax and *luwalo* became widespread, suggesting that by 1935 there were already more opportunities of earning cash.

Land tenure on most land in Kigezi was individualistic and this applied to land that was cultivated or had been cultivated. Larger groups (whether clans or lineages) were important for defence purposes, and social relations with members of these groups were important for both acquiring and gaining access to land. Ownership over land could be acquired in a number of ways, including inheritance, marriage, social networks and blood brotherhood. In addition, from early in the colonial period land could be purchased. People also gained access to land through arrangements that did not imply absolute ownership over that land: they could gain the right to use land on a temporary basis.

There are two cropping seasons per year in Kigezi, corresponding to the two rainy seasons. The main crops grown today are sorghum, peas, beans and sweet potatoes. Other crops which are grown, and which have increased in importance since the beginning of colonialism, include bananas, English potatoes, maize, tobacco and vegetables. Millet, once a major crop, and used for brewing, is much less common now. Trees are widely grown today, and indeed have been for many decades. Food crops, and peas and beans in particular, have long been traded across the region. The production decisions that farmers made as a result of their involvement in wider flows of produce were to have a significant impact on colonial efforts to introduce cash crops. In the pre- and early colonial period there were complementary food flows with neighbouring Rwanda and Congo. The royal taxation system in Rwanda and trade in non-foodstuffs, including cattle, goats, salt and bracelets, facilitated a regional trade in food crops from surplus-producing to food-deficit regions. Bordering Ruanda, being agro-ecologically diverse, being positioned on a major trading route of Katwe salt and being involved in the livestock trade (especially goats) stimulated food flows from Kigezi.[74]

This is a labour-intensive agricultural system and the main input into agriculture is labour. Crops are grown in a variety of flexible rotation systems, and both sole and mixed cropping is practised. During the colonial period officials attempted to identify 'standard' systems of rotation, which were recorded in detail together with lengths of fallow being used.[75] It is clear however, that there was no 'standard' rotation being practised, but rather a flexible and dynamic approach that allowed farmers to take into account the land and labour resources available to them. To this day agricultural techniques remain rudimentary: cultivation is entirely by hand and the only implement used is the hoe. Few purchased inputs are used, although recent agricultural policy (in particular the Policy for the Modernisation of Agriculture) is likely to result in the increased promotion of such inputs. Some farmers use small amounts of agro-chemicals for crops that are produced for sale – in particular fungicides on Irish potatoes, while traders frequently use agro-chemicals on beans to reduce damage by pests. In addition, improved varieties of seeds are purchased when available.[76] Today smallholders who own livestock may apply manure to plots close to the homestead, but this does not occur unfailingly. Agricultural staff promoted the practice of manuring crops throughout the colonial period, but with some difficulty as officials noted that Bakiga considered the idea of manuring crops to be 'repugnant'.[77] Households kept livestock, and in particular cows, goats and sheep, in small numbers. They do not form a significant part of the diet, but are kept as a form of savings, and used for brideprice payments.

In contrast to some other areas,[78] colonial officials described Bakiga agricultural methods and their hardworking nature in favourable terms: 'The

Bakiga are by nature and necessity keen agriculturalists and hard workers.'[79] Within this labour-intensive agricultural system the burden of agricultural work falls on women, a fact that was recognised, but given little attention, by colonial officials.[80] Many of men's traditional responsibilities (particularly clearing new land and constructing houses and granaries) have diminished, as there is little new land to open up, granaries are now rare and new houses are only built infrequently, with corrugated iron being common.

Men do, however, seek work outside the household and temporary migration for work has made an important contribution to Kigezi's economy for many decades.[81] The introduction of taxation in the early years of colonial rule increased the demand for cash, and many men looked to wage labour to meet this demand. At this time there was little demand for paid labourers within the district, while in southern and central Uganda demand was high. Men from Kigezi thus sought work outside the district, joining migrants from other outlying districts such as West Nile, and from neighbouring countries – in particular Ruanda-Urundi and Congo. Labour migration became common for young men from Kigezi from the early 1920s, and was both unorganised 'spontaneous' migration, and migration organised by the government through labour agencies. There were three distinct 'phases' in labour migration. In the first phase – from early 1920s to late 1940s – migration was of increasing importance to the economy of the district and led to increased cash circulation and changes in, for example, brideprice patterns. During the second phase – from the late 1940s to the 1960s – labour migration was at its peak. During the third phase – from the 1960s to the present – long-distance labour migration has declined, while shorter distance migration – for example to Kabale town – has continued, and possibly increased. These phases of migration, and the changing importance of migration to livelihoods in Kigezi, are discussed in more detail in Chapter 7.

While temporary migration has made an important contribution to Kigezi's economy for many decades, there is also a long history of permanent migration for settlement. Edel, for example, noted the 'considerable mobility'[82] of Bakiga in the 1930s. Appreciating the extent of population mobility amongst Bakiga is important to understanding their agricultural system, their reception of some colonial policies (particularly the resettlement scheme), and the complexities of their land tenure system.

Having provided some background to the district, the following two chapters consider the role and functioning of the colonial state, examining the formulation and implementation of agricultural policies and farmers' reactions to them. Chapter 2 examines efforts made by the Agricultural Department towards cash crops, while Chapter 3 explores measures related to soil conservation. Chapter 4 outlines Kigezi's land tenure system, thus laying the foundation for a deeper analysis into land and politics in the district. This is undertaken in Chapter 5 which investigates colonial policies of land reform, and the evolution of Kigezi's land tenure system. The next two chapters shift the focus of attention away from colonial policies, and towards broader changes in Kigezi's agricultural system (Chapter 6), and livelihoods

(Chapter 7). The final chapter concludes by drawing together the main themes of the study, and locating these in broader debates in contemporary development.

Notes

[1] R. Black and H. White, (eds), *Targeting Development: Critical perspectives on the millennium development goals* (London, 2004), xx.

[2] This orientation towards results can be seen in many areas of policy in the UK. For example, school, hospital and university league tables. See Black and White, *Targeting Development*, 11.

[3] D. Mosse, *Cultivating Development: An ethnography of aid policy and practice* (London, 2005).

[4] Different approaches to understanding policy processes have been summarised by Keeley and Scoones. They use different conceptual lenses to 'highlight the continuous interplay of discourse, political interests and the agency of multiple actors' (p. 39) See J. Keeley and I. Scoones, *Environmental Policy Processes: Cases from Africa* (London, 2003).

[5] Mosse, *Cultivating Development*, 8.

[6] Lord Lugard, *The Dual Mandate in British Tropical Africa* (Edinburgh, 1922).

[7] For further details see G.B. Masefield, *A History of the Colonial Agricultural Service* (Oxford, 1972), and G.B. Masefield, *A Short History of Agriculture in the British Colonies* (Oxford, 1950).

[8] D. Low and J. Lonsdale, 'Introduction: Towards a new order 1945–63', in D. Low and A. Smith (eds) *History of East Africa* (Vol. 2) (Oxford, 1976), 12. See M. Havinden and D. Meredith, *Colonialism and Development: Britain and its Tropical Colonies* (London, 1993); G. C. Abbott, 'A re-examination of the 1929 Colonial Act', *Economic History Review*, (1971), 24 1: 68–81; D.J. Morgan. *The Official History of Colonial Development* (London, 1980); J.M. Lee, *Colonial Development and Good Government* (Oxford,1967); R.D. Pearce, *The Turning Point in Africa: British Colonial Policy 1938–48* (London, 1982).

[9] See for example C.C. Wrigley, *Crops and Wealth in Uganda: A Short Agrarian History* (Kampala, 1959); E.A. Brett, *Colonialism and Underdevelopment in East Africa: The Politics of Economic Change 1919–1939* (London, 1973); S. Bunker, *Peasants against the State: The Politics of Market Control in Bugisu, Uganda 1900–1983* (Chicago, 1987); J. Vincent, *Teso in Transformation* (Berkeley, 1982); A. Richards, F. Sturrock and J.M. Fortt, *From Subsistence to Commercial Farming in Buganda* (Cambridge, 1973). See also G. Kitching, *Class and Economic Change in Kenya: the Making of an African Petite Bourgeoisie 1905–1970* (New Haven, CT, 1980); S. Berry, *Cocoa, Custom and Socio-economic Change in Rural Western Nigeria* (Oxford, 1975); P. Hill, *Migrant Cocoa Farmers of Southern Ghana* (Cambridge, 1972).

[10] See R.C. Pratt, 'Administration and Politics in Uganda, 1919–45' in V. Harlow, E.M. Chilver and L.A. Smith (eds) *History of East Africa* (Vol. 2) (Oxford, 1965), 476–542.

[11] For broad historiographical perspective on imperial environmental history see J. Mackenzie, 'Empire and the ecological apocalypse: the historiography of the imperial environment', in T. Griffiths and L. Robin, *Ecology and Empire: environmental history of settler societies* (Edinburgh, 1997). For an account of the emergence of environmental history more broadly, from its origins to the various forms it has assumed, see J. McNeill, 'Observations on the nature and culture of environmental history', *History and Environment*, 42 (2003), 5–43.

[12] R. Grove, 'Editorial', *Environment and History* 6 2 (2003), 127. He critiques scholars who see environmental history and environmentalism as having specifically North American origins. See for example D. Worster, *The Ends of the Earth* (New York, 1988); R. Nash, *Wilderness and the American Mind* (New Haven, CT, 1969); D. Worster and A.W. Crosby, *Studies in Environment and History* (Cambridge, 1995). R. Grove, *Green Imperialism: Colonial expansion, tropical island edens and the origins of environmentalism, 1600–1860* (Cambridge, 1996). R. Grove, 'Scottish missionaries, evangelical discourses and the origins of conservation

thinking in Southern Africa 1820–1900', *Journal of Southern African Studies*, 15 2 (1989), 163–87.
[13] T.R. Malthus, *An Essay on the Principle of Population* (London, 1798).
[14] P. Ehrlich and A. Ehrlich, *Population, Resources and Environment* (New York, 1970), P. Ehrlich, *The Population Bomb* (London, 1972) and D. Meadows *et al.*, *The Limits of Growth* (New York, 1972); P.R. Ehrlich, *The Population Explosion* (New York, 1990) and L.R. Brown, *The State of the World* (New York, 1992). For more recent sources see for example the 1986 study by the World Bank, *Population Growth and Policies in Sub-Saharan Africa*, and the 1989 World Bank Report *Sub-Saharan Africa: from crisis to sustainable growth* which drew attention to two trends: population growth and environmental degradation. For discussion see G.Williams, 'Modernizing Malthus: The World Bank, population control and the African environment', in J. Crush, *Power of Development* (London, 1995). Other more recent World Bank studies that adopt a similar neo-Malthusian narrative include K. Cleaver and G. Schreiber, *Reversing the Spiral: the population, agriculture and environment nexus in Sub-Saharan Africa* (Washington, DC, 1994). For a recent study of Pare, where a neo-Malthusian perspective is used to define problems, this time in a post-colonial context, see M.J. Sheridan, 'The environmental consequences of independence and socialism in North Pare, Tanzania, 1961–88', *Journal of African History*, 45 1 (2004), 81–102.
[15] D.M. Anderson, 'Depression, dust bowl, demography and drought: The colonial state and soil conservation in East Africa during the 1930s', *African Affairs*, 83 (1984), 321–43. For growth of concerns in Southern Africa context see W. Beinart, 'Soil erosion, conservationism and ideas about development: A southern African exploration, 1900–1960', *Journal of Southern African Studies*, 11 1 (1984), 52–83.
[16] In relation to such policies in Kenya see D.W. Throup, *The Economic and Social Origins of Mau Mau, 1945–53* (London, 1987); D.W. Throup, 'The origins of the Mau Mau', *African Affairs*, 84 (1985), 399–433. J. Heyer, 'Agricultural development policy in Kenya from colonial period to 1975', in J. Heyer (ed.), *Rural Development in Tropical Africa* (London, 1981), 90–120. For examples from Tanzania see A. Coulson, 'Agricultural policies in mainland Tanzania', in J. Heyer (ed.), *Rural Development in Tropical Africa* (London, 1981), 52–89; R. Young and H. Fosbrooke, *Smoke in the Hills: Land and Politics Among the Luguru in Tanganyika* (London, 1960); D.W. Malcolm, *Sukumaland, An African People and the Country: A Study of Land Use in Tanganyika* (London, 1953); S. Feierman, *Peasant Intellectuals: Anthropology and History in Tanzania* (Madison, WI, 1990); J.L. Giblin, *The Politics of Environmental Control in NorthEastern Tanzania 1840–1940* (Philadelphia, PA, 1993); G. Maddox, J.L. Giblin and I. Kimambo (eds), *Custodians of the Land: Ecology and Culture in the History of Tanzania* (London, 1996). For studies outside Eastern Africa see W. Beinart and C. Bundy, *Hidden Struggles in Rural South Africa: Politics and Popular Movements in Transkei and Eastern Cape* (London, 1987). Also S. Wallman, *Take Out Hunger: Two Case Studies of Rural Development in Basutoland* (London, 1969). K. Showers, 'Soil erosion in the Kingdom of Lesotho: Origins and colonial response, 1830s–1950s', *Journal of Southern African Studies*, 15 2 (1989), 263–86. T. Ranger, *Voices from the Rocks* (Oxford, 1999); E.C. Mandala, *Work and Control in a Peasant Economy*, (Madison, WI, 1990); K. Showers, *Imperial Gullies: Soil erosion and conservation in Lesotho* (Athens, OH, 2005)
[17] J. Mackenzie (ed.), *Imperialism and the Natural World* (Manchester, 1990), 6–8. W.M. Adams, 'Green Development Theory?', in Crush, *Power of Development*.
[18] R. Coupland, *Kirk on the Zambesi* (Oxford, 1928), 6, quoted in Mackenzie, *Imperialism and the Natural World*, 6.
[19] Grove, 'Scottish missionaries, 189.
[20] W. Beinart, 'Introduction: The politics of colonial conservation', *Journal of Southern African Studies*, 15 2 (1989), 159.
[21] Low and Lonsdale, 'Introduction: Towards a new order 1945–63'. See for example Lord Hailey, *An African Survey* (London, 1938) and E.B. Worthington, *Science in Africa*, (London, 1938). For discussion see H. Tilley, 'African environments and environmental sciences', in W. Beinart and J. McGregor (eds), *Social History and African Environments* (Oxford, 2003), 109–30.
[22] Masefield, *A History of the Colonial Agricultural Service*, 6.

[23] Beinart, 'Introduction: The politics of colonial conservation', 160; W. Beinart and J. McGregor, 'Introduction', in Beinart and McGregor, *Social History and African Environments*. See also J. Carruthers, 'Africa: Histories, Ecologies and Societies', *Environment and History*, 10 (2004), 379–406.

[24] F. Mackenzie, *Land, Ecology and Resistance in Kenya, 1880–1952* (Edinburgh, 1998). See Beinart, 'Soil erosion, conservationism'. In Northern Rhodesia the late 1920s to early 1960s was labelled the 'technical development phase'. Drinkwater notes that, despite the observation in 1961 that 'imposed technical planning has had its day', technocratic planning continued into the late 1980s in Rhodesia. M. Drinkwater, 'Technical Development and Peasant Impoverishment: Land use policy in Zimbabwe's Midlands Province', *Journal of Southern African Studies*, 15 2 (1989), 287–305.

[25] F. Mackenzie, 'Selective Silence: A feminist encounter with environmental discourse in colonial Africa', in Crush, *Power of Development*, 103 . See Anderson, 'Depression, dustbowl', 326. Re use of biological methods versus mechanical methods of control, see Mackenzie *Land, Ecology*, 120–43.

[26] Adams, 'Green Development Theory?', 90–92. See also J. Fairhead and M. Leach, *Science, Society and Power: Environmental knowledge and policy in West Africa and the Caribbean* (Cambridge, 2003).

[27] W. Beinart, *The Rise of Conservation in South Africa* (Oxford, 2003). Mackenzie, *Land, Ecology*. See also Grove, 'Scottish missionaries' and Drinkwater, 'Technical Development'.

[28] T. Ranger, 'Whose heritage? The case of the Matobo National Park', *Journal of Southern African Studies*, 15 2 (1989), 227.

[29] Mackenzie, *Land, Ecology*, 142.

[30] M. Tiffen *et al., More People, Less Erosion: Emvironmental Recovery in Kenya* (Chichester, 1994), 15, 179.

[31] Grogan, quoted in H. Tilley, 'African environments', 116. Mackenzie, *Land, Ecology*, 90.

[32] See Beinart, 'Soil erosion, conservationism', 61. Although, Beinart notes, this was not an entirely unanimous view. See also Beinart, 'Introduction', 148.

[33] Mackenzie , 'Selective Silence', 105. Also see Drinkwater, 'Technical Development', 293.

[34] Beinart, 'Introduction' , 159 and Beinart, 'Soil erosion, conservationism'. See also Tilley who argues that Agriculture Departments in the 1930s paid greater attention to African husbandry, not only because of the desire to increase production for export, but also to prevent famines and raise domestic production. Tilley, 'African environments', 115–16.

[35] W. Beinart, 'African history and environmental history', *African Affairs*, 99 (2000), 293.

[36] P. Richards, 'Ecological change and the politics of African land use', *African Studies Review* 26 2 (1983), 57. J. Ford, *The Role of Trypanosomiasis in African Ecology: a Study of the Tsetse Fly Problem* (London, 1971). W. Allan, *The African Husbandman* (Edinburgh, 1965).

[37] Note by McCombe (DAO) on Matias's (DC) Memo on 'Kigezi District: Economic Policy', Kigezi District Archives [hereafter KDA] Department of Agriculture [hereafter DoA] 11/A/1 ff11.

[38] Mackenzie , 'Selective Silence', 106.

[39] Worthington, *Science in Africa*. See Tilley, 'African environments', 121.

[40] For example see L. Cliffe, 'Nationalism and the reaction to enforced agricultural change in Tanganyika during the colonial period', in L. Cliffe and J. Saul (eds), *Socialism in Tanganyika* (Vol. 1) (Nairobi, written 1964, publ. 1972); G.A. Maguire, *Towards 'Uhuru' in Tanzania: the Politics of Participation* (London, 1969); I.N. Kimambo, *Penetration and Protest in Tanzania: The Impact of the World Economy on the Pare, 1860–1960* (London, 1991).

[41] Although see Feierman, *Peasant Intellectuals;* Showers, 'Soil Erosion in the Kingdom of Lesotho', 263–86; Mackenzie, *Land, Ecology;* J.C. de Wilde, *Experiences with Agricultural Development in Tropical Africa* (2 Vols.), (Baltimore, MD, 1967); Tiffen *et al., More People, Less Erosion*.

[42] The only literature written specifically on this subject in Kigezi is that by colonial officials: J.W. Purseglove, 'Land use in the overpopulated areas of Kigezi District, Uganda', *East African Agricultural Journal*, 12 (1946), 139–52; J.W. Purseglove, 'Resettlement in

Kigezi, Uganda', *Journal of African Administration*, 3 (1951), 13–21; and a number of studies of localised areas which focus on causes of problems – for example E.R. Kagambirwe, *Causes and Consequences of Land Shortage in Kigezi* (Kampala, 1973) but make no attempt to place these in the historical context nor assess the solutions put forward by the colonial state, or farmers' responses to them.

[43] Report of the East African Royal Commission, 1953–55 (London, 1955).

[44] H. Bernstein and P. Woodhouse, 'Telling environmental change like it is? Reflections on a study of Sub-Saharan Africa', *Journal of Agrarian Change*, 1 2 (2001), 283–324. See also A. Burton and M. Jennings, *The Emperor's New Clothes* (Manchester, in press).

[45] J.P. Platteau, 'Does Africa need land reform?', in C. Toulmin and J. Quan (eds), *Evolving Land Rights, Policy and Tenure in Africa* (London, 2000), 53. See also J.P. Platteau, 'The Evolutionary Theory of Land Rights as applied to Sub-Saharan Africa: A critical assessment', *Development and Change*, 27 1 (1996), 29–86.

[46] Beinart, 'African history', 271, 302.

[47] Tiffen *et al.*, *More People, Less Erosion.*

[48] See E. Boserup, *The Conditions of Agricultural Growth* (Chicago, 1965) and E. Boserup, *Population and Technological Change* (Chicago, 1981). Others have taken on the 'Neo-Malthusians' arguing that there are few resources which are not replaceable, See for example C.L. Jolly, 'Four theories of population change and the environment', *Population and Environment*, 6 1 (1994); D.J. Hogan, 'The impact of population growth on the physical environment', *European Journal of Population*, 8 (1992), 109–23.

[49] See for example P. Holmgren, E.J. Masakha and H. Sjoholm, 'Not all African land is being degraded: A recent survey of trees on farms in Kenya reveals rapidly increasing forest resources', *Ambio*, 23 7 (1994), 391–5. See also B.L. Turner, K. Kates and G. Hyden, *Population Growth and Agrarian Change in Africa* (Gainesville, FL, 1993).

[50] J. Fairhead and M. Leach, *Reframing deforestation* (London, 1998), 192. Also see J. Fairhead and M. Leach, *Misreading the African Landscape* (Cambridge, 1996).

[51] Beinart, 'African history', 276; Carruthers, 'Africa', 388.

[52] Mackenzie , 'Selective Silence', 101. See M. Leach and R. Mearns, *The Lie of the Land: Challenging Received Wisdom on the African Environment* (Oxford, 1996).

[53] Bernstein and Woodhouse, 'Telling environmental change'. J. Murton , 'Population growth and poverty in Machakos, Kenya', *Geographical Journal*, 165 1 (1999), 37–46.

[54] Mosse, *Cultivating Development*, 184–204. Also lecture given by David Mosse, at the London School of Economics, 2 June 2005.

[55] See J. Ferguson, *The Anti-Politics Machine: 'Development', Depoliticization and Bureaucratic Power in Lesotho*, (Cambridge, 1990).

[56] Kigezi district was divided into North and South Kigezi in 1974; then in 1980 these were renamed Rukungiri and Kabale respectively. In the 1990s Kabale was further divided into Kabale and Kisoro districts, and Rukungiri into Kanungu and Rukungiri districts.

[57] Annual Reports; J.D. Jameson, (ed.) *Agriculture in Uganda* (London, 1970) 2nd edn., 47.

[58] D. Taylor and R. Marchant, 'Human impact in the Interlacustrine region: long-term pollen records from the Rukiga Highlands', *Azania*, XXIX–XXX (1994–95), 293. Earlier research by Hamilton suggested that clearing of forests in the Kabale area started more that 4,800 years ago with further clearing around 2,200 years ago. A. Hamilton, *et al.* 'Early forest clearance and environmental degradation in South West Uganda,' *Nature*, 320 (1986), 164–7. Taylor and Marchant suggest, however, that the earlier vegetation change was likely to have had a regional cause, probably a movement towards a drier or more seasonal climate (p. 293).

[59] J. Pottier, *Re-Imagining Rwanda: Conflict, Survival and Disinformation in the Late Twentieth Century* (Cambridge, 2002), 11. Citing A. Cornet *Histoire d'une Famine: Rwanda 1927–30. Crise Alimentaire entre Tradition et Modernité.* (Louvain-La-Neuve: Centre d'Histoire de l'Afrique, Université Catholique de Louvain, 1996) 10, 39; J. Fairhead, *Food Security in North and South Kivu (Zaire), 1989* Final consultancy report for Oxfam. Part 1, Section 2 (London, 1989). For further information about mobility in Rwanda and with neighbouring regions, see Pottier, *Re-Imagining Rwanda*, 11–20.

21

[60] Uganda Government, *Population and Housing Census – provisional results* (Kampala, 2002). (246 persons/km² in 1991 Population and Housing Census). J.M. Byagagaire and J.C.D. Lawrance, *Effect of Customs of Inheritance on Sub-Division and Fragmentation of Land in South Kigezi, Uganda* (Entebbe, 1957).

[61] Rainfall data collected from Dept. of Meteorology, Kabale, Feb. 2002. Only years with complete data used.

[62] J. Bosworth, 'Land and Society in South Kigezi, Uganda' (DPhil, University of Oxford, 1995), 42.

[63] These figures are for Kigezi District. When this district ceased to exist, the combined district figures are used. Sources: Kigezi District Archives; Uganda Govt Statistical Abstracts, 1966; Uganda 1991 Population and Housing Census; Uganda 2002 Population and Housing Census 2002 (Provisional Results).

[64] Edel, *The Chiga*, 3. Example of source agreeing with Edel, see Baxter, 'The Kiga', 284.

[65] See W.R. Louis, *Ruanda-Urundi 1884–1919* (Oxford, 1963), 79–91, 194–9. Also J.M. Coote (with postscript by H.B. Thomas), 'The Kivu Mission 1909–10', *Uganda Journal*, 20 (1956), 105–12. Also H.B. Thomas, 'Kigezi Operations 1914–17', *Uganda Journal*, 30 (1966), 165–73.

[66] B. Turyahikayo-Rugyema, 'The British imposition of colonial rule on Uganda: The Buganda agents in Kigezi, 1908–30', *Transafrican Journal of History*, 5 (1976), 111–33. For wider discussion of the use of Baganda agents see A. Roberts, 'The sub-imperialism of the Baganda', *Journal of African History*, 3 (1962), 435–50; D.J.W. Denoon, 'The allocation of official posts in Kigezi 1908–1930', in D.J.W. Denoon (ed.), *A History of Kigezi in South West Uganda* (Kampala, 1972); Baxter, 'The Kiga'. The *saza* chief of Bufumbira was known as the *Mtwale*.

[67] Under the Native Authority Ordinance of 1919. See Baxter, 'The Kiga'; K.T. Connor, 'Kigezi', in J.D. Barkan *et al.*, *Uganda District Government and Politics, 1947–1967* (Madison, WI, 1977).

[68] Diary of J.R.McD. Elliot, RH MSS Afr s 1384 #28. Elliot was an official in Kigezi from 1921 to 1922. Edel, *The Chiga*, 125–7. See also Baxter, 'The Kiga', 289–90.

[69] Baxter, 'The Kiga', 289–90.

[70] Baxter, 'The Kiga', 289. See also Western Provincial Annual Reports [WPAR] 1955 and 1956.

[71] Poll Tax Rates were initially Shs 6/- (with a higher rate for Bahima and Aliens) and were increased in 1928 to Shs 7/- (16/- for Bahima and Aliens). KDA District Commissioner's Office [hereafter DC] MP136. See also, Ssebalijja, 'A history of Rukiga and other places', 14.

[72] L. S. Khadiagala, 'Negotiating Law and Custom: Judicial Doctrine and Women's Property Rights in Uganda', *Journal of African Law*, 46 1 (2002), 1–13.

[73] WPAR 1933. Ssebalijja, 'A history of Rukiga and other places', 11. Ssebalijja was one of the Baganda agents. See also WPARs, 1924, 1931 and 1935, and KDA DC GenPol.

[74] J. Pottier, 'The politics of famine prevention' *African Affairs*, 85 (1986). See also D.S. Newbury, 'Lake Kivu regional trade in the nineteenth century' *Journal des Africanistes*, 50 2 (1980); B. Lugan 'Causes et effects de la famine 'Rumanura' au Rwanda, 1916–18' *Canadian Journal of African Studies*, X 2 (1976), 347–56; R. Mutombo, 'Marchés et circuits commerciaux de la région des Masangano a la fin de l'époque pré coloniale', *Etudes Rwandaises*, 11 (1978) Numéro Special, March; B. Lugan, 'L'Economie d'Echange au Rwanda de 1850–1914', Université de Provence: Thèse de Doctorat de 3e Cycle (1976), quoted in Pottier, 'The politics of famine prevention.'

[75] For example, system of rotation recorded in southern Kigezi in 1936:

1st year	- Mtama [sorghum] followed by Bulo [millet]
2nd yea	- Maize, beans and peas followed by the same or peas alone
3rd year	- Mtama [sorghum] followed by Bulo [millet]
4th year	- Sweet Potatoes
5th year	- Fallow

Agricultural Survey of Kasheregenyi Mutala in Kigezi District. By R Wickham, (Survey conducted 1935–36, as part of one of the 19 Agricultural Surveys 1938); See also Letter of 24/1/40 to Dir of Medical Services, E'be from Stuckey, DAO KDA DoA 008.

[76] A. Kidd, *Extension, Poverty and Vulnerability in Uganda: Country Study for the Neuchâtel Initiative*, ODI Working Paper 151 (London, 2001). C. Farley, 'Smallholder knowledge, soil resource management and land use change in the highlands of southwest Uganda', (PhD, University of Florida, 1996), 89.

[77] Letter of 18/3/37 to DC and DMO from Wickham, DAO. DoA 010crops.

[78] See I. Yngstrom, 'Representations of custom, social identity and environmental relations in Tanzania 1926–1950', in Beinart and McGregor, *Social History and African Environments*. See also A. Whitehead, 'Continuities and discontinuities in political constructions of the working man in rural sub-Saharan Africa: The "lazy man" in African agriculture', *European Journal of Development Research*, 12 2 (2000), 23–52.

[79] Report for the Year, 1935, Wickham, KDA DC AGR-MNTH ff53.

[80] See, for example R Wickham, Agricultural Survey of Kasheregenyi Mutala in Kigezi District, 1935–6. For an examination of the impact of agrarian change on gender relations, and the ways that gender relations shape the course of economic change, see for example E. Francis, 'Migration and changing divisions of labour: Gender relations and economic change in Koguta, Western Kenya', *Africa*, 65 2 (1995), 197–216. See also Mackenzie, *Land, Ecology;* and H.L. Moore and M. Vaughan, *Cutting Down Trees: Gender, nutrition and agricultural change in the northern province of Zambia, 1890–1990* (London, 1994) esp. chapter 4.

[81] P.G. Powesland, 'History of migration' in A.I. Richards (ed.), *Economic Development and Tribal Change: A Study of Immigrant Labour in Buganda* (London, 1954).

[82] Edel, *The Chiga*, 18. For details of the migration of the major clans of Bakiga see B. Turyahikayo-Rugyema, 'A history of the Bakiga in south western Uganda and northern Rwanda c1500–1930', (PhD, University of Michigan, 1974), 56.

Two

Colonial Encounters with Kigezi Agriculture

Food Crops & Cash Crops

Introduction

Cash crop production was a key aim for the colonial state in Uganda, which depended on peasant production of cotton, and later coffee, to finance its own administration and to meet British industrial and consumer demand.[1] But the encouragement of cash crop production was not successful across Uganda. In Kigezi all efforts to introduce colonial cash crops proved unsuccessful and this failure of agricultural policy can partly be explained by farmer production decisions, and in part by the way that success was being defined. The colonial state failed to recognise the vibrancy and productivity of the existing production system, which centred on the production of food crops for trade and exchange. Furthermore, in a region of high localised risk, production of food crops for both consumption and exchange provided a mechanism of insurance. Inadequate attention paid by the colonial state to the importance of food production and trade, demands made on people's (especially women's) time, competing demands for land, and the role of food production in reducing risk, explain the failure to introduce colonial cash crops successfully. Moreover, in this context 'success' for the colonialists meant the introduction of a new cash crop that was marketed through the colonial state, and it was this that proved to be a failure.

In order to lay the foundation for a deeper analysis of land and politics in Kigezi, I will first outline the history of colonial agricultural development in the district, and the Agricultural Department's efforts to encourage cash crops. None of these efforts was a success. Explaining the failures of these efforts necessitates an exploration of the production of, and trade in, food crops. Bakiga responses to colonial efforts to control the export of food crops in the mid to late colonial period provide further evidence of the strength and vibrancy of the food production and trade.

This examination of the concentration on cash crops and Bakiga responses to it illustrates some of the contradictions and weaknesses of colonial agricultural policy. Kigezi was producing surpluses of foodstuffs for trade, and the failure of the administration to take this into account partly explains their inability to successfully introduce cash crops to the district. The food and cash crop dichotomy was applied to Kigezi in colonial policy, but here food crops were cash crops and the failure of the colonial administration to appreciate this was crucial. Bakiga farmers responded to opportunities that cash crops offered in ways that colonial officials sometimes found surprising. These responses are evidence that Bakiga farmers were in no way 'passive' victims of colonial state policies. Rather Bakiga farmers found ways around marketing policies that did not suit their needs and traded alternative crops to those promoted by the colonial administration.

Colonial authorities were obsessed with finding a cash crop in Kigezi, but this obsession had little to do with Kigezi itself. Rather there was a deeply ingrained colonial view that 'agricultural development' inevitably meant the development of a cash crop, that is, a low bulk, high value non-food crop suitable for export, such as cotton or coffee. Much of the interest in colonial African agricultural history has focused on the so-called 'cash crop revolution', with relatively little attention to the production and marketing of local foodstuffs. It is clear, however, that there were many regions producing surplus foodstuffs for export to surrounding areas.[2] Kigezi was one such region and the failure to introduce cash crops here needs to be seen in the context of the existing production system.

Tosh has observed that the 'success in producing a cash crop was intimately dependent on the relationship between that crop and the established complex of food crops,' and describes the effect of cash crop production on food crops as 'complex and often inhibiting'. He notes that the appeal of growing surplus food crops instead of crops for export was considerable: this was compatible with meeting subsistence needs (including in years of poor harvest), and in many parts of Africa farmers had, in fact, long been doing this. He explores the case of Lango, showing that, while the colonial government tried, with initial difficulties, to introduce cotton as a cash crop, 'the Langi already had a market crop of their own', in the form of sesame and other Lango food crops and they continued producing food surpluses. While we know that West African farmers produced food surpluses for a considerable period of time before colonialism, for the rest of tropical Africa 'the staples of everyday consumption are usually dismissed as beyond the range of market demands'.[3] Yet African cultivators planned regular food surpluses in the light of market demands, in the case of Kigezi regional food demands generated within an area of diverse ecological zones.

Kigezi: production and trade

Kigezi's cropping system has long centred on the production of food crops: surpluses of food were routinely produced and there was a vibrant trade in foodstuffs and livestock. There is substantial evidence (from colonial sources, outside observers and oral sources) that surpluses of food crops were produced and traded, undoubtedly in the very early colonial period, and almost certainly in the pre-colonial period.[4] Kigezi was tied into the wider flows of salt and livestock in the region and was an important part of this food production system and market, with the result that surplus food crops were converted into livestock with relative ease. While the salt, livestock and food trades were intricately linked, blacksmithing goods, such as hoes, and skins for wearing and ornaments made from hides (anklets and armlets) were also bartered. But for Kigezi the main products produced within the district were food crops,[5] and this had enormous implications for colonial attempts to introduce cash crops.

There were complementary food flows in neighbouring Ruanda and Congo in the pre and early colonial period.[6] This regional trade in food crops needed, as Pottier has convincingly argued, additional stimuli besides merely the presence of areas of food deficit, and these stimuli included the royal taxation system in Ruanda and trade in non-foodstuffs, including cattle, goats, salt, hoes and bracelets. The taxation system and trade in non-foodstuffs were the 'mechanisms through which the flow of food from surplus-producing to food-deficit regions was made possible'.[7] This is highly relevant for Kigezi, which is itself agro-ecologically diverse, is positioned on what was a major salt trading route (from Katwe) and was involved in the livestock trade (especially goats). Ruanda's taxation system and the trade in salt and livestock which both passed through and involved Kigezi appear, as Pottier has argued for the case of western Ruanda, to have stimulated food flows from Kigezi.[8] With the coming of colonialism there were new stimuli to food production and trade, and from the early colonial period the marketing of food crops became easier as people traded widely with more confidence of their own safety, while population increases also led to an increased demand for food crops. But colonial attention was not on the production of foodstuffs (beyond concerns that food crop production should be protected); rather, officials viewed Kigezi as a peripheral part of the Protectorate of Uganda, and they largely ignored (or were unaware of) the fact that Kigezi was a part of a vibrant food production system that crossed colonial boundaries.

Oral sources confirm that in the late pre-colonial period surplus food was commonly produced, especially by richer households, who could use it to gain access to additional labour. Alternatively it could be exchanged through bartering for a variety of goods: livestock or skins, hoes and pangas or salt from Katwe.[9] One informant noted: 'Bakiga who had food would exchange it for livestock, armlets and anklets as well as hoes and other blacksmith products.' In times of famine in neighbouring areas, people would 'come to look for food', exchanging food for livestock or at times of more extreme hardship for wives.[10]

The exchange of surpluses of food was linked to the trade in livestock (as people converted surplus food into stock, especially small stock), and to trade in other products such as hides, blacksmithing products and salt. Traders brought small stock from Ruanda to exchange for food and salt, and also sold to Ankole to the east.[11] From the early colonial period officials recognised that the trade in livestock was critical for the payment of tax and livestock was the 'main financial asset of the District'.[12] While sheep and goats formed the 'largest export business' of Kigezi there was also a 'considerable local trade' and a 'very large amount' of this small stock came from Ruanda. Officials frequently observed the importance of this trade for raising cash for tax.[13]

As well as being a medium of exchange, livestock were also a vital part of Bakiga social organisation, as cattle, together with sheep and goats, were used for bridewealth. To increase labour and reproductive power families would increase their herd, through the exchange of surplus food for small stock, which were in turn 'traded up' for large stock. While there is evidence of a thriving trade in livestock, and in particular in small stock, there are no reliable price statistics to explore changing terms of trade between different branches of the economy and their products. Nonetheless, we can presume that at times of food shortage in Ruanda (the main source of livestock) the terms of trade shifted in favour of the Bakiga, in the same way as has been observed in Kenya when famine in pastoral areas enabled Kikuyu cultivators to exchange surplus food for livestock on very favourable terms, thus acquiring more wives and household labour and increasing cultivation even further.[14]

The food and livestock trade was also linked to the trade in salt from Katwe. This long established salt trade from Lake Katwe to Ruanda passed through Kigezi, and had been observed by Captain Jack in 1910:

> The route [is] a well worn and much used one ... Large herds of sheep and goats are constantly being brought along this road and are bartered.... for the much desired Katwe salt. ... one goat would buy a packet of salt with which on the return to Ruanda two goats could be purchased, so that the trade would appear to be a lucrative one.[15]

Good has noted that in the late nineteenth century the flow of Katwe salt to Ruanda and Congo passed through Kigezi, and 'was sustained by a complementary exchange of goods collected and channelled by numerous part time traders across intertribal boundaries'. Traders from Ankole bartered Katwe salt for various goods, and Good writes that 'goats were in particular demand among young traders for dowries' and traders travelled to Kigezi 'where they would barter salt for these animals on very favourable terms'.[16] There were high profit margins in the salt trade. By the late 1920s the salt trade passed out of African hands into the hands of Indian traders using lorries, and the direct link between the salt and goat trade was also broken, with both being traded for cash.[17]

From the earliest colonial period both officials and non-officials saw the people of Kigezi as 'most industrious ... in the cultivation of their food crops'.[18] The significance of the trade in food was particularly obvious to the administration during times of food shortages in surrounding areas, although at no time did they see this trade as something to be 'harnessed' for 'agricultural development'. In 1917, as a result of food shortages in Bufumbira, people purchased food in Rukiga. A decade later Bakiga were · selling to their neighbours to the north who suffered shortage: 'The Rukiga people have been able to dispose of their surplus supplies by selling to the people in Rushenyi where there was a distinct shortage.'[19] Then in 1929 there was a shortage of food in Ruanda Belge, and people crossed the border to purchase food.[20] Even outside times of food shortage the importance of the trade in food crops was observed, for example by Roscoe who travelled through the area in 1919–20 and who noted that 'what [each woman] could spare after her household needs were satisfied she bartered for goats and sheep.'[21] Edel also described how there was 'some direct barter and sale, and rudimentary markets did exist' with women selling 'surplus products' such as grain or beer.[22] Official sources also recognised the importance of the food crops trade. In 1933 the DC observed that 'the sale of food accounts for much of the money paid in Poll Taxes', pointing to the markets which served Ankole, Ruanda and the Congo as evidence.[23] Another district official noted that

> maize, beans and peas, are sold out of the district to Belgian Congo... and Ankole. The trade is partly... by natives who walk across the district boundaries to local markets with small loads, and partly by Indians who buy up foodstuffs in large quantities at Kabale and send it through in lorry loads. There is no means of assessing the volume of this trade, but there is no doubt that the total tonnage involved is very considerable.[24]

A survey conducted in 1939 recorded that the 'large internal trade in beer' was 'one of the main sources of income' and that food crops (sorghum, beans, maize, sweet potatoes and peas) were sold at markets.[25] But despite these observations colonial officials paid little attention to the production of food crops, focusing instead on cash crops. From the time of their arrival officials sought a suitable 'cash crop', according to their definition of what a cash crop should be. What, then, drove this colonial policy?

Formulation of Uganda's colonial agricultural policy

British colonial governments saw their role as creating an environment in which market forces could work, and so lead to development. At the same time colonial governments were under pressure to be fiscally self-supporting. The publication of Lugard's *The Dual Mandate in British Tropical Africa* (1922), in which he proposed that Britain should develop her empire for both the 'advancement of the subject races' and for the 'development of its material resources for the benefit of mankind',[26] was hugely influential. Thus Departments of Agriculture were seen as 'revenue raising' departments, whose aim was to increase yields and thereby maximise the wealth of people and the revenues of colonial governments.[27]

From about 1920 the colonial administration ruled out the possibility of developing a substantial plantation sector in Uganda, and its development proceeded on the lines of a peasant economy. Wrigley's conclusion that 'people were not taxed in order that they might be made to grow cotton, rather they were urged to grow cotton in order that they might be able to pay taxes' can be applied to other cash crops.[28] Having agreed that Uganda should develop through peasant production, the Department of Agriculture set about finding suitable cash crops and persuading peasant farmers to grow them. The initial focus was on cotton, and later coffee. Working in close collaboration with chiefs, efforts were directed at increasing acreages, providing seeds and offering advice about planting. Technical innovations were few, yields per acre hardly changed and the processing and marketing sectors were placed in the hands of Asians and Europeans.

Colonial administrators at all levels, from London to Entebbe to Kigezi, were eager to raise revenues for the administration, and so agricultural policy focused on cash crops. The formulation of policy to encourage cash crops originated from outside the district, and the first task of early agricultural officers posted to the districts was to find a 'suitable' cash crop, that could be promoted in their district. Being a highland area, it was obvious to district officials that coffee should be the cash crop of choice for Kigezi. While it was felt that food production should not be displaced, little attention was paid to food crops, and the little research carried out was on famine crops.[29] The focus on cash crops continued throughout the colonial period. The impact of the Second World War on agricultural policy was twofold. First, a number of crops were considered to be high priority – and their production was to be given all possible encouragement.[30] These included pyrethrum, which was grown briefly as a plantation crop in Kigezi. Second, both country and district self-sufficiency in food was emphasised in order to reduce the necessity of imports. This policy was further reinforced by the serious famine that struck the region, particularly Rwanda, in 1943, which also led to increased controls on marketing. Following the Second World War the production of cash crops was both expanded and diversified. State-controlled marketing increased, and greater involvement of government in the development of agriculture. Uganda's economy continued to grow and cotton and coffee accounted for by far the greater proportion of exports: in 1955, 77 per cent of the value of all exports was due to cotton and coffee.[31] This growth occurred without any significant structural change in the economy or in patterns of cultivation, and the government, aware of the dangers involved in depending on these two crops, attempted to diversify agricultural production.[32]

Agricultural policy throughout the colonial period was thus geared towards fiscal viability and emphasised the development of 'cash crops' rather than food crops. The administration viewed 'agricultural development' as the development of various cash crops, which was linked to ideas of modernisation and monetarisation. While there was a sense that local food production should be protected and that cash crops should not displace food crops, the over-riding concern to find suitable cash crops encouraged an inadequate understanding of the dynamics of local economies and local agricultural and exchange systems. The search for a suitable cash crop was given highest priority in Kigezi.

Colonial attempts to introduce cash crops

Colonial officials attempted to introduce several cash crops to Kigezi, three of which will be examined here.[33] All were initially heralded as a success as Bakiga farmers took advantage of the opportunities they provided for short-term gains. However, all ultimately failed for reasons related to the labour and marketing of the new crops, and their impact on existing production patterns and arrangements. Bakiga farmers were unwilling to endanger the sustainability of their production systems, or to forgo the gains that could be made through food crop sales.

COFFEE

Efforts to find a suitable cash crop for Kigezi began before a DAO had even been permanently allocated to the district. The earliest and most significant cash crop attempted was coffee, which was first proposed in 1921. The southern part of the district, with its high altitude and ample rainfall, appeared to be ideally suited to coffee, in particular to high value arabica and for some years there were high hopes that Kigezi would develop into a highly productive coffee region.[34]   At the first meeting on the future agricultural policy for the district (held in 1923) it was agreed that coffee production should be strongly encouraged and seedling nurseries were to be established at all *saza* headquarters. Coffee seedlings were distributed first to 'all chiefs ... desirous of having them and later to *Bakopi* [peasants]'.[35] Coffee instructors were sent to the district and the expansion of coffee cultivation continued. In 1929 alone 54,000 coffee trees were planted in the district. 'Considerable enthusiasm' for coffee amongst the people of Kigezi was observed in 1930, and 1931 saw the first sales of Kigezi coffee.[36] By 1934 the demand for seedlings was so high that the policy of giving an equal number of seedlings to anyone who wanted them was abandoned. Instead those (men) considered to be more capable were given more plants and this meant that 'certain chiefs received more'.[37]

During the 1930s the acreage of coffee increased (see Figure 2.1). But optimistic rhetoric of a 'bright future'[38] for coffee changed dramatically. Following a visit to the district in 1932, Tothill, Uganda's Director of Agriculture, mentioned the pest antestia[39] as presenting 'something of a problem'.[40]   But agricultural officials felt that with careful supervision it could be overcome and they made plans for an increase in the number of trained African instructors. But, without a DAO based in Kabale, the problem of antestia became increasingly serious.[41]   By 1935 antestia was described as a 'very serious menace' and the following year the growing of arabica was

Figure 2.1 *Sales and acreages of Arabica coffee, Kigezi,* 1933–1953[42]

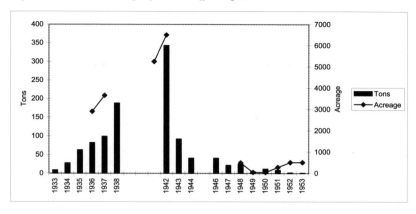

reported to be an 'uneconomic proposition' due to antestia. This news was greeted with alarm by the DC, who had not appreciated the seriousness of the situation.[43] Solutions put forward (weekly bug picking days, more resistant strains and the substitution of robusta for arabica) were to no avail and by 1939 planting had virtually ceased.[44] The quantity of coffee marketed officially continued to rise because of the slow maturation of trees until a maximum of 343 tons was reached in 1942. From 1942 the volume fell and it came to be accepted that coffee no longer had a future in Kigezi.

In other parts of Uganda, such as Bugishu, antestia, while undoubtedly a problem, did not prove to be insurmountable and was overcome through manual picking of bugs and application of insecticides. Why this should not have been the case in Kigezi is never explained. While antestia was always given as the official reason for the failure of coffee in Kigezi, the question remains as to whether there were other more fundamental problems: in particular the labour demands (especially for women) associated with coffee, and how the production and marketing of coffee 'fitted' with the existing production system, explored below.

NICOTINE TOBACCO

With the failure of coffee blamed on the antestia pest, colonial agricultural officers looked for another suitable cash crop and from 1940 tried to introduce nicotine tobacco.[45] While coffee had immediately been popular with local people the story of tobacco was more complex. Initially it was not popular. Acreage targets were set, which were often met by compulsion, and once planted the tobacco was frequently ignored by farmers, resulting in poor leaf quality.[46] A trader named Stafford had agreed to purchase the entire crop, but stood to make substantial losses when the nicotine content of the tobacco produced was lower than expected – due, he felt, to inadequate supervision by the DAO.[47] In his defence, the DAO pointed out that most of

31

those who had planted nicotine tobacco had 'done so not voluntarily but as a result of something more than gentle persuasion'.[48]

The DAO of Toro, de Courcy Ireland, was called in to report on the problems associated with tobacco in Kigezi. He found that rapid expansion with inadequate supervision had given insufficient time for growers to learn about the crop, chiefs had 'pressed' unwilling people to grow tobacco, 'varying degrees of compulsion' were used and acreage targets were expected to be met before payment was made for the previous crop. Following de Courcy Ireland's report, changes were made, notably a switch to voluntary growers and payment for the harvest before farmers planted the next season's crop. As a result, tobacco quickly became more popular and by 1946 it was not possible to meet the demand for seedlings. Acreage under tobacco was 250 acres in 1942; 484 in 1944; 998 in 1946 and over 2100 in 1948.[49] There were two crops per year and the volume of leaf produced rose considerably. Production was almost entirely on a very small scale; in 1947 the average acreage per grower was one-tenth of an acre.[50] The quality of the leaf improved, Stafford established his factory near Kabale, and production increased rapidly: by 58 per cent from 1946 to 1947, and by 63 per cent from 1947 to 1948.

The success, however, was short-lived. By 1950 it was reported that production of nicotine tobacco in Kigezi had fallen, despite increased prices.[51] In fact, as will be seen below, tobacco production continued, but the amount of tobacco sold through official channels declined. Meanwhile the price of nicotine extract fell, and this, together with the falls in sales of tobacco, meant that the operation of the nicotine extraction plant became uneconomic; in 1953 state support of nicotine tobacco ceased. From then onwards nicotine tobacco is not mentioned, although other types of tobacco grew in importance.[52] The reason for the 'failure' of tobacco in Kigezi is not analysed in colonial records but there is evidence that it was largely a failure to maintain control over the marketing, rather than a failure of tobacco production.

FLAX

In the early 1940s trials began with flax cultivation. The crop quickly became popular in both Kigezi and Ankole, and by the mid-1940s supplies to the government factory at Kisizi exceeded the capacity of the plant.[53] In 1948 a Flax Officer (Fennell) was appointed to work exclusively on developing the flax industry, giving an indication of the importance that was attached to the success of flax as a cash crop. Flax was grown mainly in northern Kigezi and was introduced through the chiefs who were to 'encourage' growers to plant it.[54] Who actually grew flax is unclear. Official records suggest that work on flax was 'shared by both sexes'.[55] This is supported by some oral sources, while others stated that it was grown by men alone.[56] Writing some years later, Fennell said that the crop 'in the main was grown by women'.[57] What is clear is that men were involved in sales to the factory (via agricultural officials) and thus controlled income from flax.

Initial predictions about the expected success of flax were optimistic, but

Figure 2.2 *Acreage of flax, Kigezi,* 1940–1955[58]

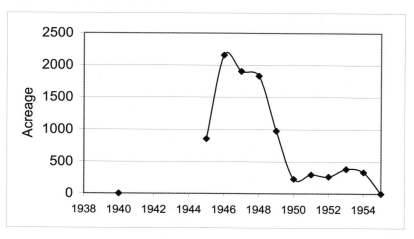

again this was short-lived. By 1948 the quality and quantity of the output proved to be 'disappointing' and in the late 1940s the presence of pasmo disease had a negative effect on the flax crop.[59]   Despite overcoming the disease, and increasing prices in 1951, both acreages and sales of flax fell, and the factory soon operated at a loss. The situation continued to deteriorate and in 1955, on the recommendation of the Flax Officer, the flax industry was abandoned altogether: the factory closed down and without a market for flax, farmers ceased growing it.

Why did cash crops fail?

These three examples show the failure to introduce cash crops to Kigezi. The official reason given for failure of coffee was the impact of antestia disease, while for the other two crops the reasons were never elucidated. However, close examination of colonial and oral sources suggests a number of reasons for these failures, related to the production patterns, land tenure, labour demands and marketing of existing and new crops.

People in Kigezi were producing food crops for exchange and sale in the wider region. These crops were grown almost entirely by women, and the agricultural system was such that the demands on their labour were high throughout much of the year. As the anthropologist Edel noted, 'the large share of all Chiga work tends to fall on women. Theirs … is the steady, unremitting daily routine of food-getting.'[60] The provision of sufficient food for the family was, and still is today, seen as women's responsibility, and women were generally able to decide how much of a food crop should be kept for family consumption and how much could be exchanged or sold. Informants repeatedly stated that as women were busy cultivating beans, sorghum and other food crops, this prevented them from taking on other crops. But even if women did contribute labour to the cultivation of cash crops, they did not have control over income earned from cash crops. Colonial agricultural officials introduced cash crops through men: they distributed seeds or seedlings to men, and purchased the harvests from men. New 'cash crops' were therefore 'seen as' (*kuzetera*) being 'men's crops'.

Although women had little say over these crops and the money they brought in, they were, in some cases, expected to make significant contributions of labour to them. For example, coffee created additional demands on women's time: in both the 'bug-picking' that the antestia problem made necessary, and also in processing coffee for sale. In 1938 Masefield, the DAO, noted that coffee hulling had become the 'limiting factor in coffee production. Many men are unwilling to pick more than a certain quantity of coffee because of the reluctance of the women to undertake the hard work of hulling.'[61] Masefield sought advice on other ways the coffee could be prepared for sale, but this was not followed up. Indeed this is the only time that the problem of the increased labour demands of cash crops, particularly for women, was recorded. But elderly women informants confirm that coffee was laborious for them, and that they had little or no control over coffee income.[62] Efuransi Batuta did not even try to stop the pest; the main reason she gave up coffee was that it was 'too tiresome and needed a lot of work'. Baryayanga noted that the coffee harvest came when women were busy planting beans and harvesting sorghum, while Bazarwa and Mukabuzungu stated 'that time [when coffee was harvested] was a very busy time – people were planting sweet potatoes in the swamps ... digging to plant beans, and harvesting sorghum'.[63] All these activities mentioned were women's tasks.

Tobacco and flax were similarly seen as men's crops, as men controlled income earned from them. In fact, as I will show, tobacco production did not 'fail' but was perceived as a failure by colonial officials, because of their inability to maintain control of its marketing. Flax, on the other hand, was a clear failure, and part of the reason why it was never popular again relates to constraints on land and labour. As with other cash crops women did not adopt flax because of the existing demands of food production on their labour, the expectations that they would produce food crops for family consumption, and because they had no control over income from flax. For men there were two major constraints, namely land and labour, as well as other more attractive opportunities to earn cash, particularly through labour migration. The land constraint is particularly interesting, as here in Kabale, as Khadiagala has convincingly argued, women's rights to control property were strong and were upheld by colonial courts (see Chapters 4 and 5).[64] On marriage a women would be allocated land by her husband, to be used for food production. If a man (or an unmarried woman) wants to grow crops for individual gain then they can do so under a system called *okwehereka* (lit: 'cultivating for self').[65] A man can either do this on *omwehereko* land (that which has not been allocated to his wives), or by negotiating use rights through his wives.[66] As land became increasingly scarce men are likely to have kept back smaller and smaller pieces of *omwehereko* land. Furthermore, gaining access to land already allocated to wives for *okwehereka* for untested and risky cash crops is also likely to have become increasingly difficult for men. In addition, men did not have full control over women's labour on land being cultivated under *okwehereka*: even if a man asks his wife to help him on his *okwehereka* plot, he must give her something in return for working for him.[67] Thus the rights of married women to use land allocated to them on marriage for the cultivation of food crops is well regarded, while their rights over their own labour for cultivation of food crops is also well protected.[68] Both sets of rights acted to constrain the production of cash crops in Kigezi.

Men were also reluctant to adopt cash crops, as by the 1930s and 1940s there were new opportunities for men to earn cash through migration. The practice of seeking work in Buganda on cotton farms began from the 1920s and grew in importance, although there are few statistics available that enable us to estimate the flow of labour from the district. But we do know that 'large numbers' of men were going to Buganda for work and oral sources suggest that temporary migration for between three and nine months was particularly popular amongst young men, who would often go with one or two friends prior to marriage.[69] Most cultivated cotton for the Baganda, and District Officials noted that 'a spirit of adventure prompted these excursions, quite as much as economic pressure'.[70] Such migration provided men with the opportunity to earn cash which did not necessitate their entering complex negotiations with their own (often female) family members for land and labour, and this may have acted as a disincentive for men to produce cash crops.

Given constraints on both land and labour it is not surprising that farmers were reluctant to adopt new crops unless they paid better, involved less labour (especially at critical times) and were more reliable. While coffee may have paid better, it involved more labour (especially at critical times for women) and disease meant it was unreliable. Prices for flax were low, and disease meant it was also unreliable. Tobacco was a reliable crop, but it only paid better if it was sold illicitly and this is what people did, which meant that in the eyes of colonial officials it was a failure. I will now explore these problems associated with marketing.

MARKETING

While food crops could be readily sold at markets that existed from the early colonial period, cash crops had to be sold through the colonial authorities that introduced them and they were subject to tight marketing controls. This is most clearly illustrated by the case of nicotine tobacco, but it is worth noting that farmers also found the marketing channels for coffee restrictive. Coffee was brought under the Native Produce Marketing Ordinance in September 1934, and markets for coffee were established in the district. The prices offered were satisfactory when compared with those in Kampala at the time, but lower than those in neighbouring Ankole.[71] By 1937 it was apparent that, contrary to marketing legislation, coffee was being smuggled out of the district as 'sellers can get higher prices in Belgian Congo, Ruanda and Ankole and can sell every day'.[72] The small fine was an inadequate deterrent and the DAO reported that local people smuggled at night. It appears therefore that there were disincentives to selling coffee, which, combined with lower prices and the labour constraints discussed above, acted to discourage coffee production.[73]

How and when produce could be sold was as important as crop prices. For example, informants suggest that delays in payments for flax discouraged farmers from growing it. Harvested flax had to be taken to a neighbouring village for collection and one farmer recalled that 'for flax you used to wait until many heaps were harvested then they would come and take it!'[74]

The importance of ease of marketing is most clearly demonstrated by the case of nicotine tobacco which (after some initial difficulties) Bakiga farmers took to well, but then chose to sell through their own channels. In 1950 it was reported that production of nicotine tobacco had fallen, despite increased prices.[75] In fact production of tobacco continued, but the amount sold to Stafford's factory declined significantly. The administration acknowledged that sales had fallen because 'a considerable amount is exported in headloads to Ankole and Ruanda for smoking or snuff,' and that 'the amount of nicotine tobacco marketed for the purpose for which the crop was originally started has been on the decline, partly because ... it is sold locally for smoking purposes'.[76] This is supported by informants, who recall selling nicotine tobacco (known as *Rwita rusyo*) against the wishes of the colonial administration. Ruheeka, for example, sold to people from Ankole, risking imprisonment if discovered. He recalled that prices were higher than those received through official channels. Bazarwa and Mukabuzungu also noted that individuals paid more than the government, and also paid in cash, and came to their farms to buy the tobacco from them.[77]

Rwita was much stronger than other varieties and colonial officials tried a number of tactics to discourage people from selling it for smoking purposes. First, it was named '*Rwita rusyo*' meaning 'kills like that' and people were told that smoking *Rwita* caused madness at best and death at worst. But this did not deter farmers, who found it to their liking, and who found a ready market from Ankole. *Rwita* was commonly mixed with other varieties (to improve its smoking quality, and also to disguise it when selling illegally):

> *Smoko* and *rwita rusyo* were most popular for growing and even for smoking. They mixed *rwita rusyo* and *smoko* and it became sweeter. ... The *bazungu* (whites) expected us to sell it to them, but we mixed it ... and then smoked it. [So] we stopped selling it to the *bazungu* and started mixing it with [other varieties] ... We still sold it – but took it to Ankole and Katwe, mixed with other varieties ... [and] sold it to other villagers. ... The *bazungu* price was small ... [and was] a fixed price, the others you would negotiate the price. I don't know [the actual] prices – but villagers' price was about three times that of *bazungu*.[78]

So, having been encouraged to grow tobacco for the factory, Bakiga farmers, much to the annoyance of officials, began to sell on the local market where the price was at least as good and marketing considerably easier.[79] Thus tobacco was successfully introduced into Kigezi, but as the government lost control of marketing and it came to be used for a different purpose from that originally intended, so it was, in government terms, 'a failure'.

This section has revealed some of the contradictions in colonial policy. While efforts to introduce cash crops were broadly unsuccessful, Bakiga farmers took up opportunities that offered good returns. They were, however, also quick to switch back to food crops if the returns on cash crops fell below those of food crops, the latter of which had the added advantage of use value as well as exchange value for farmers.[80] They were keen to grow crops over which they could maintain marketing control, which included food crops and (albeit illicitly) tobacco. There were also other possibilities for earning cash through migrant labour (especially for men) and from food crops (especially for women). This was occasionally observed by officials: 'people could make good money by selling peas, beans and English potatoes, ... so on the whole they did not see the need ... for another economic crop.'[81] Similarly officials suggested that the decline in flax cultivation was because 'the return for flax is appreciably lower than that which can be obtained from other crops or from wage earning'.[82] But these occasional observations had little, if any, impact on policy. The failure to make Kigezi into what colonial officials considered to be a 'cash crop economy' (i.e. one producing crops that were exported through official channels) would seem to be in part due to the inadequate recognition given by the administration to food production and trade.[83] Farmers felt that cash crops such as flax could not be eaten if there was a poor harvest of food crops.[84] The strength of the local market in food crops was a clear disincentive for farmers to experiment with untested cash crops.

While increased land scarcity during the colonial period might be a reason why farmers would want to focus on crops that gave them greater returns per acre, these crops would also have to 'fit' into the existing agricultural system, given existing labour demands, the gender division of labour and access to land and labour. Such crops would need marketing arrangements that suited Bakiga farmers and had been considered to be sufficiently reliable to convince people to switch. This was not the case for the cash crops on offer. The deeply entrenched belief that the production of cash crops for export was essential to 'agricultural development' meant that colonial efforts were doomed to failure. In attempting to introduce cash crops the state was trying to replace an already successful system that was producing surpluses of food crops for sale. But the colonial authorities did not entirely ignore the food crop sector, and there were significant efforts made to control marketing of food crops in the latter part of the colonial period. I will now examine Bakiga responses to these food crop marketing policies.

Food production and marketing

Kigezi's cropping system centred on the production of food crops, and there was trade in the pre-colonial period, albeit with some difficulties. The markets that existed before the coming of the British were, according to Edel, dangerous places because of interclan feuding, and travelling through areas inhabited by different clans was unsafe. At this time kin relations (whether through blood relations or marriage) and relations created through blood brotherhood were critical to ensuring the safety of traders. It is notable that many informants recall that one of the main reasons for entering into blood brotherhood was to ease movement between places. But the *Pax Britannica* of colonialism was to change this and as safety increased so trading became easier and markets became more important. [85] In 1937 officials observed that 'cultivation of food for sale appears to be increasing everywhere' and that 'large quantities' of foodstuffs were sold to mining companies in Ankole and for export to the Congo.[86] Trading in food crops, already occurring in the pre-colonial period, appears to have increased from the early colonial period, so that by the 1930s sales of food crops were critical for raising money for poll taxes, and colonial officials themselves noted that trade in foodstuffs was 'very considerable'.[87] Thus, by the time colonial officials were seriously promoting cash crops (in the 1920s and 1930s) Bakiga farmers already had a ready and profitable market for crops they grew.

Colonial policies towards maize reveal much about colonial attitudes towards 'agricultural development' and provide an interesting perspective on the food crop/cash crop dichotomy. From the mid-1930s maize was recognised as a popular crop and was one of a number of food crops earning large sums of money for the district.[88] Official policy, however, was not to encourage maize because of concerns about soil erosion and concerns related to East Africa-wide maize marketing policy. The few references in administrative records about maize make it clear that it should be discouraged.[89] Despite this, acreages of maize increased throughout the colonial period, although estimates of acreages may well be underestimated as maize is commonly intercropped with other food crops. This may also in part explain its popularity: maize is most commonly planted with beans and so could easily be incorporated into the existing agricultural system. And like other grain crops, in years of good harvest it could be sold at local markets and thus enter regional food flows. Thus, being a food crop that could be sold made maize attractive to Bakiga farmers, for whom uncertainty was an important factor in decision-making.[90] But although Bakiga farmers took to maize well, paradoxically wider colonial considerations meant it was officially discouraged.

On one hand, then, officials acknowledged the importance of beer and food sales for incomes within the district, they realised that surplus food was produced for export, and that this food was traded in exchange for goats from Ruanda. Official records show significant increases in the acreages of certain food crops, specifically sorghum, plantains and maize (see Figure 2.3). On the other hand, in relation to policy, remarkably little attention was

Figure 2.3 *Acreages of food crops, Kigezi,* 1936–62[91]

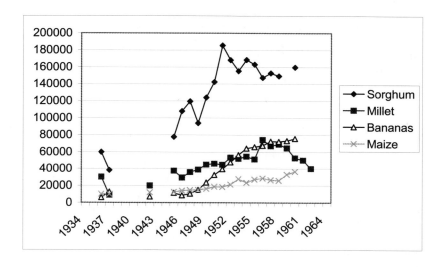

paid to the food trade, no efforts were made to further encourage or promote it, and at no time did the administration see this trade as something to be 'harnessed' for 'agricultural development'.

This indifference towards food crops shifted in the 1940s when the administration went from virtually ignoring food crops to placing tight controls on their marketing. Bakiga responses to controls on the movement of food from Kigezi provide further evidence of the significant contribution of food crops to the local economy.

MARKETING & SMUGGLING FOOD CROPS, 1940–60

While failing to acknowledge the significance of the local foodstuffs sector and believing that it was not commercially viable, the administration extended marketing controls to it .[92] As efforts to control food marketing increased, so did Bakiga efforts to get around these controls and dispose of their surpluses by smuggling. Information about the foodstuffs trade within Kigezi is very scarce and there is virtually no empirical data on local markets, but examining responses to controls on the export of food from the district sheds light on this important trade.

Colonial administrators controlled the marketing of food crops through the Native Foodstuffs Ordinance (1919).[93] They introduced controls because of a perceived need to protect African farmers from the 'greedy middleman', and a desire to maintain district food self-sufficiency.[94] This concern for both country and district-level self-sufficiency in food was re-emphasised with the coming of the Second World War, as colonial administrators sought to reduce imports. Furthermore, in 1943 there was a severe famine in the region: in neighbouring Rwanda many areas were affected and an estimated 300,000 people died.[95] Fearing food shortages as a result of the adverse weather conditions, administrators in Uganda tightened marketing regulations under the Defence (Control of Famine) Regulation (1943).[96] The purchase of African foodstuffs for resale or export beyond the district was prohibited and traders had to apply for export licences and submit monthly purchase returns to the DC. This did not affect ordinary Africans, but was aimed at large-scale traders and transporters, the majority of whom were Indians.[97] One consequence was that district officials had to detail surpluses available, giving some insight into production levels of African foodstuffs that normally went unreported. It becomes clear from these reports that the most densely populated areas of Kigezi, in particular Ndorwa and Rukiga, were indeed important food exporting counties.[98] Little or no food was officially available for export throughout 1943, although this had to be enforced through a 'strict system of frontier guards ... to prevent the export of foodstuffs from Kigezi [into Ruanda]'.[99] Furthermore, despite adverse weather conditions it was not necessary to import food into Kigezi. When the ban on food exports from the district was lifted it was replaced by a permit system for the purchase and export of food products, which continued throughout the 1940s. Whenever colonial administrators considered that local supplies were threatened, they withdrew these purchase and export permits, and this happened periodically, such as in 1946 and 1949.[100]

Throughout the 1940s, as controls over trade were tightened, so farmers circumvented these controls by smuggling their produce out of Kigezi. Although this illicit trade is difficult to quantify, there are many references to it and it was of significant proportions. Even in a bad year, such as 1948 when a 'severe drought' affected the southern part of the district, no food had to be imported; in fact, over 2,000 tons of food (valued at over £16,000) was sold for export.[101] Furthermore, this figure is probably an underestimate as it only includes produce sold legally with permits. In the same year the DAO observed that there was a 'considerable illicit trade in produce' by both Indian and African traders so that it was impossible to estimate what surpluses were being produced.[102] As a result of continued poor weather and 'the need to ensure all local food supplies', the DC cancelled all permits to export food in 1949,[103] but the substantial illegal trade in foodstuffs continued.

Smuggling was made easier by the fact that the districts had different export regulations. For example, while it was illegal to export peas from Kigezi, it was not from neighbouring Ankole where peas were hardly grown. Wholesalers in Ankole declared large quantities of peas (over 200 tons in three months in 1949, and about 500 tons in 1950), nearly all of which were believed to have originated in Kigezi.[104] The DAO in Kabale acknowledged that, despite the ban, large quantities of peas were being taken out of Kigezi without permits, by both lorries and head loads, to Ankole and beyond.[105] Officials admitted that the ban on pea exports had failed and pea exports were again allowed under permit, granted only if the *gombolola* chief was sure that 'the owner has a genuine surplus'.[106] Colonial officials clearly felt that farmers could not be trusted to judge for themselves whether they had a 'genuine surplus', despite the fact that farmers had consistently and successfully made decisions as to when it was appropriate to sell food products.

While the state attempted to regulate exports through the reintroduction of permits, trade continued illicitly without permits. [107] 'Very considerable quantities' of foodstuffs, particularly peas, sorghum and bulo were observed being illegally exported from Kigezi.[108] A market at Rwahi, Ankole, close to the boundary with Kigezi and some distance from any Ankole population, sold large quantities of foodstuffs without permits, mainly peas, beans, maize and sorghum. As this produce was from Kigezi, the DC was anxious to prevent it. Ankole's DC, however, observed that this was unfair to African traders as 'it is a known fact that the majority of the peas and sorghum come out of Kigezi by lorry and are sold to Mbarara and Masaka merchants,' a fact acknowledged by Kigezi's DC.[109] Officials estimated that during 1951 as much as 1,000 tons of peas had been 'sold and illegally exported' from the district, and the DC feared that the illegal export of peas had 'assumed alarming proportions of late and might well lead to serious consequences locally should there be a famine'.[110] When in 1952, 'sales of foodstuffs ... showed a considerable drop over the previous year, but the acreage planted did not fall proportionately',[111] it was assumed that much of this drop was accounted for by local consumption; but it seems more likely that smuggling accounted for the apparent fall.

New marketing legislation introduced in 1953, the Produce Marketing Ordinance, gave the DC continued powers to control the marketing and trade of all agricultural produce in his district.[112] The DC argued strongly that he should be able to continue to control exports of peas and potatoes, as in the densely populated areas of Kigezi 'food shortages can reasonably be termed imminent at all times'.[113] The latter, however, was no more than a colonial myth to justify continued marketing controls. These densely populated areas were, in fact, important food exporting areas where the production of surpluses of food crops was the norm. Even during the severe drought of 1943 (which had affected Kigezi in particular) no food imports were necessary and severe measures had to be taken to prevent exports. The same thing occurred in 1948 when, despite the drought, large quantities of food were exported. The assertion that shortages were 'imminent' justified marketing regulations, which acted as a constraint on production and ultimately did more harm than good.

Warnings of imminent food shortage were repeated in 1953 and 1954[114] and at this stage it is worth speculating whether shortages might actually have been *caused* by the administration's own policies. Tight controls on food exports from the district may well eventually have had a negative impact on production levels. Indeed, in 1954, the DAO observed that there were 'considerable decreases in the planting of some of the most important food crops', and he called upon chiefs to ensure that the planting of food crops was increased.[115] At no stage did officials acknowledge that the district's agricultural policy might have been responsible for this fall in production, or that increased production was obstructed by the lack of official markets for surplus produce.[116] The production of surplus food crops had long been central to the Kigezi agricultural system, and when colonial administrators introduced marketing controls on these foodstuffs Bakiga farmers responded by smuggling the food out of the district.

Conclusion

The concern of colonial authorities was to find suitable cash crops for Kigezi and agricultural officials focused their attention on export crops. From the mid-1930s a series of cash crops was tried in turn, none with any long-term success. As each new crop was introduced some Bakiga farmers seized the opportunities it offered, but this was only in the short term with no fundamental shift to cash crops introduced by the colonial authorities. Meanwhile, colonial officials paid very little attention to food crop production, while an increasing trend towards state involvement in food marketing was either ineffectual or negative.

Critically Bakiga farmers could, and did, make profits from the sale of surplus foodstuffs. The regional trade in food crops was stimulated by the presence of areas of food deficit, by Ruanda's taxation system and by trade in non-foodstuffs; the coming of colonialism provided further stimuli for food production. Understanding the centrality of food cropping within the Bakiga agricultural system is crucial to understanding agrarian change in the district, and the failure of the state to recognise the significance of food crops in the exchange economy helps to explain the failure of cash crops. Officials viewed Kigezi as a peripheral part of the Protectorate of Uganda, and they largely ignored the fact that Kigezi was a part of a vibrant food production system that crossed colonial boundaries.

Officials scarcely explored reasons for the failure of cash crops, except for coffee, where disease was blamed. I suggest that the failure may in part be explained by the relationship between the new 'cash crops' and food crops that farmers already produced for sale. Labour requirements of new crops, and how these compared with food crops, were critical. Women's time was already stretched with food production, which had the distinct advantage for women that they had greater control over food crops and their use for household consumption or for sale. Colonial officials introduced cash crops through men, and it was men who sold them and controlled income from sales. Men wishing to grow cash crops could either use *omwehereka* land, or had to negotiate access to land through their wives. Returns had to be sufficiently high, and labour demands manageable, to make this worth their while; as land became more scarce this would have been increasingly difficult. In addition, by the time cash crops were promoted, temporary labour migration by men had become popular as a source of income. There was one cash crop male farmers did adopt – tobacco – but they found they could get a better price by selling tobacco directly to Ankole. Much to the annoyance of the colonial state, they chose to market it through their own networks, rather than through official channels; consequently tobacco was not deemed a 'successful' cash crop.

Restrictive marketing also constrained the production of cash crops, particularly compared to the marketing of food crops. Food crop production was profitable and in the early colonial period wider trading networks allowed Bakiga farmers to transform their surplus food production into livestock with relative ease. Marketing food crops was considerably easier than marketing cash crops, most of which, in addition, had no use value to their producers. It is perhaps significant that maize, a crop with both exchange and use value to the growers, became popular with Bakiga farmers, despite colonial efforts to discourage it. In the postwar period, legislation to prevent food exports was more tightly enforced, and smuggling became a serious concern of the colonial administration. Colonial controls on the exchanges of foodstuffs limited farmers' outlets for their surpluses and it seems eminently possible that such policies ultimately had an adverse effect on levels of food production. The cases of tobacco and food crops thus illustrate that a 'successful' cash crop for colonialists was, in fact, a cash crop the marketing of which they could control; very different from the way Kigezi farmers would define success.

Notes

[1] See Wrigley, *Crops and Wealth*; Brett, *Colonialism and Underdevelopment*; Bunker, *Peasants Against the State*.

[2] See Pottier, 'The politics of famine prevention'. Also see R. Gray and D. Birmingham *Pre Colonial African Trade – Essays on Trade in Central and Eastern Africa before 1900* (London, 1970); J.P. Chrétien, *The Great Lakes of Africa: Two Thousand Years of History* (New York, 2003) 191–5; D. Bryceson, 'Peasant cash cropping versus self-sufficiency in Tanzania: A historical perspective', *IDS Bulletin* 192 (1988), 37–46; D.W. Cohen, 'Food production and food exchange in pre-colonial Lakes plateau region' in R.I. Rotberg (ed.), *Imperialism, Colonialism and Hunger: East and Central Africa* (Lexington, MA, 1983); J.L. Giblin, *The Politics of Environmental Control in Northeastern Tanzania, 1840–1940* (Philadelphia, 1992) esp. chapters 1 and 2; and D.S. Newbury, *Kings and Clans: Ijwi Island and Lake Kivu Rift 1780–1840* (Madison, WI, 1992). For an examination of the diverse impact of commercialisation in four contrasting rural economies see S. Berry *No Condition is Permanent: The Social Dynamics of Agrarian Change in Sub Saharan Africa* (Madison, WI, 1993).

[3] J. Tosh, 'The cash crop revolution in Tropical Africa: An agricultural reappraisal', *African Affairs*, 79 (1980), 80, 90. See also J. Tosh, 'Lango agriculture during the early colonial period: Land and labour in a cash crop economy', *Journal of African History*, 19 (1978), 415–39. For West Africa see for example C. Meillassoux (ed.), *The Development of Indigenous Trade and Markets in West Africa* (London, 1971); and A.G. Hopkins, *Economic History in West Africa* (London, 1973).

[4] It should be noted, however, that when colonial officials refer to 'trade' they usually mean trade carried out by outside traders, rather than 'internal' trade or exchange. For colonial sources see for example WPAR, 1933; District Agriculture Annual Report for 1937, Masefield, KDA DC AGR-MNTH ff98; J.W. Purseglove, 'Kitozho Mutala survey', 1940. For external observers see Edel, *The Chiga*, 89–90 and J. Roscoe, *The Bagesu and Other Tribes of the Uganda Protectorate. The Third Part of the Report of the Mackie Ethnological Expedition of Central Africa* (Cambridge, 1924), 168. For oral sources: 00/Bub/14c, 95/Muy/30b, 95/Muy/59a, 95/Muy/61a, 95/Muy/63a and 95/Bub/91a. Also see: 95/

Kab/16b, 95/Kab/17b, 95/Bub/93a, 95/Bub/94a. Interviews were conducted in 1995, 2000 and 2002. Reference system: Year/Location/Informant/Interview. See Appendix for further details.

[5] This is in contrast to, for example, Bwisha in eastern Congo, when, as Pottier and Fairhead have argued, food production was not a major source of income until after 1960. They note that prior to this, in normal periods, food had little value outside the household. But they do observe that 'within socially secured trading networks' men exchanged sorghum and tobacco, together with beer and skins, for hoes, salt and animals (p. 441). J. Pottier and J. Fairhead, 'Post famine recovery in highland Bwisha, Zaire: 1984 in its context', *Africa*, 61 (1991), 437–70. For an examination of the renegotiation of gender relations associated with the commercialisation of food production in Busoga, Uganda, see P. Sorensen, 'Commercialization of food crops in Busoga, Uganda, and the renegotiation of gender', *Gender & Society*, 10 5 (1996), 608–28. She notes that since the 1990s food crops have been 'considered to be commercial crops on the same footing of the more traditional cash crops', 616. In Kigezi this has been the case for much longer.

[6] D.S. Newbury, 'Lake Kivu regional trade in the nineteenth century', *Journal des Africanistes*, 50 2 (1980), 6–30; B. Lugan, 'Causes et effets de la famine 'Rumanura' au Rwanda, 1916–18', *Canadian Journal of African Studies* , X 2 (1976), 347–56; R. Mutombo, 'Marchés et circuits commerciaux de la région des Masangano a la fin de l'époque pré coloniale', *Etudes Rwandaises* 11 Numéro Special, March (1978), 33–45; B. Lugan, 'L'Economie d'Echange au Rwanda de 1850–1914'. Discussing the pre-colonial Great Lakes region Chrétien notes that there was both 'short-distance seasonal bartering of food and cattle products, as a function of complementarity between ecological sectors' and trade in salt, iron and jewelry that gave rise to 'truly regional trade' (191). Whether such a distinction between these two trading types is necessary or helpful is doubtful, as there was much blurring between them. See Chrétien, *The Great Lakes of Africa*.

[7] Pottier, 'The politics of famine prevention.' 231.

[8] Pottier, 'The politics of famine prevention.' See also Newbury, 'Lake Kivu regional trade'. Newbury considers the characteristics of this trade system and argues that in the Lake Kivu area 'trade was carried out on a significant scale with organised markets'. The commodities he explores include hoes, food, livestock and fibre bracelets. Similarly Andersson has observed that farming in the Uporoto Mountains of Tanganyika was not simply subsistence production, but the area was incorporated into wider networks of economic exchange. J.A. Andersson, 'Potato cultivation in the Uporoto Mountains, Tanzania', *African Affairs*, 95 378 (1996), 85–106.

[9] In exchange for labour either as food *okucwa encuro* (02/Muy/48; 02/Kbz/5d; 02/Muy/28c ; 02/Muy/T36a), or as beer (02/Muy/36c). 95/Kab/16b, 95/Kab/17b, 95/Muy/30b, 95/Bub/93a, 95/Bub/94a, 02/Muy/30d, 02/Muy/31b).

[10] 00/Bub/14c. 02/Kbz/5d, 02/Kbz/44b, 02/Muy/30d; 02/Muy/36c.

[11] Mutombo 'Marchés et circuits commerciaux' (Small stock going from Rwanda to Uganda; salt and hoes going from Uganda to Rwanda). See also 95/Muy/30b, 95/Muy/59a, 95/Muy/61a, 95/Muy/63a and 95/Bub/91a. 00/Bub/T14c; 02/Muy/30d; 02/Muy/36c; 02/Muy/13c; 02/Muy/31b; 02/Muy/31c.

[12] WPAR 1923, KDA DC MP23 and KDA DC GENPOL. See also Letter to PCWP from Adams, DC 12/10/21, KDA DC MP10 ff. 44.

[13] WPAR 1924, KDA DC MP23. Also for example WPAR, 1928 and 1929.

[14] Kitching, *Class and Economic Change*.

[15] Lecture to Royal Geographical Society, 14 April 1913. See *Geographical Journal*, VI (June 1913), 545. See also Mutombo, 'Marchés et circuits commerciaux.'

[16] C.M. Good, 'Salt, trade and disease: Aspects of development in Africa's northern great lakes region', *International Journal of African Historical Studies*, V 4 (1972), 558. See also J.W. Purseglove, 'Report on the overpopulated areas of Kigezi', 21, 561. See also WPAR, 1928 and 1929. Salt traders were also mentioned by Elliot (Diary of J.R.McD. Elliot, Rhodes House [hereafter RH] MSS Afr s 1384 #28), in WPARs, and when lorries replaced human porterage.

[17] C.M. Good, *Rural Markets and Trade in East Africa; A study of the functions and development of*

exchange institutions in Ankole, Uganda (Chicago, 1970). These profit margins were comparable to other commodities elsewhere in the region – for example *butega* fibre bracelets. See Newbury, 'Lake Kivu regional trade', 15. For further discussion of transition to lorries, see Good, 'Salt, trade and disease'.

[18] Letter to PCWP from Adams, DC, 12 Oct 1921. KDA DC MP10 ff. 44.

[19] WPAR, 1927. See also Kigezi District Annual Report 1917–18.

[20] Letter to PCWP from DC, 27 July 1928, KDA DC MP 132 ff. 109. See also Entebbe National Archives [ENA] C1376 re food exports to Ruanda in 1929.

[21] Roscoe, *The Bagesu and Other Tribes*, 168.

[22] Edel, *The Chiga*, 89–90.

[23] WPAR, 1933.

[24] Agricultural District Annual Report for 1937, Masefield, KDA DC AGR-MNTH ff. 98.

[25] Purseglove, 'Kitozho Mutala survey', 1940.

[26] Lugard, *The Dual Mandate*, 606.

[27] For further details see G.B. Masefield, *A History of the Colonial Agricultural Service* (Oxford, 1972), and G.B. Masefield, *A Short History of Agriculture in the British Colonies* (Oxford, 1950).

[28] See Wrigley, *Crops and Wealth*, 21–43; C. Ehrlich, 'The Uganda Economy 1903–45' in V. Harlow, E.M. Chilver and A. Smith, *History of East Africa* Vol. 2, (Oxford, 1965), 409–13 and 423–9; and R.M.A. Van Zwanenberg with A. King, *An Economic History of Kenya and Uganda, 1800–1970* (London, 1975), 64.

[29] Although see Masefield, *A History of the Colonial Agricultural Service*, 70. He argues that increased awareness of the extent of malnutrition in the late 1930s led to a stepping up of research on food crops.

[30] Order of priority agreed at Inter-territorial Conference in Nairobi for essential war industries in Uganda were: 1. Rubber; 2. Sugar, 3. Tin 4. Sisal and pyrethrum; 5. Timber. Letter to All DCs from Famine Commission, 19 March 1943. KDA DC MP-EOC ff. 25.

[31] Wrigley, *Crops and Wealth*, 68, 74–5. For further details of the development of policy see G. Carswell 'African Farmers in Colonial Kigezi, Uganda, 1930–1962: Opportunity, Constraint and Sustainability' (PhD, SOAS, 1996).

[32] D.A. Lury, 'Dayspring Mishandled? The Uganda Economy 1945-60' in D.A. Low and A. Smith, *History of East Africa*, Vol. 3 (Oxford, 1976), 212. The realisation that development in Uganda would not come through agriculture alone led also to a shift towards mining and secondary industries in the postwar period. For further details see Carswell, 'African Farmers'.

[33] In addition to those discussed below, pyrethrum and tea were also attempted. The former was grown as a plantation crop during the 1940s. Tea was experimented with, but was ruled out because of the lack of processing facilities in the district and high transport costs. Cotton was never attempted as much of Kigezi was climatically unsuitable for cotton. For a brief period between 1949 and the early 1950s exports of black wattle bark made a significant contribution to the local economy. However, this was shortlived as the high prices were caused by changing trading relations between India and South Africa. See Carswell, 'African Farmers'.

[34] Similar for example to Bugishu. See Bunker, *Peasants against the State*.

[35] Meeting of 8 Nov 1923 at Kabale to discuss 'Kigezi District Agricultural Development.' KDA DC MP132 ff. 15. See also WPAR, 1921.

[36] WPAR, 1930. WPARs 1924, 1929 and 1931. See also Diaries of J.D. Snowden, Agricultural Officer, Tours of Uganda, 1929–30. RH MSS Afr s 921 ff. 255.

[37] Agricultural Report by Wickham for Oct 1934, KDA DC AGR-MNTH ff. 18. See also WPARs 1934 and 1935.

[38] WPAR, 1934.

[39] Antestia is a serious coffee pest which particularly affects wetter areas, causing the coffee berries to fall off. Open pruning discourages antestia, and there are a number of effective insecticides. J.D. Acland, *East African Crops* (London, 1971), 82. See also D.S. Hill and J.M. Waller, *Pests and Diseases of Tropical Crops*, Vol. 1 (London, 1982) and J.D. Tothill, *Agriculture in Uganda*, 1st edition (London, 1940), 340–8.

[40] Letter to PCWP from Tothill, 25 Oct 1932, ENA H43/4 ff. 1.

[41] WPAR, 1932.

[42] Acreage data compiled from Kabale District Agricultural Book (KDA), KDA DC MP 4II ff. 233; ENA H43/4 ff. 10. Sales data from: WPARs; Annual Reports of the Department of Agriculture; Public Records Officer [hereafter PRO] CO 892 15/7. KDA DC AGR-MNTH ff. 17; Purseglove, Report (1945); RH MSS Perham 521/9.

[43] Report for Year 1935 by Wickham and Report on visit to Kigezi April 1936 by Stedman-Davies, Acting Senior Ag Officer, Kampala, KDA DC AGR-MNTH ff. 53, ff. 58 and ff. 58enc.

[44] Agricultural Report by Wickham for June 1935, KDA DC AGR-MNTH ff. 32. Also Report on tour of Rukiga by A.C.A. Wright (ADC) in 1937, KDA DC MP139 ff. 34. WPARs, 1935–1939.

[45] Flue- and fire-cured tobacco are both for smoking, while nicotine tobacco contains larger quantities of nicotine which was extracted for use as an insecticide before synthetic insecticides. Acland, *East African Crops*.

[46] See KDA DC MP2A. In the early stages of growth tobacco needs frequent weeding. As the plant approaches maturity 'topping' has to be performed to remove the flower heads, excess leaves and side shoots and suckers. It is thus a labour-demanding crop if a good harvest is to be produced.

[47] Letter to SAO, Masindi from Stafford, 27 April 1942. KDA DC MP2A ff. 37. Stafford had various business interests and was also involved in pyrethrum production. For further details see Carswell, 'African Farmers'.

[48] Letter to SAO, Masindi from McCombe, DAO, 12 Oct 1942. KDA DC MP2A ff. 69.

[49] Data compiled from Kabale District Agricultural Book (KDA). Reference to nicotine tobacco ceases from the mid-1950s in the District Agricultural Book, but farmers are adamant that production of nicotine tobacco continued.

[50] WPAR, 1947.

[51] WPAR, 1950.

[52] Flue-cured tobacco was grown, especially in the north of the district, and was sold through official channels, although 'large quantities' were also sold to unlicensed buyers. Department of Agriculture Annual Report, 1956.

[53] KDA DC AGR3–4. Also WPAR, 1946. For more on trials see KDA DoA 009exp-c.

[54] Letter to *saza* Chiefs from DAO 19 July 1948. KDA DC Agr3/4 ff. 1.

[55] Flax had to be planted in beds, and then transplanted, which added significantly to the labour needed for this crop. Memo on Shifting Cultivation in Western Province (by Purseglove, Oct 1951) PRO CO 892 15/7.

[56] Shared: 02/Kbz/52a and 02/Kbz/11d; 02/Kbz/42b. Men alone: 02/Kbz /44b and 02/Kbz/51.

[57] G.A. Fennell, 'Flax', in Jameson, *Agriculture in Uganda*, 228–9.

[58] Data compiled from Kabale District Agricultural Book (located in KDA).

[59] WPAR, 1948. For further details see Carswell, 'African Farmers'.

[60] Edel, *The Chiga*, 82.

[61] Letter to Senior Ag Officer from G.B. Masefield, Ag Officer, Kigezi 30/3/38. KDA DoA 11-a-1 ff. 3.

[62] 00/Muy/16a. Also see 00/Muy/T18a; 02/Kbz/42b and 02/Muy/T31c.

[63] 00/Muy/T24a. Efuransi Batuta is a particularly hard-working and successful farmer. Also see 00/Muy/37a. 02/Kbz/5d, 02/Kbz/11d and 02/Kbz/52.

[64] For a detailed account of the decline in women's legal property rights over the past fifty years see L.S. Khadiagala, 'Negotiating law and custom' *Journal of African Law*, 46 1 (2002).

[65] Married women cannot undertake *okwehereka* because 'as a woman she has to grow crops to feed the family.' 02/Muy/13c.

[66] 02/Muy/T38; Also see L.S. Khadiagala, 'Justice and power in the adjudication of women's property rights in Uganda', *Africa Today*, 49 2 (2002). 02/Muy/T30b.

[67] 02/Muy/T37.

[68] See Khadiagala, 'Negotiating Law and Custom' and Khadiagala, 'Justice and Power'.

[69] WPAR, 1923. For example 00/Kbz/26a 00/Kbz/30a, 02/Muy/T15e; 02/Muy/T34.

[70] WPAR, 1936.

[71] Perham Papers – RH MSS Perham 521/9.
[72] Annual Agricultural Report for 1937, Masefield. KDA DC AGR-MNTH ff. 98.
[73] In the early 1950s there was a revival of interest in coffee growing following price rises, but coffee was never a success in Kigezi. See Carswell, 'African Farmers'.
[74] 02/Kbz/11d.
[75] WPAR, 1950.
[76] WPAR, 1951 and 1952. Also re smuggling see KDA DoA 019/B/2 ff. 96.
[77] 02/Kbz/44b, 02/Kbz/11d and 02/Kbz/52. Also 02/Kbz/5d.
[78] 02/Kbz/51. See also 02/Kbz/44b, 02/Kbz/5d, 02/Kbz/11d, 02/Kbz/52 and 02/Muy/T31c.
[79] The ease with which farmers switch from official markets to unofficial markets has been observed by Andersson in the Uporoto Mountains. See Andersson, 'Potato cultivation'.
[80] Mackenzie has similarly observed that in Murang'a District, Kenya, maize and beans were popular as they had both 'use and exchange value.' See Mackenzie, *Land, ecology*.
[81] Report by de Courcy Ireland, written December 1942. KDA DC MP2A ff. 85.
[82] WPAR, 1952. See also KDA DC AGR3–4 and for further details see Carswell, 'African Farmers'.
[83] Nyambara observes how farmers in Southern Rhodesia in the early colonial period preferred to grow food crops, despite colonial efforts to encourage cotton, because of the extra labour demands of cotton and the greater profit associated with food crops. P.S. Nyambara, 'Colonial policy and peasant cotton agriculture in Southern Rhodesia, 1904–1953', *International Journal of African Historical Studies*, 33 1 (2000), 81–111.
[84] This was pointed out to the Flax Officer by farmers. Report to Director of Agriculture from Fennell, 19 April 1955, KDA DC AGR3–4 ff89. See also G.A. Fennell, 'Flax', in Jameson, *Agriculture in Uganda*, 228–9.
[85] Edel, *The Chiga*, 89–90. 00/Kbz/27a, 00/Kbz/29a and 00/Kbz/30b. Informants note that relations of blood-brotherhood are very rare today, as there is no 'need' for them.
[86] WPAR, 1937.
[87] WPAR, 1933 and Agricultural District Annual Report for 1937, Masefield, KDA DC AGR-MNTH ff98.
[88] WPAR, 1937.
[89] Letter to PAO from Purseglove, DAO, 20 July 1946, KDA DoA 006/A/1 ff. 139. Confidential letter to Chf Sec from A.B. Killick, Dir of Ag 15 June 1948, KDA DoA 6/A/3A ff. 15. Letter to Commissioner for Commerce from DC, 20 Sept 1951, KDA DoA 6/A/3A ff. 189. See also WPAR, 1954.
[90] Re risk aversity, see F. Ellis, *Peasant economics: farm households and agrarian development* (Cambridge, 1993), 2nd edition.
[91] Data compiled from Kabale District Agricultural Book (KDA) and KDA DC MP4II ff. 233.
[92] For examinations of marketing of food crops elsewhere and responses to colonial involvement see D. F. Bryceson, *Liberalizing Tanzania's Food Trade: Public and private faces of urban marketing policy 1939–1988* (London, 1993) (esp. chapter 3) and Moore and Vaughan, *Cutting down trees*, (esp. chapter 4).
[93] See *Laws of Uganda*, 1923, Vol. I, 590 and *Laws of Uganda*, 1935, Vol. III, 1292–6. Under the Native Foodstuffs Ordinance (1919), the purchase or barter of foodstuffs for purposes of resale or export from the district could be prohibited and the prices of any foodstuffs fixed.
[94] Letter to McEwen, Acting PAO, from Purseglove, DAO, KDA DoA 010crops, 23 May 1939. For examination of processing and marketing policy in Uganda and the role of middlemen in cotton see for example Ehrlich, 'The Uganda Economy 1903–45'; and Brett, *Colonialism and Underdevelopment* (chapter 8). For discussion of economic paternalism see Lury, 'Dayspring Mishandled'; and C. Ehrlich, 'Some social and economic implications of paternalism in Uganda', *Journal of African History*, iv 2, (1963), 275–85.
[95] The famine was known in Rwanda as Ruzagayura. See C. Newbury, *The Cohesion of Oppression*, (New York, 1988), 144–5, 158. See also I. Linden and J. Linden, *Church and Revolution in Rwanda*, (Manchester, 1977), 207. For conditions in Congo, see Gilbert, *L'Empire du silence* (Brussels, 1947), 23–29, cited in C. Young, *Politics in the Congo: Decolonisation*

and *Independence*, (Princeton, NJ, 1965), 223, all cited in Newbury, *The Cohesion of Oppression.*
[96] *Laws of Uganda*, 1943, 271. In Kigezi the crops given priority during the Second World War included pyrethrum, flax and wheat and the DAO was informed that 'every encouragement should be given in increased production of peas and beans' so that any surplus could be exported to other districts. Letter to DAO from SAO, WP, 26 Jan 1943, KDA DC MP4II ff. 154.
[97] Letter to Dir of Ag from McCombe, DAO, 4 Jan 1943, KDA DC MP4II ff. 74. Letter to various Indian traders and transporters from DC, 4 Oct 1949. KDA DC AGR4/2 ff. 4.
[98] For example see Telegram to DC from Administer, E'be, 2 Feb 1943, KDA DC MP4II ff. 136. Food Crop Notes, Jan 1943, Kigezi, KDA DC MP4II ff. 165 and Memo on Notes on Food Position in Kigezi by the DC written in February 1943, KDA DC MP4II ff. 139.
[99] WPAR, 1939–46.
[100] Letter to DAO from M.G. de Courcy Ireland, PAO, WP, 15 June 1946, KDA DoA 006/A/1 ff. 114.
[101] See KDA DoA 6/A/3A and KDA DoA 11/A/1. WPAR, 1948.
[102] Letter to the Indian Association of Kabale from DAO, 13 Dec 1948, KDA DoA 006/A/2 ff. 356.
[103] Notice by DC, 11 July 1949, KDA DoA 6/A/3A ff. 36.
[104] Table on Sales of African Agriculture produce in 1950 in Memorandum by Purseglove for EARC. PRO CO 892 15/7. Letter to PAO, Buganda from DAO, Masaka, 28 Nov 1949, KDA DoA 6/A/3A ff. 75.
[105] Letter to Dir of Ag, from Purseglove, DAO, 21 Dec 1949, KDA DoA 6/A/3A ff. 77.
[106] Letter to Dir of Ag from DC, 4 Aug 1950, KDA DC AGR/4/2 ff. 128. Letter to Dir of Supplies from Dir of Ag, 10 Aug 1950, KDA DoA 6/A/3A ff. 112. Also Letter to SecGen and All Saza Chfs from DC, 12 Aug 1950, KDA DoA 6/A/3A ff. 113.
[107] Notice from DC, 30 Jan 1951, KDA DoA 6/A/3A ff. 132.
[108] Letter to Saza Chiefs from Purseglove, DAO, 7 Feb 1951, KDA DoA 006/A/3A ff. 135. Prohibition of export under Legal Notice no 23 of 1943. For details of attempts by police to prevent exports see KDA DC AGR4II.
[109] Letter to DC Ankole, from DC (Duntze) Kigezi, 4 July 1951, KDA DC AGR4II ff. 7. Licences issued under Controlled Produce Regulations, Legal Notice No 23 of 1943. Letter from DC, Ankole, 11 July 1951, KDA DC AGR 4II ff. 11. See also Letter from DAO, Ankole to DC, Kabale, 2 Aug 1951, KDA DC MP4II ff. 12. Letter to DAO from DC Kigezi, 23 Aug 1951, KDA DC AGR4II ff. 13.
[110] WPAR, 1951. Letter to Commissioner of Commerce from DC, 2 May 1951, KDA DoA 6/A/3A ff153.
[111] WPAR, 1952.
[112] The Produce Marketing Ordinance was a complex piece of legislation which replaced the Native Produce Marketing Ordinance, the Native Foodstuffs Ordinance and parts of the Defence (Controlled Produce) Regulations. Scheduled Produce allowed the DC to control the movement from his district of produce which constituted the normal famine reserve crops. Circular Memo on Produce Marketing Ordinance, 1953. Written for guidance of Administration officers, by Commissioner of Commerce. KDA DoA 006/A/3B ff. 26. For further details see Carswell, 'African Farmers'.
[113] Letter to PCWP, from DC, 23 July 1953, KDA DC AGR4II ff. 150. Also see Letter to PC from J.A. Burgess, DC, 25 April 1953, KDA DC AGR4II ff. 137 and Letter to Commissioner for Commerce from Burgess, DC, 8 May 1953, KDA DC AGR4II ff. 139.
[114] See for example: Letter to Gomb Chfs from P.Kakwenza, Saza Chf Ndorwa, 11 Aug 1953, KDA DC AGR4II ff. 151; Letter to Saza Chf Ndorwa and Rukiga from DC, 6 April 1954, KDA DC AGR4II ff. 158; and others in KDA DoA 006/A/3B.
[115] Letter to All Saza Chfs from DAO, 23 Aug 1954, KDA DC AGR4II ff. 163.
[116] The EARC (1955) criticised the complex structure of marketing controls, which resulted in 'a degree of inflexibility which was inhibiting economic advancement'. It called for a change in policy to create more favourable conditions. For further details see Carswell, 'African Farmers'.

Three

*Soil Conservation
in Kigezi*

While colonial administrators paid much attention to finding a suitable cash crop for Kigezi, this was not, by any means, the only area of concern. With its dense population and intensive agricultural system, Kigezi has, for decades, been perceived to be at risk from serious environmental degradation. As a result of this, colonial officials in Kigezi put forward a number of policies to try to deal with problems as they saw them – namely land degradation, land shortage and fragmentation. This chapter deals with some of these policies: those of soil conservation and resettlement, while Chapter 5 explores the policies of land tenure reform, consolidation and swamp reclamation. Comparisons with other areas of East Africa will highlight how Kigezi's experience differed from other cases, and will shed light on how the soil conservation policies were successfully implemented in this district, where there was little large-scale resistance. Here I raise questions about the nature of the 'success' of conservation policies, and about the continued sustainability of the agricultural system in the face of increasing population and the social costs of the transformation that the district has undergone, which are examined further in Chapters 6 and 7.

From the 1930s the colonial state in East Africa became increasingly concerned with the environment. Such concerns can be seen all over colonial Africa and there are a number of studies of areas where these concerns played a major influence in the formulation of agricultural policy.[1] Much of the existing literature examines soil conservation policies in the context of the growth of nationalism and their role in this political process, and has thus focused on such conservation schemes as a catalyst for nationalist or local resistance.[2] Few examine in detail the methods used by the colonial state to ensure their implementation, and even fewer look at success or failure of these policies in environmental, agricultural or technical terms.[3] As a result, more mundane and pragmatic reasons for the 'failure' of such schemes in different contexts have been overlooked. While the growth of nationalism and the role of soil conservation schemes in this political process may in part have influenced the success or failure of these schemes, there were other reasons to which little attention has been paid, and I highlight the importance of these more mundane reasons. They include the nature of the measures being introduced and the methods by which they were implemented, and I show that they were of critical importance in explaining the success or otherwise of the implementation of such schemes. I also show that Kigezi, the one example of a scheme that encountered little resistance, represented a more flexible and responsive form of colonial intervention, one which was premised on a firmer understanding and appreciation of the existing socio-economic and agricultural system. This is the first study of the process of implementation and of the reception given to the policies by the local population in Kigezi.

Indigenous methods of soil conservation and early colonial encounters

Before examining policy implementation in the colonial period, I focus on Kigezi's situation during the very early stages of colonial rule: outlining indigenous methods of erosion prevention and examining early policies. Given that Kigezi is an area with a long history of agriculture and in-migration, it is probable that the pre-colonial Bakiga agricultural system was highly adaptive to demographic pressure through agricultural change, relatively innovative and included significant soil conservation practices.[4] Early administrative officers and visitors to Kigezi noted indigenous methods of soil conservation. Roscoe visited the district in 1919–20 before any colonial measures had been introduced and remarked how 'ridges' formed by gathering together weeds and stones resulted in the fields forming 'regular plateaux' that looked like terraces. An administrative officer, Elliot, wrote of the period 1920–25 that 'there was not much pressure on the land at that time but some people were already starting terrace cultivation', and that 'Even in those comparatively early days ... the Bakiga ... were growing their crops on terraces which shows they had some idea of soil conservation.' Snowden, an Agricultural Officer visiting the district in 1929, described how on the hillsides: 'cultivation starts at the bottom of the plot, so that the soil is gradually brought down and banks are formed on the foot of each plot. These banks tend to stop soil erosion to some extent.'[5] Such pre-colonial anti-erosion measures were not limited to Kigezi, but were generalised to the region. Grogan and Sharp, who travelled through Rwanda in the end of the nineteenth century, mention that the hills were terraced 'obviating the denudation of the fertile slopes by torrential rains'.[6] Another, Czekanowski, who was part of a 1907–8 German expedition that travelled through Rwanda, described how terraces, reaching 2–3 metres, were used on steep hillslopes, while people also applied dung and used irrigation.[7]

Discussing soil fertility in 1935, before any significant administrative effort had been expended in Kigezi, the Director of Agriculture wrote: 'In many densely populated counties the inhabitants have been driven by dire necessity to terrace their lands, and this practice already obtains in parts of Kigezi,'[8] suggesting that the indigenous system included aspects aimed at longer-term sustainability. The benefits of these methods were recognised and officials observed that in the Kigezi highlands 'the native has developed his own anti-erosion measures: he grows his crops in strips across the slopes, with intervening strips of uncleared land, and this system leads to the formation of natural terraces. In addition some individuals have built small terraces.'[9] The DC described the soil conservation policies that followed in the 1940s as being 'solidly grounded in traditional procedure', suggesting that some officials acknowledged that they were adaptations of traditional methods. [10]

In addition to terraces as a form of soil conservation the Bakiga agricultural system included other elements that helped protect the soil. Intercropping, both mixed and relay (serial), was widely practised, and indeed has increased. For example, maize and beans may be planted together as a mixed crop, and after the beans have been harvested sorghum is planted into the maize. The maize stalks are left in the ground after harvest and not removed until after the sorghum has become established.[11] Planting by this method has the result that the soil is never left bare, and thus is never exposed to rain and associated sheet and splash erosion.

All rotations also include significant use of leguminous plants which, with their nitrogen-fixing qualities, are important for the maintenance of soil fertility. The method of cultivating peas has the appearance of being haphazard as an agricultural officer described in 1937:

> The method of sowing [peas] is to broadcast them ... in the unweeded shambas and they are left to grow like that without any cultivation or weeding of any kind.[12]

The presence of weeds protects the soil, binding it together. When weeding is undertaken the weeds are left in the fields to decompose and are incorporated into the soil later, or they are piled along the contour, which also acts as a soil conservation measure. The incorporation of weeds and crop residues has implications for the nutrient cycling system and thus for soil fertility. Thus the use of inter and serial cropping, rough tillage, the incorporation of weeds and trash into the soil all help maintain soil fertility.

Although evidence from the pre-colonial period is scanty, there seems little doubt that at this time the Bakiga agricultural system was highly adapted to local conditions. Bakiga sited their narrow plots along the contour and left strips between plots, so that over time 'ridges' or steps formed and the steepness of the plot gradient was reduced and terraces of sorts (or at least plots of a lower gradient) built up. Shallow hoeing prior to sowing, leaving fields only half cleared, infrequent weeding and planting crops close together[13] all contributed to the protection of soil from splash erosion. Crops were planted along the contour, weeds and trash were incorporated into the soil, while the system of mixed cropping and use of legumes (with peas and beans being amongst the principal crops) helped to preserve soil fertility. The use of trash lines and

3.1 *Kigezi District, 1935, showing contour cultivation, with strips or trash lines along contour*
(Photograph by D.W. Malcolm, Secretary to Lord Hailey; visited Uganda Dec 1935 to Jan 1936).
R.H. MSS Afr s 1445 Box 4, Album III – Reproduced with kind permission of the Rhodes House
Library, University of Oxford.) A 1911 photograph by Major R.E. Jacks also shows contour cultivation
and vertical 'banks' between plots. This photograph was too poor quality to be reproduced. (Jacks was
a surveyor on the Anglo-German-Belgian Boundary Commission. PRO CO 533/57.)

'rough tillage' had the same effect.[14] Photographs from 1911, 1935 and 1938
all illustrate indigenous agricultural practices, pre-dating administrative efforts
in relation to soil conservation. They show that cultivation was along the
contour, and vertical 'banks' between plots can be made out.

The perception amongst colonial officials of there being 'a problem' with
Kigezi agriculture grew during the 1930s, and policies were put into place at a
local level to address this. As early as 1921, officials observed that land in
southern Kigezi was intensively cultivated, and in 1929 they recorded concerns
about the insufficiency of land for the population around Kabale.[15] In 1935,
the District Agricultural Officer (DAO) Wickham observed that crop yields
were falling because of soil exhaustion in a 10-mile radius of Kabale. He wrote
that it was probable that

> all crops in this area are ... deteriorating in yield, or quality. ... The reason
> for this state of affairs is clearly over population and soil exhaustion.

52

There is not enough land available for the essential item in the rotation – fallow – to be included at the proper intervals. ... nearly all the land where crops are grown is on a steep slope, causing heavy erosion.[16]

He estimated that the area cultivated by the average household had halved from 12 to 6 acres in the previous decade, and predicted that as yields fell there would be an increased tendency to encroach on land that should be left to fallow. Wickham warned that 'the position will inevitably and steadily become worse' and the area might cease to be self-supporting in food. He saw the problem as having two related aspects – soil erosion due to cultivation of steep hillsides, and soil exhaustion due to continuous cultivation.[17]

G.B. Masefield, who replaced Wickham as DAO in 1937, made similar observations and expressed concern about the effect falling yields were having on the ability to collect sufficient famine reserves.[18] In some areas he found little cultivable land resting and 'scarcely any' available for expansion, while grazing land was contracting and the number of stock increasing. Masefield quickly established a programme of propaganda and anti-erosion measures and began advising missionaries as to ways of protecting the land they leased.[19]

By late 1937, Masefield was concentrating propaganda work on anti-erosion measures. He asked the DC to help in 'spreading knowledge of these measures, whether by speaking in lukikos or otherwise'. The notes he circulated to his staff and chiefs included advice that plots should be in strips across the slope and should be no more than 30 yards down a slope (or 20 yards on steep slopes) and that there should be a 5 yard strip of grass between plots. He recommended building 'ridge terraces' at the bottom of the plot, running along the contour, and using a 'sod bank', hedges or grasses, contour rows of mulch, weeds and crop debris to help terraces form. The introduction of improved crop rotations was also advised.[20] It is clear that these measures, in particular having plots along the contour with strips of grass between plots and 'ridge terraces' at the bottom of the plots, were actually adaptations of methods already in use. This may explain why the policies were relatively readily accepted by farmers.

Masefield's policies were carried out not merely through Agricultural Department staff but largely through the network of chiefs, who, as agents of the colonial state, had substantial powers.[21] Thus, by 1938, before soil conservation policy had been formalised in Uganda as a whole, the concerns of local officials and the presence of Masefield, a recently-trained, dynamic DAO with a particular interest in soils, meant that soil conservation measures had begun in Kigezi and were one of the routine subjects discussed by officials while on tour.[22]

Masefield believed that talking about anti-erosion measures was of limited use, and so in addition to propaganda demonstration plots were also used. By mid-1938 about seven demonstration plots had been established. He suggested that the training of agricultural instructors be made more relevant, and that more attention be paid to the agricultural instruction of women.[23] Despite this, little attention was paid to women early on. In later years efforts to reach women increased and, as will be seen, they were, for example, included as participants in courses. Archival sources unfortunately failed to reveal anything specifically about the reactions of women to the conservation policies, which is regrettable as they probably did the greater proportion of physical work on fields, including for example maintaining soil conservation measures.

Masefield's successor in 1940, Stuckey, expressed concern about soil erosion on land leased to Europeans for pyrethrum cultivation and to missionaries.[24] He recommended that more land be fallowed, that strip cultivation (with bands of uncultivated land running on the contour to help check erosion) be introduced to enable land to be fallowed, and that very steep and badly eroded areas be taken out of cultivation altogether. Commenting on these recommendations, the Provincial Agricultural Officer (PAO) said that bunding had not been suggested as this would involve 'work of considerable magnitude'. He noted that 'strip cropping will serve the purpose, and if a success it will be a useful demonstration of something which ... people in Kigezi are much more likely to follow than bunding.'[25] However, as we shall see, both strip cropping and bunding were ultimately used in Kigezi, and it was bunding that was more acceptable to Bakiga farmers, being closer to indigenous methods and taking less land out of production.

At a national level, concerns over the threat of soil erosion also emerged, although Kigezi received little attention and it was not until after the Deputy Director of Agriculture toured the district in July 1941 that the extent to which anti-erosion measures were already being carried out was fully appreciated by senior officials. He reported that Kigezi was 'intensively cultivated with plots on very steep slopes. ... There has, however, been an almost spectacular development of lines of elephant grass at the tops and bottoms of plots.'[26] In 1951 the Deputy Director of Agriculture, Watson, compared the district then to 1938 when 'the farming pattern was ... a "patchwork" type, with no attempt being made to preserve or improve the land'. He noted 'it is obvious that spectacular advances have been made in the matter of reorientation of holdings coupled with a more rational type of general agriculture.'[27] His comment reveals something very important about the attitudes of colonial authorities: the failure to recognise that while the indigenous system may have resulted in 'patchwork' cultivation, it was not necessarily ignorant of soil conservation. Nonetheless, some officials such as Elliot (in 1920–25) and Snowden (in 1929), did recognise the benefits of the indigenous system, as was shown above. Another, McCombe, who was DAO in the early 1940s, saw the benefits of the system in place (such as the use of legumes) and observed that

> There is often much in the indigenous methods of cultivation which it is a mistake to ignore and to assume that the actual tillage and planting methods are easily capable of improvement. ... What I have introduced is an addition to and not a disturbance of the older system.[28]

The indigenous system of Bakiga agriculture thus included a number of important elements (legumes, rough tillage, trash lines and cultivation that led to the formation of ridges) to ensure the sustainability of the resource base. The first anti-erosion measures put into place by Masefield (elephant grass strips and recommended plot width of 30 yards) and McCombe (similar to the earlier measures but with narrower plots) were modifications to the indigenous system, and so the local population could adopt them with relative ease. The use of contour strips and 'ridge terraces' were closely related to the ridges or steps found in the pre-colonial system. As the colonial period progressed there was a gradual move towards a more orderly system of agriculture, and when Purseglove arrived he modified the system further, as will be seen below.

Development of colonial policy to 1953

Let us turn first to colonial thinking around soil conservation. I will look at the development of ideas and discussions around soil erosion in the wider colonial context, and demonstrate the growing perception in the colonial mind that soil erosion was a serious problem, up to the early 1950s when issues around land tenure came into prominence.

Anderson has examined the process by which policies of agrarian reform, and in particular those related to soil conservation, emerged and evolved during the 1930s.[29] The experiences of the 'Dust Bowl' in the USA in the 1930s clearly demonstrated the dangers of soil erosion, while the realisation that East Africa's population was growing rapidly, and the threat of drought and famine, added to these concerns. The policies that evolved in response to this and the discussion of the directions that policy should follow, were broadly similar across East Africa. As early as 1929 a conference was held to discuss soil erosion in the Tanganyikan context and the resulting lengthy report was circulated to officials in East Africa. The conference recommended that a Standing Soil Erosion Committee[30] should be appointed to consider the measures that should be adopted in Tanganyika to deal with the problem, which if left unchecked would 'result in much land becoming unfit for agricultural or pastoral purposes'. The report was sent to the CO in London, brought to the attention of Stockdale (the CO Agricultural Adviser), and the Council for Agriculture and Animal Health considered the question of soil erosion in East Africa in February 1930. The Council felt that the issue was of 'considerable importance to some of the other colonies in East Africa [and that] soil erosion should be viewed as an East African problem'.[31]

In 1932 a conference of East African soil chemists attended by Martin, Uganda's Soil Chemist, was held at Amani, Tanganyika, and the problems of shifting cultivation and soil erosion were discussed.[32] In 1935, the Teso Informal Committee was set up to investigate the situation in Teso, an area where cotton yields had been seen to fall in the previous few years.[33] In the same year Tothill, the Director of Agriculture, expressed concern that increased human and cattle populations and the expansion of cash crops had put the agricultural system, which relied on shifting cultivation to restore fertility, under great pressure. 'There are indications that the old system is not standing the strain', he wrote, citing examples from Teso. He spoke of the need for the system to be modified, and discussed changes in particular in relation to cotton and coffee, through improved rotation, planting methods, manuring and mulching.[34]

It is clear that this discussion focused largely on the situation in Buganda and Eastern Province, both major cash crop producing areas. Colonial concerns were that the standard of agriculture in these areas was low and becoming lower as farmers put increased acreages under cotton and reduced resting periods, with negative effects on yields.[35] In one of the most significant reports of this time Stockdale, the Agricultural Adviser to the Secretary of State to the Colonies, examined the problems related to increasing acreages of cotton and other cash crops. He concluded that Uganda could not hope to continue its agriculture based on the 'traditional' system of shifting cultivation as economic crops had been introduced. Noting the 'disastrous' effects of soil erosion seen in parts of the USA, he called for 'the inauguration of better systems of agriculture, involving strip cropping and the development of mixed farming in which animal husbandry plays an important part.'[36] Stockdale's report was circulated to all Agricultural Officers who were advised to 'give consideration to ... the practicability of introducing simple native cultivation rules to ensure that such crops as coffee, cotton and tobacco are only planted on sites approved by them and that the necessary measures – terracing, contour bunding and ridge cultivation – are practised, to prevent erosion [and] preserve the fertility of our soils'.[37] The focus on cash crops is clear.

Agricultural research on topics including soil erosion, was discussed at annual conferences held for Directors of Agriculture from East Africa which served to share information between colonies.[38] Ideas from further afield were also gathered: Tothill went to India and South Africa in 1938 and his notes were circulated around the Department. In 1938/39 Colin Maher, from Kenya, and H.R. Hosking, from Uganda, were sent to the USA to study erosion control measures such as contour bunding and strip cropping.[39]

Thus up to the early 1940s, Kigezi, not being a major cotton or coffee producing area, was not a part of wider national discussions about the threat of soil erosion. But measures were in fact already in place, with both indigenous practices and modifications to those practices introduced by early DAOs. The lack of attention given to Kigezi was to change quite suddenly, and before long the district's soil conservation measures were held up as an example to the rest of Uganda, indeed to the colonial world. This increase in attention took place during the Purseglove era, and the implementation of policies during that period will now be explored.

Soil conservation measures at district level: The Purseglove era (1944–53)

How, then, were soil conservation measures implemented during the Purseglove period? The state employed the stick and the carrot in introducing soil conservation policies: the 'stick' of enforcement in which chiefs and regulations played a prominent role, and the 'carrot' of propaganda, competitions and educational courses. Adverse weather conditions in 1943 resulted in food shortages across much of Uganda and a severe famine in Rwanda. Marketing regulations were tightened up and the purchase of African foodstuffs for resale or export was prohibited. The 'famine' as it was called brought Kigezi's agricultural system under closer colonial scrutiny; and the district quickly became a model for the successful implementation of conservation measures. [40] This coincided with Purseglove's arrival as DAO. He was a catalyst for many new development initiatives, in particular the resettlement scheme and soil conservation policies that collectively became known as *plani ensya*, 'The New Plan'. This phrase entered the Rukiga language, and is still remembered today. Purseglove, who has been described as a 'Pioneer of Rural Development',[41] had graduated in first position in 1936 from the Imperial College of Tropical Agriculture in Trinidad. Having developed an acute awareness of soil erosion, he was only too keen to put this knowledge into practice. He was appointed Agricultural Officer in Uganda in 1936, DAO Ankole and Kigezi 1938–39, before being appointed DAO in Kigezi in 1944, where he remained until 1952. The longevity of his stay may in part explain Purseglove's influence. His enthusiasm was also important: he learnt Rukiga and was interested in Bakiga customs. The impact he made on Bakiga farmers is striking and many informants remembered him: Byagagaire told of songs written about Purseglove,[42] while Ngologoza also praised him, recalling the nickname that Purseglove was given: 'Kyarokyezire', meaning there is plenty of ripe ready food in their area.'[43]

In 1944 a committee was established to investigate and report upon Kigezi's overpopulated areas (See Map 3.1). The Committee, comprising of officers from the Administration, Forestry, Veterinary and Agriculture Departments, had only one meeting; thereafter all the work was left to Purseglove. He carried out a series of traverses in a 12-mile radius of Kabale town to assess whether the areas were 'overpopulated', and if so to what extent. It is clear that before the study had even begun it had been decided that these areas were overpopulated, and the survey confirmed this. The population density of Kigezi district as a whole was found to be 155 people per square mile, while Ndorwa, one of the southern *sazas*, had a density of 210 people per square mile.[44]

Purseglove found that 'The main problem at the moment is soil exhaustion ... it would appear that overcultivation has resulted in soil exhaustion and a deterioration in soil structure, with a consequent reduction in the amount of water absorbed by the soil.' Quoting from Jacks and Whyte, *The Rape of the Earth* published in 1939, he stated that 'although serious erosion is not yet a problem we cannot afford to be complacent and wait for it to become so.' He concluded that the area around Kabale could not continue to support an increasing population and that it would be 'most unwise to continue under the present conditions in the hope that further soil deterioration and erosion will not take place'. Purseglove believed that grass fallows were essential to soil

Map 3.1 *Southern Kigezi, showing 'overpopulated'* gombololas *in Ndorwa and Rukiga*

fertility maintenance. He suggested moving people out of the 'over-populated' areas into less populated areas to the north in order to increase the proportion of land resting and introduce strip cropping, with every third strip resting. In the areas left behind there would be some 'reorganisation' of agriculture, the distance between bunds would be further reduced (thus narrowing the strips) and a more orderly system of alternate strip cropping would be introduced.[45] These policies, which collectively became known as *plani ensya*, differed from those of the earlier period in that they increased the proportion of land taken out of cultivation and demanded greater labour inputs.

It should be stressed that, although Purseglove played a crucial role in bringing Kigezi to centre stage, his findings were not particularly groundbreaking or innovative. On the contrary, many officials had previously discussed the problems of overpopulation, soil erosion and falling yields and by the time Purseglove arrived Kigezi's reputation as an 'over-populated' district was firmly entrenched. Purseglove, however, greatly increased the attention that was focused on the district. The reputation of being overpopulated and threatened with serious environmental degradation that Kigezi gained in this period is one that it has never been able to shake off.[46] Researchers have consistently repeated many of these ideas, often without substantiation,[47] and it is only recently that some of these myths, such as continuous cultivation, have been put to the test, as I will show in Chapter 6.[48] Yet it was these myths that shaped action.

RESETTLEMENT SCHEME

Purseglove considered that it was necessary to resettle about one-third of the population of the overpopulated part of the district, which he calculated to be 20,000 people. He assessed possible resettlement areas and selected two regions in Ruzhumbura and Kinkizi in northern Kigezi (See Map 1.2 on p. 14). It was realised that the scheme would eventually have to extend into areas outside Kigezi, and from 1953 resettlement into Ankole and Toro began. Purseglove suggested that farmers who did not cooperate with the reforms in the over-populated areas 'should be the first to move, which would thus provide a definite incentive for people to carry out the necessary reforms ... Latest arrivals ... should be the next to move.'[49] However, the District Team was less draconian in approach, insisting that 'any scheme of resettlement which was undertaken would have to be entirely on a voluntary basis.'[50]

One official noted of the Kigezi Resettlement Scheme that 'the general principle adopted was to dangle a carrot to entice settlers away from the overcrowded area whilst simultaneously applying a few pricks behind';[51] this analogy is particularly apt. A number of incentives were put forward to encourage resettlement, such as the remission of taxes for two years and the provision of transport, transit camps and food rations for the settlers.[52] The decision to provide food rations, and the occurrence of local food shortages, led to sudden increases in the numbers wanting to migrate, which forced the administration to halt further resettlement on a number of occasions for a few months. It was decided that only those settlers who could feed themselves should be allowed to migrate and fines were imposed on those who went to the Resettlement Area 'solely to get free food and without any genuine intention of settling, and who now had returned to their former homes'.[53]

But the most important incentive for people coming from an area as densely populated as south Kigezi, was the prospect of being able to lay claim to large areas of land. The precise manner in which land was allocated to resettlers remains unclear. Indeed, in the planning stages of the resettlement scheme, more attention was paid to how land that resettlers left behind would be reallocated, than how land in the resettlement area would be distributed. It was suggested that resettlers' land would be left to the chief to reallocate. However, once resettlement got underway it became clear that settlers preferred to leave their land with relatives in case they wanted to return, and the administration had to recognise this right, as will be shown.

As for land in the resettlement area itself, officials initially aimed to place as few controls and regulations on the resettlers as possible. The lack of regulations associated with resettlement is striking, particularly when comparisons are made with other schemes. Most significantly, no limit to the amount of land was set, although about 12 acres per family was recommended as sufficient. Obol-Ochola has suggested that a specially constituted Resettlement Allocation Authority which was made up of chiefs from all levels gave land to individuals.[54] No archival evidence has been found to confirm this and it appears that in the very early stages of resettlement individuals could choose the land they desired. However, this uncontrolled system could not have continued indefinitely without chaos ensuing, and some control of land distribution appears to have been given to the Resettlement Chief who was specially appointed to the area. This was in part a response to the results of a survey which found that:

> A number of people, among whom was a high proportion of people related to chiefs, had more land than was necessary but, in implementation of a District Council resolution of 1947, these people will share with their children and relations who are not yet resident in the area.[55]

Another survey in 1951 found that 'the average acreage of cultivable land taken up per taxpayer was 26.7 acres', and the PAO noticed that 'the area available for new settlers in North Kigezi was also reduced to some extent by "land grabbing" on the part of "people with influence".'[56]

The cooperation of chiefs was undoubtedly paramount to the success of the scheme,[57] and it is of more than passing interest that at least one of the chiefs benefited personally from the resettlement scheme. The Secretary General, Ngologoza,[58] was amongst the first group to claim land in the resettled area, but he did not resettle his family on the new land as was intended. Ngologoza was clearly not the only person who saw opportunities for accumulation, and the DC commented to Purseglove that it was 'too late this planting season to do anything about the absentee landlords!'[59] Thus, in the first few years of resettlement there were ample opportunities for land accumulation, and something of a land rush took place. Even when some controls were put into the hands of local authorities (either a Resettlement Chief or a broader group, such as a committee), who were supposed to allocate the land, those with power, such as Ngologoza, were still able to accumulate large areas of land. From around 1955 controls were put into place and each family was limited to 10 acres of land. The significance of the offer of unlimited land as an incentive to resettle is clear, as, soon after these controls were instituted, resettlement became less popular and settlers argued strongly to be allowed more than 10 acres.[60]

While some individuals used the resettlement scheme as an opportunity to accumulate land, there were also settlers who were not particularly wealthy or powerful. This raises the question of the extent to which compulsion was used to get people to move. The resettlement scheme has always been presented as an entirely voluntary scheme, but it is difficult to assess how much pressure was applied to individuals to migrate by local chiefs, or indeed by family members. There is some evidence of compulsion being used. For example, a medical officer who visited the resettlement area reported that there was 'dissatisfaction among settlers … some [of whom were] involuntary pioneers'.[61] In 1950 the DC expressed concern that criminals were being sent to Resettlement Areas, and informed chiefs that 'in future no person with a criminal record should be sent to Resettlement Areas without the prior approval of the Saza Chief of Kinkizi and Ruzhumbura.'[62]

A number of chiefs were told to 'instruct your people who have less than 10–20 shambas to go and take up land' and this, and the suggestion that people could be 'sent' (whether they had criminal records or not), raises many questions about how 'voluntary' resettlement was. It is extremely difficult to answer this question, and in particular to assess the levels of pressure from families, or from local chiefs. The only report that has been found of compulsion being used was that of a man who complained to the Secretary General that he was being forced to resettle despite having several plots for cultivation. In response to this complaint, Ngologoza wrote to the *gombolola* chief telling him that as the man had sufficient land he should not be forced to go.[63] This makes us wonder whether, if the man had had 'insufficient' land, as perceived by the chief or Secretary General, they would have forced him to leave.

However, it is important to stress that in Kigezi there is a long history of movement by families on their own initiative. Writing on the basis of data collected in the 1930s, Edel has noted that the

> whole picture of land use and land rights must be seen against a whole background of considerable mobility, rather than fixed relationship to a particular area of land. Any period of 10 to 20 years will normally see a total redistribution of the people in any neighbourhood. Household by household, the members of the village move away, often in different directions.[64]

Appreciating the extent of population mobility amongst Bakiga is important to understanding the reception given by Bakiga to the resettlement scheme: this type of movement was an inherent part of Bakiga life, and the resettlement scheme built upon this practice which helps explain its success.

That the scheme should in fact be seen as an extension of a process that was already occurring was acknowledged by some officials, who observed that it did 'little more than accelerate or facilitate a natural process of emigration which is continually in progress'.[65] Purseglove himself noted that unassisted resettlement continued alongside the scheme and he estimated that by the end of 1946 approximately 2,500 unassisted emigrants had moved out of Kigezi into Ankole and Belgian Ruanda. This is more than the 1,500 who moved as part of the resettlement scheme in the same period,[66] which puts the success of the scheme into context.

During the late 1940s the district administration focused its attention on the resettlement scheme and a great deal of effort was put into ensuring its success. Given this administrative effort, it is perhaps not surprising that the scheme was consistently presented as a great success.[67] While the administration wanted to resettle the landless, or near-landless, the evidence on the use of compulsion suggests that, to some extent at least, chiefs were able to send who they wanted. Juxtaposed to this aim was the desire that the scheme should be seen to succeed with farmers following soil conservation rules and making a success of their new farms. For this reason agricultural officials may have been quite happy that 'progressive' farmers were amongst those opportunists resettling and accumulating.

IMPLEMENTATION OF *PLANI ENSYA*:
THE CARROT & THE STICK

Alongside the implementation of the resettlement scheme the policies of *plani ensya* were put into place, central to which was strip cropping. Purseglove proposed taking all land on slopes of over 20 degrees out of cultivation and introducing a system of strip cropping in which land would be rested in rotation with two years cultivation and one of rest under grass (or four and two respectively).[68] The resting strip could be grazed. Plots would be a width of 16 yards on slopes of up to 15 degrees and narrower on steeper slopes, with bunds between the plots of at least three feet. Purseglove noted that 'Once the system of strip cropping ... has been established, automatic control of the number of people on the land will be accomplished. One strip in three must always be resting and this can be maintained by the minimum of supervision by the Administration, agricultural staff and chiefs.' He did, however, acknowledge that the main difficulty would be reorganising strip lines, which would cut across existing plots and necessitate some reorganisation of tenure.[69] As the 1940s progressed the soil conservation measures undertaken included strip cropping, bunding, introducing some organised fallow systems, encouraging manure use, compost pits and hedging of paths. How did the administration ensure that these measures were carried out?

Role of chiefs

By the late 1940s most soil conservation work was a matter of routine, and colonial-appointed chiefs played a crucial role in implementation. This emerges clearly from archival sources such as monthly reports sent to the DAO. For example, an agricultural officer reported that following a visit to an area where soil conservation measures had been neglected

> steps were taken by the chiefs to see that new grass strips were well laid out. ... The chiefs and the Agricultural instructors were reminded about [the use of elephant grass]. ... it is hoped that good results will be achieved if the gombolola chief and muruka chief ... remain industrious and devoted. ... progressive work about soil conservation measures ... is mainly due to the organising ability of the muruka chief.[70]

Purseglove wrote in 1948 that the success of soil conservation measures 'has been achieved through the direct approach of departmental officers and the district team generally to the peasant farmers concerned working through the medium of the native authority'.[71] Colonial authorities thus placed much responsibility on chiefs for ensuring that their 'patch' followed the required measures; if they failed to do so, they were punished accordingly. In addition, chiefs at each level (*saza, gombolola,* etc.) were responsible for ensuring that all the chiefs at the level below them carried out the work expected of them.

By working through this hierarchy the administration ensured that conservation measures were carried out, and it is clear that chiefs were punished without hesitation. In 1949 the *saza* chief of Ruzhumbura reported that he had 'dealt with' the *gombolola* chief of Kagungu, his minor chiefs and the Agricultural Instructor of the area about the 'negligency of the Soil Conservation work'. He tried the chiefs in the *saza* court and found that the *gombolola* chief was not helping his sub-chiefs and the Agricultural Instructor, and so he was warned that if he did not improve he would be fined. Just a few days later the *saza* chief took this case further, reporting that as no improvements in soil conservation measures were seen he had sacked one *muluka* chief and two *bakungu* chiefs, and fined four other chiefs.[72] Oral sources confirm that work was supervised by *muluka* or *gombolola* chiefs along with agriculture department staff.[73]

Force of law

It is widely believed today[74] that a soil conservation byelaw was in force throughout the colonial period, but in fact there was no such byelaw until 1961. Instead 'Agricultural Rules' made under the Native Authority Ordinance were enforced in the lower courts, and these Rules alone were sufficient to ensure implementation. They were only clarified in 1954 when it was decided that all rules should be 'codified', consolidated into a pamphlet and issued to chiefs.[75] The fifteen Agricultural Rules of 1954 included: width of contour strips (16 yards or 10 yards on steep slopes), width of bunds (2 yards), that bunds should be permanent, alternate strip cropping should be practised where possible, grazing areas should be set aside where possible, and grass burning should only be done with the permission of a chief.[76] The lower courts enforced the Agricultural Rules and it is perhaps for this reason that no court returns, or details of punishments imposed, have been located.

The authority that chiefs had in Kigezi is striking. If an individual failed to follow the soil conservation rules – for example if bunds were dug over and not replaced – that person was logged in the 'warning register' by the local chief and given 14 days to comply. Those who still failed to follow the rules would be taken to court and if found guilty would be fined, and ordered to comply within 7 days.[77] No archival evidence was found as to precisely how work on *plani ensya* measures was enforced and informants were inconsistent in their replies as to who actually did the work. Some said that it was just male taxpayers; while others said that women and children also worked. No court records survive of the punishments imposed for failing to carry out the measures, but oral evidence suggests that fines and short terms of imprisonment were the most common punishments, while working for the *gombolola* chief was also mentioned. It seems that the threat of a fine alone was usually enough to make a farmer implement the measures required.[78]

On occasions some chiefs were over-enthusiastic in their efforts to ensure that measures were implemented. In 1951 the Secretary General wrote to all *saza* chiefs saying that it was 'not desirable that married women should be compelled to work on the 'plani ensya' ... [nor should] ... work on 'plani ensya' be done daily. This work should be done by men, girls and boys only, and should only be done once every week.'[79] That such a warning was needed supports the view that chiefs had the authority to ensure that people turned up for *plani* and that some used this authority over-enthusiastically.[80] It is also of interest that while adult women were excused from working on soil conservation measures, it was felt that they should attend agricultural education courses. This suggests some ambivalence in the colonial policies towards women's involvement in soil conservation measures.

Following his visit to Kigezi, a Kenyan official was surprised at the successful implementation of measures in the Kigezi scheme. He was clearly particularly impressed with the degree of cooperation noting:

> The central administration seem able to persuade the tribal leaders of the desirability of soil conservation practices and good husbandry generally, and once persuaded, the chiefs and councillors seem to have little difficulty in enforcing good agricultural behaviour on their people. In the case of a particularly recalcitrant person, a fine of a shilling is apparently enough to make him change his ways.[81]

The official, who was himself in charge of Kenya's Makueni Settlement scheme (discussed below), put forward a number of suggestions for the high level of cooperation between the District Team and chiefs: first, the degree of continuity in administration; second, the power and prestige of chiefs; and third, the fact that chiefs were also members of the native courts, so that they were often both prosecutor, judge and jury. His comment on this was that, while it might 'seem an odd legal conception ... in the case of soil conservation measures, it appears to produce results. The senior native courts have powers of corporal punishment which they regularly exercise.'[82]

Education & propaganda

As well as regulations and implementation with the 'stick' there was also a great deal of effort spent on trying to persuade and encourage the carrying out of soil conservation measures through education, competitions and propaganda. Purseglove established courses at Kachweckano, an experimental farm near to Kabale belonging to the Department of Agriculture that was established 1938. Attended by chiefs, employees of the Agricultural Department, schoolteachers and others, these courses taught the rudiments of conservation methods. Chiefs had to attend at least one course, at which lectures and practical demonstrations were given by the DAO. The Secretary General explained 'The main idea of the course was that people should understand the reasons why certain agricultural operations should be done throughout the district.' In the examination held at the end of the course the emphasis was on erosion and soil fertility. Lower-level chiefs also attended lectures, given by Agricultural Assistants, on a monthly basis.[83]

Purseglove himself regarded the Kachwekano courses as 'an important factor in the scheme. ... This approach [is] of greatest significance as no lasting result can be achieved unless the mass of the people understand the fundamental reasons behind the charge [sic change].'[84] Byagagaire, an Assistant Agricultural Officer (AAO) in the 1950s, recalled that the most important thing was to 'first of all teach chiefs and public opinion leaders ... [about] why [the policies] were necessary. These are elders in the village – old men – they are not chiefs or councillors, but they are highly regarded in the village, their word is highly respected ... you had to convince them.'[85]

Oral evidence confirms the widespread impact of these courses upon chiefs and ordinary farmers alike. It is noteworthy that by the 1950s many women were attending such courses. At the same time, however, women were excused from participating in weekly soil conservation work, and it seems that colonial officials were unsure of what stand to take with regard to women's involvement in these activities. The courses were an efficient way of 'spreading the word'. As one elderly informant Bishisha recalled: 'When they came back they organised public gatherings to tell people about what they had learnt [at Kachweckano].' The fact that people were very well informed about the reasons behind soil conservation measures suggests that the propaganda campaign to explain the measures was generally effective. Many informants confirmed that explanations for the reasons for the measures, combined with the threat of punishment, together ensured that the majority of people complied. [86]

Competitions were another popular feature of the campaign. In 1946 Purseglove introduced an annual soil conservation competition, which became an important event in the local calendar. A cash prize was awarded to the *gombolola* judged to have made the biggest advance in soil conservation work during the year, which was spent on a feast attended by people living in that *gombolola* and district officials. In addition, small cash prizes were awarded to the *gombolola* chief, *muluka* chiefs and agricultural assistant,[87] which acted as an additional incentive to ensure that the measures were carried out.

3.2 *Hillside cultivation in Kigezi District in the 1940s. See additional photos in Chapter 6, showing cultivation in 1935 and 1938.*
(Reproduced with kind permission of the Purseglove family).

3.3 *Hillside cultivation in Kigezi District in the 1940s.*
(Reproduced with kind permission of the Purseglove family)

Whenever other agencies of propaganda could be employed they were harnessed to Purseglove's scheme. The missions were involved in implementing soil conservation measures in so far as it was their responsibility to follow the guidance of the Agricultural Department on land they leased. The AAO in particular worked through mission employees and teachers, school farms were targeted and in 1949 a school garden competition was introduced.[88] The Western Province Demonstration Team also had a role to play. During the Second World War Army Mobile Propaganda Units had toured Uganda giving displays and film shows and it was decided that these should be adapted for use in peacetime. There was one entirely self-contained and fully mobile team (a leader and 12 members, all Africans, mainly ex-service men) in each province. They aimed, through films, plays and demonstrations, to 'arouse interest in and stimulate action towards improved standards both in the home and on the farm'.[89] From 1947 this team worked in Kigezi giving performances on agricultural matters amongst other things. Following these performances, leaflets in the vernacular were distributed, which, for example, explained the causes of soil erosion and suggested ways to check it.[90]

The Western Province Demonstration Team played an important role in promoting one aspect of soil conservation policies that ran into particular problems: planting temporary grass leys for grazing on resting strips. The policy was introduced in 1949 and presented the administration with some of its greatest difficulties. From the beginning the demonstration teams had problems getting land on which to plant the leys and gathering people to work with them. In some areas 'much if not most' of the work was being nullified by inadequate weeding and the demonstration plots were poorly located, being too scattered over the *gombolola* for people to appreciate their existence and usefulness. The plots often belonged to people with 'very little interest in grazing them [who] therefore are not bothering to weed and maintain them properly. They seem to have very little idea of the underlying reason for the planting of these leys.'[91] As would be expected, the chiefs were criticised for not making enough effort to encourage people to maintain and graze the plots but it seems that the problems went deeper and that this aspect of soil conservation work was badly thought out. From the lack of references to the policy of planting leys in the years that followed it seems that this part of the soil conservation policies was quietly dropped from the agenda. Another aspect that largely failed was the 'reorganisation' of land left behind by resettlers, as suggested by Purseglove. This policy was also abandoned, largely because it involved changing plot boundaries and thus had implications for land tenure. In contrast to other schemes in East Africa (see below), agricultural officers in Kigezi both planned and implemented the measures to be introduced in the district. They were in a position to adapt or change the measures if problems arose and had the sense to drop interventions that were ill-conceived.

In most respects, however, soil conservation policies were implemented successfully. In 1950 the DC wrote of the 'universal adherence' to rules requiring both strip-cropping and bunding, and stated that they were 'well understood and diligently followed by the great mass of the people'. The DAO reported from Kigezi that 'cultivation has been developed on true strip cropping lines, which is now generally practised throughout the district.'[92] In this respect, the experience of Kigezi stood in stark contrast to other parts of eastern Africa. Aside from the two minor policies discussed above, no references to any widespread feelings of opposition to the policies in Kigezi have been found.[93]

Reassessment in the 1950s

From the early 1950s there was a shift in conservation policies as colonial concerns about agricultural productivity became increasingly linked to issues around land tenure (see Chapter 5). This coincided with Purseglove leaving Kigezi, and, with a change in DAO, the policies of the 1940s were reassessed. King, the new DAO, observed that the value of the resettlement scheme was often overstated, as it had never managed to keep up with the natural increase of population. From the time resettlement began to 1953, 22,000 people had been resettled, while the population was estimated to have increased by 64,280 in the same period, so that it was 'obvious that the problem had only been scratched'.[94] The scheme also failed to reorganise the agricultural system in the way suggested by Purseglove. Like officials before him, King spoke of the problems of growing land pressure and decreasing areas for grazing. With a clear hardening of attitude, he proposed further resettlement. Estimating that at least 50,000 people needed to be removed from Kigezi, he recommended that married seasonal emigrants (to Buganda and elsewhere) should be made to take their families with them. As a marked decline in the birth rate was unlikely, he felt that resettlement was the only answer, but noted that it would 'not succeed unless very strong pressure is brought to bear and severe penalties inflicted on those who subsequently return'.[95]

Other officials agreed that while the resettlement scheme had led to a 'lessening of pressure' the figures were totally inadequate. To get a 'real breathing space', about 100,000 people (i.e. 7 years increase) would have to be moved, which would 'require a colossal organisation and an expenditure of about £250,000'.[96] DC Fraser felt, however, that 'resettlement by itself is a somewhat sterile solution to the district's problems' as it would have to continue indefinitely on a very large scale. Instead, he suggested more effort should be put into finding ways for Kigezi to support a greatly increased population, and thus the emphasis on soil conservation remained.[97]

At around this time there were growing concerns over loss of grazing. The DVO Symons calculated that 'within 8 years at the present rate, there will be no uncultivated land remaining.' He was strongly critical of the strip cropping policy, observing that grass on resting strips was often of inferior quality compared to natural grazing with much weed and bush growth. Moreover it was very difficult to graze cattle, especially larger herds, on resting strips. Symons observed that often, particularly in grazing areas of northeastern Kigezi, a hill was opened up for cultivation and after three years, rather than cultivating the intermediate strips, further land was opened up higher up the hill. He wrote that 'the obvious reason for this is that the Chiefs like to produce an orderly pattern of alternate strips and the more strips then the more points they consider they will score for the Agricultural Competition. This is an obvious waste of grazing lands.'[98] The Agriculture Department itself admitted in the early 1950s that it was widely agreed that alternate strip cropping was a 'wasteful method of land utilisation' and it was virtually impossible to graze the resting strips. Instead they suggested a 'block layout' with parallel strips along the contour separated by grass washstops or bunds of about three yards.[99] This marked a return to something much closer to the pre-colonial indigenous system, and a system of horizontal plots separated by strips or bunds exists today, although the bunds or washstops are significantly narrower than three yards.

The evidence thus suggests that the system of alternate strip cropping introduced during Purseglove's time in office had been applied too broadly and over too wide an area. In applying a single formula, grazing lands had in fact been excessively reduced in some areas. As early as 1951, following a visit to Kigezi, the deputy director of agriculture proposed a shift in policy towards the promotion of block cultivation. But it was not until 1954 that experiments began in Ruzhumbura to test the effectiveness of block cultivation.[100] In 1956 they agreed that in certain areas 'better use can be made of the land if the system of alternate resting and cultivating strips is abolished and block cultivation introduced.'[101] During the mid-1950s there was an increased emphasis on a 'more rounded' approach to soil conservation, and this meant a return to something closer to the pre-colonial indigenous systems of soil conservation.

East African comparisons

To appreciate the exceptionality of Kigezi's experience of colonial soil conservation policies we need to consider the broader picture of colonial rural development programmes throughout eastern Africa (see Map 3.2). The striking difference between Kigezi and other large soil conservation schemes is the lack of opposition to the proposals in Kigezi. We therefore need to look at Kigezi's apparently anomalous position. There are a number of reasons which might contribute to the successful implementation of a soil conservation scheme, which fall broadly into three categories. First, the nature of the measures being introduced (for example, their closeness to the indigenous system of agriculture and the amount of labour required to carry them out). Second, the methods by which measures were implemented (the use of propaganda and education and the length of time taken to implement them), and third, the effects of such measures on existing social and political structures (including the effect of existing systems of land tenure and the presence of local political tensions and of nationalist politics). With these broad categories in mind, five other schemes will be outlined and contrasted with Kigezi. [102]

SUKUMALAND SCHEME, TANGANYIKA [103]

The Sukumaland Scheme was initiated as a result of growing concerns about environmental degradation, particularly related to grazing, and aimed to establish a 'sound' balance of population and livestock with resources. The scheme involved resettling people from overpopulated areas, clearing areas of tsetse, cattle marketing regulations, soil conservation practices (tie ridging) and agricultural practices that required people to adopt mixed farming and intensify their agriculture. [104] As Iliffe has observed, the policies aimed at the intensification of agriculture failed and the 'bitter hostility' aroused by the measures led eventually to their abandonment in 1958. The resettlement part of the scheme was more successful and large areas were cleared of tsetse; but, 'instead of encouraging balanced peasant husbandry, the Sukumaland scheme stimulated a capitalist land rush.'[105] Besides this expansion of the area available for grazing and cultivation (through bush clearance) most controls collapsed and there were few lasting achievements.[106] While the resettlement scheme in Kigezi also stimulated a land rush to some extent and a number of individuals claimed large areas of land, there is no evidence that this applied to the majority of settlers. Part of the reason that resettlement was a success in Kigezi was probably because migration was an inherent part of Bakiga life, while the absence of regulations and controls was also crucial.

Usually looked at in relation to the growth of nationalism,[107] there is a need to put aside the implications of the political movement for the Sukumaland scheme and to assess other influences. In this McLoughlin has observed that there were 'undoubtedly shortcomings of an economic, sociological and technical character which would in any event have greatly impaired its effectiveness'.[108] These included problems with the measures themselves, the methods by which they were implemented and the effect of the measures on existing political and social structures and divisions within the society. Although tie ridging had positive soil conservation results and improved yields, these only became evident after a long period of years. In addition, to be effective, tie ridging had to be done in January which was a busy time in the agricultural calendar and so the measure was inappropriate for the existing agricultural system, as it reduced the total area that could be cultivated by a given labour force. Attempts to introduce the use of manure into the system through mixed farming also failed as 'the additional output due to the use of manure was not worth the considerable extra labour required to produce and apply the manure.'[109] Thus, the incentives to carry out the measures were insufficient or entirely lacking.

Attempts to control cattle numbers also largely failed. According to McLoughlin the government 'probably underestimated the degree of rationality underlying the livestock holding policies of the Sukuma'[110] while

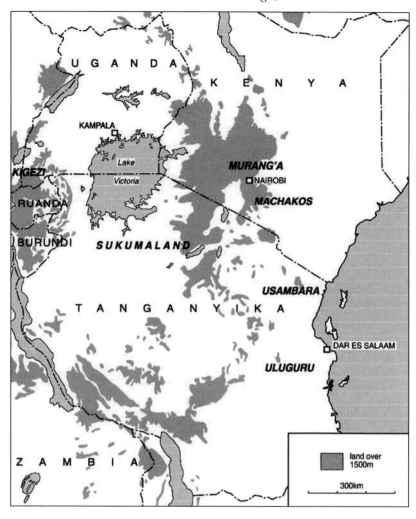

Map 3.2 *Kigezi compared: Soil conservation schemes in East Africa*

71

at the same time relying on inadequate research as to the 'carrying capacity' in what were widely variable conditions across Sukumaland. In the words of Maguire, 'it appears that Sukuma resistance to the content of specific measures, as well as to the methods of enforcement, may have been inspired as much by rationality as by ignorance, as much by economic considerations of self-interest as by politics.'[111]

In terms of the methods of implementation used, because the administration believed that there was 'neither the time nor the trained staff necessary to persuade the majority of farmers and herders of the desirability of the measures contained in the Development Scheme, primary reliance was placed on the enforcement of a series of regulations by the Native Authorities.' The tendency to enforce the policies from above through the Native Authority meant that, as hostility to the scheme grew, it developed against the Native Authority. The Tanganyika African National Union (TANU) capitalised on this discontent; the opposition to the regulations and the struggle for independence 'were mutually reinforcing and became very closely identified with each other' during the 1950s.[112] As Iliffe has observed, TANU provided the means by which the tensions within the society could be expressed.[113]

ULUGURU LAND USAGE SCHEME, TANGANYIKA

The Uluguru Land Usage Scheme (ULUS), introduced during the early 1950s, was designed to 'improve' the land in the Uluguru Mountains through the construction of bench terraces and introduction of other conservation measures. Discontent over terracing became a 'vehicle of protest against Native Authority,'[114] led to rioting in 1955, and the scheme was abandoned. Various reasons have been put forward for the failure of the scheme and the first major study by Young and Fosbrooke looks at reactions to the scheme in terms of local political dynamics and conflicts into which discontent over terracing fed. While it is impossible to say if discontent would have become apparent had it not been for the existence of these local political tensions and divisions, it is clear that the conservation scheme played a significant part. Over most of the area the difference between bench terracing and the methods already in place was much greater than was the case in Kigezi. The exception to this was in Mgeta on the western side of the mountains where, as Maack has observed, residents had practised terracing since the early 1900s, and its benefits were clear in this environment.[115] In this area the people were in general 'sympathetic with the broader ULUS'[116] and the measures were more successfully implemented, supporting the view that closeness to the existing system of agriculture was important.

The labour inputs required for the construction of bench terraces was large and colonial officials initially introduced targets of 'yards of terraces' to be built. When this failed, all taxpayers had to work on the terraces for three days a week. This was an extraordinarily high demand to make and unsurprisingly it was hugely unpopular. In addition to being very costly to introduce in labour terms, bench terraces were actually totally inappropriate for the area; indeed with the exception of the western side, they were detrimental to the soil. Tests showed bench terraces were unsuitable, given the fragility and thinness of the soil, and officers in the field themselves questioned their suitability. These officers, however, were not in a position to adapt, change or drop policies when problems arose, as were those in Kigezi. In Uluguru bench terraces had a largely negative effect on the productivity of the area with yields on treated plots actually declining. Again the exception was the western area of Mgeta, where farmers could produce high valued foodstuffs on these terraces and thus 'for them terracing was a worthwhile effort'.[117] Iliffe has suggested that the failure to offer incentives in the form of cash crops to farmers, meant it was never worthwhile farmers investing time and labour into the measures proposed and this contributed to the scheme's failure.[118] In Maack's words, 'the Waluguru resisted efforts to combat soil erosion because they derived few benefits from their labour.'[119] Overall, therefore, the measures were ill thought out and unsuited to the area, and without the incentives of high value crops to make the measures worth carrying out.

The methods used to implement these measures have not been examined in great detail and how much 'persuasion' was used is unclear. Young and Fosbrooke have observed that 'the attempt to enlist the support of the clan leaders had limited success'[120] and the speed with which the scheme was introduced may have been its greatest downfall. The scheme was first proposed in 1947 and the ambitious terracing programme was introduced in 1950. This was very different from the gradual implementation of measures seen in Kigezi and was perhaps a case of 'too much, too soon'. The presence of local political tensions and rising nationalist politics must have assisted the articulation of discontent, and Iliffe has observed that 'drudgery and political conflict also killed the Uluguru scheme.'[121] Maack has noted that the Wuluguru felt betrayed by the Native Administration at a time when new forms of political expression were becoming available. In addition, the measures became associated with loss of land (as forced migration had been discussed earlier in connection with soil conservation measures), which added to suspicions about the scheme.

Officials failed to understand fully the Wuluguru land system, which included individual rights of ownership, individual use rights and complex patron-client relationships. Unsurprisingly, farmers were unwilling to invest large quantities of time and labour on land that was not theirs. Young and Fosbrooke have observed that the ULUS 'struck at two sensitive topics: the land ... and the social system which governed the use of the land'.[122] Crucially, in Kigezi, this was avoided. Individual security of tenure was strong in Kigezi, and although measures were attempted that would have threatened the system of land tenure in place (such as the 'reorganisation' of agriculture suggested by Purseglove following resettlement) these were quickly dropped by the administration.

USAMBARA SCHEME, TANGANYIKA

The Usambara Scheme was another ill-conceived scheme introduced in Tanganyika from 1950 and eventually abandoned in 1957 due to opposition by the local population. Here the measures introduced were tie ridges on hillsides – both along the contour and down the hill, which created a grid of raised squares.[123] Working these ridges necessitated digging in a way that was dramatically different from the indigenous system of working along the hillside and the labour demands involved in building the ridges were extremely high. The scheme began in 1950 with a controversial pilot project and expanded slowly to 1952, then spread very quickly over the rest of Usambara. Over most of the area, and with little preparation, people were asked to introduce measures far removed from their system with an inadequate understanding of the reasons behind the measures. Implementation through enforcement was crucial.[124]

The agricultural system in Usambara required flexibility, and the land tenure system enabled farmers to borrow land in order to exploit the highly variable local agro-ecological environment. The introduction of tie ridges made lending land problematic as people were not prepared to build ridges on land that they were only borrowing, while someone who had invested such time and effort into their land would be less inclined to lend it. In addition, if a borrower improved some land and then continued to use it, that person would, under local rules, have established some ownership claims to the land.[125]

The feelings of discontent grew in Usambara and the scheme became 'enmeshed with opposition to the native authority'.[126] The Usambara scheme was thus another ill-conceived scheme where the measures being introduced required impossibly large labour inputs and were inappropriate and far removed from the traditional system of agriculture. The measures threatened the agricultural and land use system that was in place. The speed with which policies were introduced meant that little time or effort was spent explaining the reasons behind measures, and coercion was relied upon over persuasion, such that implementation was largely through enforcement by the Native Authority. The lack of high value crops over most of the area meant there was little incentive to carry out the measures and with rising nationalism it was unsurprising that the growing political movement should harness this discontent. [127]

MURANG'A DISTRICT, CENTRAL PROVINCE, KENYA

In Central Province a scheme of terracing was implemented through communal labour. The system of implementation was one of coercion, not persuasion, and people were required to work two mornings a week, and those who failed to do so were fined. As Throup has observed

> The alternative strategy of attempting to educate the population to follow approved techniques of 'sound' land use was dismissed as too slow, since it was considered that immediate action was necessary. Consequently the palliative anti-erosion measures were introduced without the understanding and support of the peasantry. This was a fatal error.[128]

In Murang'a narrow-based terraces, which initially took less labour to build, but in the long term had greater labour demands because of high maintenance needs, were considered by the administration to be most appropriate, but in fact were particularly unpopular. In addition, there was little incentive to carry out terracing, as production of high value cash crops was not an option for these farmers. Elsewhere – Meru and Embu – broad-based terraces and the opportunity to grow coffee meant that the measures were worthwhile and therefore more acceptable.

The high level of male migration meant that most work fell on women and they mobilised against the colonial regime. In April 1948, 2,500 women marched to the district headquarters to inform officials that they refused to do the twice weekly communal work. Kenya African Union (KAU) activists, under Kenyatta, played a crucial role in mobilising opposition to communal terracing which fed into wider discontent. Thus 'resistance to soil conservation schemes became a rallying point in the struggle against the administration, and its adherents.' By the 1950s the Agricultural Department's belief that progressive cultivators should be rewarded with the right to grow high value crops began to be accepted by the administration and there was a move towards encouragement of individual enterprise, and in 1954, with the Swynnerton Plan, a commitment to the positive role to be played by small-scale African producers. The Swynnerton Plan was in part a political device implemented as a counter-insurgency measure to the Mau Mau. However, 'compulsory terracing had destroyed any chance there might have been of gaining new collaborators as [the Kikuyu] had been irredeemably alienated from the colonial regime.'[129]

MACHAKOS, KENYA

Efforts were also made to control soil erosion in the semi-arid Machakos District.[130] The rehabilitation programme included closing areas for rehabilitation, compulsory soil conservation works and destocking. Some years earlier in 1938 a policy of compulsory destocking had met with total non-cooperation and 1,500 Akamba marched to Nairobi, camping there for six weeks until the order was rescinded and the policy abandoned.[131] This, combined with concerns about loss of land to Europeans, meant that the Akamba were deeply suspicious of government policies.

The first attempts to introduce a mechanical soil conservation unit in 1946 met with popular resistance, with people throwing themselves in front of tractors. Initially all able-bodied adults had to work communally for two days a week under the direction of chiefs and headmen but, as cultivation gave ownership rights under traditional law, people did not want soil conservation work done on their land by others even if it was for free. As in Murang'a, the type of terrace being introduced in this area was the narrow-based terrace which was easier to build initially but required a larger long-term labour input due to maintenance needs, and was subject to collapse in storms. Bench terraces were thought to be inappropriate for African farmers due to the lack of tools and the time taken to build them – but once constructed they were more permanent and stable. From about 1949 some farmers began building bench terraces for the growing of vegetables and by the mid to late

1950s, when market access had improved, the adoption of bench terraces increased. Similarly there was a 'much greater and continued interest in bench terracing in higher hill areas, when this work could be directly associated with the introduction of new and profitable crops such as coffee'.[132] Machakos in the 1940s however did not offer the attractive farming opportunities seen for example in Nyeri, where from the 1950s bench terraces became acceptable as they were associated with the introduction of coffee. This evidence therefore supports the argument that incentives in the form of market opportunities are crucial, combined with tenurial security, a persuasive approach and choice of technologies.[133]

A resettlement scheme at Makueni, in Machakos, offers direct comparisons with Kigezi. The Makueni resettlement scheme began with the clearing of bush in 1945, and the first settlers moving in 1948 on holdings of 20–30 acres.[134] Estimates of the number resettled vary, but the figure was in the region of 12,000–16,000.[135] Until 1957, the settlers got free rations for one year and had 5 acres of land ploughed free of charge. However, the holdings were too large to enable adequate bush control and with bush encroachment tsetse became a problem. Tiffen *et al.* observe that there were many rules for settlers to follow, especially related to bush clearing and rotation, and the 'ley system proved impossible to maintain because of its heavy labour requirements.'[136] This stands in contrast to the Kigezi scheme where settlers were largely left to 'get on with it', unfettered by regulations.

Conclusion

While the decision to promote cash crops in Kigezi was externally driven by administrators in Entebbe and London, policies about soil erosion were formulated within Kigezi itself. Here, in contrast to other areas, local-level officials became concerned about threats to soil fertility, and formulated local-level policies to deal with the problems as they saw them. This meant the policies began to be implemented before a national soil conservation policy had been put together, and this long run-up to the policies was important in helping explain the success of the schemes.

That soil conservation policies were implemented without opposition is in stark contrast to other areas where similar attempts were made. Comparisons with such cases highlight some of the reasons for the apparently successful implementation and lack of opposition to the measures. The degree to which measures being introduced differed from indigenous methods of erosion control; the amount of additional labour input needed to implement measures; the extent to which local conditions were taken into account in the formulation of these schemes; and the extent to which officials on the ground were able to adapt measures to local conditions were all vitally important.[137] In Kigezi the earliest colonial policies were essentially modifications of the Bakiga agricultural system, rather than a major transformation of it. The Bakiga cultivated in a manner which led to the formation of 'steps' between plots;

and when the first policy of planting elephant grass in strips between plots was introduced these were likely to have been along these ridges.

As the colonial period progressed the obsession of the colonial authorities with the threat of soil erosion and their desire for 'orderliness' in agricultural systems grew, and more far-reaching measures were brought in, which coincided with the appointment of Purseglove as DAO. But the measures began some years before Purseglove arrived, and this gradual introduction of measures was crucial to successful implementation. In comparison to similar schemes elsewhere, in Kigezi greater effort was put into education, propaganda, and the provision of incentives, and thus the reasons behind conservation measures were generally understood. Purseglove's role is also significant: not only was he a particularly dynamic individual, but his period of service in Kigezi was prolonged. By working directly through chiefs, placing responsibility on them, and giving them authority to both judge and punish, the administration was broadly successful in getting conservation measures carried out. In addition, suspicions of the government's motives, fears of losing land to Europeans and the rise of nationalism were critical ingredients missing in Kigezi, which in other areas facilitated the articulation of discontent. Finally and crucially, the Agriculture Department was flexible enough to drop those parts of the scheme that proved inappropriate (such as the planting of grass leys on resting strips and the 'reorganisation' of land left behind by resettlers), suggesting greater attention was given to local responses to policies than elsewhere. The success was such that Kigezi became a 'show piece' for the administration and a visit to Kigezi became part of many official visitors' itineraries. The 'carrot and stick' method of implementation appeared to be successful and the success story of Kigezi has been repeated many times, including by outside observers.[138]

Kigezi's soil conservation policies were successfully implemented,[139] but there are a number of different measures of 'success', and in the colonial situation manifestations of success or failure were being judged on political or social terms (as distinct from assessments on agricultural or environmental terms). It may be that Kigezi was seen as successful because the policies were introduced without strong resistance from local populations and so they were seen as politically and socially successful. In some respects Kigezi may have been no more of a success than other schemes – for example, the resettlement of 20,000 people in Kigezi was presented as a 'success', while the resettlement of 12,000 people in the Makueni Settlement scheme was presented as a failure. Whether the policies were a success in the long run in the technical or agricultural sense is, however a different question: was it the implementation of policies that was successful, or the policies themselves that were a success? Whether indigenous soil conservation practices and colonial modifications to them can be judged to be successful must depend in part on the degree to which the agricultural system continues to intensify in a sustainable manner, and what the wider implications of such intensification are for livelihoods more broadly. While there is a widely held belief that farmers have reduced the period of fallow in the face of increasing population pressure, research has shown that farmers have, in fact, continued to maintain fallow periods, with positive outcomes for the sustainability of the agricultural system, as I will show in Chapter 6. But not everyone in the district practised such environmentally positive practices homogeneously, and this and the broader social costs of the transformation that Kigezi has undergone will be explored in Chapter 7. Before doing so, the following two chapters explore land tenure in Kigezi, and assess the 'success' of land reform policies introduced from the 1950s.

Notes

[1] Anderson, 'Depression, dust bowl'. On Southern Africa see Beinart, 'Soil erosion, conservationism'. See for example Mackenzie, *Land, Ecology;* Giblin, *The Politics of Environmental Control;* Maddox, Giblin and Kimambo, *Custodians of the Land;* Beinart and Bundy, *Hidden Struggles; Throup, The Economic and Social Origins;* Young and Fosbrooke, *Smoke in the Hills;* Malcolm, *Sukumaland;* Feierman*sant Intellectuals.*

[2] For example see Cliffe, 'Nationalism and the reaction to enforced agricultural change'; Maguire, *Towards 'Uhuru' in Tanzania;* Kimambo, *Penetration and Protest.*

[3] Exceptions include Feierman, *Peasant Intellectuals;* Showers, 'Soil erosion in the Kingdom of Lesotho'; Mackenzie, *Land, Ecology;* de Wilde, *Experiences with Agricultural Development.* Also see Tiffen, *et al., More People, Less Erosion.*

[4] For a collection of detailed studies of pre-colonial agricultural technologies, including terracing, ridging and irrigation see J. Sutton *et al.,* in Special issue on 'History of African Agricultural Technology and Field Systems', *Azania,* XXIV (1989).

[5] J. Roscoe, *The Soul of Central Africa: A General Account of the Mackie Ethnological Expedition,* (London, 1922), 101. Roscoe visited Kigezi 1919–1920. Papers of J.R. McD. Elliot, RH MSS Afr s 1384, #33 and #2a. Snowden, Report to DoA on Tour of Kigezi District, 16 Nov 1929. RH MSS Afr s 921, ff. 258.

[6] E. Grogan and A. Sharp, *From the Cape to Cairo: The First Traverse of Africa from South to North* (London, 1900), 118. See also G. Honke (ed.), *Au plus profond de l'Afrique: le Rwanda et la colonisation allemande, 1885–1919* (Wuppertal, 1990), 16; cited in Pottier, *Re-Imagining Rwanda,* 142.

[7] J. Czekanowski, *Forschungen im Nil-Kongo-Zwischengebiet. Vol. 1, Ethnographie Zwischenseegebiet Mpororo-Ruanda* (Leipzig, 1917), 135–6. For photographs taken on this expedition see Vol. 3 (1911), especially plate 41 and also plates 31, 34 and 39. Also see G. Honke, *Au plus profond de l'Afrique.*

[8] 'Notes on Preservation of Soil Fertility' prepared by DoA, ENA H175/1/II ff. 5 or H218/I ff. 16(1), para 24.

[9] Tothill, *Agriculture in Uganda,* 87.

[10] Notes on the System of Land Tenure in Kigezi written by DC, for EARC, 1950. PRO CO 892 15/9 p. 47. For a discussion of attitudes to African agriculture by officials involved in earlier schemes in Southern Africa, see Beinart, 'Soil erosion, conservationism'. Here some officials 'saw African methods as insufficiently intensive to be a major threat, even if they did not recognise them as sympathetic and careful'.

[11] Today maize planted in Sept with beans; weeded once, then beans harvested in Nov–Dec, and maize harvested in Feb–Mar.

[12] Letter of 15/1/37 to SAO, K'la from Wickham. DoA 010crops

[13] This appears in a description of agriculture in the General Policy book for the district. Ironically, the unnamed official (probably H.M. Tufnell, the DC at the time) who wrote these words was describing them as 'bad' methods of cultivation. Notes on General Baraza at Kabale – 26/5/25, KDA DC Gen policy p. 96.

[14] Tothill, *Agriculture in Uganda,* 127.

[15] Letter to PCWP from J.E. Phillips, Acting DC, 26 Jan 1921, KDA DC MP69 ff. 2. Note

Soil Conservation in Kigezi

on 'Land insufficiency around Kabale', 1929, by J.E. Phillips, DC, KDA DC MP69 ff. 34.

[16] Report for Year 1935 by Wickham, KDA DC AGR-MNTH ff. 53. Wickham was the first officer to give a detailed picture about Kigezi and we rely on his early descriptions. While grazing fallow land had the advantage of spreading dung, it was also thought to compact the soil.

[17] Letter to DC from Wickham, DAO, Kabale, 5 Sept 1935, KDA DoA 009exp-c ff. 10. Note that soil 'erosion' (e.g. sheet or gulley erosion) and falling soil fertility or soil exhaustion are sometimes used interchangeably.

[18] Notes on Food Crops and Famine Reserves in Kigezi, Masefield, May 1937. KDA DC AGR-MNTH ff. 81. Masefield was DAO in Kigezi from Feb 1937 to June 1938. He had been educated at Winchester and Oxford. He received a Colonial Agricultural scholarship with his first year at Cambridge and his second at the Imperial College of Tropical Agriculture in Trinidad. From ICTA he was posted to Uganda, and after periods as DAO in Ankole, Kigezi and Mbale he was appointed Soil Conservation Officer in Buganda. Masefield recalled that his interest in soils began as an undergraduate at Oxford: 'I was thrilled with soils ... I don't know why, but I just took to soils and that is why I took to soil conservation.' Interview 18 April 1996. His career after leaving Uganda is of significance as he went on to an Oxford lectureship and wrote several books on the subject of tropical agriculture.

[19] Monthly report, July 1937, by G.B. Masefield, KDA DC AGR-MNTH ff. 87. Letter to Dr N.M. James, Church Missionary Society [Hereafter CMS], Syira, PO Kabale from Haig, SAO, K'la, 13 July 1937. Also letter of 30 Aug 1937 – Letter to SAO from Masefield, DAO) KDA DoA 009crops.

[20] Monthly Report for Oct 1937 by Masefield, KDA DC AGR-MNTH ff. 95. *Lukikos* were meetings held by officials with the local population during safaris around the district. Letter to DC from Masefield, DAO, 23 Oct 1937, KDA DC AGR6I ff. 2. Letter to DC and DMO from DAO, 18 March 1937. KDA DoA 010crops.

[21] Annual Report for 1937 for Kigezi District, by Masefield, KDA DC AGR-MNTH ff. 98. Also interviews with elderly men and women, Kabale District, July-September 1995. For details see Carswell, 'African Farmers'. Also interview with Masefield, 18 April 1996.

[22] In other parts of the colonial world, for example Southern Africa, soil conservation policy had already been formalised and ridges were being advocated. See Beinart, 'Soil erosion, conservationism'. Subjects covered at *lukikos* on safari in Kigezi included: coffee mulching, timber and black wattle planting and the planting of contour erythrina hedges to avoid soil erosion. See ADC Wright's Safari in Rukiga, 15 Feb 1937 to 3 March 1937, KDA DC MP139 ff. 34.

[23] Letter to SAO from Masefield, DAO, 26 May 1938. KDA DoA 11/A/1 ff. 4. Interview with Masefield, 18 April 1996.

[24] Planters: Letter to SAO from Stuckey, DAO, 25 Jan 1940, KDA DoA 008. Also enclosure to Letter to Stafford from H.B. Thomas, Land Officer, 23 Jan 1940, setting out conditions on which government agreed to cultivation of pyrethrum in Kigezi by Moses and Stafford. KDA DoA 008. Missionaries: Bwama Island in Lake Bunyonyi was established by the CMS as a hospital and treatment centre for lepers in 1930/31. Letter to SAO from G.F. Clay, DoA, 7 Feb 1940, KDA DoA 008. Referring to letter to DoA from Director of Medical Services.

[25] Letter to SAO, from Stuckey, 18 April 1940, KDA DoA 008. Letter to DoA from E.F. Martin, SAO, WP, 1 May 1940, KDA DoA 008. Strip cropping is the method of resting and cultivating alternate strips of land. Bunds are vertical steps between plots of land. In situations where steps or banks already exist between plots bunds are relatively easy to adopt. But introducing bunds from 'scratch' is labour-intensive and therefore more problematic.

[26] Report on Tour of Western Province, 7–19 July 1941, by Deputy Director of Agriculture, KDA DoA 11/A/1 ff. 6.

[27] Letter to DAO from T.Y. Watson, Deputy Director of Agriculture, 2 Oct 1951, KDA DC AGR6I ff. 67.

[28] Note by McCombe (DAO) on Matias's (DC) Memo on 'Kigezi District: Economic

Policy', KDA DoA 11/A/1 ff. 11. Letter to SAO from McCombe, DAO, 18 Jan 1943. KDA DC AGR6I ff. 11. For more detail re measures in McCombe's time see Letter to Saza Chiefs from McCombe, DAO, 29 June 1942, KDA DoA 11/A/1 ff. 7.

[29] Anderson, 'Depression, dust bowl'. For growth of concerns in Southern Africa context see Beinart, 'Soil erosion, conservationism.'

[30] The Standing Committee on Soil Erosion met for the first time in June 1931, then again in February in 1932, but then not again for nearly 6 years. J. Iliffe, *A Modern History of Tanganyika*, (Cambridge, 1979), 348.

[31] Report on Informal Conference to discuss soil erosion in the Tanganyikan context, held in May 1929. PRO CO 822/26/9 ff. 1. Minute by Stockdale, 27 Feb 1930, PRO CO 822 26/9.

[32] Conference of Soil Chemists, 1932. PRO CO 822/47/3.

[33] D.J. Vail, *A History of Agricultural Innovation and Development in Teso District, Uganda* (Syracuse, N.Y., 1972), 127–35. Kerr, the Commissioner for Cooperative Development, writing a memo for EARC in 1953 described some of the background to soil conservation. Kerr, an agricultural officer in Teso in 1930, wrote that he was 'struck by the loss of soil fertility and soil erosion on the agricultural experiment station and Teso District where ploughing with ox-ploughs had at that time developed extensively'. PRO CO 892 15/7.

[34] Notes on Preservation of Soil Fertility under conditions of Native Agriculture in Uganda, by Tothill, Director of Ag written July 1935, ENA H175/1/II ff. 5. Also see ENA H218 I ff. 16(1) and KDA DC AGR-MNTH ff. 44Enc.

[35] Letter to Chf Sec from Tothill 31 July 1935, ENA H218/1 ff. 16. Enclosing Notes by Tothill on 'Preservation of soil fertility under conditions of Native Agriculture in Uganda' (14pgs). See Carswell, 'African Farmers'.

[36] Report by Sir Frank Stockdale KCMG, CBE (Agricultural Adviser to the Secretary of State for the Colonies) on his Visit to East Africa, Jan–Mar 1937. Produced by Colonial Advisory Council of Agriculture and Animal Health (CO, July 1937) ENA H253. Also PRO CO 822/77/11 ff. 22. For details of Stockdale's role in the rhetoric and policy formulation see Anderson, 'Depression, dust bowl', 341–2.

[37] Letter to All AOs from A. Richardson, Acting DA 9 Oct 1937, KDA DoA 001/C.

[38] See PRO CO 822 files e.g. PRO CO822/106/5; PRO CO 822/109/various. Soil erosion was also discussed at the 1938 Conference of Governors of Uganda, Kenya and Tanganyika. Conference of Directors of Agriculture, May 1940. ENA H304 ff. 1.

[39] Notes by Tothill (DoA) on various aspects of Indian and South African agriculture, with particular reference to items of possible practical value to Uganda. (Jan–Mar, 1938) Circulated around Dept of Ag. ENA H280 ff. 1. Maher, 'A Visit to USA to Study Soil Conservation.' Department of Agriculture, Nairobi, 1940. PRO CO 892 15/7. Colonial administrators continued to look beyond East Africa to learn from the experiences of others – eg visit by Collett (Soil Conservation Officer, Basutoland) in 1955. KDA DoA 19 ff. 211 and PRO DO 35/936/Y579/12.

[40] Newbury, *The Cohesion of Oppression*, 158. Despite the adverse weather conditions in this year of 'famine', it was not necessary to import food into Kigezi. Although little or no food was officially available for export throughout 1943, this had to be enforced through a 'strict system of frontier guards ... to prevent the export of foodstuffs from Kigezi [into Ruanda].' WPAR, 1946. As was shown in the previous chapter such assertions that shortages were 'imminent' were used to justify marketing regulations.

[41] E. Clayton, *Purseglove: A Pioneer of Rural Development* (Wye, 1993). Purseglove was thus the subject of the first monograph to be produced by Wye College on important individuals in Tropical Agriculture. Further information re Purseglove from CV and Aide Memoire – RH MSS Brit Emp s 476.

[42] Interview with J.M. Byagagaire, Kampala, 21 Sept 1995. Byagagaire, from northern Kigezi, worked alongside Purseglove during vacations while doing a diploma in agriculture at Makerere. He was AAO in Kigezi 1953–57 and was the first African DAO of the District, appointed in May 1962.

[43] P. Ngologoza, *Kigezi and its People* (Kampala, 1969), 94. Ngologoza was a Mukunga Chief from 1923, rose to Gombolola Chief in 1929; Saza Chief in 1936; Secretary

General in 1946; Chief Judge in Kigezi 1956 and Chairman of Appointments Board 1959.

[44] Purseglove, 'Report on the Overpopulated Areas of Kigezi', (1945) para 17.

[45] *Ibid.*. paras 13, 93 and 94.

[46] See for example Allan, *The African Husbandman*, (Edinburgh, 1965), 182–4.

[47] For example, Ministry of National Resources, National Environment Information Centre, *State of the Environment Report for Uganda* (Kampala, 1994), 26; E.M. Tukahirwa (ed.), *Environmental and Natural Resource Management Policy and Law: Issues and Options, Summary* (Makerere Institute of Social Research (MISR) and Natural Resources and World Resources Institute, Washington, 1992); and F.D.K. Bagoora, 'Soil erosion and mass wasting risk in the highland areas of Uganda', *Mountain Research and Development*, 8 (1988), 173-82.

[48] K. Lindblade, J.K. Tumahairwe, G. Carswell, C. Nkwiine and D. Bwamiki, 'More People, More Fallow – Environmentally Favorable Land-use Changes in Southwestern Uganda', (Report prepared for the Rockefeller Foundation and CARE International, 1996). K. Lindblade, G. Carswell and J.K. Tumahairwe, 'Mitigating the relationship between population growth and land degradation: Land-use change and farm management in southwestern Uganda', *Ambio*, 27 7 (1998), 565–71.

[49] Purseglove, 'Report on the Overpopulated Areas of Kigezi', paras 96, 101. The initial areas of resettlement in Rujhumbura were in the *gombololas* of Ruhinda, Nyakagyeme and Buyanja; in Kinkizi in the *gombololas* of Kirima and Kambuga. For a detailed study of the Resettlement Scheme and in particular the effects on the family see R.E. Yeld, 'The Family and Social Change: A study among the Kiga of Kigezi, south west Uganda' (PhD, Makerere, 1969).

[50] Minutes of District Team Meeting, 8 Sept 1945, KDA DoA 11/A/1 ff. 23. The District Team consisted of the DC, ADC, DAO, DVO, and DMO. They were first created in 1945 and initially met about twice a year, then later about four times a year, to discuss district policy and progress.

[51] Memo written by Kerr, Commissioner for Cooperative Development, for EARC in 1953, PRO CO 892 15/7.

[52] Purseglove, 'Report on the Overpopulated Areas of Kigezi', para 102.

[53]Minutes of Meeting of District Team, 6 Oct 1950, KDA DoA 11/A/1 ff. 67. Free food for a number of months was part of the 'resettlement package' offered. See letter to Napire Bax, Director of Tsetse Research, Chinyanga, Tang and Dir of Tsetse Control, K'la from Purseglove, 15 March 1947, KDA DoA MP12/2 ff. 70. Also letter to Saza Chfs of Ndorwa, Rukiga, Ruzhumbura and Kinkizi from Ngololgoza, 18 Feb 1948, KDA DC MP125/1 ff. 337. Letter to all Saza Chfs from DC, 22 Oct 1949, KDA DC Dev4/1/II ff. 134.

[54] J.Y. Obol-Ochola, *Customary Land Law and the Economic Development of Uganda* (Dar es Salaam, 1971).

[55] Survey undertaken in Resettlement Area, 1950, PRO CO 536/223 40391 ff. 8.

[56] 1951 survey: Memo by Purseglove on Shifting Cultivation in Western Province written in Oct 1951. PRO CO 892 15/7. Annual Report, PAO, WP, 1961. Quoted in D.G.R. Belshaw, 'An outline of resettlement policy in Uganda, 1945–63', in R. Apthorpe (ed.), *Land Settlement and Rural Development in Eastern Africa* (Kampala, 1968).

[57] Purseglove, 'Kigezi Resettlement' 147; Purseglove, 'Resettlement in Kigezi', 17. Also letter to Dir of Ag from Purseglove, 28 April 1947, KDA DoA MP12/2 ff. 87.

[58] Ngologoza probably inherited land in Rwanyana, Rubaya (where he was born); he obtained land as part of the first group of settlers in *Gombolola* Ruhina in Rujumbura; and a decade later as part of the land tenure pilot project had 2 plots of land registered in Mwanjaari, Gombolola Kituma, Saza Ndorwa and one in Katooye. Ngologoza, *Kigezi and Its People*, 81– 99.

[59] Note to John (Purseglove) from Mat (Matias) [on safari] from Nyakageme, 10 Oct 1946, KDA DoA MP12/1 ff. 160.

[60] Report to DC from Ngologoza, SecGen 8 Oct 1955 on Visit to Bigodi in Kibale, Toro to find out why the 23 settlers rejected the 10 acres. KDA DoA 010resett ff. 98. Circular by King, DAO to SecGen, Saza and Gomb Chfs. 22 Nov 1955, KDA DoA 010resett ff. 108.

[61] Report to District Medical Officer by D.D. McCarthy, for Director of Medical Services,

7 May 1949. KDA DC MP 105/BI ff. 183.
[62] Letter to Saza Chfs Ndorwa and Rukiga and various Gomb Chfs from DC, 26 June 1950, KDA DC Dev4/1/II ff. 270.
[63] Letter to 5 Gomb Chfs from Rukereluga, Mtwale, Bufumbira, 11 Feb 1950, KDA DC MIS 12I, ff. 28. Letter to Gomb Chf Rwamuchuchu from Ngologoza, 6 Sept 1947, KDA DC MP125/1 ff. 319. Yeld examines family pressure to resettle, and suggests that those with weaker claims to land within their household were particularly vulnerable to such pressure. Yeld, 'The Family and Social Change'.
[64] Edel, *The Chiga*, 18. See also Baxter, 'The Kiga', 284.
[65] Letter to R Day, University of London, Institute of Education, from DC, 20 April 1950, KDA DC Dev4/1/II ff. 238.
[66] Report by Purseglove, Jan/Feb 1947, KDA DoA 12/2 ff. 27.
[67] On receipt of the annual reports on resettlement various officials at the CO commented in minutes on the 'strikingly successful scheme' which was a 'very great achievement.' See for example file on Settlement scheme in Kigezi District (1950), PRO CO 536/223 40391. Problems that were dealt with include the clearing of tsetse fly from the resettlement areas, dealing with health problems (especially malaria), and finding suitable economic crops to make the areas more attractive to settlers. Minutes of Kigezi District Team, KDA DoA 11/A/1.
[68] Just a few years earlier in a discussion of agricultural policy at a national level it was noted that 'strip cropping could be successfully introduced only where there is plenty of land.' Minutes of 2nd Meeting of the Rural Devt Sub-Comm, Entebbe, 19 Feb 1942, PRO CO 536 210 40287/1 ff. 20. But here strip cropping was introduced, despite this observation that it could only be successfully introduced in areas with plenty of land.
[69] Purseglove, 'Report on the Overpopulated Areas of Kigezi', paras 98–99 and 102. Details of soil conservation measures in KDA DoA 11/A/1.
[70] Report on Agriculture in Bukinda by AAO, Rukiga sent to DAO, 25 Nov 1949, KDA DoA 19/B/2, ff. 56.
[71] Letter to Provincial Agricultural Officer (PAO) from Purseglove, DAO, 9 June 1948, KDA DoA 11/A/1 ff. 51.
[72] Letter to DAO from Kitaburaza, Saza Chf Ruzhumbura, 12 Nov 1949, KDA DoA 16/A/1 ff. 87. Letter to DAO from Kitaburaza, Saza Chf Ruzhumbura, 28 Nov 1949, KDA DoA 16/A/1 ff. 90. Also KDA DC AGR6I ff. 38. There are a number of other examples of similar action being taken against chiefs e.g. Bubale, Ndorwa in 1950 – See Report by AAO, Ndorwa, 1 May 1950, KDA DoA 19/B/2, ff. 92.
[73] Interviews, Kabale District, July-September 1995.
[74] For example, amongst District Officials, Interview with Mutabazi, DAO, July 1995.
[75] Telegram to PAO from DAO 5 Sept 1950, KDA DoA 16/A/1 ff. 113. Letter to DMO, DVO, DFO and DAO from DC, 6 Jan 1954, KDA DoA 11/A/2, ff. 1.
[76] Memorandum on 'Agricultural Rules' in letter to DC from DAO, 5 Feb 1954. KDA DoA 11/A/2 ff. 5.
[77] Letter to Saza and Gomb Chfs from DC, 3 Aug 1951, KDA DC AGR6I ff. 62.
[78] Interviews in Kigezi, July–September 1995. 95/Kit/56a and 95/Kit/56b.
[79] Letter to Saza Chfs from Ngol, Secgen, 23 Oct 1951, KDA DC AGR6I ff. 70.
[80] Here the Secretary General checked the actions of over-zealous chiefs. This contrasts with the actions of Chief Tengani in the Shire Valley of Nyasaland, whose 'dictatorship' is described by Mandala and who demanded strict compliance. His zealousness succeeded in 'breaking resistance' to the scheme and Mandala shows how this generated support for the nationalist movement, raising the political consciousness of the peasantry and illustrates 'the potential of Indirect Rule for creating tyrants out of traditional rulers'. E.C. Mandala, *Work and Control in a Peasant Economy* (Madison, WI, 1990), 232–4.
[81] Balfour (Officer in Charge, Makueni, to The Commissioner, African Settlement and Land Utilisation, N'bi, 15 Sept 1950 reporting on Visit to the Kigezi Resettlement Scheme. PRO CO 892 15/8 ff. 1. Kenyan officials were interested in the scheme in the light of similar efforts being tried at this time in the Makueni and the Machakos Settlement Areas, in Kenya.
[82] Report by Balfour on Visit to the Kigezi Resettlement Scheme, 15 Sept 1950, PRO CO

892 15/8 ff. 1.
[83] Letter to Saza Chfs from Ngol, SecGen 7 Nov 1947, KDA DoA 16/A/1 ff. 50. Other correspondence in KDA DoA 16/A/1 ff. 21, ff. 31 and ff. 133. At the first course 11 Gomb Chfs; 16 Muluka chiefs and 3 instructors attended. At a second one held later in the year 17 Gomb, 20 Muluka chiefs and 6 members of Staff of Ag Dept (called 'instructors') attended.
[84] Letter to PAO from Purseglove, DAO, 9 June 1948, 'Land Utilization and Agrarian Reconstruction in Kigezi' KDA DoA 11/A/1 ff. 51.
[85] Interview with J.M. Byagagaire, Kampala, 21 Sept 1995. He also recalled that one of their policies was that they never toured the area by car, but rather always walked and camped. Similarly Audrey Richards insisted that colonial office anthropologists appointed in 1946 in Kenya and elsewhere should not have cars. (Thank you to William Beinart for this observation.)
[86] Interviews, Kabale, July–September 1995. See also articles in 'Kigezi Newsletter' (also known as 'AGANDI'). This was produced in Rukiga by the district administration from Oct 1950 – mainly about resettlement, agricultural competitions, etc. KDA DC SCW7-1-I ff. 38a.
[87] Letter to PAO from Purseglove, DAO 19 July 1946, KDA DC AGR6I ff. 14. Results of 1958 Soil Competition, KDA DoA 218A ff. 30. Also interviews.
[88] Report on Agriculture in Bukinda by AAO, Rukiga sent to DAO, 25 Nov 1949, KDA DoA 19/B/2, ff. 56. Also KDA DC AGR6I ff. 39.
[89] Memo on role of Demonstration Teams by Dept of Public Relations and Social Welfare, by C.M.A. Gayer, Dir of PR and SW, 2 Jan 1947. KDA DoA 11/A/1 ff. 38. For a discussion of the background to the creation of the Colonial Film Unit in 1939 see R. Smyth, 'British Colonial Film Policy 1927–1939', *Journal of African History* , 20 3 (1979), 437–50.
[90] Memo re organisation of WP Demo Team from Snowden, ADC, 21 May 1947, KDA DoA 11/A/1 ff. 43Enc. Letter to Purseglove from Dennis Carr, PR and SW Dept, Mbarara, 26 April 1947, KDA DoA 11/A/1 ff. 40. Leaflet on 'Soil Erosion', KDA DoA 11/A/1 ff. 40Enc.
[91] Letter to DAO from G. Symons, DVO, 27 March 1952, KDA DC AGR6I ff. 75. Letter to Gomb Chf Kitumba from Secgen, 6 Oct 1951, KDA DC AGR6I ff. 68.
[92] Notes on the System of Land Tenure in Kigezi written by DC, for EARC, 1950. PRO CO 892 15/9 pg47. Notes on Shifting Cultivation in Western Province, by Purseglove. Prepared for EARC PRO CO 892 15/7. Also letter to DAO from T.Y. Watson, (Deputy Director of Agriculture) 2 Oct 1951. Following visit to Kigezi. KDA DC AGR6I ff. 67.
[93] In the early 1950s there was some criticism in the vernacular press about soil erosion measures in Buganda. Monthly Political Surveys: Uganda (EAF 96/15/01/A) SECRET file, PRO CO 822/381 – 1951–53. Even without a vernacular press in Kigezi one might expect to find references to discontent in the district archives, in, for example, files on 'Petitions and Complaints' which were examined closely.
[94] Memo to Governor on Resettlement by Sub-Committee of Kigezi District Team (1953) KDA DoA 11/A/1 ff. 115. Letter to PAO from King, DAO, 7 May 1953, KDA DoA 012-3 ff. 8. Further assessment and reports re Resettlement Scheme in KDA DoA 012-3 ff. 11, ff. 14 and ff. 17.
[95] Letter to PAO from King, DAO, 7 May 1953, KDA DoA 012-3 ff. 8.
[96] Letter to Dir of Ag from Todd, DAO, 8 March 1954 'Kigezi Ag.al Policy'. KDA DoA 11/A/2 ff. 9.
[97] Letter to PCWP from Fraser, DC, 3 Feb 1954. KDA DoA 11/A/2, ff. 3. Letter to 'All in charge, Sazas' from DAO, 2 Sept 1954 re tour of Kigezi during August. KDA DoA 11/A/2 ff. 27.
[98] Letter to DC from G.B. Symons, DVO, 12 March 1953, KDA DoA 13/A/1 ff. 318. Also mentioned in letter to Saza Chf Ruzh from King, DAO, 8 May 1953, KDA DC AGR6I ff. 201.
[99] Annual Report of the Department of Agriculture, 1953, 42–3. Also Annual Reports for 1954 and 1955.
[100] Letter to DAO from T.Y. Watson, 2 Oct 1951. KDA DC AGR6I ff. 67. Extracts from

Minutes of Kigezi District Team Meetings in KDA DC AGR6I and KDA DoA Teammins.
[101] Letter to Secgen, Saza Chfs and Field Officers from E.W. King, DAO 23 May 1956, KDA AGR6II ff. 30.
[102] See Carswell, 'African Farmers' for further comparisons with the Pare Development Plan.
[103] For broad outlines of policies experienced in Tanganyika and reactions to them see A. Coulson, 'Agricultural Policies in Mainland Tanzania', in J. Heyer (ed.), *Rural Development in Tropical Africa* (London, 1981), 52–89. Also Cliffe, 'Nationalism and the reaction to enforced agricultural change'. Also see Giblin, *The Politics of Environmental Control*. These studies examine soil conservation measures and reactions to them, in the context of essentially political processes, and examine their influence on the growth of nationalist politics. Also see M. Stocking, 'Soil conservation policy in colonial Africa', *Agricultural History* 59 (1985), 148–61. This examined policy in nine African countries.
[104] Malcolm, *Sukumaland, An African People and the Country.*
[105] Iliffe, *A Modern History of Tanganyika*, 474.
[106] P.F.M. McLoughlin, 'Sukumaland' in J.C. de Wilde, *Experiences with Agricultural Development in Tropical Africa*, Vol. 2, (Baltimore, MD, 1967).
[107] Maguire, *Towards 'Uhuru' in Tanganika.* A study of micro-politics, the political consequences of the scheme and the development of nationalism in Sukumuland.
[108] These shortcomings are examined in detail in P.F.M. McLoughlin, 'Sukumaland.'
[109] McLoughlin, 'Sukumaland', 426, 429. Also see Coulson, 'Agricultural Policies in Mainland Tanzania', 57.
[110] McLoughlin, 'Sukumaland', 422.
[111] Maguire, *Towards 'Uhuru' in Tanzania*, 31.
[112] McLoughlin, 'Sukumaland', 419, 420.
[113] Iliffe, *A Modern History of Tanganyika*, 559.
[114] See Young and Fosbrooke, *Smoke in the Hills.*
[115] P.A. Maack, 'We Don't Want Terraces!' Protest and Identity under the Uluguru Land usage Scheme' in G. Maddox (ed.), *Custodians of the Land: Ecology and Culture in the History of Tanzania* (London, 1996), 159.
[116] See Young and Fosbrooke, *Smoke in the Hills*, 147.
[117] Maack, 'We Don't Want Terraces!', 160, 156, 158. Similarly in parts of Nyasaland there were cases of successful implementation. In Northeastern Chikwawa and on the Lulwe plateau, as well as in the Tchiri highlands, campaigns to promote ridge cultivation were successful. Mandala notes that in areas of steep hillsides farmers found it 'reasonable' to adopt contour ridging. This was in sharp contrast to the rest of the Shire Valley where opposition was strong. Thus while ridge cultivation may have 'made sense' to growers in hilly areas, it was not rational for farmers of flatter land, because ridges did not raise productivity and had high labour demands. Mandala, *Work and Control in a Peasant Economy*, 227–9.
[118] Iliffe, *A Modern History of Tanganyika*, 474.
[119] Maack, 'We Don't Want Terraces!', 153.
[120] See Young and Fosbrooke, *Smoke in the Hills*, 147.
[121] Iliffe, *A Modern History of Tanganyika*, 474. For further details of the disturbances in Uluguru see PRO CO 822/807.
[122] Young and Fosbrooke, *Smoke in the Hills*, 146.
[123] Feierman, *Peasant Intellectuals*, 181. Usambara Conservation scheme see PRO CO 822/ 1366. For further details see Carswell 'African Farmers'. This was called boxed ridging in Nyasaland. See Beinart, 'Soil erosion, conservationism', 71.
[124] Feierman, *Peasant Intellectuals*, 169–76, 188.
[125] *Ibid.*, 182–3.
[126] Iliffe, *A Modern History of Tanganyika*, 474.
[127] For a detailed examination of how political and social cleavages enabled the articulation of discontent see Feierman, *Peasant Intellectuals.*
[128] Throup, *The Economic and Social origins of Mau Mau*, 70. See also D.W. Throup, 'The Origins of the Mau Mau'. M.P.K. Sorrenson, *Land Reform in the Kikuyu Country – A study in Government policy.* (Nairobi, 1967).
[129] Mackenzie, *Land, Ecology*, 2, 152–3, 209–10.

[130] Tiffen *et al.*, *More People, Less Erosion*.

[131] For details see J.F. Munro, *Colonial Rule and the Kamba: Social change in Kenya Highlands 1889–1939* (Oxford, 1979).

[132] de Wilde, *Experiences with Agricultural Development*, Vol. 2, 97.

[133] Tiffen, *et al.*, *More People, Less Erosion*, 256.

[134] de Wilde, *Experiences with Agricultural Development* Vol. 2, 109. Throup, however, suggests that the holdings were much larger 'each settler needed 120 acres compared to the five acre plots they had cultivated in their former locations.' It is not clear if this is the acreage that each settler needed, or each was actually allocated. Throup, *Economic and Social Origins of Mau Mau*, 70.

[135] De Wilde suggests that 2,250 settler families with 12,000 people were ultimately resettled at a cost of £149 per settler, de Wilde, *Experiences with Agricultural Development* Vol. 2, 109. Although unclear if this cost is per settler family or settler individual. Tiffen *et al.* state that by 1960 there were 2,187 registered settlers which represented 12,000 to 16,000 people. Tiffen *et al.*, *More People, Less Erosion*, 53. Throup states that 664 families were moved by the end of 1952 at a cost of £18,340. Throup, *Economic and Social Origins*, 70.

[136] Tiffen *et al.*, *More People, Less Erosion*, 164. See also de Wilde, *Experiences with Agricultural Development*.

[137] Mackenzie notes that with few exceptions (all of which were in Tanganyika) 'local conservation systems, their ecological specificity and their integration of biological with technical measures, were completely ignored in attempts to resolve the growing environmental crisis in colonial Africa.' Mackenzie, *Land, Ecology*, 15. The evidence presented here suggests that Kigezi is another such exception.

[138] Wrigley, *Crops and Wealth in Uganda*, 77.

[139] There are examples of successful implementation of schemes being reported, while very little changed on the ground. See for example Thackwray Driver, 'Soil conservation in Mokhotlong, Lesotho, 1945–56: A success in non-implementation' (African History Seminar, SOAS, 1996).

Four

Land Tenure
in Kigezi

Who has authority over land, and how access to land is controlled, are key dynamics in the lives of all rural households. Outlining the system of land tenure in Kigezi, exploring what colonial officials meant by 'native customary tenure', and what this meant for the people of Kigezi, will lay the foundation for the more detailed exploration of the impact of land reform policies in the following chapter. I will argue that Kigezi has a long history of a highly individualised system of land tenure, which has endured and evolved in the face of many social, political and economic changes, and in the face of colonial land reform policies.

Colonial encounters with land tenure

Under the 1902 Uganda Order in Council and the 1903 Crown Land Ordinance (and subsequent amendments to it) all land in Uganda was declared to be Crown land, the ownership of which was legally vested in the Crown while the rights of Africans were protected. The only exception to this was land held in private title, which included grants made to non-Africans before 1902 and what was known as *mailo* land. *Mailo* land was allocated to chiefs under Agreements signed with leaders of the four kingdoms of Buganda, Ankole, Toro and Bunyoro, and did not apply outside these kingdoms.[1] With all land outside these kingdoms being declared Crown land, few changes were made to land legislation until the early 1950s.[2] This, of course, makes Uganda very different from neighbouring Kenya, where from the beginning of colonial administration grants of land were made to British settlers.

Land legislation in Uganda thus ruled out the possibility of land being alienated to outsiders, while in the Agreement States it granted land to chiefs. The 'right of natives to occupy Crown Land' was legally established, and a 1950 pronouncement on the Government's land policy on land outside Buganda stated that rural Crown land was held 'in trust for the use and benefit of the African population'.[3] But, besides this, the legislation said little about the rights of 'ordinary' Ugandans with respect to control over, and access to, the land that they used. Instead, the concept 'native customary rights' was used. Before examining what was meant by this term, I will outline the official policy at a district level.

The official policy of protecting the interests of Africans was upheld in Kigezi where there was to be no alienation of Crown land to non-Africans in freehold. There were, however, a few cases where land was granted, under leasehold, within the district. First, leaseholds were made to missions. The two missionary organisations in Kigezi, the CMS (or Native Anglican Church as it was then called) and the White Fathers Mission (WFM), were leased small areas of land for churches and schools, usually under Temporary Occupational Licences. In addition, they each had a larger area of about 300 acres at their 'headquarters'. When these areas were granted to the missions, those people living on the land were given notice prior to eviction.[4]

Second, leaseholds were granted in 1940 for the establishment of two pyrethrum estates. The decision to lease land in this overpopulated part of the district was exceptional and needs to be seen in the context of the needs of the wartime economy, with pyrethrum being declared a priority crop. The land, 800 acres in total, was leased to two Europeans under Temporary Occupation Licences, which involved a 5-year leasehold to continue thereafter from year to year. A number of conditions related to planting of firewood and soil conservation measures were imposed.[5] Production of pyrethrum at Kalengyere began in 1946, but just four years later in 1950 the American wartime stockpile was released and as a result prices collapsed. With the ending of the artificially high wartime prices pyrethrum production was no longer economic in Kigezi and the land was surrendered.[6]

Finally, some Certificates of Occupancy were granted to a number of Baganda Agents for land they held in Kigezi. Being a non-Agreement district, there were no formal links between land and chieftainships or other government-appointed positions in Kigezi – i.e. there was no *mailo* land. But these certificates were issued by the Native Authority, based on continuing cultivation, and were granted without a survey of boundaries.[7] They were also used in Toro and Ankole from the 1920s and their main aim was to

> enable any native to make use of as much Crown Land as he requires for himself, for purposes of cultivation or residence, without fear of disturbance, or the liability to pay rent, tithes etc to other natives.[8]

Although reference is made to 'any native', these were in fact granted to chiefs employed by the British administration. They were introduced to provide a sense of security, and it was hoped that this in turn would encourage people to plant permanent crops and make improvements in agriculture generally. They also provided a 'convenient answer'[9] to the occasional demands for *mailo* grants. There is some evidence that some certificates were also granted to Bakiga chiefs in the late 1920s and early 1930s.[10]

With the exception of these certificates of occupancy, and mission leaseholds and Temporary Occupation Licences, no land was alienated in Kigezi.[11] Without the threat of alienation, and with land having been declared Crown land, native customary practices with regard to access to land, and control over it, were recognised.

'Native customary tenure': the view of colonial officials

For the majority of Bakiga the declaration that land was 'Crown land' meant that 'native customary tenure' was recognised. But what did this mean, and how was it interpreted by colonial officials? This section examines the colonial view of 'customary tenure', and then explores key aspects of this system. It draws on a range of sources: colonial sources, the views of non-official visitors, including Edel, the anthropologist who worked in the area in 1933, and the views of Bakiga, mainly through oral sources.

Colonial authorities asserted state control over land in Uganda declaring it to be Crown land. The British allowed local customary law to continue alongside their own law, as this was the most convenient way of administering justice. Here the judicial basis for customary tenure was 'its recognition in statutory law and the provision made for the applicability of customary law in general'. The term customary tenure, as observed by Mifsud, 'distinguishes this type of law from western or imported law' and comprises 'a wide variety of local land laws [whose] diversity is as significant as their common features'.[12] Thus customary law was not a single uniform set of customs but rather 'the rules governing human conduct which are enforceable in a court of law'.[13] The administration gave recognition to customary law but 'interfered little with its content and application'. This 'separateness or isolation was mainly the result of the dual system of courts under which one set of courts dealt with the written legislation and the received English law and the other set, the African or native or local courts, which only had jurisdiction over Africans, primarily administered customary law.'[14] With land being declared 'Crown land', people were free to settle anywhere 'subject to the tribal rules of tenure', while disputes over occupancy rights were 'settled by native law or custom'.[15]

While customary law existed side by side with English law, 'it did not remain stagnant but developed like any other branch of law'. The dual system lasted until the 1960s when a single system of courts emerged but, as Brown and Allen observed in the late 1960s, customary law still governed the lives of the 'great majority' in Uganda'.[16] Customary civil law in Uganda was defined by the Magistrates' Courts Act of 1964 which stated that it 'means the rules of conduct which govern legal relationships as established by custom and usage and not forming part of the common law nor formally enacted by Parliament'.[17]

Customary law was thus centrally important to the everyday lives of Africans in Uganda throughout the colonial period. Colson has argued that customary law in Africa was not traditional, but rather was created:

Colonial officials expected the courts to enforce long-established custom rather than current opinion. Common official stereotypes about African customary land law thus came to be used by colonial officials in assessing the legality of current decisions, and so came to be incorporated in 'customary' systems of tenure.[18]

As Chanock has observed, 'custom became a resource ... of government [which] gradually incorporated it. ... Governments and lawyers gradually sought to control it and make it part of the hierarchic order of government.' Thus custom was transformed from 'a way of representing and manipulating the world into a set of government rules'.[19] While Chanock argues that colonial administrators codified local custom and in doing so imposed rigid rules and an individualist ethos on formerly fluid, communal and egalitarian societies, Berry claims that his conclusion is shaped by his methodology, interpreting the writings of government officials and anthropologists, rather than records of actual land disputes and transactions. Berry notes that in practice 'land-tenure rules have remained ambiguous, and rights in land are subject to ongoing reinterpretation'. She writes: 'in pre-colonial times Africans' rights to use land and other natural resources were usually contingent on their membership in social groups and/or their allegiance to traditional authorities.' [20] This did not mean that all members of the group enjoyed equal access to land, or that its use was communally controlled. Whatever the rights in principle, in practice the exercise of those rights had to be negotiated with local authorities. The exercise of rights to land was liable to change: 'rights to land were contested and/or renegotiated in the course of changing patterns of settlement and structures of authority, and the security of tenure was linked to the overall security of social and political life.'[21] In Pottier's words, 'land is socially embedded .. [the] site of complex interlocking tenurial rights.'[22]

During the colonial period it was observed that customary tenure varied, and that 'in a few crowded areas, native cultivators exercise individual rights of a proprietary character on land which is nominally and legally Crown land.'[23] This was certainly the case in Kigezi, and below we shall see that colonial officials and other observers, such as Edel, recognised the existence of individualistic tenure in Kigezi from the 1930s. Indeed, no-one who had worked in the area disputed this. In the post-colonial period, however, lawyers have argued that in 'overcrowded' areas such as Kigezi, customary law 'has been inadequate to meet the needs of the people'. Here

> the law is uncertain and confused ... [and] the lower courts ... have been unable to apply law to the facts because there have been only a few confused rules to apply. For example, in customary law the sale of land was an unknown concept. But as land became scarce in certain areas an occupier of land would find in practice that he could sell his land.[24]

Customary law of inheritance was also blamed for being the principal cause of excessive fragmentation in Kigezi.[25] But suggesting that sales of land were 'unknown' and that customary law was inadequate to meet the needs of the people implies that customary law was static and unchanging. There is, in fact, a good deal of evidence to the contrary.[26]

What 'customary land tenure' meant for the people of Kigezi

What then did 'customary tenure' mean for the people of Kigezi? Who had authority over land, how did people acquire control over it or gain access to it? It will be seen that sources differ as to the roles played by 'clans', 'lineages' and household heads in relation to land. This section will briefly describe how land was accessed in the early, and as far as it is possible to reconstruct, the pre-colonial period, and explore changes to tenure associated with colonial rule. Before doing so we need briefly to reflect on the terminology being used. Scholars have recently noted that 'land tenure in Sub Saharan Africa is more usefully conceptualised in terms of rights of access and control than of ownership.'[27] This conceptualisation is adopted here, as I review how people both acquired control over land, and accessed it, but it should be noted that many early sources (such as Edel, and colonial sources) refer to ownership, and where discussing these sources, this terminology will be used.

The earliest written description of the system of land tenure in Kigezi comes from an unofficial source, that of Roscoe, who visited the district in 1919–20.

> The members of each village claimed as their own the side of the hill on which the village was built, and any intrusion by strangers was fiercely resented and often led to strife and bloodshed. ... Anyone who intruded on [land] or questioned the owner's right to it ran a grave risk of being speared down on the spot.

Roscoe also observed that the most frequent cause of the common wars between clans was 'intrusion upon clan land'. If a stranger tried to claim what Roscoe called 'clan land' there would be a 'fiery dispute' and the 'real owner' would 'appeal to his village for help in expelling the invader'.[28] His evidence, although rather fragmentary, suggests that kinship groups (which he terms 'clans') were an important grouping for defence purposes and in particular the protection of land rights. The use of the term 'real owner' also suggests that some degree of individualism was recognised at this time.

One of Kigezi's first DCs, Phillips, also referred to clans in relation to land. In 1919 he noted the 'extremely strong feeling among the clans as to the alienation of their lands, whether fallow or cultivated'.[29] The role of the clan is stressed by Geraud, a White Father based in Kigezi, who wrote that 'in the past the clan was also a political organisation with territorial boundaries. The chief of the clan was the chief of the land.'[30] Geraud, however, gives no details of what authority such a person would have, or how they reached this position. The only published account by a Mukiga is that by Ngologoza, and he refers only to the role played by lineages, stating that Bakiga 'settled disputes according to lineages'.[31]

Edel's anthropological study of 1933 gives the most substantial account of the system of land tenure. She recorded that a man established his claim over land by marking its boundaries with a hoe, and having acquired title by doing this (even if he did not work the field) he 'retains it indefinitely, that is, as long as precise memory remains'. She stated that

> Ownership [of land] is essentially individualistic ... individuals, particularly adult male family heads, have exclusive claim. This claim is acquired through manufacture, gift, certain forms of seizure, purchase or inheritance. The owner is in all cases free to dispose of an article recognised as his in many different ways. ... [He] has the privilege, denied to others, not merely of using it, but also of delegating its use or leaving it unused.[32]

Edel noted that the patrilineal clan itself 'does not share actively in land ownership' as land rights were 'essentially individual household rights'. She continues:

> The lineage whose members live in a particular area guarantees their common security by defining the locus of probable good relations and peaceful settlement of most disputes. But it does not assign or regulate land, which is acquired by its different component segments on the basis of individual claims stacked out when the area in question was first settled.[33]

Taylor agreed that, while the system of ownership was individualistic, the membership of lineage 'guaranteed the common security of individual owners by peaceful settlement of most disputes'. He also notes that although it was not discussed by Edel it was 'likely ... that strangers wishing to settle in a lineage area would seek the permission of the head of the extended family or lineage.'[34]

The earliest detailed descriptions of the land tenure system in Kigezi from colonial officials come from two *mutala* surveys carried out in the late 1930s. These also suggest that land tenure was individualistic. Wickham's survey of Kasheregenyi *mutala* found that land was cultivated 'on an individualistic basis,' while Purseglove's survey of Kitozho stated that land ownership was individual, not communal.[35] Both Purseglove and Wright noted the increasing authority being given to government-appointed chiefs, a point that will be returned to in the following chapter. Officials in Kigezi were adamant that both ownership and cultivation of land were individualistic. In 1937 the DC Kigezi corrected an official from outside the district who had thought tenure was communal.[36] The DC noted that 'a peasant has a good title to all land which he is cultivating or which is lying fallow. The native courts are very jealous of the rights of a cultivator to his land and deal severely with any attempted usurpation.' Even if a person asked for assistance in clearing land or gathering a harvest, both the plot and the harvest belonged to the individual, not the community. The DAO echoed these views, noting that in all the surveys they had conducted in Kigezi they had 'found cultivation to be entirely on an individual basis'.[37]

While these early sources suggest that land ownership was entirely individualistic, land was not considered to be wealth (which was in the form of wives and cattle) worthy of accumulating for its own sake. Edel states that, while there were considerable differences in the amount of property owned by individuals, there was no class differentiation and no political significance in patronage as no patron was powerful enough to benefit from the relationship.[38] Oral sources, however, suggest that such individuals could be sufficiently powerful to gain from the relationship in the sense of being able to accumulate more labour (in the form of wives) and thus cultivate larger areas of land, and in turn acquire more livestock in exchange for produce. Individuals that had power, and from that the ability to accumulate wealth, were priests, medicine men, rain-makers, and to a lesser extent diviners, as they were widely feared by the population.[39] Oral sources confirm that the fears raised by these individuals, and threats of physical or supernatural violence, were sufficient to ensure that they had the power to accumulate. In the words of Kazeene: 'those you went to consult (called *abafunu* and *abarogi* etc.) were very rich, and they got their wealth because when you went to consult them you went with a cow or daughter.'[40] Vokes has argued convincingly that the Nyabingi spirit cult, while best known for the role it played in anti-colonial struggles in the early twentieth century, had a critical role to play as a medium of exchange. These exchanges, of livestock, beer, grain, as well as women, were central to the function and meaning of the cult. Large quantities of an extensive range of goods were given to the mediums of the Nyabingi, and Vokes notes that 'particularly successful consultants of Nyabingi are presumably able to build up substantial amounts of wealth.' He goes on to argue that the mediums also passed goods on, and in this way the system was a redistributive one.[41]

Bakiga perceptions of the land tenure system in the pre- and early colonial period can be revealed through interviews with elderly farmers. Informants agreed that individuals had full control over their land: they had the right to do whatever they wished with their land, and this fundamental right has changed little. In the words of one interviewee, Kamuyebe, 'everybody had to use his land in any way he wanted' and this included the right to transfer ownership. But oral sources were inconsistent about the role played by clans, and clan elders in connection with the allocation of unoccupied land. Andrea Nyakarwana and Ebriahim Kagangure said that clan elders had the power to allocate unoccupied land to migrants who wanted to settle. Christopher Karubogo said that a stranger coming into an area (if he had not been brought there by a friend) would not start cultivating without permission from (more broadly) 'old people'. With regard to dispute settlement, oral sources suggest that clan elders played a role, but that this was simply rooted in memory and experience. Esther Ellevaneer Bushoberwa and Andrea Nyakarwana made it clear that the role of clan members was only advisory and they had no power to ensure that their decisions were implemented. In the words of David Mashoki: 'In the past there were old people in the clan and those used to settle people's disputes and what they decided was done [because] they were respected.'[42]

Box 4.1 – Tenure of swamp land

Not all land types had the same rights. Swampland, in particular, was not individually owned in the way that land on hillsides was. Swamps were essentially a common property resource, used for the extraction of papyrus and other materials for housing. In addition, during times of low rainfall swamp edges could be cultivated by households on an individual basis, and as such they provided an important 'insurance' for Kigezi farmers. In the late 1940s the DC described the tenure on swamps as being 'no-mans-land with no hampering traditional, hereditary or other rights existing over them except as regards communal rights to take out residual papyrus and sedge.'[43] The rights to use swamp resources such as papyrus was open to all people living in the area. Disputes arose when individuals or institutions tried to claim a part of the swamp as their own for the gathering of these resources, but this appears to have been relatively rare.[44]

The communal rights were important to the people of Kigezi, and what proved to be a more serious threat to them was the policy of swamp reclamation. This was to lead to dramatic changes in both the use of swamp land and the system of tenure. In addition, when the land reform was proposed, see Chapter 5, one of the major concerns of many of those asked to express an opinion, was about what would happen to swamp land.[45]

The consensus amongst colonial officials, non-officials (e.g. Edel, Baxter and Taylor[46]) and Bakiga sources (Ngologoza and oral sources) was that land ownership was strongly individualistic.[47] Other land types, such as swamps, had different tenure arrangements (see Box 4.1). But larger groups (whether clans or lineages) were important for defence purposes, and, as will be shown below, social relations with members of these groups were important for both acquiring and gaining access to land. The remainder of this chapter will look at how people acquired control over land or gained access to it in the pre- and early colonial period, and how this changed with the coming of colonialism.

LAND: ACCESS & CONTROL

Throughout the colonial period the most important way of gaining control over land in Kigezi was through inheritance. Access to land could also be through marriage, social networks (especially for in-migrants), blood brotherhood and purchase, as well as through arrangements that did not imply absolute control over that land: people could, for example, gain the right to use land on a temporary basis, through non-cash- (and later cash-) based arrangements. Gaining access (to use) land could precede acquiring greater control over it, and because acquiring control over and gaining access to land were often closely entwined, they will be explored together.

Acquiring land through inheritance (*okuhungura*[48]) has long been the most important way of acquiring land in Kigezi. At the time of his marriage a young man would be allocated land by his father, from that part cultivated by his mother; never land cultivated by his mother's co-wives. He would then distribute most of his land to his wife or wives for cultivation. Having acquired land in this way a woman's rights over that land were not inconsiderable, and were recognised by the colonial courts, as will be seen below.[49] This system remains unchanged although it has undergone some modifications, particularly in relation to the use of written statements. It is now common practice for a man wishing to distribute his land to call witnesses together and make a public statement, which is often written down. Precisely when this practice came into being is unclear. Informants state that signed statements became common practice as it was realised they prevented land disputes, and were recognised by the courts.[50] Khadiagala, who draws on colonial court records, notes that it occurred in the 1950s, and emphasises the importance of increased literacy. In addition, the propaganda effort associated with land reform policies of the 1950s is likely to have encouraged this practice. While inheritance by sons is the norm, it is also possible today for women to inherit land and, as Khadiagala explains, if there were no sons, then daughters inherit.[51] Research also uncovered recent cases of daughters inheriting land, even when there were sons, but this appears, in part at least, to depend on whether brideprice was paid for her marriage.[52] It is striking that brideprice payments are increasingly uncommon.[53]

But inheritance was not the only way of acquiring control over land. Kigezi was an area of 'considerable mobility',[54] and exploring how in-migrants to an area acquired both access to, and control over, land reveals much about 'customary land tenure'. The existence of a survey from 1939 with detailed information on how newcomers to an area acquired land enables us to assess the importance of different methods (see Box 4.2).

In 1939, Wright, an Assistant DAO, surveyed 172 households in Kitozho and of these he classified 49 as 'foreigners', detailing how they had acquired land. His survey highlights the range of methods available in the late 1930s for in-migrants to acquire land: from in-laws through marriage, blood brotherhood, by 'begging', as well as through purchase and by allocation by government chiefs. Of the 49 'foreign' households eight got their land through their father-in-law or other in-law, while four got it from another relative (such as maternal uncle, grandmother's nephews, etc.), and six acquired land after making blood brotherhood with a resident of the area. Four 'begged' land from a man of a different clan, and seven got land through a combination of 'begging' from someone of a different clan and by marrying into that clan. Methods associated with the coming of colonialism also proved to be important: 13 were allocated land by the chief, while six were using land temporarily as part of their government or church positions and one purchased the land[55] (see Figure 4.1).

While it is generally the case that men are allocated land by their fathers, and women migrate to their husbands' area on marriage, there is substantial evidence that this is not always the case. As Wright's survey highlights, acquiring land through marriage was clearly important for men: not only did 16 per cent of households acquire land from their in-laws, but a further 14 per cent got land through marriage combined with other strategies. Wright details a number of marriages that enabled land to be acquired, with, for

---

Box 4.2 – The Kitozho and Kabirizi Surveys

1939
In 1939 two colonial officials, Purseglove and Wright, conducted a survey of Kitozho *mutala* which included demographic information of the 172 households living in the area, and details of settlement history as well as agricultural practices.[56] The survey was written up in two parts (by Purseglove and Wright), and is referred to as Kitozho Survey (1939) throughout this book.

2000[57]
In 2000 a follow-up survey was conducted in Kabirizi, a part of Kitozho. Kabirizi was selected as a smaller, more manageable part of Kitozho, which was known to the author from previous research visits. For this follow-up survey a questionnaire was conducted with all 48 households living in the area that was previously inhabited by 22 households listed in the 1939 survey. Settlement histories of these households and their ascendants were collected. In addition, the whereabouts of the descendants of all the households listed in the 1939 survey were identified and migratory patterns in the area explored. It was found that about two-thirds of households that lived in Kabirizi at the time of the 1939 survey had descendents still living in the immediate area. The remaining one-third of households had either moved away or died out.[58] Furthermore, there is no-one currently living in Kabirizi who is not directly descended from the households living there in 1939: there has thus been no 'new' in-migration to the area since 1939.

All households currently living in Kabirizi were allocated a wealth rank (WR) 1–7, with WR1 being the richest, and WR7 being the poorest. The definitions of wealth rank were based on local definitions of wealth (including size of land holdings and banana plantations, involvement in formal employment and use of additional labour) and the allocation itself was done through a wealth ranking exercise with a group of key informants. This survey is referred to as the Kabirizi Survey (2000), throughout this book.

---

example, the grandfather of Nyamachunda 'seeking refuge' with his in-laws, having been 'driven [from Muko] by the raids of the pigmy Batwa'.[59] This is further supported by oral sources, which confirm a significant number of marriages between Basigi women and Babwiga men in the early years of settlement through which Babwiga men were able to gain access to land in Kabirizi.[60] One of the richest men in Kabirizi in the 1930s, Kabunga, allocated land to his daughter Samalie, on her marriage to Rwangaza, while at least two of Kabunga's sisters married men from within Kabirizi who were also given land through the female line.[61] This is also illustrated in the case study of Rwakira Constant (see Case study 4.1). Similar arrangements were found in other parts of Kigezi. For example, in Muyebe Kazeene recalled that his father moved to Muyebe, married a woman born there, and was given land by his father-in-law, Bukirwa, one of the richest men in the area. Kazeene himself was also allocated land by his father-in-law, Bugugu.[62]

The example of Rwakira Constant is typical. Being very poor, Rwakira probably initially worked for Kabunga in return for food only (*okucwa encuro*).

Figure 4.1 *Means by which 'foreigners' gained access to land, Kitozho,* 1939[63]

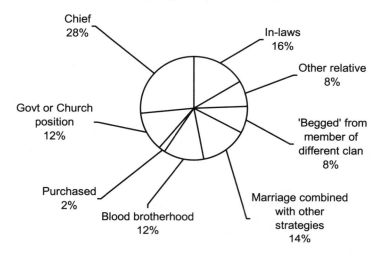

Chief
28%

In-laws
16%

Other relative
8%

Govt or Church
position
12%

'Begged' from
member of
different clan
8%

Purchased
2%

Marriage combined
with other
strategies
14%

Blood brotherhood
12%

Case study 4.1 – Rwakira Constant

Rwakira Constant is an elderly man, probably in his 80s. He was born in nearby Mpalo, a member of the *abusingola* clan and his parents died when he was a young man. Poor, and with no animals with which to pay brideprice, Rwakira moved to Kabirizi, where he had a maternal uncle called Kabunga. Kabunga was a very rich man, with a number of wives, large numbers of livestock and a lot of land. Rwakira began to work for Kabunga, and was lent some land by him. After some time Rwakira married a niece of Kabunga, and in time he was allocated land by Kabunga.[64] For the rest of Kabunga's life Rwakira worked for him. Having worked for Kabunga, and been given land by him, this land 'became mine forever'.[65] Indeed it was striking that in lengthy discussions about land rights resulting from a land dispute that involved Rwakira's son and daughter-in-law,[66] who were divorcing, no-one (even the grandchildren of Kabunga) questioned Rwakira's right to the land given to him by Kabunga.

Without any livestock to pay brideprice Rwakira would either have been given livestock by Kabunga for his brideprice, and worked for him in return. Or he may have worked for his father-in-law under an arrangement known as *okutendera*, whereby a poor man would work for his father-in-law for an agreed period (often of a year or two) *in lieu* of paying brideprice. Such arrangements enabled poorer individuals to gain access to wives. The fathers of such women, wanting to be sure that their daughter (or niece) had land to cultivate, would usually allocate land to her new husband – this was thus a way for men to gain access to land through marriage. In this way an in-migrant could become established in a new area. The example of Rwakira

Constant also shows how one arrangement could be used to initially gain *access* to land, and then later another one to acquire full control over it. In this case, Rwakira initially worked for Kabunga in return for the use of some land. Later, having married a close relative of Kabunga, he continued to labour for him and he thus gained 'ownership' of land through marriage. Marrying a close relative of his host enabled Rwakira to acquire control over land. Such arrangements, which involved the exchange of labour in return for other key resources such as land and wives, changed with the coming of colonialism.

While marriage was one way for an in-migrant to acquire land in the pre- and early colonial periods, it was not the only way and social networks were important. Gaining access to land through social networks has been described by Edel who stressed the importance of giving gifts to the land owner. She notes that people would sometimes give the use of land on what she described as a 'kind of patronage basis'. In this case, the borrowers would do a day's work for the owner, give the owner a basket of the harvested crop and share their beer with him when they brewed. This relationship appears to have been of a long-term nature, although 'there is always the risk that he may ask for the land to be returned. This sort of relationship is most usual for a man who is living away from his own kinsmen in a semi-dependent status.'[67] Wright refers to the 'begging' of land from men from different clans, and in his survey 8 per cent of households used this, and it was also used in combination with marriage and other strategies by a further 14 per cent.

But who were these individuals with whom in-migrants would form such relationships? They appear to have been well-established men from whom protection could be sought, and who themselves had good social networks, making them suitable to act as 'hosts' to an in-migrant.[68] Such hosts were not necessarily the wealthiest people in the area, although they might be wealthy in terms of land and livestock, but they were also likely to be labour-poor. Those who gained reputations for being 'successful consultants with Nyabingi' would build up 'substantial amounts of wealth'[69] and this combination of reputation and wealth may have made them important hosts.[70] Hosts 'introduced' a person to an area, and historically a relationship with such a host appears to have been essential for an in-migrant to an area to acquire land. The host would benefit by gaining labour and the in-migrant might initially merely work for their host in return for food (*okucwa encuro*). Some time later the host would lend the migrant some land and in return the migrant would labour for the host (under an arrangement called *okwatira*).[71] In-migrants might also form other relationships with their hosts: whether fictive kin relationships (such as blood brotherhood, or adopted son), or kin relations such as marriage. The relationship between the in-migrant and host would thus change with time, and may not necessarily have been of a permanent nature, as the in-migrant would seek to form other relationships. This fits in with Vokes' argument, that people were multiply located, maintaining membership of several different networks at any one time.[72] It should be stressed that such arrangements were neither fixed nor inflexible: the precise nature of each arrangement varied and could change over time. While relationships with hosts have continued to be important, *who* the hosts were has changed. With the coming of colonialism authority over land has become increasingly formalised, and in particular chiefly authority over land changed. Wright's study suggests that even by the late 1930s obtaining land through government-appointed chiefs, or through government and church positions, was an important strategy. This must have been a relatively recent phenomenon associated with the coming of colonialism. Changing chiefly authority over land will be explored in the following chapter.

Another important method of acquiring land, according to Wright, was through blood brotherhood. Blood brotherhood was entered into by two men of different clans, and the principal motivation for this arrangement appears to have been that it facilitated safe movement through areas populated by different clans. Edel asserts that, given the context of inter-clan fighting, combined with a need to negotiate marriages between clans, or to move into other parts of the country during times of difficulty or famine, blood brotherhood provided individual safety. She notes that its purpose was primarily to 'establish relationships across clan lines, rather than to strengthen existing bonds'. [73] Oral sources confirm these reasons as the primary motive behind creating blood brotherhood ties. Ruheeka said that as a young man he had done it with three people so that if he went outside Kabirizi then he would be safe. Similarly Bazaara Nelson stated 'The main reason that people did this was because there were many killings at that time, so if you went to a different area to people of different clans they would kill you. But when you had a friend that you had this with, then you would be safe.'[74]

Wright suggests that a significant number of the households (12 per cent) had acquired their land having entered into blood brotherhood. But, other sources disagree and strikingly Edel does not mention blood brotherhood as being used to gain access to land. Similarly most oral sources also suggested that blood brotherhood was not commonly entered into as a means of gaining access to land. While some informants ruled this out categorically, others suggested it might occur, but only temporarily as this land was lent and not given outright.[75] An explanation for this contradiction might be found in the Rukiga words used. According to informants today, the term that Wright gives for blood brotherhood, *omukago*, simply means friendship, with *omukago gwashagama*, meaning 'friendship with blood'.[76] Others refer to different terms for blood brotherhood: Edel calls it *omunywani*, meaning 'the one I drank with reciprocally', while one informant, Bazaara Nelson, used the term *okusharanahana* which means 'cutting stomach'.[77] It is possible therefore that the relatively high percentage of people accessing land through blood brotherhood found by Wright is as much related to a problem with translation as anything else. Furthermore, as blood brotherhood does not imply people of different status, it is likely that people would prefer to be thought of as blood brothers, rather than anything that might imply lower status.

While inheritance, marriage, social networks and blood brotherhood were all used to acquire control over land, another method also existed during the colonial period, and has grown significantly in importance during that period: purchases (*okugura*). Land sales have a long history in Kigezi: the earliest record of a land sale comes from Edel. Having worked in the district in 1933, she noted that 'while permanent transfer of land did not happen very often, it was possible. One man ... and his uncle, who shared a common plot of land, had sold it to another man for a goat; this gave the purchaser full and permanent rights to it.' Giving a further example, she states: 'There was some disagreement as to whether such outright transfer of land was a standard traditional form, though no-one doubts its present validity.' [78] Obol-Ochola records the role that Baganda agents played in the development of a land market: when they left the district from the 1920s onwards they sold the land they had been using, and this was emulated by Bakiga. He also notes that according to some informants land bartering occurred prior to the arrival of Europeans and it was *cash* sales that increased from the 1930s.[79] Certainly by the late 1930s sales were occurring, albeit on a small scale, and Wright's study mentions one purchase.[80] During the colonial period land purchases became increasingly common and in 1940 the 'recent tendency towards the sale of land in the Bakiga areas' was noted by colonial officials.[81]

Land sales have increased in importance, such that today a very significant proportion, and some studies suggest a majority, of plots are acquired through purchase. Bosworth found that in southern Kigezi in the early 1990s inheritance and purchase were 'equally important', while a study in Kabale district conducted in 1996 found that just over half of plots (52 per cent) had been purchased.[82] Another survey conducted in Muyebe, southern Kigezi in 2002 found that 23 per cent of households had bought land in the previous two years.[83] Oral sources indicate that it is considered normal to acquire land in the early part of the household cycle, and to sell off these plots later when cash demands increase. As Isaaye Kellen Turyagenda, of Muyebe, explained 'Since we got married we have bought 30 pieces of land, [but we] don't have them all now. We sold them because of school fees and now have 20 left ... we haven't bought any land in the last ten years and can't buy when they are still studying.'[84]

Such sales need to be distinguished from 'distress' sales, to meet unexpected cash needs, typically medical fees. Bosworth argues that land sales were 'largely a result of economic distress'.[85] While evidence from Muyebe supports the fact that most sales occur to meet cash needs (planned or unplanned), it also suggests that these exchanges are largely occurring amongst the richer half of the population. Between 2000 and 2002 all land purchases were undertaken by richer households, while all but one of the land sales were also by richer households (see Figure 4.2. WR1 is the richest wealth group, and WR7 the poorest). This suggests greater involvement of the richer half of the population in the land market, but as they are also selling land it would not appear that they are simply accumulating land. Rather, they seem to be using the land market as a means of saving: purchasing land when they have funds available, and selling it when they need cash. The increased prevalence of purchasing as a means of acquiring land has the potential for

Figure 4.2 *Land purchases and sales, Muyebe* 2000–2002[86]

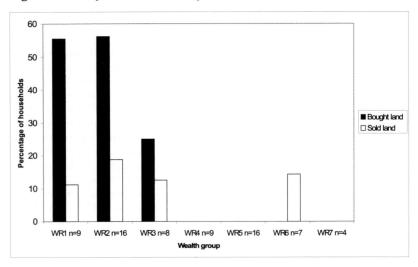

significantly altering the opportunities for women to acquire land. Oral sources suggest that women can buy land if they have the money and there are many well-recorded cases of this occurring, as will be seen below.[87]

There were also arrangements that enabled people to gain temporary use of land, that is, access to it.[88] Just as there is evidence of a long history of cash purchases of land, so there is a long history of lending people land for temporary use, in return for labour, some kind of 'gift', and later in return for cash (*okupangisa*). In the pre-and early colonial period a variety of such non-cash-based arrangements existed that were typically arranged between individuals who had a kin or fictive kin relationship, or were between hosts and in-migrants, and land would be lent in return for labouring (*okwatira*) or for part of the harvest (*ekitenga*). Edel's research found that 'a man ... can rent [his field] to someone else ... but no-one else may use it without his permission.' She notes that temporary transfers (of one or two seasons) were more common that outright transfers of land, and in this case a small fee (such as a hoe) would be agreed upon. Alternatively 'the loan may be described as a gift, for which ... some return would be expected.'[89] Wright also refers to the giving of gifts of part of the harvest, which he interprets as being 'not so much a form of rent as a recognition of overlordship and a claim for protection'.[90] He explains that once the man had established himself permanently and collected a group of 15–20 people around him he would be recognised as a family head and would cease to make the payment. According to Wright, the establishment of an administration had tended to 'wipe out this system of seasonal gifts, which might have developed into a system of renting'. In fact the system did not simply disappear, as we shall see.

By the 1950s gifts were still given, but rent in cash could also be paid. Writing in 1956, Byagagaire, then Assistant Agricultural Officer in Kigezi, described how land could be loaned for a short period of time (one or two crops), in which case the borrower, known as *'enturami'*, would give the owner gifts of part of the harvest and beer as a sign of appreciation, a type of loaning Byagagaire referred to as 'free'. Alternatively 'rent' known as *'isoko'*, could be paid to the owner in the form of cash or free labour by the tenant.[91] This practice of 'leasing' land was noted to be 'widespread' throughout Kigezi.[92]

Oral sources confirm that the giving of gifts of part of the harvest (*ekitenga* or *entende yo bulo*) was common as a sign of appreciation for the loaning of land.[93] Byagagire is not alone in referring to such lending of land as 'free': informants frequently stated that *'okwatira'* was lending for free, before continuing that the borrower would often work for the land owner.[94] Such arrangements were not formalised and how much work was expected was open to negotiation. Furthermore, this arrangement might very well be transformed into another arrangement, such as *okutendera* (labour in lieu of payment of brideprice), as occurred in the case of Rwakira Constant (see Case study 4.1).[95] But the evidence suggests that working for hosts in return for using, and possibly eventually acquiring greater control over, land was common.

Today the renting of land, for cash (*okupangisa*), is common. A 1996 land use survey conducted in Kabale found that, in the year prior to the survey, 45.8 per cent of households rented land, most of them renting land for an entire year. Bosworth also found significant temporary transfers of land, with 27 per cent of households renting land.[96] Renting land does not appear to be correlated to wealth group, or to the size of household land holdings. While renting is important for those with small land holdings, it is also undertaken by people who want to gain access to different land types. Women (whether married, divorced or widowed) also commonly gain access to land by renting, and the arrangement is no different from those made by men who rent land.[97]

Thus although rental in its current form (for cash) is relatively new and associated with the coming of colonialism, the temporary transfer of land in return for something is not new. There has been a gradual shift in leasing arrangements, towards arrangements based on cash. The frequency of renting land for cash has increased, probably in association with a decline in other, non-cash-based arrangements. Today non-cash-based arrangements such as *okwatira* (using land in return for labouring for the land owner) are rare, although Bosworth found that they did occur occasionally.[98] People who would, in the past, have used land in return for labouring for the land owner (*okwatira*) are now more likely to rent land for cash, and also to work for other households for cash.

WOMEN & LAND

Thus far this chapter has only explored methods of gaining access to land that were negotiated between different households, but access was also negotiated between members of the same household. While colonial sources reveal little about women and their rights to land, many references are made which would suggest that male heads of households were always seen as the land owners. It is ironic that while records frequently state, for example, 'a peasant has good title to all land which *he* is cultivating,'[99] it was of course women members of the households who did the majority of the agricultural work. Edel also uses the male he/him, and states that 'adult male family heads have exclusive claim.' She does, however, note that while 'the owner is the head of the household, ... when a wife or borrower cultivates the field it is known as hers or his.'[100] That rights to land were claimed by clearing it, and that clearing of new land was, and is, a male task would also contribute to men being 'seen as' the owners of land. Today, both men and women state repeatedly that land is 'seen as' *kuzetera*, being owned by men, with women's access to land being mediated by relations with different male relatives: her father, husband, sons or brothers. But, as we will see below, women's rights over land (and not just the use of land) were in fact strong, and were upheld by the colonial courts.

For women the most important way of gaining access to land continues to be through marriage. How this happens has changed little from the pre- and early colonial period: on marriage a woman is allocated land by her husband, on which to produce food. He would normally distribute most of his land to his wives, keeping only a little for himself. The land that he keeps for himself is called *omwehereko* land, and anything produced on that land is seen as his own. If he wishes to grow crops for himself, then he does *okwehereka* (lit: 'cultivating for self'). Assuming he had *omwehereko* land, then this is straightforward, and he can cultivate on it. But the rest of his land, having been allocated to his wives, cannot be used. If he had no *omwehereko* land then he would have to negotiate with his wives to be allowed to use some of the land allocated to one of them.[101] The rights that married women had over the land allocated on marriage, were upheld by the colonial courts, while married women's rights over their own labour for the cultivation of food crops were also well protected.[102] The need to pay 'more attention to the way that land and labour intersect' has been noted,[103] and other studies have also found this link between land and labour. Yngstrom has observed that 'In a context where labour is frequently a key limiting factor of production, and where women can and do provide a significant share of this, especially in terms of household food provisioning, the obligation by men to acknowledge their wives' contribution and to provide land for food is critical to the farming and household enterprise.'[104] As Chapter 2 showed, these factors proved to be critical when attempts were made by colonial authorities to introduce cash crops.

While broadly the system by which women gained access to land has changed little, the extent to which the legal system has supported these rights has changed. During the colonial period a woman's rights over land allocated to her on marriage were not inconsiderable: she would make all decisions over cultivation, and had strong usufruct rights which were related to her responsibilities of providing for the household. But Khadiagala argues, using detailed analysis of colonial court records, her rights went further than this and women 'had the right to control property to the exclusion of husbands and co-wives'. Concerns about food security, and the perception that female authority was a guarantor of social order, led colonial courts to interpret customary law in terms that were favourable to women. 'The courts accorded women extensive autonomy over land through the principle of gifting – once a man had allocated property to a wife's "house" the courts made it difficult for him to take it back.'[105] It was the concept of property rights known as the house-property complex, which organised assets around autonomous female-headed households, that guided the colonial courts. In addition, the fact that women were responsible for food supply and that they worked the land further fostered a legitimate right. Succession patterns (with sons inheriting from land used by their mothers) and the institutionalisation of women's property in the tax system (with men having a tax book for each wife, which recorded all land and livestock held by that wife) further contributed to the women's perception of ownership. During the colonial period the courts protected women's rights over the land gifted to them at marriage and saw such land transfers as irreversible. Men who sought to sell a wife's land or to transfer parcels among co-wives received sharp rebukes from the courts. Thus women's rights over land, in terms of access and control, were upheld. More recently, however, as will be discussed below, women's rights have declined, despite the rhetoric about increasing them.

But even when women's rights over property were strong and upheld by the colonial courts, women were still left vulnerable in situations of divorce or widowhood, particularly in terms of control over land. Khadiagala notes that, while the courts did protect women when adult sons and levir husbands sought to grab widow's assets, this was in part because of inheritance patterns that tie the future security of children to the property rights of women.[106] A widow was therefore particularly vulnerable if she had no children. Good relations with her in-laws were also important. This appears to have changed little today. A widow does not have full rights over land: rather, she is seen to be 'looking after' her deceased husband's land on behalf of her children to whom it would be distributed later.[107] Her rights over that land are limited and, in particular, she cannot sell it, as 'she has to keep it for the children'. A widow with no children is particularly vulnerable and the expectation is usually that she would return to the place of her birth, accessing land there through her father or brothers. The land she had used would thus return to her husband's family, often to his brothers.[108]

There is less evidence about women's rights over land in situations of divorce. Khadiagala provides no insights, while oral evidence suggests that a divorced woman would normally seek to gain access to land through her father or brothers. Today women note that the only way for a divorced woman to access land is through her father, and if he did not give her any (or was deceased) she would turn to an uncle or brother – but she could only get access to land through a male relative.[109] While returning to their place of birth might enable divorced women to gain access to land, it is rare for them to get full control over that land. Aida, for example, returned to her place of birth when she divorced. She uses land that was her father's, but she cannot give it to her children.[110] But this is an area of legislation undergoing change, and new legislation was supposed to give divorced women greater rights over property. Although women recalled having heard about a law that property should be divided, few had ever heard of this actually happening.[111] Informants noted that today women would at least try to claim some of the property, whereas before they would simply leave when they got divorced. However, even when the courts rule in favour of women, implementing such ruling is not always easy, as Case study 4.2 illustrates.

The case of Milka illustrates the ways that women can acquire and gain access to land in Kigezi today. First, she cultivated the land allocated to her and her husband by her father-in-law. Second, she cultivated land belonging to her brothers. (This is relatively unusual as not only is it uncommon for a woman to be living in the place of her birth, but also she had two brothers who were working away from Kabirizi and who had land which she could use). And third she purchased land. But, as was common practice, Milka put her husband's name on the agreements. Despite this, when the cases came to court, no-one questioned that the land was purchased by Milka using money she had saved.

While there is ample evidence of women acquiring land through purchase,

---

Case study 4.2 – Milka: when 'winning' is not enough[112]

Milka was born in Kabirizi and married Banduhizi Fabius (also born in Kabirizi) in 1985. At the time of their marriage Banduhizi's father allocated them three plots of land. Banduhizi joined the army and so was often away. Milka came from a relatively wealthy family, and had two brothers who were teachers, working away from Kabirizi. They let her cultivate their land and by selling the crops Milka was able to accumulate sufficient cash to start investing in land. Milka bought a number of plots using the money she had saved, but, as was the practice at that time, she bought the land in her husband's name. Land purchases were commonly formalised through the writing of an 'agreement' and as her husband was absent she would leave a space for his name on the agreement.

Banduhizi returned from the army and their relationship deteriorated. Milka's health had declined and to reduce the amount of agricultural work she was doing she wanted to set up a small business. They bought a shop, but soon afterwards Banduhizi took a second wife and this was when the real problems began. Banduhizi tried to give some of the land that Milka had purchased to his second wife. Milka objected and took the case to various courts: over the past three years it has been taken from the level of LCI (Local Council 1, the lowest level of local administration) up to the High Court in Kabale. During this time she has also divorced him. Milka has consistently won these court cases, which ruled that the land is hers. But despite this, she is still not using the land due to Banduhizi's intimidation and threats of violence against her and her children. These threats are very real and have, on one occasion, been carried out, which resulted in Milka's eldest daughter being injured with a *panga* by her father. When Banduhizi has seen Milka going to her fields, for example to harvest matoke, he chases her away and she has frequently had to hide from him.

the degree to which they gain control over it is more complex. Even when a woman states that she has bought land, her husband's (or other male kin's) name is written onto any agreement.[113] One woman noted that she had never seen a woman own land on her own, while Efuransi Batuta said that she had bought land with her own money, and although she had bought it, 'when they made the [written] agreement, they put it in her husband's name.' She explained that 'people have no respect for women' and as the husband is the head of the family, if he is alive it must be in his name.[114] Bosworth, also notes that 'almost exclusively, land purchases and sales are transacted between male household heads', and that while several women regarded themselves as land purchasers, there were no women who had bought land entirely independently. Even a divorced woman who had bought land with money earned from her own business had named her father as purchaser in the purchase agreement.[115] This practice does, of course, make women extremely vulnerable should conflicts arise over that land.

Khadiagala has shown that women's rights over land, well protected during the colonial period, have undergone a 'precipitous' decline more recently. In the colonial era men who tried to transfer land from one wife to another received 'sharp rebukes' from the courts. A shift to a more patriarchal vision of family and towards the perception of female authority being a source of social chaos from the 1970s, has contributed to this, such that by the 1990s entrenched in judicial doctrine was a legal presumption that property belongs to the male head of households. The subordination of women in legal precedent was entrenched in a 1993 land dispute. Courts increasingly emphasised the responsibilities of men to ensure a sufficient supply of land to each wife, and the corresponding right to redistribute land from one wife to another. Furthermore, 'while oral testimony had biased the courts towards women, as the daily users of land, written proof skewed it toward men.'[116] But Milka's case is interesting because it is an exception, and Milka has actually won her court cases. When Banduhizi took a second wife he attempted to allocate some of Milka's land to her. The courts ruled that Banduhizi had no right to redistribute land that Milka had bought to his second wife.[117] But critically, while numerous court rulings have supported Milka, and maintained that the land she purchased is hers, she has been unable to use that land. For Milka, winning in court is not enough as there is no way for her to ensure that the court's rulings are implemented. Furthermore, Milka is in a relatively strong position: Kabirizi is the place of her birth, and all her brothers are local 'big men'.[118] But despite her unique position, and despite all the court rulings, she still cannot use her land. This is consistent with Berry's arguments that rights to, and security over, land are linked to overall security in social and political life. [119]

Social relations with key individuals continue to be important today, particularly in relation to dispute settlement. Disputes are initially taken to LC1 councils and today it is relations with members of these councils that are critical. Khadiagala has shown that giving LC1 councils judicial powers and making them the first port of call for all disputes has created significant difficulties for women in land dispute cases. With marriages being patrilocal and LCs usually dominated by men, a woman is likely to be confronted by a council filled with her husband's friends and relatives. LCs also act as 'gatekeepers' – to both higher-level LC courts, and to the formal magistrates courts, making it difficult for people to appeal against decisions of the LC1 court. This, combined with a more 'patriarchal view' of the family and increased reliance on written evidence, has reduced the legal protection of women, which has undergone a 'precipitous decline.'[120] Thus in Kigezi, as Berry has argued, 'people's ability to exercise claims to land remains closely linked to membership in social networks and participation in both formal and informal political processes.' The case of Milka (Case study 4.2) is in many ways an exception that proves the rule. Milka was able to take her case up through all levels of the courts, and won consistently. Her success can, in part at least, be explained by the fact that she still lives in her place of birth, and her social networks in this area, and with members of the LC1 council, are very strong. But Milka's case illustrates something further for, despite winning, she is still unable to actually use the land. As Berry has noted, 'official policy and local practices often differ'[121] and there are a number of other examples of women 'winning' law suits but being unable to execute the rulings of the court.[122]

Conclusion

I have outlined Kigezi's land tenure system, showing that early colonial officials encountered a highly individualised system of land tenure. Land was most commonly acquired through inheritance, while for in-migrants to an area social relations with more established households were essential. These could be relations formed through marriage or blood brotherhood, and such relations formed with 'hosts' by newcomers to an area gave them the protection of more established households. Access to land, and control of it, were thus mediated through the relationships formed with such households. But this was to change with the coming of colonialism, as authority over land became increasingly formalised. Whereas previously relations could have been sought with a wide range of 'hosts', with colonialism chiefs were given formal authority by colonial powers and thus became important individuals with whom relations had to be sought. Indeed by the time of the 1939 survey, getting land through a chief was the single most important means by which land was granted to newcomers to an area. I will return to this in the following chapter.

Social relations, and particularly local power relations, continue to be critical and any number of laws will not change this. As Whitehead and Tsikata have noted, insufficient attention is paid to power relations in the countryside and their implications for social groups, such as women, who are not well positioned and represented in local-level power structures.[123] While rulings can be made, and new laws can be put into place, these are not necessarily reflected in changes on the ground. The implementation of laws and execution of rulings are areas of research and policy that require further examination. The twentieth century has seen Kigezi's land tenure system evolve in a number of ways. Most notably, purchasing has increased significantly, and there is ample evidence of a strong and vibrant land market.[124] Today a significant proportion (and some studies suggest a majority) of plots are purchased, but there is evidence that this has a long history dating back to the early colonial period. Inheritance still occurs in much the same way, although written statements have become increasingly common. Other methods that were once important, such as blood brotherhood and *okutendera* (working in lieu of brideprice payments), that enabled people (particularly in-migrants) to initially access, and later to acquire, land from their hosts, are no longer practised. While social relations are still important, who they are with has changed over the course of the colonial period. In particular the role of chiefs has been central as they were given authority over land, and this will be explored in the following chapter, illustrated by the case study of swamps. More generally there has been a shift in the way that land is acquired from non-cash-based arrangements (such as blood brotherhood and *okutendera*) to cash-based arrangements, that is, purchase and rental, with land rental for cash being undertaken by between a third and a half of the population. This increase in cash-based arrangements can be seen in other aspects of livelihoods, as will be seen in Chapter 7. While Kigezi's land tenure systems have evolved in particular ways, the colonial administration put into place a number of land reform policies that had the explicit aim of changing land tenure – with both intended and unintended effects – and it is to these that the following chapter turns.

Notes

[1] For more details see Hailey, *An African Survey*, 2nd edition, 723–6 and 786–8. West, *Land Policy in Buganda*; C.K. Meek, *Land Law and Custom in the Colonies*, 2nd edition (London, 1949).

[2] There were periodically discussions about the possibility of introducing new legislation around land. These discussions arose in part for political reasons, and in part out of the belief that agricultural productivity could only increase if there was a move towards individualism in land tenure. For example discussions about African land tenure during the mid-1940s see: PRO CO 536 215 (40336) – Land (Tenure) Legislation, 1944–46.

[3] Minute to Mr Nunsam from J.H. Harris about land legislation in Uganda, discussion of despatch to J. Griffiths (S of S for C) from J.H. Hall 16 March 1950, Land (Tenure) Legislation 1950–51, PRO CO 536 223/40336. Land Policy of the Protectorate of Uganda, *Uganda Gazette*, Vol. XLIII, No 30, 1950. This was made shortly before the EARC and changes to government policy with respect to land, which will be examined further in Chapter 6. For further details see PRO CO 536 and PRO CO 822/345. For further details on colonial thinking re African land tenure see *Journal of African Administration*, special issue on land tenure, October 1952.

[4] KDA DC LAN 9I. Also see KDA DC GENPOL BK. There is some oral evidence that compensation was paid when households were evicted, but it is not clear whether this was for the land itself, or merely for the loss of crops. Interviews: 95/Kab/2a, 95/Kab/

2/b and 95/Kab/5/a.

[5] Enclosure to Lloyd S of S for C, 27 Jan 1941 – PRO CO 536/208 40060 (Alienation of land) ff2. Letter to Stafford from H.B. Thomas, Land Officer, 23 Jan 1940. KDA DoA 008. See also KDA DC MP4II, and PRO CO 537/1508 (40342/1).

[6] Kigezi pyrethrum scheme, written Kampala, 20 Dec 1955, KDA DC AGR3–7 ff2A. For further details see Carswell, 'African Farmers'.

[7] For example Abdulla Namunye, former agent in Kigezi, granted land in Bufumbira in 1921. KDA DC MP58 ff134. In addition, some were allocated *mailo* land in Buganda, eg Erasito Musoke, Political Agent, Kigezi granted land in Buddu in 1937. KDA DC MP58 ff1.

[8] Letter to DC Ankole and Toro from Sandford, PCWP, 29 Nov 1937. KDA DC MP60A ff31.

[9] *Ibid.*

[10] KDA DC MP57 ff57, KDA DC MP69 ff20, KDA DC MP58 ff3 and ff4.

[11] There were also a few evictions for government purposes, such as when the government experimental farm at Kachwekano was established in 1937. Three households living within the farm boundaries were given notice but no compensation for the land. For full details see KDA DoA 009exp.

[12] F. M. Mifsud, *Customary Land Law in Africa*, (Rome, 1967), 6, 1.

[13] As distinguished from custom which is 'merely social usage' Brown and Allen, 29. For a discussion of characteristics of customary law from a legal point of view see D. Brown and P. Allen, *An Introduction to the Law of Uganda* (London, 1968).

[14] E. Cotran, 'The place and future of customary law in East Africa', *East African Law Today* 5 (1966), 75.

[15] C.K. Meek, *Land Law and Custom in the Colonies* (London, 1946), 137.

[16] Brown and Allen, *An Introduction to the Law of Uganda*, 28–9.

[17] Uganda Magistrates' Courts Act, No 38 of 1964 quoted in Cotran, 'The place and future of customary law', 73.

[18] E. Colson, 'The impact of the colonial period on the definition of land rights', in V. Turner (ed.), *Profiles of Change: African Society and Colonial Rule* Vol. 3 of L. Gann and P. Duignan, *Colonialism in Africa* (Cambridge, 1971), 196.

[19] M. Chanock, *Law, Custom and Social Order – the Colonial Experience in Malawi and Zambia* (Cambridge, 1985), 47. See also M. Chanock, 'Paradigms, Policies, and Property: A Review of the Customary Law of Land Tenure', in K. Mann and R. Roberts, *Law in Colonial Africa* (London, 1991).

[20] Berry, *No Condition is Permanent*, 102–5.

[21] *Ibid.*, 105.

[22] J. Pottier, '"Customary land tenure" in Sub-Saharan Africa today: meanings and contexts', in C. Huggins and J. Clover (eds), *From the Ground Up: Land rights, conflict and peace in Sub-Saharan Africa* (Pretoria, 2005), 56.

[23] Meek, *Land Law and Custom in the Colonies*, 137.

[24] Brown and Allen, *An Introduction to the Law of Uganda*, 79.

[25] J.M. Byagagaire and J.C.D. Lawrance, *Effect of Customs of Inheritance on Sub-Division and Fragmentation of Land in South Kigezi* (Entebbe, 1957).

[26] See for example S.F. Moore, *Social Facts and Fabrications: Customary Law on Kilimanjaro 1880–1980* (Cambridge, 1986); Chanock, *Law, Custom and Social Order;* Mann and Roberts, *Law in Colonial Africa.*

[27] F. Mackenzie, 'Land tenure and biodiversity: An exploration of the political ecology of Murang'a district, Kenya', *Human Organization* 62 3 (2003), 255–66. See also P. Shipton and M. Goheen, 'Introduction – Understanding African land-holding: power, wealth and meaning', *Africa*, 62 (1992), 307-26; H.W.O. Okoth Ogendo, 'Some issues in the study of land tenure relation in African agriculture', *Africa*, 59 1 (1989), 6–17; P. Bohannan, '"Land", "Tenure" and "Land Tenure"', in D. Biebuyck (ed.), *African Agrarian Systems*, (London, 1963).

[28] Roscoe, *The Bagesu and other Tribes*, 163–4, 174.

[29] Copy of letter to PCWP, from Phillips, DC 5 Sept 1928, KDA DC General Policy Book,

Land Tenure in Kigezi

Quoting declaration by Phillips made in 1919 which was ratified by PCWP in letter to DC Kigezi, 7 Oct 1921.

[30] F. Geraud, 'The Settlement of the Bakiga', in D. Denoon (ed.) *A History of Kigezi*,(Kampala, 1972) 29.

[31] Ngologoza, *Kigezi and its people*, 8.

[32] M.M. Edel, 'Property among the Chiga', *Africa*, 11 (1938). Edel undoubtedly had an influence on colonial officials and references to her ideas can be found in Wright's *mutala* survey, although not references specifically to land tenure. Her research was conducted in 1933, some was published in 1938, and her book in 1957.

[33] Edel, 'Property among the Chiga', 331; Edel, *The Chiga*, 99. Also see M.M. Edel 'The Bachiga of East Africa' in M. Mead, *Cooperation and Competition among Primitive Peoples* (New York, 1937), 127–52.

[34] B.K. Taylor, *The Western Lacustrine Bantu*, (London, 1962) 122.

[35] R.T. Wickham, 'Agricultural survey of Kasheregenyi Mutala', (1938); Purseglove, 'Kitozho Mutala Survey.' See J.D. Tothill, *Report on Nineteen Surveys* (1938).

[36] Letter to DCs Toro, Ankole and Kigezi from PCWP, 31 May 1937, KDA DC MP60A ff26.

[37] Letter to PCWP from DC, 16 June 1937, KDA DC MP60A ff28; and Letter to DC from Masefield, DAO, 5 June 1937. KDA DC MP60A ff27.

[38] Edel, *The Chiga*, 106–9. Also M.M. Edel, 'Property among the Chiga'.

[39] For example 02/Kbz/11c; 00/Kbz/30b; 00/Muy/23a. Also see Tibenderana who suggested that the fear of the supernatural was crucial to methods of peacekeeping in the nineteenth century, and because of their strong belief in spirits, Bakiga 'successfully manipulated supernatural forces to control interpersonal relations'. P.K. Tibenderana, 'Supernatural sanctions and peacekeeping among the Bakiga of western Uganda during the 19th century', *Journal of African Studies*, 7 (1986), 150.

[40] 02/Muy/30d. See also 02/Kbz/44b; 00/Muy/T23b and 00/Kab/T5b.

[41] R. Vokes, 'The Kanungu Fire: Power, patronage and exchange in south western Uganda' (PhD, Oxford, 2003),159. See also R.Vokes, 'The Kanungu Fire: Transformations of the Nyabingi Spirit Cult', Paper presented at 'Qualities of Time', ASA Conference 2002, Arusha. Vokes also discusses confusion around the different terms being used: Nyabingi, emandwa and others. See also E. Hopkins, 'The Nyabingi Cult of Southwestern Uganda', in R.I. Rotberg and A.A. Mazrui, *Protest and Power in Black Africa* (New York, 1970), 258-336.

[42] Interviews with 95/Muy/60a; 95/Kab/12a and 95/Kab/16a; 95/Kit/55a.; 95/Kab/1a and 95/Bub/97a; 95/Kab/6b and 95/Kab/12a and 95/Muy/59a. See also 95/Kit/56a and 95/Kit/65a.

[43] Two memos to DAO from DC Burner. Undated. Probably June 1948. KDA DoA 11/A/1 ff50.

[44] There is a recorded case of this from 1957, when a dispute arose between an individual and the Catholic Church over the right to take papyrus from a swamp that the church claimed as its own. This individual complained that grass he had collected from the swamp had been taken from him and he questioned how the church had been able to take the swamp. The DC believed that this swamp was supposed to be communal land which could not be reserved exclusively for the church, and when the *gombolola* chief investigated the case it was found that the swamp was indeed not Catholic Church land, and the church was ordered to pay back the grass. See Letter to Saza Chf Ndorwa from A. Kasilingyi (Muluka Kigongyi, Gomb Kabale) 26 March 1957. KDA DC LAN8/I ff122; Letter to Saza Chf, Ndorwa from DC, 4 April 1957, KDA DC LAN8/I ff123; and Letter to Saza Chf Ndorwa from Mr A. Kasilingye (of Muluka Kigongyi, Gomb Kabale) 9 April 1957, KDA DC LAN8/I ff126.

[45] KDA DC Lan12EAR. Letters from *gombolola* chiefs, 1956.

[46] For example Edel, *The Chiga*; Baxter, 'The Kiga'; Taylor, *The Western Lacustrine Bantu*, 122. There is, however, one notable exception: Obol-Ochola, writing in the early 1970s, takes an opposing view on individualism. He argues, based on interviews with Bakiga elders, that land holding was based on, and determined by, membership of clan and was

not individualistic. He asserts that clan elders were regarded as land controlling and allocating authorities, but provides little evidence to back up this claim. Obol-Ochola, 'Customary Land Law', 223. Obol-Ochola was not a Mukiga, but was from Northern Uganda.

[47] That there was no institutionalised political authority over land is in contrast to neighbouring areas. For example see J.R. Fairhead, 'Fields of struggle: towards a social history of farming knowledge and practice in a Bwisha community, Kivu, Zaire' (PhD, SOAS, 1990). Here households were annually allocated land which reverted back to wider communal control when it was fallowed (60). Lineage councils of elders decided on the fields to be used, crops to be planted and land to be allocated to each household. There is no evidence of similar controls in Kigezi. For details of other neighbouring areas see Taylor, *The Western Lacustrine Bantu*, 122.

[48] *Okuhungura* to inherit; *okusigira* to bequeath, and *okuraga* to make a will. The more general *okuha* (to give) can also be used.

[49] See L.S. Khadiagala, 'Negotiating Law and Custom: Judicial Doctrine and Women's Property Rights in Uganda', *Journal of African Law* 46 1 (2002), 1–13. See also E. Francis, 'Gender, migration and multiple livelihoods: Cases from eastern and southern Africa', *Journal of Development Studies* 38 5 (2002), 167–190.

[50] Another modification is that today the distribution of land sometimes occurs prior to marriage. See also. Khadiagala, 'Negotiating Law and Custom'.

[51] Khadiagala, 'Negotiating Law and Custom', 3 and 10. See also L. S. Khadiagala, 'Justice and Power in the Adjudication of Women's Property Rights in Uganda' *Africa Today* 49, 2 (2002), 101–21.

[52] 02/Muy/T29b and 02/Muy/GAW – Case of Margaret and her sister, Namara. Margaret had married with the payment of brideprice, and when her parents died her brothers gave her some land. Brideprice had not been paid on her sister's marriage, and she got nothing. Margaret noted: 'My sister tried to fight the case, but the brothers and older sisters hadn't benefited from her, because there was no brideprice paid for her. That was the main reason they refused.'

[53] There are two types of marriage widely recognised today: 'proper' marriages called *okuhingira*, and 'unofficial' marriages known as *okweshagara* (literally means 'to take for yourself; also referred to as 'going at night' because the woman goes to join the man at night). In Muyebe out of 61 marriages for which information could be obtained 61 per cent were *okweshagara* (Muyebe Survey, 2002; see Appendix). In Kabirizi out of 67 marriages for which information could be obtained 78 per cent were *okweshagara*. (Kabirizi Survey, 2000; see Appendix). In *okuhingira* marriages brideprice (*enjugano*) is agreed, and usually paid, before the marriage. For *okweshagara* marriages brideprice (and a fine called *omutango*) might be paid after the event, but this is not always the case. Informants state that *okweshagara* marriages and 'marrying for free' have become more common (00/Kbz/29a; 02/Muy/49).

Bosworth describes an *okusigura* marriage as one made without exchange of brideprice and gifts, and often without informing and getting the consent of the girl's parents. She describes how the woman would go to the man's house late at night, and in the morning the couple would be considered married. After some weeks or months the couple would present themselves to the woman's parents and brideprice would be discussed. She notes that this type of marriage is not a new phenomenon and cites cases of it occurring in the 1930s and 1940s, but the reasons for it have changed. The cases from the 1940s were entered into in order to speed up the formal process of marriage. In contrast, more recently it would be entered into in order to avoid, or at least to postpone, brideprice payments. She notes that the 'prevalence of *okusigura* ... may represent a major transformation in Kigezi society ... If the non-payment of brideprice ... weakens the marriage bond, there could be serious implications for the land system and the social structure.' (p. 174.) *Okusigura* marriage has become 'generally accepted' although she notes that it is rejected by some men as lacking in security, since when brideprice has not been paid it is easier for a woman to leave her husband. Bosworth, 'Land and Society in South Kigezi', 173–7.

Edel also mentions elopements, although she does not give them a name. She explains that if a girl runs away and stays at a man's home for a few days this is considered to be a *de facto* marriage, which can be legitimised subsequently with the payment of a bride price (Edel, *The Chiga*, 56–7) suggesting that such marriages have a long history.

[54] Edel, *The Chiga*, 18.

[55] Wright considered foreigners to be all those belonging to clans other than *abasigi* and *abazigaba*, the two dominant clans in the area, who according to oral tradition had been settled in the area longest. While it is likely that his definition was also based on local perceptions of 'foreignness', this data is useful in showing us how people new to an area could acquire land. Wright, 'Kitozho Mutala Survey', Appendix IV.

[56] The survey was written up in two parts: J.W. Purseglove 'Kitozho mutala survey' (1939) and A.C.A. Wright, 'Kitozho mutala survey' (1939). Purseglove's report focuses on agriculture, while Wright's explores social and demographic issues.

[57] This research visit was undertaken with the generous support of the British Institute of Eastern Africa. Significant research assistance was ably provided by Rhiannon Stephens. The research also explored changes to livelihoods activities and changes more broadly. Some follow-up research was also conducted in the same area in 2002, supported by the Leverhulme Trust. Kitozho is an area that is on the edge of the densely populated highland region of southern Kigezi: it can be seen as something of a transition zone between the highlands of the south, and the drier and less densely populated north (Rujhumbura) (See Maps 1.2 and App. 1).

[58] 14 out of 22 and 8 out of 22 households respectively.

[59] Other examples include: 'Korumbona obtained land ... from his father in law Bahikira; Rukara married Nyanza, sister of Mikaro, and obtained land from him; Y. Byabasheija married Muzana ... cousin of Nyamachunda from whom he received land; ... Bujiji married Nyabakongo, daughter of Buhazi, from whom he received land.' Wright, 'Kitozho Mutala Survey', Appendix IV.

[60] 00/Kbz/29a and 00/Kbz/30a.

[61] Kabunga's two sisters were D. Muzana (who married Byabasheija) and M. Nzinebuhe (who married Birabiremu). Both stayed living in Kabirizi and were given land by Kabunga. Wright, 'Kitozho Mutala Survey', Appendix IV, and family trees compiled 2000.

[62] 02/Muy/30c.

[63] Wright , 'Kitozho Mutala Survey', Appendix IV.

[64] Kabunga was therefore both his maternal uncle and his wife's uncle.

[65] Most of this story was told by Rwakira Constant (02/Kbz/6). However, some aspects of his life required careful collaboration with other sources: working in return for food or in lieu of brideprice implies extreme neediness and low status, and is not easily or openly discussed. Further details of Rwakira Constant's story told by Kivabulya (02/Kbz/12b) (grandson of Kabunga) and Lydia Kakuru (02/Kbz/8) d-in-l of Kabunga.

[66] Milka Namara (02/Kbz/47a), a granddaughter of Kabunga.

[67] Edel, *The Chiga*, 102. Roscoe refers to 'annual rent' of beer. Roscoe, *The Bagesu and other Tribes*, 163–4.

[68] I have avoided the term patron because while wealth differentiation might have been an important element of the relationship, it was not *the* most important element. Rather what was critical was having lived in a place for a long time, and being well established and well connected. This was in part informed by useful discussions with Richard Vokes, to whom I am very grateful. Vokes critiques the model of patronage usually used in the case of Ankole. He argues instead 'horizontal networks of influence' were key (27), and that these involved local forms of exchange which 'invariable involve mutual and equivalent rights and duties between giver and receiver (42), 'The Kanungu Fire' (2003).

[69] Vokes, 'The Kanungu Fire' (2003), 157–8. While arguing that these never constituted a 'leadership', Vokes notes that 'some mediums certainly did build up sizeable reputations as particularly successful communicants with the spirit' (170) and given the exchanges of goods, such people may have been able to build up wealth.

[70] 02/Muy/30d and 00/Muy/T23a. Furthermore, given that people often migrated following misfortunes (such as famines or Batwa raids), and following Vokes' argument

111

that Nyabingi increased at times of misfortune, we can speculate that an in-migrant might very well approach a Nyabingi medium, who in turn would become his host.
[71] The term for going out looking for land under this arrangement is called *okwatisa.*
[72] Vokes, 'The Kanungu Fire' (2003), 28.
[73] Edel, *The Chiga*, 26–27. For discussion of blood brotherhood in East and Central Africa see L. White, 'Blood brotherhood revisited: kinship, relationship, and the body in East and Central Africa', *Africa*, 64 3 (1994), 359–72.
[74] 00/Kbz/27a and 00/Kbz/29a. Also see 00/Kbz/30a and 00/Kab/9d.
[75] 00/Kbz/27a and 02/Kbz/6a.; 00/Bub/T14a.
[76] 00/Kbz/30a. Vokes argues that in Ankole *omukago* is more than a generalised form of friendship, as it 'places the two parties in a permanent and binding relationship involving a series of clearly defined reciprocal rights and obligations.' However he notes that '*Obukago* used to be forged through the two parties consuming a mixture of each other's blood' although today a female animal is given on the understanding that the first offspring will be returned to the giver (65–7). This evidence might suggest that, historically at least, *omukago* was a form of blood brotherhood.
[77] Edel, *The Chiga*, 27; 00/Kbz/29a.
[78] Edel, *The Chiga*, 100–2.
[79] Obol-Ochola, 'Customary Land Law', 233–4.
[80] Wright, 'Kitozho mutala survey'. Of the 49 households classified by Wright as 'foreigners' one had purchased land. Unfortunately he did not investigate how non-foreigners had acquired land. Appendix IV.
[81] Letter to PCWP from DC, 29 March 1940, KDA DC MP60A ff32.
[82] Bosworth, 'Land and Society', 142. A 1996 study found that 41 per cent had been inherited from parents. The remainder had been obtained from the government or obtained through some other means. These results were similar when total acreage rather than the number of plots was considered. All of the swamp plots had either been purchased (33.3 per cent) or obtained from the government (66.7 per cent); none had been inherited or donated by parents. Lindblade *et al.*, 'More People, More Fallow', 40
[83] A survey of 69 households living in Nyamurindira and Kabuyenja in Muyebe *gombolola* was undertaken by the author in 2002. This is referred to as the Muyebe Survey, 2002 throughout this book.
[84] 02/Muy/49.
[85] Bosworth, 'Land and Society', 193. Example of distress sale to meet medical costs: 02/Kbz/8a.
[86] Muyebe Survey, 2002.
[87] Interviews with 95/Kab/2a and 95/Kab/2b; 00/Kab/T4a, 02/Muy/13c, 02/Kbz/42b, 02/Muy/T28 b and 02/Muy/T65.
[88] Other ways that people might gain access to land include borrowing it for free. Nowadays this happens only occasionally (7 per cent of households, Muyebe Survey, 2002) and is almost entirely from close relatives (such as in-laws), or in one case, from the Church. Finally, some people also access land through their jobs, for example teachers and catechists. It is well recognised that this land does not belong to the users, who have full usufruct rights for as long as they hold the position. This also appears to have declined in importance. (In the 1939 Kitozho survey 12 per cent of land was being used as part of a government position, while in 2000 a survey of the same (but smaller) area found one household (out of 48) (2 per cent) using land as part of her position as a catechist. (Kabirizi Survey, 2000). Muyebe Survey (2002) found just 2 households out of 69 (2.9 per cent) were using land as part of their jobs, in this case as school teachers.)
[89] Edel, *The Chiga*, 100–2.
[90] Wright, 'Kitozho Mutala Survey' (1939), 12–14.
[91] Note on Background of Land Fragmentation in the Over-Populated Areas of Kigezi District by J.M. Byagagaire, AAO Kigezi. 1956. KDA DoA 12/b ff153.
[92] J.M. Byagagaire and J.J.D. Lawrance, *Effect of Customs of Inheritance on Sub-Division and Fragmentation of Land in South Kigezi, Uganda* (Entebbe, 1957).
[93] *Ekitenga*: gift brought after harvesting to the owner of the land. 02/Kbz/5a; *Entende yo*

bulo: gift of millet given to land owner. 02/Kbz/5a. See also 02/Muy/T37 and 02/Muy/T38.

[94] 02/Muy/T37 and 02/Kbz/6.

[95] This was done by Rwakira Constant (00/Kbz/33a and 02/Kbz/6) who worked for Kabunga and later married one of his daughters. See also 02/Muy/T15b, 02/Muy/T37 and 02/Muy/T38.

[96] Bosworth, 'Land and Society', 213.

[97] See Muyebe Survey, 2002 and Lindblade *et al.* 'More People, More Fallow', 42. 00/Kab/7a.

[98] Bosworth, 'Land and Society', 213–14. She notes that the amount of labour varies greatly, and most people engaged in this form of borrowing are women, often those in particularly difficult circumstances, e.g. young widows etc.

[99] Letter to PCWP from DC, 16 June 1937, KDA DC MP60A ff28. My italics.

[100] Edel, 'Property among the Chiga', 325–41. Introduction by Abraham Edel in Edel, *The Chiga*, 2nd edition, xxviii. This new edition includes an introduction by Abraham Edel containing extracts of letters from May Edel during her time in Kigezi and four additional chapters. This quote appears in the introduction, and seems to be an extract from a letter, although this is not entirely clear.

[101] 02/Muy/T38; 02/Muy/T30b. 02/Muy/13c. Unmarried women could also do *okwehereka*, typically on land borrowed from their mother. Married women cannot undertake *okwehereka* because 'as a woman she has to grow crops to feed the family.' Also see Khadiagala, 'Justice and Power'. Byagagaire and Lawrance define *okwehereka* as the piece of land which a man keeps for himself when allocating land between his wives, from which he derives his own cash income. Byagagaire and Lawrance, *Effect of Customs of Inheritance*, 19.

[102] Khadiagala, 'Negotiating Law and Custom' and Khadiagala, 'Justice and Power'. Also 02/Muy/T37.

[103] See Pottier, 'Customary land tenure', 68.

[104] I. Yngstrom, 'Women, wives and land rights in Africa: Situating gender beyond the household in the debate over land policy and changing tenure systems', *Oxford Development Studies*, 30 1 (2002), 21–40. See also M. Kevane and L.C. Gray, 'A woman's field is made at night: Gendered land rights and norms in Burkina Faso', *Feminist Economics*, 5 1 (1999), 1–26.

[105] Khadiagala, 'Negotiating Law and Custom', 1–3.

[106] *Ibid.*, 4.

[107] 02/Kbz/42b.

[108] 00/Muy/40a and group interview with men, 02/Muy/GAM.

[109] 00/Kab/7a and 00/Muy/40a.One male informant noted that on divorce a man might divide his land so that his children got some of it, but not his ex-wife. 02/Muy/GAM.

[110] 02/Muy/48.

[111] Interviews in Kabirizi and Muyebe (including 02/Muy/GAM and 02/Muy/GAW). The Land Act of 1998 and the Domestic Relations Bill were both initially believed to be going to give women greater rights in law, but so far neither has done so. The Domestic Relations Bill 'languished' in the Land Reform Commission and then in Parliament', see Khadiagala, 'Justice and Power' 118. The Land Act included an amendment to deal with the question of married women's rights to ownership of land (the joint marital-property clause), but when the Land Act was published it did not include this Amendment, which has since been referred to by campaigners as the 'Lost Amendment'. It is unclear whether the amendment had indeed been passed (as claimed by some) or not, and some stated it had in fact never even been formally put before Parliament. See McAuslan, *Bringing the Law Back In*, Chapters 12 and 13.

[112] Based on various interviews: Milka (02/Kbz/47a and 47b); LC3 hearing (Land dispute between Milka and Banduhizi Fabius; 02/Kbz/46); Bruce Natakunda (02/Kbz/9c) and Kivabulya (02/Kbz/12b Milka's brother). Rwakira Constant (02/Kbz/6; Banduhizi's father)

[113] Interviews with 02/Kbz/46, 00/Kab/7a, 02/Muy/13c. And in one case a woman

113

reported going with her grandfather to buy land 00/Kab/T4a.

[114] 00/Kab/7a and 02/Muy/13c.

[115] Bosworth, 'Land and Society', 191, 205.

[116] Khadiagala, 'Negotiating Law and Custom', 8.

[117] The land that Banduhuzi's parents had allocated them was not under dispute – only the land purchased during their marriage.

[118] It might, indeed, be because of this that the LC1 rulings have been in her favour, see L.S Khadiagala, 'The failure of popular justice in Uganda: Local Councils and women's property rights', *Development and Change*, 32 (2001), 55–76. Furthermore, Banduhizi is unusually poorly connected: his father came to the area as a client of Kabunga, and he has virtually no relatives in the area.

[119] Berry, *No Condition is Permanent.*

[120] Khadiagala, 'Negotiating Law and Custom'. Also see Khadiagala, 'The failure of popular justice in Uganda'.

[121] Berry, *No Condition is Permanent,* 104, 103.

[122] A review of files of legal cases stored at Kabneto – a legal aid project based in Kabale – found a large number of cases of (usually) women, who reported that the courts had ruled in their favour, but they had been unable to execute them. (For example cases: 59/1996; 20/1996; 144/1997; 36/1997; 1/1998; 19/1998 and 014/2002.)

[123] A. Whitehead and D. Tsikata, 'Policy Discourses on Women's Land Rights in sub-Saharan Africa: The implications of the return to the customary', *Journal of Agrarian Change*, 3 1 (2003), 67–112. In this review of contemporary policy discourses on land tenure reform in SSA they argue that there are considerable problems with so-called customary systems of land tenure and administration for achieving gender justice with respect to women's land claims.

[124] Purchases may even occur between close family members. Take the case of Tofus Kigatire who bought land from her brother; he had migrated, and when their parents died he returned to the area and sold all 'his' land to two of his sisters: one (Tofus Kigatire) had remained in the area when she married and bought two plots. The remainder was sold to her sister, who had returned to the area on her divorce (95/Kab/2a and 95/Kab/2b).

Five

Land Reform Policies
& Chiefly Authority

Land reform policies

From the early 1950s the main focus of the colonial administration shifted from agriculture and soil conservation to policies of land reform. Following the report of the East African Royal Commission, 1953–5 (EARC), major changes to land tenure were proposed and land reform was to be the most significant element of the colonial encounter with Kigezi in the postwar period. Focusing on these most ambitious and far-reaching policies, I will show that the implementation of these policies proved to be rather different from that seen with soil conservation policies. The conservation policies were largely successfully implemented, being firmly grounded in systems of soil fertility maintenance that were already in use in the agricultural system. The general success of soil conservation policies can be contrasted sharply with notable failures in land reform, but in each case there were winners. I will look at different policies of land reform – titling, consolidation and enclosure – all of which failed in Kigezi. Moreover, post-Independence policies have largely failed to be anything more than rich in rhetoric. All these land reform policies were used by prominent individuals, often chiefs or those with strong links to the colonial state, to strengthen their control over land. This chapter is thus about the nature and reception of colonial policy and practice, the endurance and evolution of Kigezi's land tenure system, and the political nature of land tenure and land reform.

Wider political concerns drove the formulation of land reform policy in Kigezi, and in this policy arena it was political issues in Kenya that were particularly influential. Sir Philip Mitchell, the Governor of Kenya, was concerned about land shortage amongst the Kikuyu, [1] and an investigation into agriculture and land across East Africa was proposed. Lyttleton, the Secretary of State for the Colonies, explained that the rapidly increasing African population was causing 'severe over-crowding' which was leading to some Africans demanding land from European farmers, particularly in the

White Highlands. He noted 'We cannot agree to this, nor would it be any solution to the agricultural problem. Something, however, must be done to meet the real African difficulties which come not only from the present shortage of fertile land, but also from the need to adjust the traditional African life to modern social and industrial conditions.'[2] The Mau Mau emergency was declared in October 1952, and the Commission was to investigate not just agriculture and land tenure, but also the measures necessary 'to achieve an improved standard of living'. It was specifically asked to make recommendations with reference to the 'economic development of the land already in occupation by the introduction of better farming methods' and 'adaptations or modifications in traditional tribal systems of tenure necessary for the full development of the land'.[3] It thus set out with the purpose of recommending changes to land tenure systems.

While the stimulus for an investigation into land tenure came from Kenya, colonial officials in Uganda had in fact themselves recently made a pronouncement on land tenure. The 1950 pronouncement stated that rural Crown land was held 'in trust for the use and benefit of the African population'.[4] When the EARC was proposed, outside observers within Uganda were not convinced of the need for it. An editorial in the *Uganda Post* declared that there was no reason for the EARC to visit Uganda as 'land in Uganda … is already in the hands of the natives and, therefore, there is no need for external interference.'[5]

The Report of the EARC was published in 1955, and was enormously influential. It argued that economic growth and the involvement of the market were key to the future of East Africa. Contending that efficient mixed farming would be impossible under traditional systems of land tenure, it reasoned that there should be a move towards properly demarcated smallholdings, individualisation of land ownership, mobility in the transfer of land and encouragement of 'progressive farmers'.[6]

The findings of the EARC Report were discussed in great detail in London,[7] as well as in Uganda. Governor Cohen, of Uganda, admitted in private correspondence that he was 'very disappointed' with the report, although he conceded that the land tenure section was 'very valuable'.[8] However, the Uganda administration accepted the recommendations of the report, and published the Land Tenure Proposals on 6 January 1956. These put forward the proposal of confirming individual customary tenure by adjudication of the land and registration of title.[9] The aim was to 'introduc[e] … a system of individual land tenure which will be more suited to the efficient development of farming than the customary systems of tenure'.[10] The Ministry of Lands was created shortly afterwards, with Mungonya appointed as Minister.

The formulation of land reform policy was not without debates and struggles between colonial officials in London and those in Entebbe. Those in the Colonial Office were surprised at the speed with which the Uganda Government published the Land Tenure Proposals, believing that more discussion might have been beneficial.[11] Opinions were also divided about the proposals: Simpson, the CO's land tenure expert, criticised the use of 'active and forceful propaganda' as being the wrong approach, saying 'if the people *really* do not want it, why bother?' He was also critical of Uganda's use of the term 'granting' of title – which he said 'gets them utterly and completely on the wrong foot'. Instead they should be 'recognising' title and until they did so they would 'continue to receive the hostility which they describe'. [12] The EARC itself spoke of the 'confirmation' of individual land rights.

Through policies put forward in the Land Tenure Proposals, the EARC had the potential of making a profound impact on ordinary farmers in Kigezi, as colonial officials attempted to implement its recommendations through the granting of titles, consolidation and enclosure. In fact, this potential was never fulfilled, but it was still influential as individualisation of land tenure was confirmed. Moreover, the policies enabled some people to strengthen their control over, or increase their access to, land.

TITLES – SPORADIC TITLES & THE LAND TENURE PILOT PROJECT

From the 1950s an essential part of the modernising project of colonialism was the strengthening of individual land tenure through the granting of titles. The EARC and the colonial administration viewed titles as modern, efficient, and, critically, as a way of increasing agricultural productivity. This policy of land reform was to have a number of stages, which are examined in turn: the granting of sporadic titles, a pilot project, followed by policies of enclosure and consolidation which it was hoped would lead to a broader programme to grant titles in the district. Before the pilot project could begin, the colonial administration had to turn around opposition by Kigezi's District Council to the Land Tenure Proposals. They succeeded in doing this, and the turn-around by the Council appears to be related to a decision to grant titles in southern Kigezi to eight individuals, including some of the most senior African chiefs in Kigezi. The titles granted to these eight individuals were 'sporadic' titles – that is, they were parcels of land that were physically isolated from other land being granted titles and were outside the pilot project area. Officials of the Land and Surveys Department were not at all keen on the idea of sporadic grants, one noting that they were something that 'the politicians were trying to foist onto us'. [13] Lawrance (Uganda's Permanent Secretary to the Ministry of Land) admitted that sporadic grants were being given 'for "political" reasons.' [14] But it was felt that sporadic grants might stimulate support for titling more generally and should therefore go ahead. [15] District officials noted that the more important the person being granted sporadic title, the more likely it was that other people would follow his (they were only men) example. Therefore 'priority should ... be given to senior chiefs.' [16] Applications for sporadic titles were made some months before the resolution approving the granting of freehold titles had even been passed by the District Council, and in this way sporadic titles acted as an incentive for senior chiefs to approve the Land Tenure Proposals.

Sporadic titles were granted to eight people, for 13 parcels of land all within a four-mile radius of Kabale. The process by which sporadic titles were adjudicated was ostensibly the same as for systematic grants, but in practice this was not the case. Sporadic grants were given 'special treatment'; for example, surveying began before the adjudication process was complete.[17] It appears that, in return for having their land adjudicated and titles granted before the pilot project had even begun, these influential individuals lobbied in support of the Land Tenure Proposals, and helped to persuade more junior chiefs that the district should go ahead with the proposals.

The majority of titles in Kigezi were granted systematically as part of the Land Tenure Pilot Project (LTPP). Officials within Kigezi considered the district to be wholly unsuitable for the LTPP: the topography made surveying difficult and costly, while most of the district had a highly fragmented land use pattern.[18] But there was a strong desire that the pilot project should be seen to succeed, and so the area chosen for the pilot project was one where implementation would be easier. The area was Nyakaina *muluka*, *gombolola* Buyanzha located in Ruzhumbura *saza* in the northeast of the district (see Map 5.1). Ruzhumbura was quite different from Ndorwa, Rukiga and Bufumbira in the south of the district in terms of population density, agro-ecology and agricultural system. Here it was possible to avoid 'unduly difficult terrain and ... fragmented or severely subdivided areas'.[19] The area was also a resettlement area: plots of land were large and there was no need to consolidate land before titles were granted. The desire for security of tenure on this newly acquired land is likely to have been particularly strong. Furthermore, the District Commissioner observed that 'the vexed problem of ownership of the grazing areas will not arise on any large scale in this particular muluka.'[20] Thus the area chosen for the pilot project was not typical of Kigezi as a whole. The LTPP began in September 1958, and progress was steady. The project, however, never extended beyond Ruzhumbura and so, with the exception of the sporadic grants, no titles were granted in southern Kigezi.

While the District Council approved the LT Proposals, the question remains as to whether the population as a whole was convinced of the value of titles. A large number of applications for titles might suggest strong support for them. The Secretary General stated that 'many people'[21] were applying for titles but the only evidence found in archival sources is of chiefs and ex-chiefs applying for titles: few ordinary farmers applied.[22] *Gombolola* chiefs were asked their opinions about titling and the responses of these lower-level chiefs, which are likely to have been closer to the concerns of ordinary farmers, are revealing. A number of *gombolola* chiefs asked why there was a need for titles as everyone knew their own land, an opinion expressed to this day:

> I don't have [a title] because nobody can interfere with my land and it is in one place. As far as my land is concerned, I wouldn't like to have a title, because I don't like to keep paying for nothing when the land is mine. That is useless.[23]

Other *gombolola* chiefs were concerned about how titles could be given to people who had fragmented land. The fragmented nature of land holdings in southern Kigezi is recognised by farmers, and frequently referred to as a

Map 5.1 *Kigezi District, showing LTPP and site of consolidation experiment in Bufumbira*

constraint on titling: 'most people didn't get titles because their land was not all in one place.'[24] The other major concern expressed by *gombolola* chiefs was about other land types, and what type of title they would get. In particular, questions were asked about swamps and forests and grazing and watering areas: what sort of titles these land types would get and who would be responsible for them. I will show below that the *gombolola* chiefs were right to be concerned.

Both archival and oral sources suggest therefore that there was not a clamouring in support of titles, nor a rush to get them. Rather, most of the people for whom titles would have been available (men) saw little need for them. They felt secure in their control over their land, and the most popular feature of titles was the marking of boundaries. Ironically the group for whom titles might have provided increased security over land, women, were not being offered them. All levels of the administration and Bakiga themselves only ever considered that land titles would be in the names of men.[25] No reference was made to the use of land by women and there is no evidence that the issue of female-headed households was even considered.

In contrast to many soil conservation and other agricultural policies, the policy to encourage consolidation and offer land titles is a little remembered area of British colonial policy.[26] This is perhaps not surprising given the focus of attention on the LTPP area in northern Kigezi, but even within the LTPP area up-take of titles was slower than expected.[27] By the time the LTPP scheme was completed in March 1962, 6000 plots had been adjudicated, and 6,400 had been demarcated and surveyed. But by April 1968 only 1800 titles had actually been paid for and collected and most registered proprietors continued to sell and lease land under customary law without registering these arrangements.[28] Thus the LTPP was a success only in so far as titles were successfully granted in the area. But critically, the majority of those for whom titles had been prepared chose not to buy them. This suggests that there was in fact little demand for titles.

Colonial policies around titles can be remarked upon as much for what they did not achieve, as for what they did achieve. The LTPP and granting of sporadic titles did not lead to an increased demand for titles, and did not in fact have any major impact on the majority of the population. A study undertaken in the LTPP area as to whether titles had a positive impact on investment and productivity (the main reason behind the EARC's support for land titles) was inconclusive as to whether registration stimulated increased investment.[29] Despite these inconclusive results, policy towards titling has continued in the same vein in the post-Independence period with an assumption that titling is associated with increased investment in agriculture, as will be seen below. One 'achievement' was that the granting of sporadic grants enabled a handful of influential individuals to strengthen their control over their land.

ENCLOSURE & CONSOLIDATION

The granting of sporadic titles and the LTPP were supposed to be just the beginning of a broader programme to grant titles in Kigezi. But titling would be prohibitively expensive unless air surveys were carried out, which in turn required plots to be enclosed by hedges visible from the air. Moreover most land in southern Kigezi was so highly fragmented that consolidation was an essential precursor to enclosure. From the mid-1950s therefore, consolidation – bringing together scattered plots – took over as the principal aim of the Department of Agriculture, having shifted away from soil conservation.[30]

Attempts in the 1950s to consolidate land in southern Kigezi were not the first such efforts. Some years earlier, as part of the resettlement scheme, agricultural officials had hoped to consolidate land that settlers left behind. However, people chose either to sell their land or leave it with relatives, and as a result consolidation as part of resettlement failed completely, and was quickly dropped from the agenda. By the mid-1950s, following the EARC and Land Tenure Proposals, consolidation was firmly back on the agenda. Farmers were to consolidate their land and enclose it with hedges and would then be able to apply for titles. Enclosure was not to be encouraged in areas of severe fragmentation. As with other policies, the Department of Agriculture worked through the hierarchy of chiefs and *saza* chiefs were informed 'If people are to secure titles over the next few years it is important that enclosure should start *now*, on consolidated holdings.'[31]

Propaganda advised of the advantages of enclosed land, which included providing security of boundaries, and so reducing boundary disputes and associated litigation.[32] But all did not proceed smoothly, and despite an 'intensification of propaganda towards land consolidation and enclosure',[33] there was virtually no demand for consolidation. Furthermore, people began to enclose land that had not been consolidated, much to the concern of the DAO who noted that enclosing scattered plots 'makes good land use impossible [and] will also hinder if not prevent any subsequent grant of title'.[34] Thus while there was support for enclosure and households readily enclosed plots of land with hedges, this support did not extend to support for consolidation. To make matters worse for the administration, they were unable to stop enclosure going ahead on unconsolidated land.

There were also problems with land being enclosed over which people did not have recognised rights. Cases arose of the enclosure of 'common' or 'grazing' land, particularly in northern Kigezi, which had extensive areas of grazing land. Such disputes over the use of communal grazing land also arose in the densely populated south of the district where there was much less communal grazing land available.[35] Thus the concerns that *gombolola* chiefs expressed in their questions about the Land Tenure Proposals around the enclosure of grazing land and swamps proved to be absolutely correct.[36]

Endeavouring to 'kick-start' consolidation, the Agriculture Department focused its attention on a small area of Bufumbira in the far south of Kigezi (see Map 5.1). But even this approach proved a complete failure; and the department acknowledged that it was 'difficult to get people to agree to consolidation'.[37] As the department became increasingly desperate incentives were offered: farmers with consolidated holdings were to be given priority when coffee seedlings were issued. Still this did not stimulate consolidation.

It was then decided that people with over two acres of land would be the first to be offered titles, in the hope that this might encourage them to consolidate.[38] Finally in December 1959 it was decided that five sporadic grants should be made 'to prominent persons having economic, unfragmented holdings in order to provide a "bait" to other people to consolidate'.[39] But despite continued propaganda, and incentives in the form of coffee seedlings and titles, all the efforts of the administration came to nothing and it proved impossible to implement consolidation in southern Kigezi.

The belief that consolidation, enclosure and the granting of titles were vital for greater agricultural efficiency was central to colonial thinking from the mid-1950s. Consolidation, however, proved to be a major stumbling block for the colonial state. Incentives to consolidate were offered – including titles – and so ironically titles became not only the end goal, but also the means by which consolidation was to be carried out. On a number of occasions the efforts of individual chiefs to promote consolidation were lauded,[40] but for most people consolidation of their fragmented holdings was simply not feasible.

Consolidation essentially failed because farmers in Kigezi need plots in different places to take advantage of the great variability in soil types and topography. This was recognised by at least one official, T.F. Ellis, a junior agricultural officer, who travelled extensively around the highly fragmented counties of Ndorwa and Rukiga. He discussed consolidation with a 'representative collection of the community' and found broad agreement on the subject. He noted that practically everyone had land scattered across hilltops, hillsides and in valleys, which provided them with a mixed variety of soil types and soil depths. This, and local variations in climate (particularly rainfall which is frequently very local), meant that they considered that they could grow a greater variety of crops with scattered plots. Many were suspicious of losing out during exchange for consolidation, and the general feeling was that they were better-off as they were:

> Consolidation might have some advantages, but these in their opinion do not outweigh the disadvantages, the idea of all their eggs in one basket does not appeal to them. They prefer to walk miles to work, and in some instances even living near their hill top plots for some months away from home in temporary grass huts, than to run the risk of having a farm with much the same soil, or plots of all one elevation, or all in a valley. Who they wonder wants all hill or all valley, as it is with a variety one has a far better chance of some success.[41]

Ellis's analysis of the situation was absolutely correct, and had officials paid more attention to it they might well have abandoned the whole policy of consolidation before it had even begun. But for reasons that are unclear his report was ignored. As Ellis observed, a cropping system in an area as variable as that of Kigezi needed scattered plots to reduce the risk of serious crop loss. Being able to take advantage of different soils and micro-climates is essential to the success of the system. Accessing land of different types was so important that, as Byagagaire and Lawrance observed in the 1950s, people would often rent parcels of land to enable them to do this.[42] Farmers today express similar views. While many informants note the advantages of consolidation (in particular time saved in walking between plots), they were all too aware of the impossibility of exchanging plots, due to the variability of fertility. One informant stated, for example: 'we cannot consolidate our land because the fertility is not the same.'[43] Farmers are well aware that these barriers to consolidation also prevent them from acquiring titles. It is not uncommon for informants to reply to a question about titles with a response about fragmentation and consolidation. Thus, when asked if he had a title to his land, Kazlon Ntondogoro replied simply 'It is not together.' When the question was repeated in a follow-up interview he again responded with fragmentation: 'a title would be good, because ... my wife ... walks a long distance.'[44] Thus in the minds of some informants, titles and consolidation were interconnected: while the impossibility of having a title on fragmented land was well known to farmers, the enormous difficulties of consolidating land in Kigezi were also recognised.[45] The policy of consolidation proved, therefore, to be a complete failure in Kigezi.

There were other reasons too for this failure, which can be highlighted through comparisons with other land reform efforts: politics, resources and timeliness.[46] Comparing Kigezi with Central Province, Kenya, highlights the importance of resource levels in the context of a politically charged situation. In Central Province, in the light of Mau Mau, high levels of resources were allocated, compared to Kigezi. The policy of villagisation and the powers of the emergency regulations, combined with staffing and finance levels that Kigezi would never approach, meant that Central Province's administration could push through a policy that may have been unpopular.[47] Officials from Uganda acknowledged that they lacked the powers that Kenyan officials had to enforce the policy, observing that 'the detention of large numbers, the large-scale security measures and closer administration had resulted in a greater compliance of the population.'[48] This unique administrative and political situation was very different form that of Kigezi and meant that there was a certain inevitability that the scheme would proceed successfully in the Kenyan example.

Timeliness also helps explain the failure of consolidation and titling in Kigezi. In Kigezi land was both so fragmented, and tenure already highly individualised, that consolidation was virtually impossible to achieve. Exchange would have disturbed too many vested interests: there were simply too many permanent houses and wood lots, as well as too many fragments. Local farmers could foresee that consolidation in this situation would have caused such disruption that they rejected it outright. Kigezi was well ahead of other areas of colonial Africa in the effects of population pressure: such changes to tenure that were beginning in Kikuyuland were already well under way in Kigezi.[49] The strength of individual tenure made consolidation much harder to achieve, and can in part explain the failure of this part of colonial land reform.

SWAMP RECLAMATION

The final colonial land policy to be explored is swamp reclamation. Papyrus swamps occupied many of Kigezi's valley bottoms: nearly 9 per cent of Kigezi's 2,040 sq miles was occupied by swamps, mostly in the densely populated south of the district (see Map 5.2). They had many uses, most importantly as sources of papyrus and grasses for thatching, ropes, baskets and mats. The margins of swamps were also important for dry season cultivation and were an important reserve of land used during particularly dry years.[50] Swamps were used for the watering of cattle, but were not important grazing areas.[51]

Table 5.1 *Area of swamps in Kigezi, and areas suitable for reclamation*[52]

Swamps	Total area in acres	Acreage suitable for drainage and cultivation
Kiruruma South	5,950	4,300
Kiruruma North	3,000	1,870
Kashambya	2,020	1,830
Kigyeyo	6,250	470
Others	7,700	3,500 (approx)

From the earliest years of colonial rule the possibility of reclaiming swamps in Kigezi was discussed. In 1935, the DAO, Wickham, suggested reclamation in response to declining acreages of available cultivable land. No action was taken, however, until after the 1943 famine, which brought swamps into prominence. The planting of sweet potatoes on swamp edges was observed to have made the 'greatest contribution to averting a food shortage'.[53] The practice was adopted as official policy: whenever food shortages were predicted orders were made that sweet potatoes be planted on swamp edges. In fact Bakiga farmers had long been using swamp edges for cultivation during dry periods. But it suited agricultural officers to present swamp cultivation as a colonial initiative that they had successfully implemented, and the administration's efforts to encourage swamp cultivation are also remembered by many informants.[54]

Swamp reclamation occurred in two ways: first, on a small scale by individual farmers without the practical support of the administration. This was essentially an extension of the cultivation of swampland during dry years that had long been occurring. Second, reclamation occurred on a larger scale at the initiation, and with the advice and technical assistance, of the colonial administration. There were two distinct phases in reclamation by the administration. Up to 1956 reclamation occurred in a somewhat piecemeal fashion. Colonial officials disagreed as to the best way forward and this period was characterised by serious technical difficulties. In 1956 a report by Sir

Alexander Gibb and Partners on water resources in Uganda recommended the drainage and development of over 80 per cent of Kigezi's swamp.[55] From then onwards official policy was in favour of large-scale reclamation, and in the late 1950s and early 1960s much reclamation occurred. This policy can therefore be seen as successful insofar as swamps were reclaimed. But its success in terms of what happened to that land (and in particular whether it was made available for subsistence agriculture for people living around the swamps) is another question to which I will return below.

POST-INDEPENDENCE POLICIES

Since the coming of independence land tenure policies in Uganda have been rich in rhetoric, and weak in practice. In the years immediately prior to independence the World Bank Commission to Uganda (1960–61) endorsed the recommendations of the EARC, including the registration of individual ownership of land, and 'it was passed that individuals who wanted land titles were to register at the district headquarters'.[56] The familiar arguments (that individual tenure facilitated increased investment, and thus agricultural productivity) were used in the post-independence period. The Crown Land Act of 1962 converted crown land into public land, under the control of the government, but on the ground there was little change. Similarly the Public Lands Act of 1969, which provided that no customary tenant could be evicted without his or her consent, and that compensation had to be paid, also led to few changes on the ground.[57]

The 1975 Land Reform Decree (Decree No 3 of 1975), during the presidency of Idi Amin, declared all land in Uganda public land under the control of the Uganda Land Commission in accordance with the provisions of the Public Lands Act (1969). The Decree thus significantly changed the legal basis of land tenure, and had the potential of leading to major changes to land tenure in Uganda. This was particularly the case for tenants on *mailo* land in the Kingdoms, as it 'radically altered' relationships between landlords and tenants on *mailo* land. Customary tenants became tenants at sufferance. Freeholds were abolished and converted into leaseholds of 99 or 999 years. The decree, however, was never fully implemented and the majority of tenants continued to occupy land without legal protection. Indeed it has been argued that 'customary tenants on state land continue[d] to enjoy an adequate level of security of tenure.'[58]

A more recent phase of land reform began in Uganda with the National Resistance Movement (NRM) government. Scholars have argued that the impetus to begin land reform came from external bodies such as the World Bank, while it has also been noted that 'land marketability was one of the key driving forces in the land reform process.'[59] McAuslan has observed that there were two forces behind the 1998 Land Act: one, the World Bank, representing the force of the market, and the other, the Constitution, representing political forces.[60] In the late 1980s the World Bank and USAID funded a major study of land tenure and agricultural development carried out by the Wisconsin Land Tenure Center, together with the Makerere

Institute of Social Research. The study concluded that the Land Reform Decree of 1975 should be abolished and land tenure policy in Uganda should support the emergence and smooth functioning of a free land market to enable progressive farmers to gain access to land for development on a commercial basis. Its conclusions were therefore remarkably similar to those of the EARC, which reported some thirty years earlier. The system should protect land rights, and should provide for the evolution of a uniform system of land tenure across the country. It came to these conclusions despite the fact that this part of the study was limited to Buganda, and few efforts were made to draw in findings from other areas in Uganda.[61] Furthermore, Roth *et al.*'s study of the LTPP (part of the broader LTC-MISR study) found that land registration had a negligible effect on the use of credit from banks and that few investments accrued from the security of tenure.[62] But this conceptualisation of land tenure 'evolving' towards greater individualisation and formalisation (or the Evolutionary Theory of Land Tenure) has been a powerful one which continues to be influential amongst policy-makers today.[63]

In addition, there was the constitutional dimension to land reform. The process of drawing up a constitution began in 1992 and a number of provisions related to land tenure were adopted by the constitution. The 1995 Constitution vested all land in Uganda in the citizens of Uganda with customary tenure among the land tenure systems recognised (others being freehold, *mailo* and leasehold). Under the constitution the state no longer held absolute title to land; all citizens owning land under customary tenure may acquire a certificate of customary ownership, and such land may be converted to freehold land ownership by registration. The constitution thus indicated that government policy was that 'most land in Uganda should be held on individual freehold tenure'.[64]

The reforms brought about by the constitution were to be made operational by a new land law. Following a consultation process the drafting of this land law began and between 1996 and July 1998, when the Bill was finally passed as law, five versions of the Bill had been drafted.[65] The Land Act 1998 (Number 16 1998) provides the legal framework governing land tenure, land administration and the settlement of disputes in Uganda. It grants tenure rights to customary holders of land, who can now get certificates of customary ownership thus gaining immediate titles to the land they occupy. Certificates of this nature can be obtained at three levels: individual, family or community.[66] This certificate of ownership gives the holder the right to lease, mortgage or sell that land (S. 9 (1) and (2)). The Act also permits holders of land in customary tenure to convert it to freehold tenure (S.10). This can be done with or without the certificate of customary ownership. The act recognises the role of traditional authorities in land administration and dispute resolution, providing that traditional authorities will determine disputes over customary tenure by acting as mediators alongside the formal land tribunal system (S.89). The Land Tribunal can also advise parties to settle their case through mediation to enable the services of traditional authorities to be utilised. The Land Act provides that 'any decision taken in respect of land held under customary tenure ... will be in accordance with the custom, traditions and practices of the community ... except that a decision which denies women ... access to ownership or use shall be null and void' (S.28 of the Land Act, Article 33 of the 1995 Constitution). Section 40 provides for consent by spouses or children in any transaction on land where a family ordinarily resides or derive its sustenance.[67] An amendment to deal with the question of married women's rights to ownership of land was proposed, but the published act did not include this amendment. It is unclear whether the amendment had indeed been passed (as claimed by some) or not, and some stated it had in fact never even been formally put before parliament.[68]

The scale of the new land administration machinery being put into place in Uganda following the Land Act has been described by Manji as 'remarkable'. It involves 45 new District Land Boards and 9000 Parish Land Committees, and a Land Tribunal for each sub-county, which will have jurisdiction over land disputes. Appointed by the District Council, Parish Land Committees will be responsible for the initial consideration of certificates of customary ownership, applications for grants of land in freehold, and applications to convert customary tenure to freehold tenure. Having determined any applications for certificates of customary ownership, the recommendations of the Parish Land Committee are then confirmed, rejected or amended by the District Land Board. From here appeals can be made to the Land Tribunal and from there to the High Court.[69] The District Land Boards are therefore responsible for confirming, rejecting or varying the recommendations of land committees. The recording of customary land rights and settling of any disputes that might arise are thus the role of administrative bodies, rather than the courts. Coldham notes that 'the success of the land reform programme will depend in large part on the effective operation of these committees', while McAuslan has described them as playing an 'absolutely fundamental role in the implementation of the act'.[70] He notes, however, that it is 'unclear' what powers and duties the Parish Land Committee will have or how it will verify customary rights while there is little indication of how the committees will be established. More generally, McAuslan has criticised the Bill for being 'over broad', noting its 'lack of clarity, the very wide and unstructured powers given to new public bodies being established in the Bill and the rather poor definitions of key terms used in the Bill'.[71]

Indeed while it is one thing to pass such a land act, it is quite another to implement it. Implementation of the Land Act has been slow, and as Busingye noted in 2002, 'not much in terms of implementation of the provisions in the Land Act has happened ... No single certificate of ownership has been issued as yet and the status quo on the ground remains the same.'[72] Manji, who explored the problems of implementation, notes that, in addition to those barriers of implementation that are easy to identify (such as lack of clear policy directives, shortages of qualified personnel, etc.), there are others which need consideration, such as 'lack of political will, community conflicts and the actions of individual implementers'.[73] McAuslan observes that the

Act requires decentralisation of resources to districts and parishes, while 'those at the "centre" feel their power and status is threatened.' He continues that 'any process of land reform which aims to devolve resources and power therefore requires a major component of restructuring and re-educating central government officials so that they can see a new and useful role for themselves.'[74]

Perhaps the biggest challenge to implementing the Land Act is establishing and making operational the many new institutions created. District Land Boards were supposed to be established by January 1999, by which time only 19 out of 45 had been appointed, and while 43 had been appointed by March 2000 they were not in a position to issue certificates of ownership as few Parish Land Committees were in place.[75] In the light of these difficulties, proposals have been put forward to amend the administrative machinery, including shifting land committees from parish to sub-county level (thus reducing the number of committees from over 4,000 to around 1,000) and using existing LC3-level courts at sub-county level for the resolution of land disputes.[76] How these changes will affect the working of the Act remains to be seen.

Post-colonial land reform has thus been rich in rhetoric, but weak in practice. The 1975 Land Reform Decree had the potential for dramatically changing land tenure, but insecurity and lack of capacity meant that the existing system continued little changed. More recently the Land Act of 1998 has the potential to bring in enormous changes to land tenure. It involves a huge new land administration machinery and grants tenure rights to customary holders of land, who will be able to get certificates of customary ownership of their land. There has been notable criticism of the Land Act and recent studies from other parts of Uganda suggest that implementation has been slow at best. For example, Green has written of the 'failed implementation' of the Act in Buganda in 2005, while Adoko and Levine note that at the time of their research (late 2004) no Land Committees had been formed, and none of the structures prescribed by the Act were functional in Apac District, Northern Uganda. It is therefore too early to say what the impact of the Act on the ground will be.[77] Having reviewed policies of the colonial and post-colonial periods, the following section will now explore how these policies affected chiefly authority over land, and how some individuals attempted to use these policies to increase their access to, and power over, land.

Chiefly authority over land

While land ownership in Kigezi has been essentially individualistic for many decades, social networks are also important for both acquiring control over land, and gaining access to it. In the pre- and early colonial period social relationships and relations of kin or fictive kin were important. With the coming of colonialism and the appointment of colonial chiefs, authority over land became increasingly formalised. Up to the 1950s chiefs had considerable powers over everyday issues, such as agriculture, bride wealth and tax collection, and were also given certain powers over land, in particular related to the allocation of 'abandoned' land, dispute settlement, and approving land transfers. These powers, and the relationship between political authority and land more generally, will now be explored.

The relationship between political authority and control over land can be seen, firstly, in terms of a direct relationship (i.e. people being allocated land because of their position within the colonial state) and, secondly, in terms of the power that those with government positions had over other people's land. The first of these is of less significance in Kigezi as, with a handful of exceptions, there were no formal links between the position of chieftainship and land ownership.[78] But the power that chiefs had over other people's land was of very great relevance in Kigezi. The present section will look at how changes to chiefly authority affected different aspects of land tenure: how people acquired land (the role that chiefs played in allocating land to in-migrants); how people disposed of their land (whether chiefly authority has had any impact on inheritance); and the role that chiefs played in dispute settlement. I will show that initially chiefly authority over land increased in the early part of colonial rule, and thus, while social relations continued to be important, who these were with underwent change. As authority became linked to the position of chieftainship, so relations with chiefs became important. But over time constraints were placed on chiefly authority, and in response to this some chiefs tried to reassert their power – using particular policies (such as swamp reclamation), and emphasising the role of 'clan elders'.

From the early colonial period chiefs were given authority to allocate land, thus taking over the role played by hosts (see previous chapter). But many chiefs appointed in the early years of colonialism would themselves have previously acted as hosts: being well connected and well established individuals, they shared the key characteristics of hosts. There was thus a shift in how land was allocated: from a system whereby well-connected individuals could form relationships with in-migrants, act as their hosts, and benefit from their labour, to a system whereby colonial appointees – by virtue of their position – could allocate land. As the individuals involved were, initially at least, the same, this should be seen as a shift, rather than a dramatic change and there was thus something of a formalisation of authority.

One role given to chiefs was to allocate 'unused' land. In the early colonial period, because their salaries were determined by the number of people they administered, chiefs had a strong incentive to encourage people to settle in their area: chiefs 'were out and out for more and more people'.[79] For in-migrants relationships with chiefs became crucial as they had formal authority to allocate unused land, and Wright's 1939 survey of Kitozho showed that at this time the allocation of land by chiefs was the single most important way for in-migrants to the area to acquire land, making up 28 per cent of the land acquired by in-migrants.[80] But the term 'unused' is ambiguous, and in some cases chiefs allocated land that had an owner. Ngologoza, himself a chief, noted that chiefs took land away from people to 'give it to newcomers' and they would tell the owner that 'he had no land since all of it was Crown land.'[81] The case of Nkulikimana, a CMS teacher, illustrates this well. On the death of his father in the late 1920s chiefs took away his father's land, claiming his mother was unable to cultivate it. The land was later reallocated by the local chiefs, with the explicit support of colonial officials.[82]

Questions over tenure of 'abandoned' or 'unused' land were of particular significance in a district of such dense population, and one in which, as will be seen in the following chapter, fallow was so central to the agricultural system. Agricultural officers were particularly concerned about how long land could be left before being considered 'abandoned', as insecure tenure of fallow land would be a barrier to maintaining fallow periods. In 1937 the DC noted that the decision as to whether land had been abandoned depended on whether the person's house had been abandoned, in which case the chief would allot it to any applicant. [83] Elsewhere no mention is made of the significance of abandoning the house, and later statements appear to be contradictory. For example, in 1938 Purseglove wrote: 'there was an absolute security of tenure to the peasant cultivator and his heirs *so long as he keeps the land under cultivation.* The peasant is protected from anyone encroaching on his fallow land, *for having once cultivated it he has permanent rights.*'[84] Whether land had to be cultivated for tenure to be secure is unclear from this statement, but Wright's more detailed 1938 study of the same area sheds more light:

> A man can own as much land as he can cultivate and defend with the assistance of his clansmen. This became modified, with the establishment of a settled administration to the principle that a man can own as much as he can cultivate in a year, together with as much as he can prove was the area of his cultivation in previous years. This latter will no doubt be further slowly modified by a lukiko decision not to recognise fallow land for more than 7 years unless the land is hedged.

The involvement of the *lukiko* suggests that land rights were being increasingly formalised. Wright continues:

> the matter [of loaning land] however (except for those plots which the peasants actually occupy) has ceased to be in [the peasant's] hands but is in the control of the mukunga chief who distributes land ... The chief has a right to apportion abandoned land (*itongo*) to persons who are in need of land to cultivate but he has no right to do this with fallow land; it is however, upon the original occupier to establish his claim that it is fallow land and not bush.[85]

With the authority to allocate unused and abandoned land, chiefs were important figures for those wanting to acquire land. In-migrants or people seeking additional land would have to approach chiefs, who quickly became the most important route to land. Good relations with these colonial appointees were clearly therefore very important for anyone who wanted to acquire more land, as is also illustrated by the case study of Kalengyere pyrethrum estate (see Box 5.1).

Box 5.1 – Kalengyere pyrethrum estate

The Kalengyere estate was leased for the cultivation of pyrethrum during the Second World War. When the site was abandoned the land was distributed amongst the local population. This case study illustrates how those in positions of authority, or those with links to such people, were able to gain access to this land when it was distributed.

The land on which the Kalengyere estate was established was located next to the Echuya Forest Reserve and was uncultivated, being considered marginal for food crops due to crop raiding. In 1940 the land was leased to a European planter under a Temporary Occupation Licence to grow pyrethrum. Production began in 1946, but just four years later the American wartime stockpile was released and as a result prices collapsed. The ending of the artificially high wartime prices meant that pyrethrum production was no longer economic in Kigezi and in late 1952 the Kalengyere estate came to an end.[86]

From mid-1952 the estate was effectively abandoned, it was formally surrendered in late 1954 and the reallocation of land took place in 1956. But prior to official allocation some people began to use the land – most notably the *gombolola* chief, Mbuguzhe, who used it for both grazing and cultivation, while preventing others from doing so. Mbuguzhe, who it was noted 'had little difficulty in controlling an apathetic council',[87] used his position as *gombolola* chief to gain access to a large part of the estate in the months before the land was reallocated.

Once formal reallocation began in June 1956 Mbuguzhe again found ways of gaining access to a large proportion of that land. The total area to be distributed was 290 acres, which was to be divided up between 30 individuals. A list of 30 men was drawn up but there is no evidence from the time as to how these individuals were chosen. A Department of Agriculture official noted that

> The Gombolola Chief Mbuguzhe was ... allowed to select his own plot ... Only friends, relatives and servants of the gombolola chief or ALG were allocated land. The piece of land selected by Mbuguzhe was in the middle of the block of some 60 acres. By means of threats and physical violence he has obtained control of all this land.[88]

Oral evidence supports this and informants noted two methods of gaining land: either through kinship relations with Mbuguzhe, or through bribery. The bribes were not necessarily cash, as some people worked for Mbuguzhe, in return for being given land. Archival sources also confirm that Mbuguzhe used communal labour for his own purposes.[89]

There is no doubt that Mbuguzhe thus used his position of *gombolola* chief to successfully acquire more than ten acres of land at Kalengyere. Attempts to persuade Mbuguzhe to return the land failed, and by April 1958 he had at least 60 acres. He used his knowledge of colonial officials' own developmental and modernist arguments, and of colonial policies (such as consolidation, mixed farming, individualisation of land tenure) to argue that he should be allowed to keep the land.[90]

Mbuguzhe, however, went too far. His land acquisition led him into disputes with more senior chiefs and the colonial administration. In July 1957 he was fined and threatened with dismissal, and in April 1958 he resigned.[91] There is no archival evidence of what happened next, but at some point between 1958 and the 1980s Mbuguzhe obtained a title to the land that he had acquired at Kalengyere. Because of this Mbuguzhe had the last laugh: this title meant that he was the only person able to retain his land when everyone else was evicted by the government in the 1980s, and his children still use it to this day.[92]

131

The power of chiefs to allocate abandoned land did not continue unchallenged, and the resettlement scheme of the 1940s brought the issue sharply into focus. Before this scheme was launched (see Chapter 3) it was unclear whether land left behind by settlers would be 'allocated by the chiefs to people with insufficient land' or whether migrating individuals would themselves transfer ownership of their land.[93] In the event, it became clear that people left their land to relatives or friends so that they could reclaim it if they wished to return, and colonial efforts to redistribute land left by settlers failed. The practice of *okusigira eitaka* ('the assumption of authority to dispose of land which a man proposes to abandon') was noted to have developed around 1946, as land left by settlers 'was not re-allocated by chiefs, elders or clan-heads but by the direct designation of its late occupiers'.[94] Settlers appointed deputies or *abasigire* who were often relatives to look after their land in case they wished to return in order to 'ensure that the chiefs cannot say the land has been abandoned'.[95] Thus chiefs were excluded from any decision-making over settlers' land and their authority to allocate abandoned land was challenged. In 1953 the ADC wrote: 'the right to leave land and yet retain ownership of it by appointing a deputy is ... a completely new right, which is now well recognised by the courts.'[96] Hence, in response to a threat to individuals' rights to allocate their land on migration a new practice was incorporated into 'customary tenure', a practice which was quickly recognised by the courts. This highlights well that, whatever 'customary tenure' was, it was certainly not static, but evolved in the face of changing conditions. Moreover, it illustrates that chiefs' powers over land were beginning to be restricted in some areas of land tenure by the late 1940s.

As population increased, less and less land was available for allocation in southern Kigezi. But when new land did become available – for example when swamps were reclaimed – chiefs played an important role, and thus relationships with chiefs remained critical for gaining access to this land. This is illustrated in Box 5.1 and in the following section.

In addition to having power to allocate land, chiefs were also given authority over land sales. By 1940 it was necessary to gain the consent of the chief prior to making a sale but whether this was merely a case of informing the chief, or whether permission had to be sought is unclear.[97] In 1951 the District Council passed a resolution 'allowing' sales of land. In fact land sales had, by this time, long been occurring, but by passing the resolution chiefs were formalising their involvement. Furthermore, the District Council stressed that it was the duty of the chief to see that land was not sold to anyone who was not a 'native of Kigezi',[98] and oral sources confirm that chiefs had authority over decisions as to who could buy land. Physs Rwakabirigi's husband wanted to buy some land from his brother who was migrating. However, his brother planned to sell it to someone who was unrelated. Her husband went to the *muluka* chief who ruled that somebody outside the family was not supposed to buy land if there was a brother who was able to buy it.[99] Thus in relation to sales of land there appears to have

132

been increasing (and increasingly formalised) involvement of chiefs up to at least the early 1950s. As Purseglove noted in 1951, 'the authority of the chiefs in the allocation of land and their interest in land generally … in Kigezi has been strengthened.'[100] This may have been the case in many areas, but, as we have seen above, it was not the case for the allocation of land left by resettlers.

Finally, chiefs also had authority over land through their involvement in dispute settlement and their work in the courts. In 1929 the DC observed 'frequent … litigations' over land,[101] suggesting that people quickly began to make use of more formalised systems of authority. Land disputes were 'taken in the first instance before the Muluka Council' and, although this body had no legal powers, most cases were settled at this level. If they could not be solved at *muluka* level they were taken up to the *gombolola* courts.[102] Thus government-appointed chiefs were given increased powers over other people's land through their involvement in dispute settlement, and this continued up to the late colonial period.

Thus courts had significant powers over land through dispute settlement, and in the early years of colonialism, when chiefs ran the courts, it was the chiefs who had this authority. Getting their power from their colonial positions, chiefs in the early colonial period had authority in settling disputes, allocating increasingly scarce unoccupied land to newcomers and allocating so-called 'abandoned' land. But these powers did not last, and the resettlement scheme saw the first major challenge to chiefly authority: a system developed whereby 'deputies' were appointed so that chiefs could not claim that land had been abandoned. More formal limits continued to be placed on chiefly authority over land, and in 1952 the District Council decided that 'a chief has no power to give away a man's land, no matter how long he stays away.'[103] And then from the mid-1950s the separation of the judiciary and executive began, which further eroded the powers of chiefs.

While limitations were being placed on the authority of chiefs over land, chiefs themselves tried to reassert the authority of 'clan elders' as a way of reclaiming authority over land. The EARC of 1953–55 presented an opportunity for prominent individuals to present customary tenure as they saw it. In oral evidence to the EARC, Ngologoza (then Secretary General) mentioned 'clan land-givers' who could allocate land to people in need. A memorandum drawn up by senior Bakiga chiefs and others for the EARC stated that 'whenever there were land transactions between individuals they would get the approval of Clan Elders.' [104] Thus as chiefs saw their power over land being squeezed, they sought ways to re-define their authority by re-creating this authority through their position as clan elders.

This reassertion appears to have had some success. During discussions over membership of adjudication committees (for the granting of titles for the LTPP in the late 1950s) it was noted that, while 'there is nothing to prevent muluka councillors from forming the basis of the committee … every effort must be made to include those clan elders who are normally associated with land matters.' The desire to include 'some representation of traditional land authorities'[105] implies that officials did believe that some individuals had authority over land matters, elsewhere referred to as 'traditional land allocators',[106] but officials never spelt out who these might be, or precisely what their role was. Similarly, it was suggested that clan leaders should be involved in the system of certification of heirs that was necessary once the LTPP began.[107]

Oral sources suggest that in practice people 'played' different sources of authority off against each other: for example, relatives, elders or chiefs.[108] Whilst informants agreed that British-appointed chiefs were given power over land (most notably over land disputes and the allocation of unoccupied land), a number of informants noted that when disputes arose they would initially approach clan members, and only if they were dissatisfied with the decision of the clan members would they take the dispute to government chiefs. Phyllis Rwakari and David Mashoki said that chiefs would not try to settle land disputes without first approaching family members and elders, and that this remains unchanged to this day.[109] Mackenzie makes similar findings in Murang'a, noting that 'people draw ... on whichever legal resource they can' in the contestation of land rights, giving rise to a complex picture.[110]

In sum, chiefs' power over other people's land changed over the course of the colonial period. Up to the mid-1940s these powers increased steadily: chiefs allocated land taking over the role played by 'hosts' in the pre-colonial period. But initially the change may not have been obvious as many of those appointed to be lower-level chiefs would have been the type of persons who would have acted as hosts: well connected and well established individuals. Thus the powers given to them by colonial authorities were a formalisation of authority rather than a major change to it.[111] Chiefs also played a role in dispute settlement through their involvement in the courts and were given the authority to give 'consent' to sales. But from the time of the Resettlement Scheme these powers began to be reined in and the allocation of migrants' land was left in the hands of those migrating. As the 1950s progressed chiefs' powers were further eroded: there was an increase in elected members on local councils and from the mid-1950s the separation of the executive from the judiciary further reduced the power of chiefs. In the face of this erosion in their powers, chiefs did two things. First, they tried to hold on to any power that they had over land, with older chiefs reasserting the authority of clan elders. Second, chiefs switched their attention to land that they had previously ignored. The intensified interest in swamps, which had not previously been the focus of their attentions, illustrates this well.

POWER, POLITICS & PATRONAGE:
THE CASE OF SWAMPS

The case of swampland shows how chiefs tried to hold on to powers over land, and to assert authority over such 'new' land as did become available. Using evidence from the three largest swamps in Kigezi (Kashambya, Kiruruma North and Kiruruma South – see Map 5.2), this section will show that the involvement of chiefs in the machinery put into place by the colonial administration to distribute reclaimed land enabled them to retain some of their powers over land. I will also use the case of swampland to illustrate how links with the colonial state proved to be an important means of acquiring land, with individuals using these links to increase their ownership of land, which contributed to the highly differentiated ownership of swampland that is found in Kigezi today.

Swamp reclamation began in Kigezi on a small scale and took off with colonial support from 1956. Initially the administration paid little attention to the question of how swampland would be distributed. Chiefs, on the other hand, did raise the issue: noting that natural swamps were communally owned and could 'be used freely by anyone' and asking how rights to reclaimed swampland would be determined and plots distributed.[112] District officials believed that chiefs should allocate the reclaimed land to private owners living in the vicinity of the swamp. In contrast, officials of the Ministry of Natural Resources in Entebbe argued that, given the costs of reclamation, the government should 'retain some control over land use or allocation in order to insure optimum productive use of the land'.[113]

Despite this difference of opinion, it was agreed in 1958 that the district team would establish local machinery to ensure that the swamps were developed efficiently and productively. Establishing this machinery was slow and it was not until May 1959 that it was decided that a 'development plan' should be drawn up for each swamp before reclamation work began.[114] Swamp Planning Committees were established with overall responsibility for swamps, and in particular for zoning (which areas were to be cultivated, grazed and left for papyrus). But the power of these committees is open to question: the committees themselves had no statutory authority to make reallocations or remedy what had already taken place.[115] In fact, as we will see below, many of the powers over swamps remained with *gombolola* councils and chiefs. Furthermore, the actual allocation of land was the responsibility of chiefs: land in small swamps was controlled by *gombolola* chiefs, while in the three large swamps it was allocated by the *saza* chief with the colonial Field Officer's advice.[116]

While agreement was made as to the *process* by which allocation of land would take place, the *principles* of allocation remained ambiguous and were debated throughout the late 1950s. On the one hand, there was a concern that land distribution should be fair and equal, while, on the other, there was a wish to increase agricultural productivity by encouraging progressive farmers. Initially the desire to increase land for food production drove swamp reclamation: the consultant engineers recommended that swamps be used for subsistence crops, and they planned to allocate swampland in plots of 0.25 acres.[117] But before long the possibility of encouraging 'economic sized' farms began to be mentioned. There were clearly differences of opinion within the administration. In a meeting held by the Natural Resources Sub-Committee of the District Team in November 1959 some members argued that swampland should be allocated in small units of 0.25 acres, with the object of using swamps as food reserves. Others, however, disagreed,

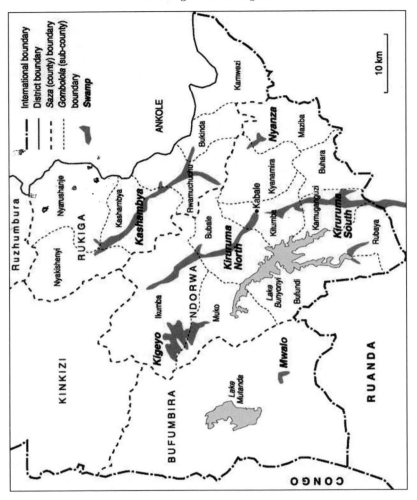

Map 5.2
Southern Kigezi,
showing swamps

136

considering that swampland should be allocated in units of an economic size with the object of creating mixed farms.[118] Before long those in favour of larger mixed farms, supporting the 'progressive' farmer, had prevailed. Official policy outlined in January 1960 noted: 'The ultimate objective of policy will be to turn the cultivated parts of planned swamps over to proper economic sized mixed farms in the hands of those who have proved themselves most capable of using the land to best advantage.' [119]

As a result of the differences of opinion within the administration, issues were blurred in the first few years of reclamation. Thus, while a maximum of five acres per household was agreed, it was later noted that the amount allocated would 'depend ... upon the need of a man and his family and his capacity to develop the land properly' which opened the way for exceptions to be made.[120] The differences of opinion on the part of the administration meant that officials were inclined to turn a blind eye to farmers they considered to be progressive who laid claim to larger areas of land. Furthermore, the swamp committees, with overall responsibility for swamps, were very often set up too late, and even once established they were often ineffectual. Allocation did not proceed as planned and there were 'irregularities in procedure,' with the result that much swampland was distributed highly inequitably.[121]

For chiefs swamp reclamation represented an opportunity to hold onto powers over land, powers that elsewhere were being diminished. Plans for the swamps were drawn up by Swamp Planning Committees, on which chiefs sat. *Gombolola* chiefs commented on the plans and were also responsible for ensuring that they were complied with. Furthermore, reclamation could not go ahead without the approval of *gombolola* councils. *Gombolola* chiefs distributed reclaimed swampland in the smaller swamps, while in the larger swamps the *saza* chiefs were initially responsible, although this was reduced to *gombolola* level from July 1962.[122] Some chiefs claimed land for themselves – for example in Kiruruma South a number of *miluka* chiefs reserved large areas for themselves, which they refused to share out.[123] And even those chiefs who did not benefit personally undoubtedly had increased power over swampland. For individuals who wanted land in the swamps their relationships with chiefs were crucial. This was observed when, for example, the *saza* chief of Rukiga was seen as not being impartial in his decisions over Kashambya swamp. Swampland can thus be seen as a remnant of chiefly power over land and this is confirmed by oral sources, which note that it was chiefs who distributed, and had significant powers over, the reclaimed swampland.[124]

Many people claimed swampland before it was officially allocated by the chiefs. For example, in Kashambya swamp people began cultivating swampland before it was allocated. Those who were able to invest labour in draining and clearing the swamp avoided the restrictions on the amount of swampland that could be held.[125] Similarly in Kiruruma South, complaints that people were taking land 'without proper arrangements' were made almost as soon as drainage began in 1957, and efforts to prevent people claiming land prior to allocation failed.[126] The same occurred in Kiruruma North with large pieces of land being claimed prior to allocation. Here about 50 people claimed land including Batuma with over 50 acres, Bagacwa with 30 acres, 35 people with land of between one and 2.5 acres, and 12 people with plots of under one acre.[127] Although this was seen as a 'complete breakdown of the traditional system whereby these swamps were regarded as communal until such time as they were reclaimed and allocated through Chiefs',[128] no attempt was made to overturn this. Rather, it was decided that those who 'had invested money and labour in swamp land and were using the land they claimed, or were capable of using it, effectively and beneficially ... had a moral right to be confirmed in their occupation of that land'.[129] The 37 people with plots of over one acre were allowed to keep their land, while the 12 others, all with plots of under an acre, lost their land but were promised plots when more had been drained.[130]

But, critically, many of these individuals who claimed large pieces of land had links with the colonial administration, and therefore access to information, knowledge and the money to pay wage labourers to assist in the clearing of the swamps. For example, Batuma (one of the largest landowners today) was a Veterinary Officer and sat on two swamp committees. Makara, another large landowner, also worked for the colonial administration, while Kibirigi, who had a large plot in Bubale, was *gombolola* chief for Ikumba.[131] One informant noted the importance of links with the administration when it came to swamp allocation: 'My husband was working with the bazungu ... and he was able to get a big swamp land.' Not only did such individuals have knowledge of swamp reclamation, through their links with the colonial state, but they also had cash incomes, so could employ labourers to clear the reclaimed land. Oral sources confirm that, while some allocation of equally sized plots occurred, there was a good deal of land grabbing of larger plots. Some informants suggested that all was not legitimate: one said that 'those who had money got bigger land,' while another claimed that chiefs on the committee had been bribed: 'they wanted porridge.' Areas that were zoned to be left as papyrus were later cultivated: 'the rich people wanted more parts and they used [these parts].' Another told of how 'the rich said that the government said that land is theirs and so they put there their cows. [We] kept quiet, [and] ... did not report it anywhere.'[132]

Swamp reclamation represented a perfect opportunity to claim access to additional land for those who foresaw future pressure on land. In some cases such individuals did not have the labour to cultivate the land, and so instead planted trees on it to confirm their rights to it.[133] Planting trees on newly reclaimed swampland went against the advice of the Hydrological Department and so was investigated closely.[134] In one instance 13 people were investigated for having planted trees, and of these seven resided in Kabale or Rugarama (the CMS headquarters located just outside Kabale), some distance from Bubale.[135] This suggests that many of those being allocated swampland were not local to the area, and swampland was being used as an opportunity by well-placed individuals to increase their land. This area of

5.1 *Large dairy farms around Bubale*
(© Grace Carswell, 1996)

Present-day Kabale, showing different cultivation patterns in swamps

5.2 *Small plots of sweet potato cultivation in south Kiruruma*
(© Grace Carswell, 1996)

Kiruruma North has since been the scene of many transactions of swamp-land. Today the swamp around Bubale is made up of large dairy farms of exotic cattle owned by a few individuals, resulting in highly differentiated ownership of land.[136] The aim of increasing land available for the cultivation of food, was thus not entirely successful.

The policy of swamp reclamation that began in the colonial period and continued after independence was successfully implemented in the sense that swamps were indeed reclaimed. But this policy saw mixed success in terms of its original aim of increasing land available for food production for people living around the swamps. The initial colonial desire for the 'fair' distribution of swampland sat uncomfortably alongside the policy of encouraging progressive farmers, which ultimately took over as official policy. Partly as a result of this contradiction, and also because of the inadequacies of the structures put into place to ensure equality, large areas of reclaimed swamp fell into the hands of a few farmers. Being high-potential land, and the only new land that has become available since the 1950s, the value of swampland has risen with increased population pressure. Some individuals foresaw the potential it held and used their links with the colonial state, and with chiefs, to gain access to large pieces of reclaimed land. The outcome was thus a concentration of swampland ownership.

The story of swamp reclamation illustrates how colonial policies affected chiefly authority over land and this in turn had implications for land distribution. Here a common property resource was transformed into highly inequitably individually owned agricultural land.[137] The costs of reclamation therefore include increased land differentiation, the loss of a valuable reserve of land and the loss of other resources that swamps held. Some Bakiga had expressed fears about losing these resources when swamp reclamation was first suggested,[138] and these fears proved to be well founded, as on reclamation swampland became privately and individually owned. The swamp case study also demonstrates how chiefs attempted to maintain their control over land. As their powers began to be restricted from the late 1940s, so chiefs tried to reassert their authority over land, by reasserting the authority of 'clan elders', and shifting attention to new land as it became available. The involvement of chiefs in swamp reclamation meant that they were well placed to do this.

Conclusion

In stark contrast to earlier colonial policies around conservation, the land reform policies introduced in Kigezi from the 1950s were implemented with mixed success. The LTPP was a 'success' in that the area was adjudicated and titles were granted, but this success needs to be seen in light of the fact that colonial officials wanted to be seen to succeed and so selected the LTPP area specifically because it would be easier to implement the policy there. But it failed in that few of these titles were taken up by their owners and used.

Furthermore, the idea of titles did not catch on, and colonial propaganda failed to stimulate a demand for titling more generally. Indeed the only titles granted in the south of the district were those few sporadic titles granted to local 'big men', which were granted to try to stimulate support for the LTPP, to ensure that the land tenure proposals were approved by the District Council, and to kickstart consolidation in Bufumbira.

The policies of consolidation and enclosure largely failed. While enclosure proved to be popular amongst Bakiga, it was consolidation that was impossible to implement, and in the minds of colonial officials enclosure was impossible without consolidation. The region's great agro-ecological variability and Bakiga concerns to minimise risk, mean that there are significant advantages in having a number of scattered plots: advantages that clearly outweigh the disadvantages in the minds of Bakiga both today and in the past, and which led to consolidation's failure.

The policy of swamp reclamation was a success in so far as swamps were reclaimed. But it was not a success in the sense of the initial aim of equitably increasing access to land for the cultivation of food crops to the surrounding populations. But over the course of the implementation of this policy, its aims changed (to one of reclaiming land for use in 'economic sized' units by progressive farmers), and thus the policy could still be presented as a success. There were also unintended consequences of colonial land reforms. Thus, swamp reclamation provided opportunities for influential individuals and chiefs (who found their authority over land being challenged) to reassert their authority over land, and increase their control over it. Swamp reclamation led to changes in the tenure over that land, and has contributed to increasingly skewed ownership of land, as will be discussed in Chapter 7. Land reform policies of the post-colonial period have had little impact on the ground thus far, while it is too early to assess any effects of the 1998 Land Act.

Colonial land reform policies were being implemented as part of a broader modernising project in order to facilitate a land market, which should have – it is argued – positive impacts on agricultural productivity. But here in Kigezi a land market already existed: land tenure in Kigezi has long been highly individualised and land could be bought and sold in the early colonial period – long before these land reform policies began. This was a land tenure system that was constantly changing and evolving to suit the characteristics of Kigezi. Thus, for example, migrants to resettlement areas developed an arrangement that enabled them to retain control over the land that they left behind. Also, farmers rejected consolidation as they favoured fragmented land holdings, which suited the highly variable agro-ecological environment of Kigezi. Indeed, one reason why people rent land is to gain access to different land types. Kigezi's land tenure thus evolved in particular ways, in the face of a changing socio-economic context, and in response to colonial policies. While policies such as consolidation, enclosure and titling were introduced in order to facilitate a land market, here in Kigezi a land market already existed, rendering the policies somewhat irrelevant or superfluous.

That there is a vibrant land market is not to deny that social networks continue to be important for gaining access to land. With whom these networks are formed has changed over time: from hosts who were well established and well connected individuals in the pre- and early colonial period, to colonial appointed chiefs for much of the colonial period, to councillors and other elected officials more recently. Controlling access to higher-level courts, these officials are crucial, and women's legal protection has declined as a result. Furthermore, even when women win court cases, they are often unable to execute the rulings of the court. It is clear therefore that claims to land are still 'socially embedded',[139] albeit differentially.[140] While methods of accessing land have changed over time, there have also been changes to the agricultural system itself. Given the rapid increases in population, there are widely held beliefs about how Kigezi's agricultural system has changed over the past 50–100 years. These will be explored in the following chapter, which will show that changes have indeed been occurring, but some of these are most unexpected.

Notes

[1] Mitchell published an article in *The Times* on 'Land and Population in East and Central Africa', (published on 24 and 25 Sept 1952 to coincide with announcement of the EARC) which outlined some of the problems that the EARC would examine, as seen by the Kenyan administration. The timing of the announcement became linked with Kenyan political difficulties, see PRO CO 822/709. See also PRO CO 822 147/1, PRO CO 822/708, and PRO CO 822/711.

[2] Minute by Lyttelton to PM, 6 March 1952, Re Proposed RC. PRO CO 822/708 ff9.

[3] *Report of the East African Royal Commission, 1953-55* (London, 1955), xi.

[4] Land Policy of the Protectorate of Uganda, *Uganda Gazette*, Vol. XLIII, No 30, 1950. This related to land outside Buganda. For more re colonial mind and African land tenure during the mid-1940s see: PRO CO 536/215 (40336) – Land (Tenure) Legislation, 1944–46. Also PRO CO 822/345. Also see *Journal of African Administration*, special issue on land tenure, October 1952.

[5] Editorial in *Uganda Post* by J.W. Kiwanuka, *African Affairs Fortnightly Review*, 30 Oct 1952, PRO CO 822/424 ff39.

[6] *Report of the East African Royal Commission*, 428.

[7] See for example PRO CO 822/874 and PRO CO 822/877.

[8] Letter to Perham from Cohen, 2 Aug 1955, RH MSS Perham 514/5 ff38+.

[9] Uganda Government, *Land Tenure Proposals* (Entebbe, 1955). For more details of the Uganda Government's reaction to EARC see PRO CO 822/1613.

[10] 'Brief for Debate in House of Lords on a Motion by Lord Hudson. Land Use in Uganda, Summary, Confidential.' Enclosed in letter to W.A.C. Mathieson from Cohen, 16 June 1956, enclosing brief for Lord Hudson's motion in the House of Lords, which Hudson was persuaded to postpone. PRO CO 822/946 ff7 and ff7Enc.

[11] The Secretary of State for the Colonies had not even seen the Proposals. See Telegram to Cohen from Lloyd, 9 Jan 1956. (Immediate, Secret and Personal) PRO CO 822/877 ff7. For further details of CO reactions to Land Tenure Proposals see PRO CO 822/877. Evidence on district officers' views of the proposals is sketchy.

[12] Comments by Simpson re Note for Brigadier Hotine's visit to Uganda, enclosed in letter to Simpson from Smith, 23 Oct 1957. Comments for information only – not to be sent to Uganda. PRO CO 822/1407 ff20B & ff20D. His emphasis.

[13] Letter to Simpson (CO's Land Tenure Specialist) from Smith, Land and Surveys Department, Uganda 23 Oct 1957. PRO CO 822/1407 ff20A. The eight people who got sporadic titles were Paulo Ngologoza (Chief Judge, ex-Sec Gen), Paulo Kakwenza (Saza Chief, Ndorwa), John Lwamafa (Legislative Council Rep for Kigezi), Petero R Ntungwa (Gombolola Chief, Kyanamira), Sebastiano B. Rwabyoma (Gombolola Chief, Kamwezi), Gabrieri Tiragana (Dispenser, Medical Dept, Kabale), Tadewo Mbafundizeki (position unknown) and Coronerio Rukuba (position unknown).

[14] Letter to Simpson from Lawrance, 28 May 1958, PRO CO 822/1407 ff27.

[15] *Report of the EARC*, 351.

[16] Record of Meeting held at Kabale to discuss land tenure policy, 29 March 1957. PRO CO 822/1407 ff7. Furthermore, evidence from archives suggests that some of this land was occupied by other people, referred to as 'tenants'. KDA DC LAN 12 II ff148.

[17] Note on 'Land – Kigezi District' (Record of Discussions: Director of Lands and Surveys; Perm Sec Land Tenure; DC Kigezi and others, April 1958) PRO CO 822/1407 ff23Enc. There was actually a complaint in late 1958 against one of these sporadic titles, that of Ngologoza concerning his land in Katokye. The complaint was made after the one month given for appeals, and so was dismissed. Letter to Gomb Chf Kyanamira from Ngologoza, 3 Dec 1958. KDA DC LAN 12/5 ff12. and Letter to Chf Judge from DC, 8 Dec 1958 ff14.

[18] J.C.D. Lawrance, 'A Pilot Scheme for grant of land titles', *Journal of African Administration*, 8 (1956), 137. For further details of the LTPP see Carswell, 'African Farmers'.

[19] Lawrance, 'A Pilot Scheme for grant of land titles', 137.

[20] Letter to Perm Sec, Min of Land Tenure from DC, 3 May 1958, KDA DC LAN12-1I ff1.

[21] Letter to Tomasi Rwomushana from SecGen 20/4/57. KDA DC LAN12/II ff83

[22] For example Tomasi Rwomushana (*ex-saza* Chief Rukiga) (KDA DC LAN12/II ff82); William Rutankundira, (Asst SecGen, (KDA DC LAN12/II ff163).

[23] 95/Kit/53a. Other interviewees expressed similar sentiments. See various letters to DC from *gombolola* chiefs re LT Proposals, KDA DC LAN12/II.

[24] For example 00/Muy/23a 12/8/00. Also see letter from *gombolola* chief, Kumba, KDA DC LAN 12 II. See also interviews with 95/Kit/56a, 95/Kit/65a, 95/Kit/67a, 95/Kit/70a, 95/Muy/23a, 95/Muy/30a, 95/Muy/32a, 95/Muy/57a, 95/Kab/3a, 95/Kab/6a and 95/Kab/8a.

[25] For example, the responses of *gombolola* chiefs to the land tenure proposals show that there was a strong belief that land titles would be in the names of men.

[26] For example 00/Muy/16a and 00/Muy/20a. The area of the LTPP itself was not visited.

[27] Minutes of Meeting of Kigezi Land Board, 13 July 1962. KDA LAN 8/6I ff. 105.

[28] Commissioner for Lands, quoted in Obol-Ochola, 'Customary Land Law', 307–8.

[29] M. Roth, J. Cochrane, and W. Kisamba-Mugerwa, *Tenure security, credit use, and farm investment in the Rujumbura pilot land registration scheme, Rukungiri District, Uganda*. University of Wisconsin-Madison. Land Tenure Center Research Paper 112 (1993), 38–9.

[30] Consolidation and enclosure were administered by the Department of Agriculture, while surveying and the granting of titles were administered by the Department of Land and Surveys.

[31] Letter to all Saza Chfs, Kigezi from King, DAO, 14 Oct 1958, KDA DoA 154 ff6. Also KDA DoA 218A ff94. See Carswell, 'African Farmers'.

[32] Circular Standing Instruction, No 3 of 1959 – Enclosure on Agricultural Land, Issued by Ministry of Natural Resources, E'be, 10 Feb 1959. KDA DoA 154 ff89. Chiefs were instructed in December 1957 that all ALG holdings should be enclosed with live hedging (after they had ensured that there were no disputes over it). Letter to Saza and Gomb Chiefs from SecGen, 30 Dec 1957, KDA DC LAN8I ff170. Churches were also advised to enclose all their church and school land. Note on 'Land – Kigezi District', April 1958. PRO CO 822/1407 ff23Enc.

[33] Minutes of First Meeting of Natural Resources Sub-Committee of Kigezi District Team held 2–3 Dec 1957; Appendix B – Land Policy: Kigezi Draft, KDA DoA ADMIN 2/1 ff22.

[34] Letter to Sec Gen, all Saza and Gomb Chfs and Mission Supervisors, from King, DAO,

3 Sept 1958, KDA DoA 154 ff2. See also Letter to Gomb Chf Kyanamira from DAO, 19 May 1958, KDA DC AGR 6II ff89. See also Letter to all Saza Chfs from King, DAO 9/5/58 KDA DC Agr 6II ff. ff88; Letter to All Saza Chfs, Kigezi from King, DAO 14/10/58 KDA DA 154 ff6.

[35] See for example cases of enclosure of grazing land in Kanyinya and Kebisoni, Ruzhumbura 1960, KDA DC LAN12VA ff10–14 and KDA DC 155 ff31. See also Interview with J.M. Byagagaire, 21 Sept 1995. Note on 'Land – Kigezi District', PRO CO 822/1407 ff23Enc. Re southern part of district: For example see Letter to Field Officer, Ndorwa from DVO, 3 March 1959 – re land dispute in Kyanamira. eg KDA DoA 154 ff50.

[36] KDA DC Lan12EAR. Letters from *gombolola* chiefs, 1956.

[37] Minutes of meeting of Natural Resources Sub-Committee, 30 Dec 1958, KDA DoA Team Minutes. Letter to Fraser, DC from Whittaker, 6 Jan 1959, KDA DC LAN 12/II ff154. For further details see Carswell, 'African Farmers'.

[38] Letter to Field Officer, Bufumbira from DAO, 13 March 1959, KDA DoA 154 ff55. Minutes of meeting of Natural Resources Sub Committee of Kigezi District Team, 6 July and 2 Nov 1959, KDA DoA Team Minutes. Note (no author) on letter to Mtwale Bufumbira from DC, 24 Oct 1959, KDA DC LAN 12/2 ff7.

[39] Note on 'Land – Kigezi District' prepared by Ministry of Land and Mineral Devt. Sent to DAO for comments, 1 Dec 1959, KDA DoA 154 ff90. Also see Minutes of Meeting of Natural Resources Sub Committee of Kigezi District Team, 4 Jan 1960, KDA DoA Team Minutes. Record of Meeting on Consolidation and Land Titles in Kigezi, 6 Jan 1960. KDA DC ADM 9/7 ff40.

[40] Letter to J.C.D. Lawrance, Officer of Minister of Land Tenure, from E.W. King, DAO, 27 May 1958, KDA DoA Saf1/3 ff77.

[41] Letter to DAO from T.F. Ellis, Field Officer, Ndorwa and Rukiga, 28 July 1956, KDA DoA 17A-2 ff34.

[42] Byagagaire and Lawrance, *Effect of Customs of Inheritance*. See also Mifsud, *Customary Land Law in Africa*, 81.

[43] 95/Kab/6a. See also 95/Kab/8a and 95/Kit/56b.

[44] 95/Kit/56a and 95/Kit/56b. See also interviews with 95/Kit/65a; 95/Kit/70a.

[45] Similarly Tiffen has noted that in Machakos the Akamba refused titling for as long as consolidation was a condition, as they 'valued having land in different ecological niches'. Tiffen, 'Land and Capital: Blind spots in the study of the "resource-poor" farmer', in M. Leach and R. Mearns (eds), *Lie of the Land* (London, 1996)', 175.

[46] For further details see Carswell 'African Farmers'.

[47] See Sorrenson, *Land Reform*; and B. Berman and J. Lonsdale, *Unhappy Valley – Conflict in Kenya and Africa. Violence and Ethnicity.* (Book 2) (London, 1992).

[48] Observations by J.C.D. Lawrance and E.W. King (Department of Agriculture, Uganda) in Sorrenson, *Land Reform*, 239–40.

[49] See de Wilde, *Experiences with Agricultural Development* Vol. 1. Kigezi was included in the study, but the results from Kigezi were not ready at the time of publication and so there is no detailed discussion of the findings.

[50] Interviews with 95/Kab/20b, 95/Kal/90a, 95/Bub/92a, 95/Bub/98a and J.M. Byagagaire 21 Sept 1995. 95/Muy/24b, 95/Muy/63a, 95/Bub/91a, 95/Bub/92a. See also WPAR, 1933 and other Annual Reports.

[51] Purseglove, 'Kitozho Mutala Survey.' See also Edel, *The Chiga*, 2nd edition, 213.

[52] Sir Alexander Gibb and Partners (Africa), *Water Resources Survey in Uganda 1954–55* (Entebbe, 1956). PRO CO/822/886 (57/6/014).

[53] Report for Year 1935 by Wickham, KDA DC AGR-MNTH ff53. See also correspondence from 1930 in KDA MP105; 1936 KDA DoA 009-EXP-C and also WPAR, 1938. Food Crop Notes, Jan 1943, Kigezi, KDA DC MP4II ff165. See also Letter to Famine Commissioner from DC, 25 Feb 1943, KDA DC MP-EOC.

[54] For example see Letter to all Saza and Gomb Chfs from Duntze, DC, 7 Jan 1951, KDA DC AGR4II ff39. Letter to Dir of Ag from DAO, 17 Aug 1953, KDA DoA 6/A/3B ff12. Also Letter to All Agric Staff in Charge, Sazas from AO, 9 June 1955, KDA DC AGR4II

ff170 and Letter to all Saza Chfs and AOs from T.F. Ellis, DAO, 4 May 1962, KDA DC AGR4II ff189. 95/Muy/24b, 95/Muy/63a, 95/Bub/91a, 95/Bub/92a. Also 95/Kab/ 8a, 95/Kab/13a, 95/Kab/20b, 95/Kab/21b, 95/Kit/55a, 95/Kit/56a, 95/Muy/62a, 95/Kit/71a, 95/Kit/76a, 95/Kit/79a and 95/Bub/94a.

[55] Sir Alexander Gibb and Partners (Africa), *Water Resources Survey*. PRO CO/822/886 (57/6/014). For further details see Carswell, 'African Farmers'.

[56] N. Xavier, *Land Privatisation, Security of Tenure and Agricultural Production: The Ugandan experience* (Institute of Social Studies Working Paper), (The Hague 163, 1997), 16.

[57] Xavier, *Land Privatisation*. For further details of major legislation in the pre- and post independence period see also P.J. Nkambo Mugerwa 'Land tenure in East Africa – some contrasts', *East African Law Today* 5 (1966), 101–14. N. Bazaara, 'Civil society and the struggle for land rights for marginalized groups: the contribution of the Uganda Land Alliance to the Land Act 1998' (draft mimeo, no date. Produced for Civil Society and Governance Project, IDS and Ford Foundation.) Also see Roth *et al.*, *Tenure Security*.

[58] M. Marquardt and A. Sebina-Zziwa, 'Land reform in the making' in H.B. Hansen and M. Twaddle, *Developing Uganda* (Oxford, 1998), 177. See also J. Bosworth, 'Uganda Case Study' Paper presented at Regional Workshop on Land Issues in Africa, Kampala, 2002; W. Kisamba-Mugerwa, 'Institutional dimensions of land tenure reform' in H.B. Hansen and M. Twaddle (eds), *Changing Uganda* (London, 1991).

[59] H. Businge, 'Customary Land Tenure Reform in Uganda; Lessons for South Africa' *International Symposium on Communal Tenure Reform*, (Johannesburg, 2002), 2. A. Manji, 'Land Reform in the Shadow of the State: the implementation of new land laws in sub-Saharan Africa', *Third World Quarterly*, 22 3 (2001), 327–42.

[60] P. McAuslan, *Bringing the Law Back In: Essays in Land, Law and Development* (Aldershot, 2003), 281.

[61] MISR and LTC Wisconsin, *Land Tenure and Agricultural Development in Uganda* (Madison, WI, 1989). For a critique of this study see E. Ddungu, *A review of the MISR – Wisconsin Land Tenure Center Study on Land Tenure and Agriculture Development in Uganda*, CBR working paper 11 (Kampala, 1991).

[62] Roth, J.P. *et al.*, *Tenure Security*; see also Xavier, *Land Privatisation*, 49.

[63] See J.P. Platteau, 'The evolutionary theory of land rights', *Development and Change*, 27 (1996); C. Toulmin and J. Quan, *Evolving Land Rights* (London, 2000).

[64] S. Coldham, 'Land reform and customary rights: the case of Uganda', *Journal of African Law* 44 (2000), 67. See also McAuslan, *Bringing the Law Back In*, 283–5.

[65] P. McAuslan, 'Supporting local rights: will the centre let go? Reflections from Uganda and Tanzania', in Workshop report: *Securing Customary Land Tenure in Africa: Alternative approaches to the local recording and registration of land rights.* (Workshop held at IIED, 2000); R. Mwebaza, *How to Integrate Statutory and Customary Tenure: The Uganda case*, IIED Drylands Programme Issue paper, 83 (London, 1999). An early draft of the land bill implied the promotion of an entirely free market in land through the transformation of the whole country into individually-owned leasehold and freehold estates. Liz Wily has described it as 'one of the harshest transformations into western tenure yet seen in Africa, which would open the door to rapid accumulation and land speculation'. Quoted in R. Palmer, *Oxfam GB's Land Advocacy Work in Tanzania and Uganda: The End of an Era* (Oxford, 1998), 3.

[66] Coldham, 'Land reform and customary rights'. Businge, 'Customary Land Tenure Reform in Uganda', 6. In contrast, McAuslan says ownership could only be at individual or group level, and not at household or family level. McAuslan, *Bringing the Law Back In*, 287.

[67] Businge, 'Customary Land Tenure Reform in Uganda'.

[68] For a discussion of the process of amending the Bill in early 1998 and in particular re the 'Lost Amendment' see McAuslan, *Bringing the Law Back In*, Chapter 12. The Land Act (Amendment) Bill, 2003, introduced the concept of security of occupancy for spouses. See A. Tripp, 'Women's movements, customary law, and land rights in Africa: the case of Uganda', *African Studies Quarterly*, 7 4 (2004) [online]. Also D. Hunt, 'Unintended Consequences of Land Rights Reform: The Case of the 1998 Uganda Land Act', *Development Policy Review*, 22 2 (2004), 173-91.

[69] Manji, 'Land Reform in the Shadow of the State', 336. E. Nsamba-Gayiiya, *Implementing Land Tenure Reform in Uganda: A complex task ahead*, IIED Drylands Programme Issue paper 84 (London, 1999). The District Council will also have a District Land Office with Planner, Land Officers, Valuer, Surveyor and Registrar of Titles. Coldham, 'Land reform and customary rights'.

[70] Coldham, 'Land reform and customary rights', 70; McAuslan, *Bringing the Law Back In*, 315.

[71] McAuslan, *Bringing the Law Back In*, 287, 305.

[72] Busingye, 'Customary Land Tenure Reform in Uganda', 8. Palmer has noted that the problem of implementing new land reform has been overlooked, as attention has been on the debating and passing of new land laws. Palmer, 'Oxfam GB's land advocacy work in Tanzania and Uganda'.

[73] Manji ,'Land Reform in the Shadow of the State', 335.

[74] McAuslan, 'Supporting local rights', 1. For example, central government officials think they should have increasing resources over time (with district funds decreasing) and wanted the Land Fund to be the central component of the implementation process. But this Land Fund, set up through the Land Act to provide funds for people to acquire land, was found in a study by DfID to be 'unworkable'. It was argued that it should be abandoned.

[75] Nsamba-Gayiiya, *Implementing Land Tenure Reform*. McAuslan, *Bringing the Law Back In*, 324–5.

[76] Bosworth, 'Uganda Case study', 28–29. The Land Act Implementation Study concluded that implementing the Act was 'beyond the financial capacity of the Government of Uganda and even when modified in ways proposed in the Study, would still involve a considerable financial burden for the country in respect of which there were no clear and identifiable social or economic benefits to be gained', p. 327. The report was, however, 'more or less buried' by the Directorate of Lands and Environment (Ministry of Water, Lands and Environment) for whom, as McAuslan has shown, the Act 'turned the world upside down'. Overnight officials of the DLE had been stripped of their powers of land management which were vested in the District Land Boards, and this was accompanied by loss of control over resources (pp. 331–2). The DLE responded by fighting to maintain control over resources, a battle that they eventually won and having done so they allocated 80 per cent of projected funds to the centre and less than 20 per cent to the decentralised local agencies which were mandated by the Act to implement the Act (pp. 333–4). He concludes that 'Laws relating to land involve issues of governance … and governance involves the exercise of power and the use of public money by public officials. Any fundamental changes in those laws, particularly changes designed to remove powers from and therefore access to and use of public money by public officials are likely to be opposed by those officials unless they can see some specific benefits flowing to them from the reforms.' McAuslan, *Bringing the Law Back In*, 348.

[77] E.D. Green, 'Ethnic Politics and Land Tenure Reform in Central Uganda', LSE *DESTIN Working Paper*, 05-58 (2005); J. Adoko and S. Levine, 'A Land Market for Poverty Eradication? A case study of the impact of Uganda's Land Acts on policy hopes for development and poverty eradication' (Land and Equity Movement in Uganda, Kampala, *mimeo*, 2005). See also McAuslan, *Bringing the Law Back In*.

[78] The exceptions were a small number of certificates of occupancy granted to chiefs in the early colonial period. Some chiefs did try to gain land through their positions. On appointment chiefs used African Local Government (ALG) land, and there are a number of cases of chiefs attempting to continue using, or selling, ALG land when they retired or were transferred. See for example K KDA DC LAN8/6/1 ff69. Of the various disputes involving land and chiefs the best documented is Kalengyere (see Box 5.1) but there were others, such as a long and complex dispute that arose in 1956 between Ngologoza (Secretary General 1946–56) and Kitaburaza (who succeeded Ngologoza as Secretary General), (see KDA DC MIS 12 (Pt6) and KDA DC LAN 12-II ff95). There were also disputes over the enclosure of land by individuals (including chiefs) who did not own that land. (See KDA DC MIS 12, KDA DoA 154 ff50, and KDA DC AGR 6II ff119.)

[79] Memo drawn up by Kigezi Special Meeting held in Kabale Council Hall on 8–9 Dec

1953 to be presented to EARC through DC re land tenure in Kigezi, KDA DC LAN 12/ I ff29enc.

[80] Wright, 'Kitozho Mutala Survey.'

[81] Ngologoza, *Kigezi and Its People*, 74.

[82] Letter to DC from Rev. Orpwood (CMS) 3 Jan 1935, KDA DCMP57 ff83enc. While there was some disagreement as to whether Nkulikimana needed the land, colonial officials did not question the right of the chief to allocate the land. Draft reply to Orpwood from DC, KDA DC MP57 ff83enc. Probably drafted by ADC.

[83] Letter to PCWP from DC, 16 June 1937, KDA DC MP60A ff28.

[84] Purseglove, 'Kitozho mutala survey.' Emphasis added.

[85] Wright, 'Kitozho mutala survey', 14, 17.

[86] Kigezi pyrethrum scheme, written Kampala, 20 Dec 1955, KDA DC AGR3–7 ff2A. See also KDA DC MP4II, and PRO CO 537/1508 (40342/1). Enclosure to Lloyd S of S for C, 27 Jan 1941. PRO CO 536/208 40060 (Alienation of land) ff2 Table A – Return of Grants of Freehold and leases of land.Letter to HM Syndicate from Land Officer (E'be), 10 Dec 1952, KDA DC LAN 8I ff38. Interviews with 95/Kal/73a, 95/Kal/84a, 95/Kal/86a and 95/Kal/89a.For details see Carswell 'African Farmers'.

[87] Notes by NBC, March 1956 and by G.R. Barnes, Feb 1957. KDA DC Chiefs File. Letter to Chairman, Kigezi District Council from C.A.R. Mbuguje, Gomb Muko, 11 April 1955, KDA DC LAN8I ff154

[88] Letter to DC from DC Collin, Field Officer, Rubanda,3 June 1959, KDA DoA 154 ff70. Also KDA DoA 17A-2 ff257.

[89] 95/Kal/ 89a, 95/Kal/87a and 95/Kal/72a ; 95/Kal/85a, 95/Kal/89a, 95/Kal/83a and 95/Kal/84a. Statement read to the Appointments committee meeting of 19 July 1957. KDA DC Chiefs file. See also KDA DoA 012B ff37.

[90] Letter to A. Mbuguje Gomb Chf, Muko from SecGen, 13 July 1957. KDA DC LAN8I ff148. See also KDA DC LAN8I ff149. Letter to Ministry of Local Government from Mbuguje, 29 July 1957, KDA DC Chiefs File. Report dated 27 Sept 1957 by Sec Gen on visit to Kalengyere Estate on 25 Sept 1957. KDA DC LAN8I ff164. Letter to Sec Gen from Mbuguje, 1 April 1958, KDA DC LAN8I ff179. In addition to this there were also tree plantations. Letter to Sec Gen from Mbuguzhe (Gomb Muko), 15 Nov 1957. KDA DC LAN8I ff165. Letter to Ministry of Local Government from Mbuguje, 29 July 1957, KDA DC Chiefs File.

[91] Statement read to the Appointments committee meeting of 19 July 1957. KDA DC Chiefs file.

[92] At the time of allocation the government was supposedly relinquishing all rights of ownership of this land. However, from the 1970s there was renewed government interest in the land at Kalengyere as a possible site of a highland crop research station. In 1982 the Ministry of Agriculture was formally assigned the land, and evictions took place in the late 1980s, without any compensation being paid. Today the area forms the Kalengyere Highland Crops Research Station, under government administration. For further details see Carswell, 'African Farmers'. See also KDA DC AGR3–7 and 95/Kal/83a and 95/ Kal/72a.

[93] Purseglove, 'Report on the overpopulated areas of Kigezi district', 72.

[94] 'Problems in each district from Land Tenure and custom', Memo #6 – Notes on the System of Land Tenure in Kigezi, written by DC, 7 March 1953 (6pgs), Preliminary Information for the Royal Commission on Land and Population, 1953, PRO CO 892 15/9.

[95] Notes on Land Cases in Kigezi for Information of EARC, by APS Sheridan, ADC. KDA DC LAN 12/I ff32.

[96] *Ibid.*

[97] Letter to PCWP from DC, 29 March 1940, KDA DC MP60A ff32.

[98] Extracts from Kigezi District Council Minutes, KDA DC LAN 12/I ff69A. Resolution 14/51.

[99] 95/Kit/82a.

[100] Memo put forward to EARC on Shifting Cultivation in Western Province, by Purseglove, 16 Oct 1951 (33 pp. + appendices), PRO CO 892 15/7.

[101] Note on 'Land. Insufficiency, round Kabale, for population.' 1929. KDA DC MP69 ff34.

[102] 'Problems in each district from Land Tenure and custom', Memo #6 – Notes on the System of Land Tenure in Kigezi, written by DC, 7 March 1953 (6pp.), Preliminary Information for the Royal Commission on Land and Population, 1953, PRO CO 892 15/9. Purseglove, 'Report on the Overpopulated Areas of Kigezi', para 68. Purseglove drew heavily on Wright's *mutala* survey in his description of the early colonial Bakiga land tenure system.

[103] Extracts from Kigezi District Council Minutes, KDA DC LAN 12/I ff69A. Resolution 6/52. Chiefs were also given some powers over land in relation to the policy of 'farm planning'. For further details see Carswell, 'African Farmers'.

[104] Oral evidence collected at Meeting of Hudson, Gaitskell and Sykes of the EARC and the Standing Committee, Kigezi Local Government, 22 Dec 1953, PRO CO 892 16/6, Memo #18, evidence of Ngologoza, SecGen. Memo drawn up by Kigezi Special Meeting held in Kabale Council Hall on 8–9 Dec 1953 to be presented to EARC through DC re land tenure in Kigezi, KDA DC LAN 12/I ff29enc. In readiness for the arrival of the EARC efforts were made to gather relevant information and a meeting, attended by senior chiefs and others, was held with DC to discuss Land Tenure see: Letter to DC from Sec Gen, 5 Dec 1953, KDA DC LAN 12/I ff22.

[105] Land Tenure Policy: Grant of Title: Kigezi. Record of Meeting held at Kabale, 29 March 1957 (Confidential) PRO CO 822/1407 ff7.

[106] Letter to Mathieson from Lawrance, 7 Nov 1957, 25 Oct 1957, PRO CO 822/1407 ff18. Another reference to 'clan elders' came from Watts, a member of the Lands and Survey Department, who referred to the adjudication process saying that 'The original grants were decided by clan leaders on the basis of occupation and ratified at huge meetings on the ground.' Papers of Mrs A.G. Watts (née Budge) (Worked in Lands and Survey Dept 1945–47 and 1955–60) – Women Administrative Officers in Colonial Africa; Uganda: RH MSS Afr s 1799, Box VIII (40).

[107] Record of a Meeting between the Minister of Land and Min Devt and General Purposes Committee and Land Tenure Committee of the Kigezi District Council on 5 Jan 1960. KDA DC ADM 9/7 ff46enc. Also see Record of Meeting of Kigezi District Council Standing Committee, 5 Jan 1960 KDA DC ADM 9/7 ff46.

[108] Similarly Vokes recounts how today people will turn either to the LC system for dispute settlement, or to other individuals outside the system who have a good reputation for settling such cases. Vokes,'The Kanungu Fire' (2003), 83–5.

[109] See 95/Muy/59a, 95/Kab/1b and 95/Muy/30b.

[110] F. Mackenzie, 'Land tenure and biodiversity', *Human Organization*, 62 3 (2003), 258.

[111] By the time that a 'new' type of chief was more widely in place (younger and, more importantly, literate) the powers of the chiefs were being restricted, which occurred from the late 1940s or early 1950s. See Baxter, 'The Kiga' and K.T. Connor, 'Kigezi', in J.D. Barkan, *et al.*, *Uganda District Government and Politics, 1947-1967* (Madison, WI, 1977).

[112] Quoted in enclosure to letter to DC from P.P. Howell, Min of Natural Resources, 20 March 1957, KDA DC DEV4–5A ff147Enc. For further details of Kigezi's experience of swamp reclamation see Carswell 'African Farmers'.

[113] Letter to Perm Sec Natural Resources from DC, 6 Nov 1957, KDA DC DEV4–5A ff188. See also ff147Enc and ff166. Draft Memo by Ministry of Natural Resources. Water Resources Sub Committee re Work in Kigezi, 24 Oct 1957, KDA DC DEV4–5A ff181.

[114] Natural Resources Committee – Land Use Sub-Committee, Entebbe, 6 Jan 1958. KDA DoA 001/2 ff18. Minute of Water Resources Sub-Committee, Min of Natural Resources, 6 May 1959, KDA DC DEV4–5B ff69.

[115] Minutes of Natural Resources Sub Committee of Kigezi District Team on 7 Sept 1959. KDA DoA Team mins. Committees were to be made up of three administrative officers (ADC, Water Devt Officer, Field Officer) *saza* chief, and the relevant *gombolola* chiefs. KDA DC DEV4–5B ff68. Also KDA DoA 218–A ff55. Some Committees also had *miruka* chiefs on them. KDA DC DEV4–5B ff147.

[116] Memo on Swamp Land issued by DC to all Saza and Gomb Chfs, 22 Jan 1960, KDA DC DEV4–5B ff111.

[117] Some Observations on Swamp Reclamation in Kigezi. Recommendations of the Consulting Engineers. Written by P.P. Howell 14 March 1957. KDA DC DEV4–5A ff147Enc. See also Sir Alexander Gibb and Partners, *Water Resources Survey in Uganda*, PRO CO/822/886 (57/6/014).

[118] Minutes of Natural Resources Sub Committee of Kigezi District Team on 2 Nov 1959 Minute 14/59 – Swamp Reclamation. KDA DoA TeamMins. This Sub-Committee consisted of DC, DAO, Sec Gen, DVO, Field Officers, Forestry Superintendent.

[119] Memo on Swamp Land issued by DC to all Saza and Gomb Chfs, 22 Jan 1960, KDA DC DEV4–5B ff111.

[120] Minutes of Natural Resources Sub Committee of Kigezi District Team on 2 Nov 1959. KDA DoA Team mins. Memo on Swamp Land issued by DC to all Saza and Gomb Chfs, 22 Jan 1960, KDA DC DEV4–5B ff111. Indeed this was the argument that Batuma used to explain why he was allocated more land. 95/Kab/99a.

[121] Letter to County Chfs Rukiga, Ndorwa, Rubanda from DC, 22 July 1961, KDA DC DEV4–5B ff152. Letter to Gomb Chfs of Kashambya, Buhara, Kamuganguzi, Kitumba, Bubale, Ikumba from DC, 10 June 1960, KDA DC DEV4–5B ff117. Extract from Minutes of Meeting of Natural Resources Sub-Comm, 3 July 1961, KDA DC DEV4–5B ff151.

[122] Letter to Saza Chf Ndorwa, Collin (Field Officer), Kabega (Water Devt Eng); Gomb Chfs Buhara, Kamuganguzi and Kitumba, 23 May 1959, KDA DC DEV4–5B ff70. Memo on Swamp Land issued by DC to all Saza and Gomb Chfs, 22 Jan 1960, KDA DC DEV4–5B ff111. For further details about opposition to reclamation from some *gombolola* councils, and successful colonial attempts to overturn this opposition see Carswell, 'African Farmers'. These concerns were largely because of the need to maintain supplies of papyrus and other grasses. See also KDA DC DEV 4–5D ff. 40.

[123] Letter to Saza Chief from Exec Eng WDD, 3 July 1961, KDA DC DEV4–5B ff150. The outcome of this dispute is unclear. Letter to DC from Saza Chf Ndorwa, 13 July 1961, KDA DC DEV4–5B ff153.

[124] Memo by ADC re Minutes of Swamp Comm Meeting held at Kashambya Gomb HQ on 21 Aug 1961, KDA DoA 218-B ff98. 95/Kab/6a. Also see interviews with 95/Kab/ 8a, 95/Kab/22a, 95/Muy/24a, 95/Muy/24b, 95/Muy/26a, 95/Muy/27a, 95/ Muy/ 28a, 95/ Muy/29a, 95/ Muy/30b and 95/Muy/32b. 95/Muy/57a, 95/Muy/58a, 95/Muy/59a, 95/Muy/61a, 95/Muy/62a and 95/Muy/63a.

[125] See for example Minutes of Kashambya Swamp Comm, 5 April 1962, KDA DC DEV4/5C ff225. Letter to Saza Chf Ndorwa from DC, 18 Oct 1961, KDA DC DEV4/ 5C ff180. In this case one of the churches had acquired more than 5 acres of swampland, and argued to be allowed to keep it all. See Carswell, 'African Farmers'. Letter to DAO from Asst AO, Rukiga, 9 Jan 1962. KDA DoA 218-B ff153. Also see Minutes of Meeting of Kashambya Swamp Comm, 20 Jan 1962, KDA DC DEV4/5C ff205.

[126] Letter to DC from Kitaburuza, SecGen, 12 March 1959, KDA DC DEV4–5B ff54. Letter Saza Chief, Ndorwa from Collin, Field Officer, 12 March 1960, KDA DC DEV4–5B ff112.

[127] Minutes of Natural Resources Sub Committee of Kigezi District Team on 7 Sept 1959. KDA DoA Team mins. Letter to DC from Gomb Chf Bubale, 12 Sept 1959, KDA DC DEV4–5B ff91. John Batuma trained to be a veterinary assistant and worked in various parts of Uganda, before returning to work for the Veterinary Department in Kabale. His land at Bubale is a plot of 160 acres on which he has a freehold title. In total he has about 240 acres of which some he described as being 'leased'. Interview with John Batuma, 14 Sept 1995 (95/Kab/95a).

[128] Minutes of Natural Resources Sub Committee of Kigezi District Team on 7 Sept 1959. KDA DoA Teammins.

[129] Record of Meeting on Land Allocation in Kiruruma North Swamp held at Bubale Gomb HQs on 14 Sept 1959, KDA DC DEV4–5B ff90. At this meeting the committee was appointed. It consisted of the saza chief Rubanda, the Field Officer Rubanda, gomb chief Bubale and two Bubale councillors.

[130] Letter to Saza Chf Rubanda from DC, 30 Nov 1959, KDA DC ADM 9/7 ff26. See also KDA DC DEV4–5B ff143. Claiming reclaimed land before it had been allocated

continued to occur – for example in June 1961 'large numbers' of people moved into recently cleared swamp. (Letter to Saza Chf Rubanda, from DC, 14 June 1961, KDA DC DEV4–5B ff145.) Allocation by the chief was hastily arranged, with 80 people being allocated land. Letter to DAO from Gomb Chf Bubale, 27 June 1961, KDA DoA 218 - B, ff72. Throughout 1961 official policy that no-one should cultivate the swamp before it had been allocated continued to be re-stated, but this was not universally applied.

[131] Batuma was on the Kiruruma North Swamp Committee by virtue of being a councillor in the area (KDA DC Dev4–5B ff147) and was on the Rubanda Swamp Committee as a Veterinary Assistant. He was actually Veterinary Asst of Ndorwa and had managed to get on the Swamp Committee of Rubanda, because the Veterinary Asst Rubanda did not have much experience in swamps. (Letter to Saza Chf Rubanda from J.C. Allen, DVO Kigezi, 8 Dec 1961, KDA DC DEV4/5C ff190). 95/Kab/94a. KDA DC DEV4–5A ff158. Another government employee was the Asst AO mentioned in R.J. Tindituuza, 'Study on Land Tenure at Nyarurambi Parish'. See Carswell, 'African Farmers'.

[132] Various interviews in Bubale, 1995. Names obscured to protect the confidence of the informants.

[133] For example Mujingo and Nyakashezo. Letter to Saza Chief, Ndorwa from Collin, Field Officer (Ag), 12 March 1960, KDA DC DEV4–5B ff112. See also Letter to Gomb Chfs of Buhara and Kashambya from Kitaburaza Sec Gen, 7 Nov 1960, KDA DC DEV4–5B ff130. See also interview with J.M. Byagagaire, 21 Sept 1995. (95/Kam/100a)

[134] KDA DC DEV4–5B ff120 onwards. Also see Letter to Gomb Chf Bubale, from saza Chf Rubanda, 20 Oct 1960, KDA DC DEV4–5B ff129. This was a particular problem around Bubale: Minute of Natural Resources Comm, 5 Sept 1960 Minute 30/60 – Swamp Reclamation ff129A. Also see Letter to Saza Chf Ndorwa from DC, 24 Aug 1960, re meeting at Bubale on 20 Aug 1960 re planting trees, KDA DC DEV4–5B ff126.

[135] Letter to Gomb Chf Bubale and Saza Chf Rubanda, from DC, 17 Jan 1961, KDA DC DEV4–5B ff134.

[136] For further details about allocation and distribution of swamp land in Kashambya, Kiruruma South and Kiruruma North swamps see Carswell, 'African Farmers'.

[137] Some swampland was owned by cooperatives in the early post-colonial period. Most later entered private hands, but how it was originally given to coops, and then how it got into private hands, is unclear.

[138] Fears were expressed about losing the resources that the swamps held, particularly papyrus. July 1948 – Monthly reports of the Dept of Agriculture, KDA DoA 007. Letter to DC from Kakwenza, Saza Chf Ndorwa, 19 Jan 1953, KDA DC DEV4–4II ff124. For further details see Carswell, 'African Farmers'.

[139] Yngstrom, 'Women, wives and land rights', 24; Mackenzie, 'Land tenure and biodiversity'; Berry, *No Condition is Permanent.*

[140] Pottier, 'Customary land tenure', 71; H. Musahara and C. Huggins, 'Land reform, land scarcity and post-conflict reconstruction: A case study of Rwanda', in C. Huggins and J. Clover (eds), *From the Ground Up: Land rights, conflict and peace in Sub-Saharan Africa* (Pretoria, 2005); P. Peters, 'Inequality and social conflict over land in Africa', *Journal of Agrarian Change* (2004) 3 1/2: 269–314.

Six

Changes
in the Agricultural System

Having examined colonial encounters with Kigezi agriculture in terms of attempts to introduce cash crops, soil conservation measures and land reform and the responses to these measures by local populations, I will now look in more detail at the agricultural system of Kigezi. Questions about the sustainability of Kigezi's agricultural system, and specifically about its ability to cope with an increased population, were raised from the earliest colonial period, and continue to the present.[1] Drawing on evidence from a study conducted by Purseglove in 1945, and a repeat survey conducted by the author and a team of researchers in 1996,[2] I examine land use change over this period.

With its dense population and intensive agricultural production system, Kigezi has a reputation as an over-populated district that would experience severe environmental damage if no interventions were made.[3] These apparently indisputable beliefs go back many decades: during both the colonial and post-colonial periods concerns about sustainability have been continually reiterated, and the concept of Kigezi as an 'over-populated' district on the verge of disaster is one that has become firmly entrenched in the minds of both researchers and Bakiga themselves. However, while there is clear evidence that the population of the district has grown consistently, none of the envisaged environmental disasters has struck. Predictions of major environmental catastrophe, food deficit and the unsustainability of the agricultural system, have not materialised. Rather, it appears that the district has successfully avoided such problems and absorbed an increasing rural population. These two factors taken together would lead us to infer that local farmers have found ways of managing their land in such a way that productivity is maintained whilst serious degradation is avoided.

Examining agricultural change over a 50-year period, I argue that, contrary to various models of intensification, to popular belief and to the opinions of many researchers, fallow periods have increased in terms of both length and frequency. The models of agricultural change that the chapter draws on include the one by Esther Boserup[4] which argued that population growth

151

and increasing population density are a stimulus for both a reduction in fallow and the introduction of innovations associated with intensified land use. According to this view, provided the rate of population increase is not too rapid, people will adapt their environment and cultivation practices and so increase yields without degrading the resource base. This counters the more pessimistic 'agricultural involution' model associated with Geertz.[5] With this model agricultural output is maintained under increased population pressure by increasing the input of labour, so that while output per hectare increases, output per capita does not. No new methods are introduced, but existing methods are intensified, thus giving rise to diminishing returns to labour. Contending that Kigezi farmers have successfully and sustainably increased agricultural production, I contribute to debates concerning positive land use changes associated with increasing population densities.[6]

Other studies have also shown that established opinion about environmental problems may be poorly founded. These have resonance for Kigezi as policies founded on environmental orthodoxies, narratives and received wisdoms have proved both harmful to African farmers and ineffective in ecological terms.[7] These 'received wisdoms' have had the effect of promoting external intervention in the control and use of natural resources, which in turn can have negative consequences for local people.

Population and environment narratives

Kigezi's reputation as an area suffering from the effects of overpopulation is deeply ingrained.[8] From the time the British first arrived in the district, agriculturalists and environmentalists have written extensively about the threat of environmental disaster.[9] The earliest concerns expressed by colonial officials were about land shortage and over-population. In the 1920s it was observed that land in Kigezi was intensively cultivated and 'barely suffices for present needs'.[10] By the mid-1930s the problems being discussed focused more specifically on the threat of soil exhaustion and the problem of reduced fallow. These concerns need to be seen in the context of a growing obsession with soil erosion, and the threat of land degradation resulting from high population growth, that was occurring all over colonial Africa from the 1930s.[11] There are a number of studies showing how these environmental concerns played a major influence in the formulation of agricultural policy across East Africa.[12]

Concerns about the threat of soil erosion were expressed at a district level from the late 1920s, and in 1935 Wickham, the DAO, commented on problems of overpopulation and soil exhaustion. He specifically drew attention to the fact that fallow was not being included in the rotation at proper intervals. [13] Later DAOs expressed similar concerns throughout the 1930s and 1940s. One of these officials, Purseglove, proved to be particularly influential, and following his detailed survey of Kigezi's 'overpopulated' areas he stated that 'although serious erosion is not yet a problem we cannot afford to be complacent and wait for it to become so'. He concluded that the area around Kabale could not continue to support an increasing population and that it would be 'most unwise to continue under the present conditions in the hope that further soil deterioration and erosion will not take place'.[14] These findings confirmed the earlier fears that serious environmental degradation was likely to occur in the area unless dramatic steps were taken, and soil conservation policies and a resettlement scheme were put forward in response, as discussed in Chapter 3. In the case of soil conservation policies, Kigezi presents a rather unusual case, as here soil conservation measures were implemented successfully, with little resistance from local populations, in contrast to other parts of colonial Africa.

The reputation that Kigezi gained in the colonial period is one that it has never been able to shake off. Rather, it has been continually reiterated and elaborated upon and the environmental degradation narrative remains little changed. The views of colonial officials about 'primitive' agricultural systems are perhaps not surprising in the context of the colonial system, but it is striking how little this has changed in the post-colonial period: indeed statements made in the 1990s could be almost verbatim quotes from colonial reports written 50 or 60 years earlier.

In the immediate post-independence period influential writers such as Allan commented on the 'very serious congestion' in Kigezi, observing how 'all the usual symptoms of over-population' were evident, including 'almost continuous cultivation and consequent soil degradation, subdivision and excessive fragmentation of land'.[15] Studies conducted by Makerere University staff reiterated the familiar concerns, adopting the same environmental degradation narrative. Thus, for example, Kagambirwe observed that soil had deteriorated, referring to 'an assumption that there is considerable population pressure on the land'. Without questioning this assumption he refers to 'the cry for land for cultivation' and the 'exhausted hillslopes', thus adopting the same environmental degradation narrative.[16] Other Makerere studies conducted in the 1970s include that by Langlands, who noted that population pressure in some parts of the district was such that 'it is improbable that further increases could take place under existing technological practices', while Kateete observed that fallowing was limited due to too much pressure on land. [17]

After a lull in research outputs in the 1980s, research and publication began again in the late 1980s and 1990s and again the picture presented is similar to that of the 1940s and 1950s. These reports and publications espouse a neo-Malthusian environmental narrative which suggests that over-population leads to severe land shortage, which in turn leads to reductions in fallow, increasing soil erosion and reducing fertility. The 'failings' of local people are often implicit in the statements made. Thus Joy Tukahirwa has written that in the highlands of Uganda high population growth has led to heavy pressures on the highland environment, and points in particular to:

indiscriminate cutting and burning of vegetation, over-cultivation and overgrazing, and ... lack of attention of soil erosion control measures. ... soils are overcultivated with very little fallow. [18]

These observations, however, are not based on any scientific data and in fact no source for them is cited. Similarly, the 1994 *State of the Environment Report* for Uganda claims that the major causes of soil erosion and degradation were 'poor farming practices and high population pressure.'[19] The report notes that in Rukiga county 'soil erosion and degradation has reached alarming proportions on steep slopes due to poor cultivation techniques.' It is, quite simply, the farmers' fault.

A number of researchers have focused on the dangers associated with shortening fallow. Were has noted that 'fallow periods have become too short to allow soil to regenerate. ... The decreasing use of fallow system to restore soil fertility and lack of effective soil conservation measures combine to threaten the region's food security.'[20] Were reached these conclusions despite his own findings that 77 per cent of farmers said they had some of their land under fallow, and he was not able to support his claim that fallow periods had decreased. Other studies make similar claims, often without substantiation.[21]

Donor agencies have also adopted these beliefs about reduced fallow. CARE International, which works with farmers living in the vicinity of two National Parks in southwest Uganda, notes that 'with serious soil degradation from continuous cultivation and soil erosion, crop production is now declining in most areas . . . Traditional fallowing practices could conserve soil and restore fertility but fallowing has largely been abandoned because of increasing land pressure.'[22] Other agencies make similar assumptions: the International Centre for Research on Agroforestry (ICRAF), which has a project operating in Kabale District under their Agroforestry Research Networks for Africa (AFRENA) programme, has noted:

> Permanent cultivation, with short rotation periods, prevails. ... Soil deterioration and crop yields decline are a common consequence of such farming practices ... The sustainability ... [of the system of agriculture] is seriously threatened by the rapid decline in soil fertility ... The reduction in farm size long ago resulted in the abandonment of fallowing practices and continuous cultivation is now common in the area.[23]

But it is not only outside agencies which have adopted this environmental narrative. Today's DAO observes that 'fields are cropped every season without a rest' while the *District Environment Profile* records that 'there is continuous cultivation of land without rest leading to soil degradation and exhaustion.' Again, the negative role of people is observed: 'soil erosion has also largely been accelerated by human activities. The district experiences continuous cropping of land without ample rest and ... is carried out without appropriate soil and water conservation measures.'[24]

But despite being described in apocalyptic terms for over fifty years, this densely populated area of Uganda has not succumbed to serious environmental catastrophe and the extent of environmental degradation in the district is highly debatable. What then is the evidence for this neo-Malthusian narrative? The existence of Purseglove's detailed land use survey, conducted in 1945, enabled us to test some of these statements, and in particular to examine changing patterns of fallow use.

Two land use surveys – 1945 and 1996

In January 1945 Purseglove, the DAO, carried out a detailed land use survey in southern Kigezi to assess whether the area was overpopulated, and if so to what extent. The study was carried out to provide empirical support for colonial policy and provided a spring board for the stepping up of the soil conservation policies and resettlement programme of the mid-1940s explored in Chapter 3 above. Purseglove conducted 14 transects totalling more than 34 miles (52 km) in the southern part of Kigezi (in the area within a 12-mile radius of Kabale town) to measure the land under cultivation, swamps or woodlots (see Map 6.1). Along these transects he calculated the slope of each piece of land, recorded land use (whether under cultivation, crop combinations, swamps or woodlots) and estimated the length of time which land had been left to fallow (by looking at weed types). He randomly selected 34 households and collected information on household size, livestock, income-generating activities, crops stored, total acreage and number of plots.

A repeat survey was conducted in January 1996 by the author and a team of researchers following (and elaborating) Purseglove's methodology. All 14 of Purseglove's original transects were relocated and the survey repeated. Land use along the transect was recorded and length of fallow estimated (using a weed succession table based on that of Purseglove). In addition, household interviews were conducted with fifty households living along the transect, gathering information about their land and farming methods. Information was also gathered through 'field interviews', community Rapid Rural Appraisals and interviews to gather information on land holdings, livelihood strategies and farm management practices. This range of methods enabled us to collect quantitative information on land use change since 1945, community perceptions of change, and detailed field histories as recalled by individual farmers. The two surveys were carried out in the same month, used the same methodology, and covered the same territory, and the study thus set up a diachronic comparison that enabled an assessment to be made of land use and agriculture at two points in time over a 51-year period. [25] These findings will be discussed here, while the broader effects of changes to the agricultural system are discussed in the following chapter.

Land use change over fifty years

The results of the research were surprising and suggested that land use had changed in unexpected ways. Changes in land use over the 51-year period are summarised in Figure 6.1.

Cultivated land was, as would be expected, the predominant land use in both 1945 and 1996. But perhaps surprisingly, given the significant increase

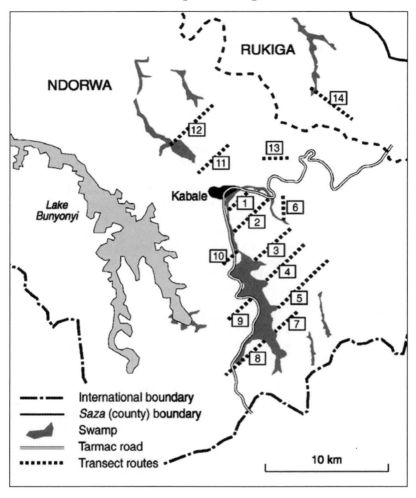

Map 6.1 *Southern Kigezi, showing transects followed in 1945 and 1996*

Figure 6.1 *Changes in land use: 1945 to 1996*[26]

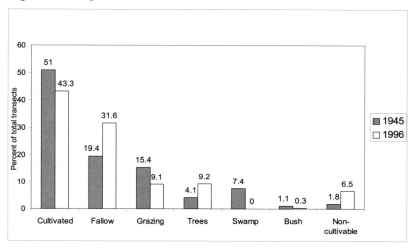

in population over this period, the proportion of land cultivated had fallen from 51 per cent to 43 per cent. Related to this is the most striking finding: that of changes in the proportion of land being fallowed.

FALLOW

The survey found that the proportion of land left to fallow increased from 19 per cent in 1945 to 32 per cent in 1996. This was entirely unexpected, particularly given the overwhelming belief that fallow has declined or disappeared altogether. But household interviews confirmed the findings, suggesting that 29 per cent of land was being rested at the time of the interview. Thus this result is verified, with a high degree of confidence, because more than one method of data collection was used. Furthermore, not only has the proportion of land left to fallow increased, but also the length of time that fields are rested has also increased, as is shown in Figure 6.2.

This shows a clear shift in the pattern of fallowing. In 1945 just under 50 per cent of fallow land was being rested for less than 6 months, and by 1996 almost all land being fallowed (95 per cent) was being rested for more than 6 months, most of it being rested for between 6 months and a year. The average time land was left to fallow increased from 9.4 months in 1945, to 14.2 months in 1996. [27]

Whether land was fallowed or not depended on a range of factors, including the plot location (in particular, distance from the homestead) and the size of the household's total landholdings. Fields far from the homestead were more likely to be resting and other farm management practices that require little labour, such as the construction of trash lines, were more common on distant plots, while those requiring a lot of labour (use of manure, compost) decreased

Figure 6.2 *Changes in fallow length: 1945 – 1996*[28]

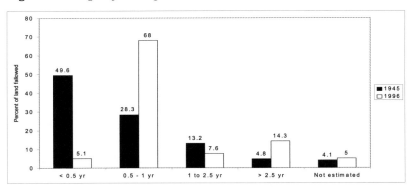

rapidly with distance from the homestead. Other practices, such as mulching and incorporating crop residues, were similar on all fields irrespective of distance to plot.

Significantly, not all households are fallowing land equally. On the contrary, it appears that while more land is being fallowed, this is predominantly the land of the richest and the poorest of the population. The survey found that households with most land fallowed the most, but significantly those with least land also fallowed a lot. The largest landowners (of 11 acres and above) had 31 per cent of their land under fallow; owners of 5–11 acres had 17 per cent fallowed, and owners of less than 5 acres had 25 per cent of land fallowed.[29] Households that are land-rich are able to fallow because they have sufficient land, they know the benefits it gives to the land, and they can afford to leave greater portions of it fallow. In order to make up for the loss of productivity associated with leaving land out of production, these households hire labour to increase production through labour intensive methods: intercropping, weeding more, etc. In addition, some richer households rest their own land, and at the same time rent additional land. The vibrant rental market for land enables them to do this, and also enables households to take advantage of ecological 'niches', for example cultivating particular crops in swamps.[30]

At the other end of the scale those with *least* land also fallow but for very different reasons. They have very little land, but are actually working it less intensively: they fallow it more, and intercrop less. This is essentially because of labour shortages: as we will see in the following chapter, they are working so hard as wage labourers on the land of richer households that they have less time to invest in their own land. While the high fallowing of the land of poorer households may be good for environmental sustainability (with more fallowing seen to be a 'good' thing), it may not be so good for livelihoods. This is because productivity is also probably lower because they are also intercropping less and not investing labour in weeding, etc. Furthermore, we find that these poorer households buy in a greater proportion of their food:[31]

they are coping through high involvement in the market, by selling their labour, and buying their food.

Households in the middle are a particularly interesting category. This group seem to work their land more (and thus fallow less) compared to those in the poorest or wealthiest categories, and this may have a negative impact on environmental sustainability. [32] Therefore, if environmental sustainability is the main concern, then it is probably this group of farmers that policy-makers should focus on. While many of them still need to supplement their incomes with off-farm income, such as working on the land of richer households, it will be seen in the following chapter that they are able to get involved in wage labour through arrangements that have much higher returns than the poorest households.

Some of the loss of production from increased fallow may be recouped through increased intercropping. The proportion of fields with two or more crops at the same time increased from 37 per cent in 1945 to 47 per cent in 1996. Others have also observed that loss of production resulting from land being taken out of production is 'made up' through intercropping. Grisley and Mwesigwa found that a significant number of households used fallowing as a fertility improvement methodology and that 'intensification of production through intercropping was directly related to an increase in fallowing.' [33] Of the farms they surveyed 76 per cent had some cropland in grass fallow, with 26 per cent of the total crop land under fallow. Although the authors observe that 'fallow periods may be reduced or even eliminated to satisfy an increase in the demand for food,' which is the widely held belief about the situation in Kabale, they go on to say, 'at the same time, however, as soil fertility deteriorates from more intensive use, households may be forced to resort to more, not less, fallowing to maintain a viable level of fertility.'

Other changes in land use uncovered by the survey provide further evidence that challenges the neo-Malthusian narrative. We found that, rather than population growth having led to a depletion of woody biomass, the area covered by woodlots had more than doubled, from 4.1 per cent in 1945 to 9.2 per cent in 1996. This supports other work in East[34] and West Africa[35] that suggests that higher population densities are associated with higher woody biomass. While it is usually assumed that deforestation has occurred as a result of relatively recent population pressure,[36] there is evidence that this occurred much longer ago. While agriculture concomitant with more permanent settlements was probably established around 2,000 years ago,[37] Taylor and Marchant note that forest clearance was highly localised and that lower altitudes were permanently cleared of forest about 1000 years ago, while higher altitudes were cleared before then.[38] Thus by the time colonial officials arrived, forests had long been cleared and hence the population increase of the past century cannot be blamed for Kigezi's deforestation. Furthermore, today it is often assumed that the planting of trees by farmers is a new practice introduced from outside.[39] But, in contradiction of such beliefs, farmers have actually been growing trees for many decades. Evidence from colonial archives suggests that in the early 1930s woodlots were common, 'coppices of wattle trees, planted on the hill-tops, along the roads, and around the homestead,' forming 'a marked feature of the landscape'.[40] A striking two-thirds of families surveyed in southern Kigezi in 1935–6 had their own source of wood fuel – mainly black wattle plots (*Acacia meansi; burikoti*).[41] Today eucalyptus (*Eucalyptus spp; karutusi*) is the preferred tree crop, and these are planted in wood lots and along boundaries.

SWAMPS

The policy of swamp reclamation and the opportunities it offered for individuals to gain access to additional land were explored in the previous chapter. Here, the implications of changes to swamp usage for the agricultural system itself will be explored. At the time of the 1945 survey 7.4 per cent of land surveyed was classified as natural swamp, with the majority of swamp (85 per cent) being undrained. [42] But by 1996 there had been a dramatic change, and the survey confirmed that agriculture had been extended into previously uncultivated swampland, with just 0.05 per cent of land surveyed classified as natural swamps. What had once been swamp is now being put to use: 51.3 per cent being used for grazing; 8.5 per cent for cultivation; 39.1 per cent 'currently resting'; and 0.6 per cent for trees. [43] In the early 1940s swamps were largely uncultivated as the labour required to drain them was too large to render this a viable option. However, about a decade later the situation in some areas had changed and swamp cultivation was taking place with the support of the colonial state. Those with plentiful household labour, and those with cash incomes who could employ waged labour, were thus able to cultivate the swamps. The latter were often employees of the colonial state, who had better access to knowledge about the potential of swamps for cultivation. By 1996, with virtually all swampland in the district cultivated or grazed, there is no more land to extend cultivation into.

The extension of agriculture into reclaimed wetlands may have recouped some of the loss of production resulting from increases in fallow discussed above. Cultivation is an important use to which swampland is put – 8.5 per cent of swamps are currently cultivated, while 39.1 per cent are resting.[44] The most popular crops grown on swamps are Irish potatoes and sweet potatoes (grown on raised beds) (see photo 5.2) and maize and commercial vegetables. But more important is grazing, and today just over half of swamps are grazed, and the use of valley bottoms for grazing in the 1990s is in stark contrast to grazing patterns in 1945. Overall the survey found that there was a decline in the proportion of land used for grazing, associated with a change in the areas used for grazing with a switch from marginal land on steep back slopes in the 1940s to valley pastures reclaimed from swamps in 1996. In 1996 grazing land was predominantly (75 per cent) located in reclaimed swamps and this shift has also been associated with changing patterns of livestock ownership, and in particular increased differentiation. Many of the relatively small number of farmers who gained access to swamp land have converted it into high quality pasture, and since the 1960s the rearing of exotic cattle for milk production has become a feature of the district's wetlands.

While this may have had positive impacts on the area's overall agricultural productivity, two points need to be highlighted. The first is around issues of differentiation and distribution, and will be explored in the following chapter, while the second is around the environmental impacts of reclamation.

The reclamation of swamps has undoubtedly had a negative impact on biodiversity, and this is an issue highlighted by international conservation agencies in recent years.[45] The extent of the ecological significance of this loss and the impact of draining wetlands on other aspects of environmental quality, such as water quality and quantity, microclimate and soil fertility in the former wetlands has not been evaluated. [46] Nor is it possible to say whether drainage of wetlands has degraded the economic productivity of land in the district. Kigezi has experienced a long history of concerns about environmental sustainability, which in most policy arenas has resulted in a strong degree of continuity of policy.[47] In the case of swamps, however, there has been a complete reversal of policy. While in the colonial (and early independence) period the rhetoric around overpopulation and land shortage led to swamps being reclaimed to provide additional land, today they (now called wetlands) are being protected due to concerns about the protection of biodiversity. But such concerns are to a large degree externally driven by international conservation organisations such as IUCN, which has been heavily involved in the wetlands programme. This reversal of policy reflects broader continuities with the colonial period in the articulation of development narratives. Whilst the particular narrative has shifted, the momentum for that shift, as with earlier narratives on soil conservation, land degradation and so forth, has occurred from outside the country.[48] It is striking that in both the colonial and independence periods development narratives have been created from outside, and imposed by external agencies without sufficient regard for local conditions. [49] Paradoxically, the expression of concerns about biodiversity in swamps came too late, as, by the time they were being articulated, most of the swamps had already been drained.

SOIL EROSION & FERTILITY

A key element of the neo-Malthusian narratives is that high population pressure has had negative consequences on soil fertility and erosion. What is the evidence that soil erosion is a serious problem? The one significant published survey to which many reports refer is that by Bagoora, who surveyed four areas within one *gombolola* of Kabale District. Although a measure of soil erosion was calculated (number of landslide scars per square kilometre), the hills that were investigated were purposively selected as areas on which severe erosion could be visually identified. Furthermore, while the study area was quite small, results were generalised not only to the region of Kigezi but to all highland areas in Uganda. Despite the limitations of this study, Bagoora concluded:

> Most slopes are seriously affected by all forms of soil erosion and conservation measures are needed to prevent irreversible calamity. ...

The highlands of Kigezi are a particularly noteworthy example of the induced risk of accelerated erosion in Uganda ... This form of land use [in practice in Kigezi] has done indelible damage to nature in some parts of the highlands. [50]

This study is cited by almost every author who writes about soil erosion in south-western Uganda and is often their only source that attempts any objective quantification of the extent of soil erosion. The small, purposively selected sample cannot, however, be assumed to be representative of the district. [51]

Although it was not possible to assess changes in soil fertility, due to lack of comparative data, current assessment of soil fertility was possible. Analysis of 151 soil samples collected from plots along the transects found that 'according to standards for tropical soils, except for phosphorus, most of the samples were above the critical levels of other nutrients; less than two per cent of samples were deficient in all nutrients.' [52] Thus overall the soils of Kabale do not appear to be completely degraded: although they are generally phosphorus-deficient and many are too acidic, their proportion of organic matter, nitrogen and potassium appears to be good. While farmers complain of declining soil fertility due to over-cultivation, with more in-depth questioning about specific soil types, they admit that they have taken action which has actually improved fertility on a number of plots. Soil erosion had never been noted on more than 54 per cent of fields surveyed. More than 45 per cent of the fields visited were reported to have increased in fertility or to have experienced no change. Although there is no doubt that soil fertility could be improved, it is clear that it is not at all-round disastrous levels. It is also apparent that, despite population pressure for land, farmers are being proactive in their land management by choosing to fallow before fertility levels decline to disastrous levels. [53]

Other researchers have reported that the soils of Kabale are resilient and resistant to erosion. In contrast to the prevailing viewpoints on soil erosion, laboratory analysis of soil from the area conducted by Magunda found the soil to be well aggregated, with a stable structure and high organic matter levels. He concluded that the soil was particularly resistant to erosion. [54] Another more recent study has examined accelerated erosion using 12 natural runoff plots on which soil loss and erosion features were measured. Again, in contrast to conventional wisdom about soils in the Kabale area, results from this study indicate that land cover rather than slope is a more important factor in determining extent of soil erosion, and that, due to low rainfall intensity and highly permeable soils, erosion is much less than would be expected. [55] This study does not, however, appear to have been taken up by other observers, who continue to write about the high levels of erosion (see, for example, *Kabale District Environment Profile*, 1995). Thus while there are few detailed studies of soil erosion, those that do exist suggest that soil erosion is actually much less than would be expected in an area with such steep slopes and continuous cultivation over decades.[56]

YIELDS

The final aspect of the neo-Malthusian narrative to be explored here is the discussion around falling yields. While no data have been found that would enable comparisons of yields in Kabale today and in the past, Kabale's yields can be compared with the national average. See Figure 6.3.

Figure 6.3 *Comparison of harvested yields: Kabale District and Uganda national average, 1992*[57]

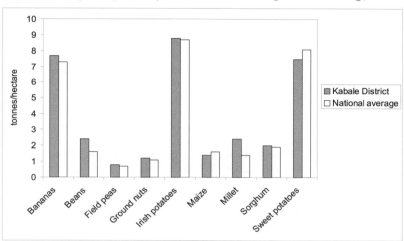

This shows that, for most crops, yields in Kabale in 1992 were as high or higher than the national average, and provides further evidence that Kabale may not be close to catastrophe due to low yields caused by environmental degradation resulting from population pressure.

Questions raised, comparisons and conclusions

The outcome of this research seriously challenges the overwhelming view that population growth in the region has resulted in reduced fallow, which is in turn associated with environmental degradation. Both researchers and policy-makers often repeat that both the longevity and frequency of fallow periods has consistently fallen for several decades. This would fit with models of intensification that suggest that, when there is no longer land to extend cultivation into, farmers intensify production by increasing the intensity of cultivation (by reducing fallow) and increasing other inputs and technologies such as labour and intercropping.[58] It is also recognised that, unless counteractive measures are taken, shortening fallows will lead to the depletion of soil fertility and will lead inevitably to lower yields.[59]

The findings suggest that in Kigezi, an area of dense population, land use changes have occurred that, in conjunction with local farm management practices, have contributed to the lack of severe land degradation in the area. Rather than cultivation techniques being the cause of problems of environmental degradation (as, for example, the *State of the Environment Report* suggests), there is evidence that in fact these very techniques contribute to the success of the agricultural system. Land use changes (increase in fallow and woodlots, and the relocation of grazing) and land management practices (including intercropping, rotation, mulching, etc.) have helped to mediate the impact of population growth on the environment. The results demonstrate that common assumptions about population growth and its effects on the environment do not necessarily hold true upon more in-depth analysis.

Close examination of earlier research suggests that other studies have in fact found a high prevalence of fallow, but this result is not highlighted in the findings. Even Were, who stated that fallows have reduced and are now too short to allow soils to regenerate, found that 77 per cent of farms had some land under fallow, and provided no evidence of decreasing fallow periods.[60] Grisley and Mwesigwa's survey also found a high prevalence of fallow: of the farms surveyed 76 per cent had some cropland in grass fallow, with 26 per cent of the total cropland under fallow. Their research suggested that, while increasing population density resulted in a decrease in the amount of land fallowed, this occurred at a rate significantly lower than the corresponding increase in population density.[61]

Kigezi farmers have, against all predictions, managed their farms in such a way as to maintain production, while they have simultaneously avoided serious environmental degradation. This is not to say that absolutely no such environmental degradation exists, rather that it has not reached the proportions envisaged. Realising that to maintain the soil fertility they cannot afford to reduce fallow periods, farmers have found other ways of increasing production through both intensification (using increased intercropping, and the use of manure and household wastes) and by extending cultivation into areas of land not previously considered suitable, such as swamps. Prior to reclamation these swamps were owned and utilised on a communal basis. Their edges were cultivated during dry years as a mechanism for reducing risk of crop failure. As land pressure rose, spontaneous reclamation began, which was soon to be supported by the colonial state. Once reclaimed, they became privately owned and used for cultivation and grazing by a small minority of the population.

The case of Kigezi thus illustrates the existence of parallel processes of agricultural change: extension into previously uncultivated land such as swampland and intensification in the face of population pressure in areas already under cultivation. These dual approaches have been adopted since the late 1940s in order to maintain production. But they have not been occurring in an undifferentiated fashion. I have shown that undertaking environmentally positive agricultural practices is socially differentiated and people fallow for different reasons: while rich households have enough land to be able to fallow, poor households fallow at least in part because of labour shortages (they depend on working as casual labourers for other households for much of their income). Thus, here in Kabale where the main investment in agriculture is labour, and where casual wage labour is an important source of income for many households, it is the labour of poorer households that is used to increase labour invested in the land of richer households. It is therefore the labour of land-poor households that drives agricultural intensification on the land of rich households. Land differentiation is clearly important in the effects that it has on environmental sustainability, as examined in the following chapter.

Furthermore, extension into previously uncultivated land has also been characterised by accentuating differentiation. The move into swamps has proved to be particularly beneficial to those with existing resources (see Chapter 5). Associated with the increased cultivation of swampland has been a shift to improved livestock for milk production by a small number of farmers, which has been accompanied by an increased differentiation of livestock ownership. However, the extension of cultivation has now reached its limit and there are no more swamps to drain and no more land to extend into. It is possible to speculate therefore that southern Kigezi has reached another critical moment, which will necessitate a shift in which intensification will predominate.

The findings support research that suggests that global correlations between population growth and environmental degradation cannot necessarily be extended to the local level. This is in line with a growing body of literature – of which the best known is the study of Machakos[62] – that illustrates the dangers of making simple assumptions regarding the impact of population growth on environmental degradation. In Machakos District, Kenya, increases in population density over a sixty-year-period, combined with a favourable policy environment, actually induced environmentally positive changes in land utilisation. Farmers were able to reverse land degradation, conserve and enhance their livestock, invest in their farms and improve productivity. The technological achievements in Machakos resulted from an endogenous process whereby the farmers selected and adapted new ideas from multiple sources.

Further research conducted in Machakos raises a number of questions related to livelihoods and the broader social costs of environmental and agricultural change. Murton looked at the effects on livelihoods (i.e. not just environmental sustainability) of the environmental change documented by Tiffen *et al.* While he agrees that there have been environmental improvements in Machakos, his research suggests that these have been accompanied by a polarisation in land holdings, differential trends in agricultural productivity and a decline in food self-sufficiency with farmers becoming more dependent on non-agricultural sources of income. [63] Those households with access to urban derived non-farm income are able to undertake agricultural innovation and accumulate land. On the other hand, those who depend on agricultural

6.1 *Shores of Lake Bunyonyi, 1935, showing contour cultivation. Taken by D.W. Malcolm (Secretary to Lord Hailey, who visited Uganda Dec 1935 to Jan 1936). RH MSS Afr s1445, Box 3, Album II.* (Reproduced with kind permission of the Rhodes House Library, University of Oxford)

6.2 *Shores of Lake Bunyonyi, 2000, showing same part of the shoreline of Lake Bunyonyi, illustrating more developed bunds.*
(© Grace Carswell 2000)

167

6.3 *Across Lake Bunyonyi, 1938, showing 'steps' in background on hills around Lake Bunyonyi. From collection of Miss Edith Baring Gould, Church Missionary Society Acc 28z5.*
(Reproduced with kind permission of the CMS collection, Birmingham University)

6.4 *Across Lake Bunyonyi, 2000, showing development of tree lots and terraces in the background. (© Grace Carswell 2000)*

labour markets are finding it difficult to cope with the changes. Thus when the Machakos experience is examined at a household level it is shown to be neither a homogenous experience nor an unproblematic one. Murton's work suggests that there were two phases of agricultural intensification. The first of these required no monetary inputs and almost all households followed it. The second phase required capital availability and so has been adopted only by those who can afford them. Boserupian intensification on richer farms and a form of Geertzian involution on poorer farms are seen to be proceeding side by side within the same village. The Kigezi case similarly suggests dual processes of agrarian change that involves intensification (though increased labour inputs, associated with, for example increased intercropping) and the extension of agriculture into land that was previously uncultivated, such as swampland. These dual processes enable farmers to continue to fallow, which they realise is necessary to maintain fertility.

Farmers in Kigezi have successfully risen to the challenges faced by their agricultural system, and thus the research suggests that favourable agricultural changes have occurred over the past fifty years. But today the agricultural options are increasingly limited: many intensification strategies have been used and extension into uncultivated land is no longer available. Furthermore, the highly differentiated nature of this latter aspect of agricultural change and the increased vulnerability of the majority of farmers associated with this increased differentiation must mean that the next few decades are critical. Murton's work emphasises the importance of looking at the broader costs of environmental change in terms of livelihoods, and the following chapter explores the broader social impacts of the transformation that Kigezi has undergone, looking in particular at the changing role, patterns and importance of livelihood diversification and remittances and changing patterns of social differentiation.

Notes

[1] Purseglove, 'Report on the overpopulated areas of Kigezi', *State of the Environment Report for Uganda 1998*, National Environment Management Authority (Kampala, 1999).

[2] Purseglove, 'Report on the overpopulated areas of Kigezi'. Lindblade *et al.*, 'More People, More Fallow'.

[3] NEMA, *State of the Environment Report*, 55.

[4] Boserup, *The conditions of agricultural growth*.

[5] C. Geertz, *Agricultural involution: the process of ecological change in Indonesia* (Berkeley and Los Angeles, 1963).

[6] Tiffen *et al.*, *More People, Less Erosion*.

[7] Fairhead and Leach, *Reframing Deforestation*; Leach and Mearns, *Lie of the Land*.

[8] G. Carswell, 'Continuities in environmental narratives: the case of Kabale, Uganda, 1930–2000', *Environment and History*, 9 1 (2003), 3–29.

[9] Purseglove, 'Report on the overpopulated areas of Kigezi'; NEMA, *State of the Environment Report*.

[10] Letter to PCWP from J.E. Phillips, Acting DC, 26 Jan 1921, KDA DC MP69 ff2.

[11] Anderson, 'Depression, dust bowl'.

[12] See for example Mackenzie, *Land, Ecology*; Giblin, *The Politics of Environmental Control*;

Maddox, Giblin and Kimambo, *Custodians of the Land.*

[13] Report for Year 1935 by Wickham, KDA DC AGR-MNTH ff53.

[14] Purseglove, 'Report on the overpopulated areas'.

[15] Allan, *The African Husbandman.*

[16] Kagambirwe, 'Causes and consequences of land shortage'.

[17] B.W. Langlands, *A Population Geography of Kigezi District*, (Makerere, Department of Geography, Occasional Paper 26, 1971); B.M. Kateete 'Land tenure and land use in Humurwa parish, Ikumba sub-county, Rubanda County, Kigezi District' in R. Tindituuza and B.M. Kateete, *Essays on Land Fragmentation in Kigezi District* (Makerere, Department of Geography, Occasional Paper 22, 1971).

[18] J.M. Tukahirwa, 'Soil resources in the highlands of Uganda: Prospects and sensitivities', *Mountain Research and Development* 8 2/3 (1988),165–172.

[19] Ministry of National Resources, National Environment Information Centre, *State of the Environment Report, Uganda* (Kampala, 1994).

[20] J.M. Were, *Population Pressure, Land Use Changes and Consequences on the Environment in Kabale District* (Makerere University Department of Geography, Kampala, 1992).

[21] See for example J. Y. K . Zake, *Report of the Soil Fertility Survey of South Western Region Kabale and Rukungiri*, South-west Regional Agricultural Rehabilitation Project (Mbarara, 1991); A.B. Cunningham, 'People, park and plant use: Research and recommendations for multiple-use zones and development alternatives around Bwindi-Impenetrable National Park, Uganda', Report prepared for CARE-International (Kabale, 1992); E. M. Tukahirwa (ed.) *Environmental and Natural Resource Management Policy and Law: Issues and Options, Summary* (MISR and Natural Resources and World Resources Institute, Washington, DC, 1992); African Highlands Initiative (AHI) C and D Uganda Team, 'Natural resource management constraints and prospects in Kabale District' (Kampala, 1998).

[22] CARE 'Development Through Conservation project proposal, 1992–1993 A proposal to USAID.' (Kabale, 1992).

[23] See for example AFRENA, 'Agroforestry Research Networks for Africa Uganda National Taskforce. Agroforestry potentials for the land-use systems in the bimodal highlands of eastern Africa: Uganda.' AFRENA Report No. 4. International Centre for Research on Agroforestry (Nairobi, 1988).

[24] National Environment Information Centre, *Kabale District Environment Profile* (Kampala, 1995).

[25] Lindblade *et al.* 'More People, More Fallow'.

[26] *Ibid.*

[27] *Ibid.*

[28] *Ibid.*

[29] *Ibid.*

[30] For example 02/Muy/Q10, 02/Muy/Q2 (both in richest wealth group) and 02/Muy/Q1, 02/Muy/Q21 and 02/Muy/Q46 (all in second richest wealth group) all rent land in the swamp.

[31] Lindblade *et al.* 'More People, More Fallow', 47–8.

[32] Lindblade *et al.* 'More People, More Fallow', 40, 54.

[33] W. Grisley and D. Mwesigwa, 'Socio-economic determinants of seasonal cropland fallowing decisions: Smallholders in south-western Uganda', *Journal of Environmental Management*, 42 (1994), 81–89.

[34] P. Holmgren and E.J. Masakha and H. Sjoholm, 'Not all African land is being degraded: A recent survey of trees on farms in Kenya reveals rapidly increasing forest resources' *Ambio*, 23 (1994), 390-5.

[35] R.A. Cline Cole, H. A. C. Main and J. E. Nichol, 'On Fuelwood consumption, population dynamics and deforestation in Africa', *World Development*, 18 4 (1990), 513–527.

[36] See for example National Environment Management Authority (NEMA), *The National Soils Policy for Uganda* (Kampala, 1998). Africare, 'Baseline Survey', (Kabale, 1997); NEMA, *State of the Environment Report for Uganda 1998* (Kampala, 1998); *Kabale District Environment Profile* (1995).

Changes in the Agricultural System

[37] D. Taylor, 'Late quaternary pollen records from two Uganda mires: Evidence for environmental change in the Rukiga highlands of southwest Uganda', *Palaeogeography, Palaeobotany and Palynology*, 80 (1990), 283–300. D.L. Schoenbrun, 'The contours of vegetation change and human agency in Eastern Africa's Great Lakes region: ca 2000 BC to ca AD 1000', *History in Africa*, 21 (1994), 302. Also see P. Robertshaw and D. Taylor, 'Climate change and the rise of political complexity in western Uganda', *Journal of African History*, 41 1, (2000), 1–28.

[38] Taylor and Marchant, 'Human impact in the Interlacustrine region', 294. See also D. Taylor, P. Robertshaw and R.A. Marchant 'Environmental change and political-economic upheaval in precolonial western Uganda', *The Holocene*, 10 4, (2000), 527–36; A. Hamilton, *et al.* 'Early forest clearance and environmental degradation in South West Uganda', *Nature*, 320 (1986), 164–7.

[39] W.M. Bamwerinde, S.B. Dickens, J. Musiime, and T. Raussen, 'Sharing local knowledge: farmers from Kabale (Uganda) study tree pruning systems and agroforesty in Embu (Kenya)' (Kabale, 1999), 4; Africare, 'The Status of UFSI' (Kabale, 2000); D. Miiro *et al.*, 'Participatory Rural Appraisal Report, Bubaale Sub-county, Kabale District' Indigenous Soil and Water Conservation Project (Kabale, 1998).

[40] WPAR, 1932.

[41] Agricultural Survey of Kasheregenyi Mutala in Kigezi District. By R. Wickham, (Survey conducted 1935–36, as part of one of the 19 Agricultural Surveys, 1938)

[42] Overall 9 per cent of the land surveyed was swamp (including cultivated, resting and natural, or undrained, swamp). Lindblade *et al.* 'More People, More Fallow', 19.

[43] Lindblade *et al.* 'More People, More Fallow'.

[44] A far higher proportion of swamp soil (*eryofunjo*) is rested: cultivated compared to other soil types. See Lindblade *et al.* 'More People, More Fallow', 44.

[45] The National Wetlands Conservation and Management Programme is implemented by the Department of Environment Affairs, with the support of the IUCN and the World Conservation Union.

[46] There is also some debate about the health implications of the drainage of swamps, and informants frequently state that this has brought malaria to the area. A study of differences between reclaimed and non-reclaimed swamp land suggests that 'replacement of natural swamp vegetation with agricultural crops has led to increased temperatures, which may be responsible for elevated malaria transmission risk in cultivated areas.' See K.A. Lindblade, E.D. Walker, A.W. Onapa, J. Katungu, and M.L. Wilson, 'Land use change alters malaria transmission parameters by modifying temperature in a highland area of Uganda', *Tropical Medicine & International Health* 5 4 (2000), 263–274.

[47] G. Carswell, 'Continuities in environmental narratives: the case of Kabale, Uganda, 1930–2000', *Environment and History* 9 1 (2003), 3–29.

[48] *Ibid.*

[49] E.M. Roe, 'Except Africa: Postscript to a special section on development narratives', *World Development*, 23 6 (1995), 1066.

[50] F. D. K. Bagoora, 'Soil erosion and mass wasting risk in the highland area of Uganda', *Mountain Research and Development* 8 2/3 (1988), 173–82.

[51] Lindblade *et al.*, 'More People, More Fallow'.

[52] *Ibid.*, 45.

[53] Lindblade *et al.*, 'More People, More Fallow'.

[54] M. K. Magunda, 'Influence of some physico-chemical properties on soil strength, stability of crusts and soil erosion', (PhD, University of Minnesota, 1992).

[55] J. M. Biteete-Tukahiirwe, 'Measurement, Predictions and Social Ecology of Accelerated Soil Erosion in Kabale District, South-West Uganda' (PhD, Department of Geography, Makerere University, Kampala, 1995).

[56] See also C. S. Farley, 'Smallholder knowledge, soil resource management and land use changes in the Highlands of southwest Uganda' (PhD, Department of Geography, University of Florida, Gainesville, 1996).

[57] Ministry of Agriculture, *Report on Uganda National Census of Agriculture and Livestock (1990–1991)* (Entebbe, 1992).

171

[58] Boserup, *The Conditions of Agricultural Growth.*
[59] Geertz, *Agricultural Involution.*
[60] Were, *Population Pressure.*
[61] Grisley and Mwesigwa, 'Socio-economic determinants of seasonal cropland fallowing decisions'.
[62] Tiffen *et al., More People, Less Erosion.*
[63] Murton, 'Population growth and poverty'.

Seven

Livelihoods, Labouring
& Differentiation

Introduction

Farmers in Kigezi have found ways of avoiding serious environmental degradation, supporting research from elsewhere that suggests that global correlations between population growth and environmental degradation cannot necessarily be extended to the local level. As other research, such as Tiffen *et al.*'s Machakos study, has shown, the impact of population growth on the environment is more complex than a simple neo-Malthusian explanation would suggest. But further research undertaken in Machakos by Murton highlights the importance of looking at livelihood change more broadly when investigating the relationship between population growth and the environment.[1] There are other, broader social costs to such changes, and I will now explore these, looking at livelihood change in the broader sense in Kigezi.

While diversification activities have become notably more visible, it is not simply that they have become more important. While there is a literature that suggests that livelihood diversification is increasing,[2] in Kigezi these activities have long been there, but being non-monetarised were hidden from view. More specifically people laboured for others as part of a complex set of social relations that enabled them to gain access to land, and other key resources. These arrangements were particularly critical, given the high level of mobility of people in Kigezi, and where working for others was a means of establishing a household in a new area. Such arrangements have decreased over time, and this has been associated with an increase in cash-based arrangements, such as labouring for others for cash. Other arrangements involving cash that have increased include renting and buying land (see Chapters 4 and 5). Examining the changing role, patterns and importance of migration, and changes to differentiation, in particular land and livestock ownership, I will ask how these changes have affected livelihoods more broadly in Kigezi.

Livelihood diversification

There is a growing literature on the importance of non-agricultural activities – an area of research of increasing interest to both researchers and development agencies. After many years focusing their attentions on agriculture, policy-makers have recently given increased consideration to the contribution made by livelihood diversification to rural livelihoods. The importance of earnings from non-farm activities has been highlighted by research undertaken throughout Sub-Saharan Africa and the wider world.[3] In Kigezi many households rely on different income sources, and this broader picture needs to be considered to ensure a firm understanding of changes to the agricultural system.

The literature on livelihood diversification, which crosses several related fields and disciplinary approaches, is characterised by many terms and definitions. Here, the definition of livelihood diversification chosen by Ellis is used:

> Rural livelihood diversification is defined as the process by which rural households construct an increasingly diverse portfolio of activities and assets in order to survive and to improve their standard of living.

People diversify by adopting a range of activities. Thus income sources may include 'farm income', 'non-farm income' (non-agricultural income sources, such as non-farm wages and business income), and 'off-farm income' (wages of exchange labour on other farms – i.e. within agriculture, including payment in kind).[4]

Ellis deals in detail with conceptual issues around livelihood diversification. Livelihood diversification activities are commonly categorised on the basis of their roles as mechanisms for coping, adaptation, and accumulation. The differences between livelihood diversification of poor people who are struggling to survive, and that of better-off individuals who are diversifying to accumulate, have been observed. Ellis draws attention to the dangers of such superficially attractive typologies, noting that 'diversification obeys a continuum of causes and motivations that vary across families at a particular point in time, and for the same families at different points in time.'[5] While this distinction is not used here case studies of individuals diversifying will illustrate how people from different wealth groups choose particular activities. While different people might do the same activity (e.g. labouring for others), the institutional arrangements through which the activities are organised may vary and this has major implications for the returns to be made from that activity. Diversification activities make an important contribution to livelihoods, and historical data show that this is not a new phenomenon, merely more obvious than ever before. This is because many activities that might today be referred to as 'diversification activities' have long been undertaken, but were not a part of the cash economy, and were tied up with complex institutional arrangements that enabled access to resources, such as land, and thus were hidden from view. The research therefore highlights the importance of an historical approach for a firm understanding of livelihood change.[6]

LIVELIHOODS & LABOURING: EVIDENCE FROM KABIRIZI

The contribution of non-agricultural activities to livelihoods, and how these have changed, was explored in a 'livelihoods survey' conducted in Kabirizi in 2000. Kabirizi is located in Rwamucucu *gombolola*, a distance of some 50 kilometres from Kabale town. This area was included in the 1939 survey of Kitozho (see Box 4.2), and the existence of this historical data enabled changes over time to be assessed.

Sources of income

A range of different sources of income is available in Kabirizi today. While sales of agricultural products are the first or second most important source of income for over 80 per cent of households, casual labour (on other people's farms) is an important source of income for 50 per cent of households (particularly as a secondary source).[7] Thus, 'off-farm income', especially wage labour on other people's land, is extremely important for half the population. Other 'non-farm' income sources include formal work and trading.

Households in Kabirizi were categorised into different wealth groups, based on local definitions of wealth (which included size of land holding, size of banana plantations, involvement in formal employment and use of additional labour). The importance of different sources of income varies for different wealth groups[8] and for male or female-headed households. A larger proportion (just over 80 per cent) of the richest half of the population get most of their income from agricultural produce compared to the poorer half of the population (just under 60 per cent). Casual agricultural labour is very important for poorer households: work on other people's land is the first or second most important source of income for over 50 per cent of poorer households (compared to about 25 per cent of richer households). Labouring for others, and how it has changed, will be returned to below. Formal work, brewing and trading are more important for richer households compared to poorer; while remittances and basket/mat making are more important for poorer households. There are similar patterns for male and female-headed households.[9] Sales of agricultural and livestock products, and formal work, are more important for male-headed than female-headed households, while casual labour and remittances (see below) are important for more female-headed households. The only other source of income which is significantly more important for female-headed households is basket and mat making, but this is only ever as a secondary source of income.

Changes to sources of income: 1939 to present

Today different income sources are important for different groups, but whether this has always been the case is key to understanding whether there has been an increase in livelihood diversification. Bryceson has argued that diversification activities have increased in importance in rural Sub-Saharan Africa, which, she suggests, is becoming less rural in character. Associated with this process of 'deagrarianization' is a declining reliance by many rural households on income from farming, and a rising reliance on non-farm income sources.[10] She argues in particular that the implementation of Structural Adjustment Programmes and economic liberalisation has 'coincided with the rapid expansion of rural income diversification'[11] and reports research findings from a number of countries in Sub-Saharan Africa that indicate a 'surge' in non-agricultural income sources over the past 15–20 years.[12] She notes that 67 per cent of involvement in non-farm activity in a site in Nigeria was initiated over the past 15 years, and 43 per cent had had no previous economic activity before then.[13] In a study in Tanzania over 50 per cent of existing non-agricultural activity began in or after 1990, a third began in the 1980s, while only 16 per cent of respondents were involved in non-agricultural activities in the past.[14] Other research has also found that diversification has increased, but suggests that Structural Adjustment has made diversification possible, rather than having negative effects on livelihoods.[15] But whether for negative or positive reasons, such studies suggest increases in diversification.

Whether there has been such an increase in diversification activities in Kigezi can be explored using historical sources. Comparing data from today with the 1939 survey would suggest that there has been an increase in the range of sources of income, but this does not say anything about their prevalence or importance. Unfortunately the 1939 survey does not give any detail of the importance of different sources of income. It does, however, refer to sales of agricultural produce and brewing (for sale), noting there was a 'large internal trade in beer'.[16] The survey also makes reference to labour migration in Buganda (see below) but at this time the only people with regular cash incomes were catechists and government employees such as chiefs. Some men worked as porters building roads and the report also makes passing references to pottery (which was apparently seldom sold) and basket work. The range of income sources available today is therefore somewhat wider than in the past, as is illustrated in Table 7.1. This table also shows the range of activities undertaken in Kabirizi in 1939 and 2000, and in Muyebe (a *gombolola* immediately to the south of Kabale town) in 2002.

The table shows that today there are just three more sources of income available to households in Kabirizi compared to 1939: retail trade, carpentry and renting out land. Agricultural labour has increased significantly from being 'very occasional' to being common today, and will be discussed further below. In contrast, in Muyebe there are many additional activities available: firewood and timber sales, selling second-hand clothes, brick making, fishing, healing, providing transport (bicycle *boda bodas*), and profits earned from lending cash and savings groups. Households in Muyebe had an average of 2.75 different sources of income (compared to 2.21 in Kabirizi), and with twenty different sources of income (compared to 12 in Kabirizi) Muyebe is more

Table 7.1 *Sources of income in Kabirizi (1939 and 2000) and Muyebe (2002)* [17]

Kabirizi, 1939	Kabirizi, 2000	Muyebe, 2002
Agricultural produce	Sales of agricultural products	Sales of agricultural produce
Trade (Beer)	Sales of livestock produce	Sales of livestock produce
Brewing	Trading	Trading
Labour migration	Brewing	Brewing
Govt employees	Remittances	Remittances
Catechists	Formal work	Formal work
Labour on roads	Casual (non-agricultural) labour	Casual (non-agricultural) labour
Basket work	Basket / mat maker	Basket / mat maker
Agricultural labour ('very occasionally')	Agricultural labour	Agricultural labour
Pottery	Shop owner	Sales of food, drink (*hoteli, duka*)
	Rent out land	Rent out land
	Carpenter	Carpenter
		Mason
		Painter
		Firewood / tree / charcoal sales
		Selling clothes
		Transport (*boda boda*)
		Healer
		Brick making
		Fishing
		Lending cash
		Profits from savings/lending group

diversified than Kabirizi. Case study 7.1 illustrates how some of the different sources of income are combined in one household. The most likely explanation for why Muyebe is such a highly diversified economy compared to Kabirizi is location.[18] Muyebe is located just 7 kilometres from Kabale town, and being just a few kilometres from the tarmac road has good transport links to the town. Many of the activities in Muyebe are dependent of its proximity to Kabale town and the main road: transport provision (bicycle *boda bodas*) is largely to take people into Kabale town, bricks supply the building boom in Kabale, while fish, firewood and timber are all sold in Kabale. Involvement in the second-hand clothes trade is largely dependent on Muyebe's proximity to one of the region's largest markets at Mwangari just south of Kabale town, which is held twice a week.

Habaasa is an example of someone who has successfully diversified into a range of highly profitable activities. The success of these can in part be explained by his location close to the Kabale-Gatuna road (see Map App. I). This provides Habaasa with easy access to markets in both Kabale town and Rwanda.[19] Habaasa was able to begin his first business thanks to the

---

Case study 7.1 – Habaasa

Habaasa was born in Muyebe, is married to one wife, and has three children. Habaasa is aged about 30 and has a fairly small plot of land, no cattle and no formal job. He is, however, classified as one of the richest men in Muyebe, and this is largely because he is involved in a number of different activities. He was in the army from 1986–1992, and when he left he got a 'retirement' package, with which he started up his first business. This was as a motor-bike *boda-boda* driver in Kabale town from 1992 to 1997. During this time he also got involved in other activities, including brick making, and he employed people to work with him making bricks. In 2000 he sold his motor bike and started making *waragi* (local spirit). He sells the *waragi* to bar owners and this became a very profitable business. There are also opportunities for making even larger profits by providing *waragi* for the illicit trade into Rwanda, a trade that both the Rwandan and Ugandan armies are heavily involved in. Habaasa has diversified into other activities: he keeps pigs, and also takes mudfish for sale in Kampala. He has recently bought a mobile phone, and will charge people to use this. Habaasa employs two people on a monthly basis who help him, mainly collecting water and carrying firewood for the *waragi* business. He also employs people to collect mudfish, paying them per fish caught.[20]

'retirement' package he received when he left the army, which he invested in the motorbike. But he also noted that when he began the *waragi* business his personal relations were very important: another *waragi*-maker based in Gatuna, on the border with Rwanda, has been particularly valuable. This man helped him to get established, supplies him with raw ingredients and has lent him money when he needed it. It is possible that his relations with soldiers and other ex-soldiers have also provided him with links to the lucrative trade smuggling *waragi* into Rwanda.

Labouring

It can be seen therefore that the range of income-earning activities has increased, particularly in areas close to towns. But today one activity stands out as being particularly important to livelihoods: labouring for others. Demand for labour is high: labour is used to cultivate land more intensively (through increased intercropping and weeding, etc.) and this contributes to the high demand for labour.[21] The Kabirizi 2000 survey found that casual agricultural labour (i.e. working on other peoples' farms) was extremely important for poorer households, forming the first or second most important source of income for over 50 per cent of poorer households. Nor was it insignificant for richer households, forming the first or second most important source of income for about 25 per cent of richer households.

High rates of involvement in casual agricultural labour are confirmed by findings from a 1996 survey which found that over 50 per cent of households had engaged in casual agricultural labour during the previous 12 months. The same survey found that a significant proportion (64 per cent) of households hired labour, suggesting that hiring labour is not something only carried out by a small minority of very rich farmers.[22] But it is the case that the households with more land were more likely to hire labour than households with less land: 89 per cent of those owning more than 11 acres hired labour, compared to 78 per cent of those owning 5.1 to 11 acres, and 52 per cent of households owning less than 5 acres.[23] Similarly, the Muyebe survey (2002) found that 55 per cent of households had hired labour in the previous 12 months. Again it was found that although this was much more common amongst richer households, with 88 per cent of those in the richest group hiring labour, it was by no means something that only richer households did, with just over one quarter of the poorest group hiring labour.[24]

The following case studies highlight how people of different wealth groups are involved in the same activity – labouring for others – but in different ways and with very different returns. There are various arrangements for labouring for others: working individually (this is often piece-work, paid for by the plot), or working as part of a labour group. There are many types of labour group, the two most important being:

> Labour-rotation group – People work together, usually once a week, and take it in turns to receive all the money that they are paid.[25]

> Labour-loaning group – People work together and all the money is pooled. This money is then lent out to group members, at a high rate of interest. Once a year all the money (original payments, plus interest collected) is divided up amongst the members.

By acting as loaning groups some labour groups make large profits for their members, as we will see below.

Rovince is an example of a typical wage labourer who is diversifying to meet immediate cash needs. Because she cannot wait to get her money, she is excluded from being involved in labour-loaning groups. As such she misses out on the advantages of getting a share of the profits made from lending out that money, and having access to money for loans. In contrast, Muchore, who can afford to wait for payment, works in a labour-loaning group and so gets a share of the money earned from interest from those who borrow. He

---

Case study 7.2 – Rovince

Rovince is in her early twenties, and is married with five children. Her husband lives in Kabale town, visiting rarely, and she believes that he has another wife there. He contributes no money to the upkeep of Rovince and her children, and Rovince was classified as 'poor'. She owns no livestock and has a small plot of land which she cultivates, but her most important source of income is working for others. She works as an individual, rather than in a group. In the past she worked with a labour-loaning group, but she stopped because she could not afford to wait to the end of the year before getting her money. Working individually she gets paid immediately. She finds it difficult to combine cultivating her own plots and working for others because of the timing: 'When I am busy there is work available, and when I am available there is no work.'[26]

Case study 7.3 – Muchore

Muchore is a man in his late twenties who has a range of livelihood diversification activities. He does agricultural work in a group, as an individual, as well as non-agricultural labour individually, and he also buys and sells sorghum. Although he makes more money doing non-agricultural labour [27] he prefers to do agricultural labour in a group. The group he works with always finish their work at 1pm. It also acts as a loaning group: the money earned is not distributed immediately, but is instead lent to members of the group who pay 10 per cent interest per month. With such high rates of interest being charged the money quickly builds up and at Christmas the money and all the interest are divided up. [28]

---

is also able to borrow from the group, and has used loans to buy and sell sorghum, making very large profits. Thus, while the poorest often work individually, those who are a little better-off frequently work in groups, as well as individually. Another advantage of working in groups is that they finish work at 1pm, whereas working individually is often piece-work (i.e. paid per plot), and is seen to be harder work for the same money.[29]

Not only is there a great variety of labour groups, but there are also many ways of working individually, as will be illustrated by the following case study.

Case study 7.4 – Baryayanga[30]

Baryayanga is one of the richest men in Kabirizi who employs a number of people under different arrangements. He notes that 'as long as you have money, you can always get labour'. Baryayanga employs:
* A man who works on the *matoke* plantation and who also sometimes digs. He is from the area and so stays in his own home. He used to work for Baryayanga on a daily basis, but is now employed on a monthly basis and is paid 30,000/- per month, and also gets his lunch.
* A man who looks after Baryayanga's livestock. He is from outside Kabirizi, and so lives with Baryayanga, and is provided with food. He has been working for about one year, and is paid 15,000/- per month.
* Women who are employed on a daily basis to dig. He employs two or three of them – usually twice a week. During busy times (such as the sorghum harvest) he will employ them more often. Baryayanga employs different women who are all from the area, depending on who is available, but he knows them all well, and noted that he did not even need to supervise them. He pays them 1000/- for a day's work. Baryayanga observed that he never employs women on more than a daily basis, because women 'have to go to their own gardens, so can't dig for someone else for a month'.
* Men who come from around Muhanga (a small trading centre south of Kabirizi) and who move around looking for work. They stay for two to three months, and are paid cash.
* Apollo, a young man living with Baryayanga, who works for him. He was born in the area to a very poor family. He is not paid in cash, but instead he is fed, clothed and his school fees paid. Baryayanga has also lent Apollo some land which he cultivates for himself (*omwehereko*).[31]
* A man who is working for a few days. He does not get paid, but gets food to eat. He is a cousin of Apollo.

Baryayanga employs many different people under various working arrangements: a man who is paid monthly, women paid on a daily rate, and men who are fed and clothed, but not paid cash at all. This range of arrangements, and the different types of labour groups that have been discussed above, illustrate that 'labouring for others' is a highly flexible term that can mean many different things. A few patterns are clear. First, because of the need to work on their own plots, women can only work on a daily basis (whether individually or in a group). This means that they are excluded from longer-term, and more secure, arrangements. Second, the very poorest individuals accept arrangements under which no cash is paid, but they are fed and in some cases assisted in other ways. Finally, poorer people with immediate cash needs find it impossible to participate in those labour groups with the highest returns, i.e. those that also function as loaning groups. The exorbitant rates of interest charged ensure that rates of return are high.[32] Secondary benefits of belonging to such groups are that members are able to borrow money from the group (albeit at these high rates of interest) and people such as Muchore have done so, making large profits by buying and selling sorghum. Thus it can be seen that while, superficially, people from both poor and less-poor households labour for others, how this is organised varies, and with this, so the returns vary.

Changes to labouring for others

While the most important source of off-farm income today is labouring on other people's land, it is striking that the 1939 survey does not mention income from agricultural labour as a source of cash income. The report states that 'hired labour is not normally used', but then continues 'very occasional[ly someone] may pay labour by the day – for example may pay a girl 20 cents to cultivate for a day.'[33] This suggests that at that time working on other people's land occurred, but was uncommon; and thus comparing the 1939 survey results with more recent surveys would imply that off-farm activities, and in particular wage labour, have indeed increased.

More detailed historical research, however, suggests a more complex picture than a simple increase in the prevalence of off-farm activities. Labouring for others was being undertaken, but not as part of the cash economy. Rather, such labouring was tied up with complex arrangements that enabled people to access key resources such as land, and in this way it was obscured from immediate view. A number of arrangements existed under which people worked on other people's land. Chapter 4 showed how recent migrants to an area would work for a host in return for food (*okucwa encuro*) or for land (*okwatira*).[34] While people often state that *okucwa encuro* is no longer practised,[35] cases of it were uncovered – see, for example, Case study 7.4 above. Baryayanga himself stated that *okucwa encuro* is much less common now, but is still practised. He also noted that while people do still work in return for food, the term *okucwa encuro* is rarely used, as it is regarded as being low status.[36]

Under *okwatira* an incomer to an area would get some land in exchange for giving labour (and part of their first harvest) to the giver of the land. Oral sources frequently refer to the practice of labouring for richer neighbours, particularly in the first years of settlement in a new area and migration was common amongst the Bakiga. Today, people no longer expect to be allocated land after working for a host. Apollo (Case study 7.4), for example, has been lent a small piece of land by Baryayanga to cultivate for himself (*omwehereko*). But he knows his rights over this land are only usufruct and temporary: 'The time will come when I'll be stopped! Baryayanga's sons feel bad when they see me cultivating it.' He is also sure that he will not get any land from Baryayanga: 'he has his own sons – I'm not his son. I think that even his sons don't want me to be here ... because I am eating their share.'[37]

The 1939 survey refers to the practice of *okutendera*, that is, labouring on the land of in-laws in lieu of brideprice payment.[38] People also worked in return for beer and for livestock.[39] Thus labouring was a common means of gaining access to key resources, and a whole set of relationships existed, under which members of poorer households (men and women) would work for richer, more established, neighbours – in order to gain access to land, beer, livestock and wives. While there is no doubt that these arrangements existed, studies such as the 1939 study have little or no reference to them, and certainly no attempt is made to quantify them.

Such arrangements, which were neither fixed nor inflexible, have undergone major transformation since the early colonial period, having become significantly less common, and being largely replaced by cash-based arrangements. Oral sources repeatedly stated that there is no longer any need to enter such arrangements 'because there is money'. Thus, for example, working in return for livestock became less common as 'when money came, people started working and buying livestock.'[40] Precisely when the transition began is unclear, but the evidence suggests that by 1939 a shift towards cash payment for labour was beginning.[41] Oral sources suggest that *okutendera* (working in lieu of brideprice) declined once labour migration increased in prevalence in the 1930s and 1940s. Others dated the decline specifically from the Second World War, when 'people started working for money and using it for brideprice.'[42]

The transition from institutional arrangements that did not involve cash, to the cash-based arrangements of today has a number of implications. In social terms the shift to cash is perceived to be better for the labourer: working for food or brideprice was regarded as low status. As Cosia Rutabyaama said: 'People now prefer to work for money and buy food rather than *okucwa encuro*' (working for food). Similarly, Charles Beisakanwa observed that 'when money came, they considered it better to work for money and buy land or cows instead of *okutendera*. The person who did *okutendera* would do all kinds of work, he would even do the grinding, ... [and] collect water.'[43] Today, working for wages is done by many people, and there is no social stigma attached to it, and so from a social point of view the transition to cash-based arrangements can be seen a something of an improvement for people's livelihoods.

Whether the shift to cash has benefited the workers in terms of increasing income and other aspects of livelihoods is another matter. Whilst today there is a widely recognised wage rate,[44] it is impossible to compare these rates with the returns in earlier non-cash based arrangements, if only because the latter were open to negotiation. Informants recall that 'rates of pay' were not fixed under non-cash-based arrangements: 'there was no measure. They would just work and when the [rich one] felt [like it] they would give, for example, a cow, and they would continue going there [to the rich man] once in a while to help them.'[45] In this way they were 'tied' to someone, which may have restricted their choices. Today's cash-based arrangements appear to give greater flexibility to workers: they can work for one person, and rent land from someone entirely different. High demand for labour, the well recognised rates of pay of today, the greater flexibility workers have acquired and the increased social status associated with cash arrangements would suggest that the commodification of labour has been associated with an improvement in the conditions of workers.

Thus while it is true that today labouring for cash is both a key 'diversification activity' and a critical income source for poorer households, this practice is a modification of earlier arrangements that enabled poorer, less powerful households to access resources such as land, suggesting a more complex picture than a simple increase in off-farm activities. It is not a straightforward story of diversification activities increasing in importance, as labouring for other people has long existed in Kigezi as part of the complex social arrangements and networks that enabled people to access key resources. Under arrangements such as *okwatira, okucwa encuro* and *okutendera* people have long been working for other households. These arrangements were not a part of the cash economy, being socially embedded and tied up with arrangements that enabled access to, for example, land, and thus were hidden from view. But whereas in the past most labouring for others was undertaken as part non-cash arrangements, today it is only the poorest individuals who labour under these arrangements.

In the example of Machakos, Murton has argued that agricultural labour, generated by richer farmers growing new labour-intensive crops, 'creates a lifeline to poorer households enabling them to cling onto their stake in the rural economy'.[46] Similarly in Kigezi agricultural labour is generated by richer farmers, and is used to increase the investment of labour into the land of richer farmers. And similarly agricultural labour (for which demand is high) enables people to 'cling onto their stake in the rural economy'. But this research has shown that there is a long history of labouring for other people in Kigezi, and what has changed is that this activity has become commodified. It is therefore difficult to say whether or not labouring on other people's land has increased, but we can say that labouring for cash has increased. In turn labouring for other people without cash being exchanged has decreased. Hence diversification activities have certainly become more visible, but this is not the same as becoming more common. But critically for those who labour, the commodification of labour has been associated with reduced social stigma, improved status, greater flexibility and widely recognised rates of pay for workers.

Migration

In many parts of Sub-Saharan Africa remittances earned from migration make an important contribution to livelihoods.[47] Some studies have also shown that remittances play a crucial role in the agricultural system.[48] Murton, for example, found that remittances were important in explaining the patterns of agricultural intensification seen in Machakos.[49] He observed two phases of agricultural intensification and conservation technology, with the second phase being increasingly dependent on inputs of urban derived capital. The first-phase practices (e.g. terracing and mulching) only required labour, and no monetary input, and were adopted by most households. Second-phase practices such as manuring and use of inorganic fertiliser required capital and were therefore only adopted by those that could afford them. Thus those with access to urban-derived non-farm income could undertake agricultural innovation in the longer term and accumulate land. Whether remittances have played a similar role in Kigezi is a key question, and in particular whether urban-derived non-farm income has 'driven' positive environmental changes.

There have been three phases of labour migration in Kigezi: it grew in importance up to the late 1940s, was at its peak from the 1940s to the 1960s, and since then has declined and undergone changes in its nature. In the first phase – from the early 1920s to the late 1940s – increasing migration contributed to an increase in cash circulation in the economy and led to changes in, for example, brideprice arrangements. From the early colonial period, the need to pay taxes and the lack of job opportunities within Kigezi encouraged many men to look for wage labour further afield in southern and central Uganda where demands for labour were high. This demand stemmed from the needs of government, planters and African (particularly Baganda) farmers. [50] The colonial administration therefore encouraged labour migration from outlying districts – in particular West Nile and Kigezi – and from neighbouring countries – in particular Ruanda-Urundi and Congo.[51] From the early 1920s the practice of seeking work in Buganda on cotton farms, and later on municipal works, and in mines in Ankole, became more common for young men from Kigezi. In 1923 'large numbers' of men were reported to be going to Buganda for work and a road count in September 1924 of migrants moving into Buganda found that 65.4 per cent were from the Western Province. [52] Wright's 1939 survey of Kitozho found that 22 per cent of the men counted on the day of the survey had worked in Buganda at some time in their lives. If those who were away at the time of the survey were added in then the figure rises to 37 per cent.[53] The majority of migrants spent more than six months away, typically between six months and three years.[54] Unfortunately there is no discussion of remittances, and the amounts of remittances brought back are not recorded.

In the second phase, from the 1940s to the 1960s, labour migration was at its peak and made an important contribution to the economy of Kigezi

District. Informants recall migrating to work on cotton and coffee farms in Buganda, sugar plantations in Busoga, tea plantations and copper mines in Toro. Unfortunately migration from Ruanda-Urundi and Congo into Uganda overshadowed migration within the country, and there is relatively little information about internal migration.[55] Most men migrated on their own, or in small groups, to farms of the Baganda. In 1951 colonial officials reported alarm at the 'ever increasing exodus of adult males' from Kigezi and it was estimated that in this year over 29,000 left the district; in 1954 the figure was out at between 30 and 40,000.[56] These rates seem to have continued throughout the 1950s, and it was estimated that between 40 and 50 per cent of the total adult male population migrated each year. [57] In 1952 it was observed that 'apart from the incentives of gaining money this migration to Buganda is becoming something of a tradition and the younger generation look upon it as the recognised thing to do before settling down in the district.'[58] Oral sources suggest the temporary migration for anything between three and nine months was particularly popular amongst young men prior to marriage.[59] Bosworth's research confirms these high figures: around 50 per cent of men in her study sites were involved in labour migration during the 1950s and 1960s.[60]

In addition, some migration was organised through a recruiting office. This was opened in 1946 in Kabale, and in that year 1000 men were recruited to work on sugar estates in Busoga.[61] The Kigezi Recruitment Agency provided transport for workers who signed up to work in the plantations and mines and Bakiga were considered to be good workers. [62] The recruiting agency expanded its activities: in 1952 6,700 recruits were despatched by the Agency and this increased to a maximum of nearly 16,000 in 1955 before falling off to 8–10,000 in the late 1950s.[63] Colonial officials were extremely supportive of labour migration organised in this way, noting that greater attention could be paid to the welfare of the migrants, in contrast to those who went of their own accord, who often had to 'live in very primitive conditions and receive a very irregular and often unsuitable diet'.[64] This support for organised migration contrasts strongly with their attitudes to unorganised migration, suggesting some ambivalence about migration more generally. Concern was expressed about 'social problems' resulting from the absence of such a high proportion of the adult men, and it was noted that when migrants returned they had sufficient money for their needs, and so had 'no need or inclination' to work locally.[65] To deal with these 'social problems' and in response to the familiar concerns about overpopulation, the administration were keen to encourage family migration, but this did not prove to be popular. This is unsurprising, as leaving a family (and in particular a wife who would cultivate the land) was essential to maintaining claims to land.

Unfortunately there is no data concerning how much money was brought back by migrants, but there is evidence that these sums were not inconsiderable. In the early 1950s an underground worker at the Kilembe mines earned Shs 36 per month together with his food, while a Bakiga working in Buganda of their own accord could earn as much as Shs 60 to Shs 80 per month. In addition, they usually grew some cotton of their own. Both these figures, particularly the earnings to be made in Buganda, were considerably higher than the rates available for work within the district, where the average paid out for agricultural, government and local government work was between Shs 19 and Shs 25.[66] Informants recall that they migrated to earn money for tax, brideprice and to buy land or livestock, often going with a very specific purpose in mind.[67] This would support evidence discussed above that suggested that non-cash-based arrangements (e.g. *okutendera* and *okwatira*) declined during this period. One elderly informant, Daniel Ruheeka recalled that he went to Buganda 'to look for brideprice and tax', and after two trips of six months each he had earned enough to pay for them both.[68] Clearly then, returns on labouring in Buganda were high.

The third phase of labour migration, from the 1960s to the present, has seen a decline in the prevalence of long-distance migration. The reason given for this is that 'people got involved in their own activities and could get money around here, so there was no need to go to Buganda.'[69] While long-distance migration has reduced, migration of a different sort continues: today young men commonly migrate to regional trading centres, such as Kabale town, working, for example, as casual labourers on building sites. Like the migration to work on Buganda farms that was common in the second phase of migration, this migration is often carried out by young men prior to, and in the early years of, marriage. Bosworth explains the decline in migration to Buganda as being a result of the deteriorating economic situation throughout the country in the 1970s and civil unrest, both of which reduced the availability of work.[70] While this has no doubt been important, also significant are the increased opportunities for earning closer to home. In the 1970s and 1980s Kigezi benefited from its proximity to Rwanda as cross-border trade grew,[71] while since the 1990s Kabale town has undergone an economic boom resulting in increased opportunities for casual labour.

While long-distance labour migration (rural to rural) has declined, working away from home still occurs, suggesting that migration is still important, but the nature of it has changed since the first and second phase. A 1996 survey found that 27.5 per cent of household heads (all men) had worked away from home for at least one day in the previous 12 months. Men with less land migrated more than men with more land.[72] Bosworth found that 12 per cent of household heads had been labour migrants in the previous two years, while the Muyebe survey found that 13 per cent of households had a member who had worked away from home in the previous 12 months.[73] They were away for an average of 21 weeks, most of them working in towns in south, and especially south-western, Uganda. In stark contrast to migration in the second phase discussed above, none were working on Buganda farms. Both Bosworth's study and the Muyebe survey were conducted in sites close enough to Kabale for people to go to work there daily. In more distant sites even higher rates of migration would be expected: in Kabirizi nearly half of all households had a member who had worked away from home at some time in the past.[74] This varied from men who had worked for a few months in

Kabale, to people who permanently straddled between Kabirizi and their place of work. This straddling between rural and urban areas has been observed elsewhere.[75] Here in Kabale some 'straddlers' are individuals with more education who migrate for jobs in the formal sector – such as teachers or NGO or government employees. Such migration is often of a more long-term nature, but the migrants maintain links with their rural area, often having a wife in both the town and the rural area. Although this type of migration is not common in terms of absolute numbers, it makes an important contribution to the economy of rural areas, as we will see below.

The existence of migration alone does not imply that migration is important for rural livelihoods, as it says nothing about the significance of remittances. While there is little data on levels of remittances, Bosworth's study noted that 'almost all those households with members currently involved in labour migration received remittances on a regular or irregular basis', while the elderly, particularly women or widows also received cash remittances, often from their children. Although she did not attempt to quantify remittances, she does note that 'they were usually small and used only for day-to-day living and other services such as medical care or school provisions.'[76] This is confirmed by the Kabirizi survey, which suggests that today 28 per cent of households receive remittances, but only 8.5 per cent of households classified remittances as their most important source of income.[77] While overall female-headed households are no more likely to receive remittances than male-headed households, a greater proportion of those who classified remittances as their most important source of income were female-headed.[78] The Muyebe 2002 survey made similar findings: 23.2 per cent of households had received remittances during the previous 12 months, but only 11.6 per cent said that remittances were their first or second most important source of income.[79] Furthermore, many households with members who migrated recorded receiving no remittances.

Patterns of labour migration have thus changed: rural-to-rural migration increased during the colonial period to very high levels, but in the most recent phase the nature of migration has been rather different. Men still migrate, but instead of going to work on Buganda farms they tend to go to small towns closer to home. Furthermore, the use to which remittances are put has changed. In the first and second phases of migration remittances were used for specific investments – especially for purchase of land and/or livestock by young men prior to marriage.[80] In contrast, today remittances are more likely to be used for subsistence purposes and everyday expenses, such as taxes and school fees. Remittances rarely form the most important source of income, although elderly women dependent on absent children for cash income are an obvious exception.

Thus, today remittances are generally not used for investment in agriculture. While remittances were often used in the first two phases of migration to buy land and livestock, this enabled young men to establish a household independently, free from family ties. More generally, remittances earned from labour migration allowed people to access resources such as land and livestock without having to depend on non-cash-based arrangements. This concurs with the more general findings discussed above, that there has been a move away from non-cash-based arrangements to access key resources, to arrangements based on cash, such as buying and renting land, and wage labour.

While generally therefore remittances do not appear to be 'driving' the agricultural changes, as Murton found, there are, however, important exceptions, particularly in relation to 'straddlers'. These individuals 'straddle' between towns where they have formal jobs, or other businesses, and rural areas. Many of them have links with the government and they are often the very same individuals who gained access to large areas of swamp land (see Chapter 5).[81] While relatively few in terms of absolute numbers,[82] they have made a significant impact on Kigezi's agriculture and landscape and make an important contribution to the rural economy. They do this in two ways. First, they use their urban-derived non-farm incomes to employ labourers, to increase the investment of labour in their land, which has positive environmental consequences. These richer households fallow more, and also use their land more intensively by investing more labour in it, and it is here that hired labour is critical. Second, some of them have used urban-derived non-farm incomes to invest in dairy farming, which is highly capital-intensive. But this has had negative environmental consequences, in terms of loss of habitat and the impacts that has on biodiversity.[83]

One aspect of labour migration that should be examined is the impact of male migration on women. This is an area that has received much attention in the southern Africa literature,[84] but in Kigezi many informants felt that women were little affected by men migrating, because women did most of the agricultural work anyway. Rather, it was women whose husbands stayed away for a long time who were affected.[85] It is certainly the case that, with women responsible for the bulk of agricultural activities, the loss of male labour might not be very great. The most significant male task was the clearing of land, and by the time that men started migrating in large numbers in the mid-colonial period there was relatively little 'new' land needing heavy clearing. Those who would have been most affected were those who wanted to extend into new areas of land such as recently reclaimed swamps. Indeed a number of informants recall 'missing out' on being able to claim reclaimed swamps, because their husbands were away and they were unable to clear the land.[86] But this is the only time that the negative effects of men's absence were observed.

The ability, or otherwise, to claim reclaimed swampland is just one factor that has had an impact on changing patterns of differentiation, and it is to this that we now turn. Murton's research highlighted the importance of considering non-agricultural activities for their role in contributing to a sustainable agricultural system. Thus while he showed that positive environmental changes had occurred at a regional level, this was partly due to contributions from the non-agricultural sector. The research presented above shows that people from Kigezi have a long history of labour migration. But in contrast to Machakos, remittances in Kigezi were not used simply for investment in agriculture but were used by young men to establish households without having to depend on their parents. More recently a small but significant minority of people who straddle urban and rural areas have used urban-derived incomes to invest in agriculture. This has been through investment in additional labour (with positive environmental impacts) and investment in dairy farms, which have been argued to have negative environmental consequences. In addition, dairy farms have contributed to increased differentiation in the area, which the following section explores.

Differentiation

LAND OWNERSHIP & DIFFERENTIATION

Murton's work suggested that the environmental improvements highlighted by Tiffen *et al.* in Machakos were accompanied by increased polarisation of land holdings. In 1965 the richest quintile of farmers owned 40 per cent of the land, a figure which had increased to over 55 per cent by 1996. The poorest quintile had owned eight per cent of the land in 1965, and this was reduced to three per cent in 1996. But Murton found that this increase in differentiation of land ownership was driven largely by differential access to urban wages and capital. Whatever was driving it, we need to ask whether the same thing has happened in Kigezi.

The existence of the 1939 Kabirizi survey enables us to explore changing patterns of land ownership.[87] Today, unsurprisingly, land ownership is closely associated with wealth group: with households in the richest quartile owning an average of 3.75 acres compared to households in the poorest quartile who own only 0.6 acres.[88] The close relationship between land ownership and wealth group that is found in Kabirizi today is shown in Figure 7.1.

The figure also indicates how much land people actually cultivate, compared to how much they own and it is clear that wealthier households do not cultivate all the land they own, while poorer households cultivate more than they own. Ownership of land is only one means of accessing it, and today 30 per cent of households in Kabirizi use more land than they own by entering into borrowing, and more usually renting, arrangements.[89] The importance of accessing land by renting for cash again illustrates the shift towards cash-based arrangements, and the vibrant land market and high rates of land rental. Other surveys have made similar findings.[90]

Land ownership patterns have changed. The Kabirizi survey showed that the average acreage of land owned per household fell: from 2.82 acres in 1939, to 1.25 acre in 2000.[91] But some households have successfully maintained their ownership of land, and Figure 7.2 illustrates the degree to which land ownership is differentiated, and how this has changed.

Showing the percentage of population against percentage of land owned in both 1939 and 2000, Figure 7.2 demonstrates that land ownership is differentiated, and indeed always has been. But there is a suggestion that it has become more differentiated over the past 60 years: a change that has

Figure 7.1 *Land ownership & use, by wealth group, Kabirizi 2000*[92]

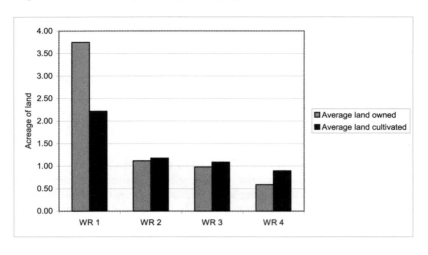

Figure 7.2 *Land differentiation in Kabirizi, 1939–2000*[93]

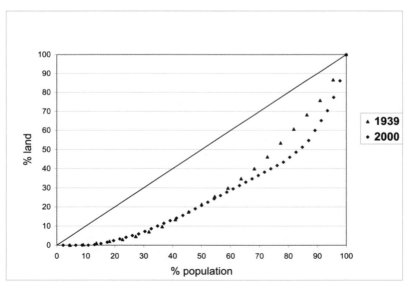

occurred at the richer end of the spectrum. At the poorer end the poorest 20 per cent of the population owned less than 3 per cent of the land in both 1939 and 2000: there has been little change.[94]   But at the rich end of the spectrum there has been a shift and the richest 20 per cent of the population have increased the proportion of the land that they own – from about 41 per cent in 1939, to 54 per cent today.[95]   This would suggest that, while the rich have got richer, the poor have not necessarily got any poorer.

Other surveys have had similar findings of highly differentiated land ownership. A 1996 survey found that the wealthiest group of landholders (who owned over 11 acres) owned 55.5 per cent of the land, while they made up only 18 per cent of the population. At the other end, households in the poorest group (owning 0 to 5 acres of land) made up 62 per cent of the population, and owned only 23.5 per cent of the land. [96] Data from Muyebe (2002) found an even more differentiated pattern of land ownership, with the richest 20 per cent of the population owning 72 per cent of the land, while the poorest 50 per cent of the population owned only 11 per cent of the land. As was shown above, Muyebe is the site of a large range of livelihood diversification activities, and it is possible that this has contributed to increased differentiation of land ownership.[97]

Furthermore, the same data presented differently tells us more. Figure 7.3 shows the acreages of land owned by all the households in the two surveys in Kabirizi conducted 61 years apart, with each dot representing one household. It shows that the prevalence of landlessness has increased, from 4.6 per cent in 1939 to 10.9 per cent today.[98] Furthermore, there has been an increase in 'near landlessness' – that is the numbers of people owning one acre or less

Figure 7.3 *Land owned, Kabirizi 1939–2000*[99]

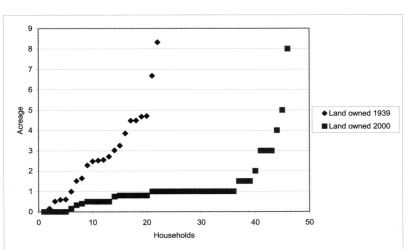

today, compared to 1939.[100] So while the rich have got richer, and the poor have not got poorer, there do appear to be *more* poor than before. Thus, while land ownership has declined for everyone, it has done so to different degrees. Some households have successfully maintained their ownership of land, while others have declined significantly. While the richest have increased the proportion of land that they own, there is more landlessness and near landlessness, indicating increased differentiation of land ownership. Moreover, there also appears to have been increased differentiation of particular types of land owned – in particular swampland. Swamp reclamation has been associated with increasingly differentiated patterns of both land and livestock ownership, and it is to the latter that we now turn.

LIVESTOCK OWNERSHIP & DIFFERENTIATION
Historical data and contemporary surveys indicate that livestock ownership has declined since the colonial period, as illustrated in Table 7.2.

Table 7.2 *Livestock ownership, Kigezi district, 1939–2002*

	Kabirizi, 1939[101]	Kabirizi, 2000[102]	Kabale, 1996[103]	Muyebe, 2002[104]
Percentage of households owning:				
Cattle	55	23	31	20
Goats	59	43	25	41
Average number of livestock owned:				
Cattle	2.6	0.6	1.1	1.0
Goats	3.9	1.2	1.1	2.9
Sheep	1.6	0.8	0.9	1.0
Chickens	2.2	2.1	3.5	4.3

Table 7.2 compares data from the 1939 Kabirizi survey, and three surveys conducted between 1996 and 2002. It demonstrates that both the percentage of households owning livestock, and the average number of livestock owned per household, have declined since 1939.[105] There are a number of reasons for such falls: today there is less grazing space available, livestock appear to be less important as a means of saving, cattle are only used symbolically for bridewealth (the majority of the payment being in cash), and finally, informants say that with children going to school there is no-one to look after livestock.[106]

The reduction in grazing, frequently mentioned by informants, is confirmed by findings in relation to changes to grazing outlined in the previous chapter: from 1945 to 1996 there has been a shift in grazing areas from the steep back-slopes and hilltops to swampland.[107] Associated with this shift are changes in the ownership of grazing land: while previously no grazing land was owned on an individual basis, [108] today grazing land which is predominantly in swamp, is almost entirely individually owned. Chapter 5 showed how the colonial desire to encourage 'progressive' farmers led them to move away from a policy that would have distributed swampland in small plots for subsistence farming. Instead, those who were considered most likely to be able to develop the swampland into 'economic' units were encouraged so that such people were able to claim larger areas of swampland. Thus some individuals (many with links to both the colonial and/or post-colonial state) laid claim to large areas of reclaimed swamp, which they turned over to high quality pasture grazed by exotic cows for milking. Today just over 50 per cent of swamps are used for grazing. [109]

Dairy farmers form a distinctive group of livestock owners, having established dairy farms on reclaimed swampland. [110] Many of them are the same individuals who gained access to this land through their links with the state. Others have purchased land more recently. [111] This high quality grazing land is only used for dairy milk production, which is highly capital-intensive. Thus while livestock ownership has generally declined since the colonial period, it has become increasingly differentiated, with small numbers of rich farmers owning large numbers of high quality dairy cattle grazed on former swampland.

These results suggest some interesting changing patterns of differentiation. There has been an increase in the number of people who are landless and who own no livestock, and both land and livestock ownership has become increasingly differentiated. A few rich farmers own large numbers of high value livestock, which are grazed on what is now individually owned high quality grazing land. Ownership of this grazing land in the former swamps is highly differentiated, much of it having been acquired through links with the colonial and post-colonial state.

Livelihoods and well-being

Thus far we have explored three key aspects of livelihoods, and changes to them: labouring, migration and differentiation. But these changes need to be located within the debates about livelihoods in their broadest sense. As Murton has shown, at a household level, the Machakos experience is neither homogenous nor unproblematic, and he draws attention to the importance of exploring 'livelihood sustainability' as well as 'environmental sustainability'. While he examines access to non-farm income, land differentiation and differential trends in agricultural productivity, he does not look at some of the other aspects included in the concept of livelihoods, and it is to these that we now turn.

Sustainable livelihoods approaches place people, and the priorities that they define, at the centre of any analysis, and such approaches have been extremely influential. [112] The concept of sustainable livelihoods builds upon participatory approaches to development, and the recent 'paradigm shift' in development policy towards participation, empowerment and capacity-building is striking. The rationale for participatory development is clear: 'only when the supposed beneficiaries of intervention participate in the planning and implementation of projects which are intended to benefit them will they have any interest in making development projects succeed.'[113] How poor people themselves view development, and indeed how they define poverty, is increasingly seen as being important – in contrast to externally imposed views and definitions. [114]

Contemporary approaches, being more systematic and holistic, recognise the multiple strategies that people adopt and the multiple outcomes that they pursue, while understanding the dynamic nature of livelihoods.[115] These multiple outcomes are key: using the concept of livelihoods ensures that not only are issues of income, food security and natural resource sustainability considered, but also issues of well-being and vulnerability. [116] More importantly, people themselves define the criteria that are important. It is clear that people value non-material goods, and their sense of well-being is affected by numerous factors, including for example, self-esteem, security, and a sense of control and inclusion, as well as more conventionally measured material concerns.[117] The multi-dimensionality of poverty needs to be stressed.[118] One study, for example, suggests that core components of poverty are a state of dependence and a lack of psychological well-being. There are multiple aspects of well-being: material, bodily, security, social and freedom of choice and action. Non-material components of poverty, incorporating self-respect, dignity and freedom to make decisions, are less commonly considered by outsiders, but are critical from the point of view of the poor.[119] Work by Sen has put forward the concept of development as freedom: the freedom to choose a life that a person values. He argues that it is not merely utilities nor the primary goods that need to be understood, but the substantive freedoms to choose a life one has reason to value. Thus development is the process of expanding the real freedoms that people enjoy.[120]

So how have livelihoods, in this broad sense that encompasses well-being and vulnerability, changed in Kigezi? The evidence suggests that in some key ways livelihoods have improved for many poorer households: first, in terms of self-esteem, second, in relation to knowing what to expect, or a sense of 'predictability', and third in terms of being free to make decisions. In Kigezi many of the non-monetarised arrangements (such as *okucwa encuro* and *okutendera*) for gaining access to resources had some social stigma attached to them, thus contributing to low self-esteem, and a lack of psychological well-being. In contrast, working in return for cash – which has increased and is now undertaken by all but the very richest and very poorest – has no social stigma attached to it, and indeed is valued positively.

The second key negative aspect of non-monetarised arrangements for the poor was their fluidity and 'open-endedness'. Most notably labourers would not know how much work they would have to do before, for example, getting an animal. Similarly, getting land in return for labouring was highly negotiable – indeed the term *okwatira* is often initially translated as 'for free' before people explain that the person would be expected to work for the land-owner. The amount to be worked was usually undefined, and a person who wanted to continue to enter such arrangements would have to ensure that he maintained good relations and thus their negotiating position would have been weak. But it was the 'not knowing' that made life difficult. In contrast, today there is a widely recognised rate of pay, and people have a clear idea of how much work they will have to do for the said payment.

Finally, the increase in monetarised arrangements has been associated with increased freedom to make decisions, with positive implications for the livelihoods of the poor. Being involved in many of the non-cash-based arrangements effectively 'tied' a person to their host – such that they were not free to decide who they bought livestock from, or accessed land through. The increased opportunities to earn cash were mentioned by both rich and poor informants as having led to improvements in the lives of the poor: they can 'migrate to other places … sell crops more easily today than in the past and can go and work for money'. Or as one poor man said, 'the life of the poor [has] got better of course, because now we can go and work for money to improve our welfare.'[121] People are free to decide who to work for, and for how long. In addition, informants felt that involvement in non-monetarised arrangements meant that poor people had little freedom to make more 'everyday' decisions – such as when to eat meat: 'In the past poor people only ate meat if given it by the rich. Now poor can eat meat because they can work for money.' Today people who work for cash are free to decide how to spend it, and, for example, being able to buy livestock was frequently cited as evidence that life has got better for poor people.[122] Being free to make decisions such as when and from whom to buy livestock, from whom and for how long to rent land, and when to eat meat, all contribute to a sense of well-being.

Thus for many poor people the shift towards cash-based arrangements has led to a number of improvements in their well-being. Working for cash, and in turn buying food for cash, is not seen as low status and has no social stigma attached to it. While not necessarily meaning that the (economic) standard of living of the poor has improved, such changes have significantly improved well-being more broadly. The poor have increased opportunities of earning cash, which is a highly valued activity, have a much clearer idea of what the returns to their labour will be and have increased freedom to make decisions. Changes to such intangible and difficult-to-measure factors, such as status and self-esteem, are critically important to a feeling of well-being, and thus to livelihoods, and need to be understood and included in any analysis of livelihood change.

Also in need of greater understanding and further research are the negative aspects of the shift from non-monetarised arrangements. Such arrangements were two-sided and, while the shift towards cash has in some ways benefited the poor, there may also have been negative effects of the transition. What might be called the 'patronage' side of the relationship has fallen away with the transition to cash, and the effect of this on the poor is unknown. Poorer households would, for example, have been able to turn to their 'hosts' in times of need. Informants noted that in the past the rich were 'very sympathetic to the poor', whereas today the 'rich don't give to the poor'. [123] While this might be a romanticised view of the past, others noted that today there is less interaction between the rich and poor: 'in the past you [a poor person] would go to work there [for the rich person] and ... the rich would invite you ... and you would spend a day drinking together but now there is no interaction. The rich interact with their fellow rich.'[124] Being able to work, rent land, or buy livestock from anyone might give people greater flexibility, freedom and self-esteem, but it might also result in the loss of relationships that provided protection. The switch to cash may thus have loosened these ties and so increased vulnerability. Furthermore, such freedoms are only an advantage if labour demand is high.[125] Should further changes occur to the agricultural system, or the economy more widely, that significantly reduce labour demand, then the positive aspects of cash-based arrangements may become less pronounced. Finally, there is likely to be a gender dimension to how the shift towards cash-based arrangements is experienced. More particularly, the seasonality of labour demands is felt less by men (who can and do also seek work in urban areas), than by women (who rarely go to towns for work). It may therefore be that women feel the negative aspects of the shift – such as loss of patronage – more strongly, while benefiting less from the positive aspects.

Conclusion

In Kigezi positive environmental practices are undertaken, but these are not carried out by everyone homogeneously. While overall more land is being fallowed, which is good for the environment, there are broader changes to livelihoods which must be considered. People in Kigezi today engage in a range of livelihood activities. While sales of agricultural produce are the most important source of income for most households, other activities are important, particularly in areas close to urban centres, or with good transport links. In all sites demands for labour are high and labouring for other people is common, while for poorer households labouring for other people is a critical source of income. But labouring for others is not a new phenomenon: it has long been occurring, but was not a part of the cash economy and, as such, was hidden from view.

Furthermore, labouring for others is, in fact, an activity with very variable returns. People across the wealth spectrum are involved in labouring for others, and different arrangements give them different returns, as well as different levels of security. Richer individuals labour as part of labour-loaning groups, gaining access to money for credit, and higher returns through the interest collected on such loans. In contrast, poorer individuals are more likely to work as part of simple labour-rotation groups, or individually at a daily rate. There are also other arrangements by which people worked for others in the past, which did not involve cash, and the labour was exchanged in return for access to land, livestock or food. These have declined in importance, and in some cases disappeared, and at the same time there has been an increase in monetarised arrangements, such as buying and renting land, purchasing livestock, and labouring for cash. Having said that, the very poorest do still get involved in such arrangements, with all the social stigma that they involve.

While livelihood diversification activities have become more visible with this shift towards cash-based activities, there have also been shifts in the nature of migration, historically an important income-earning activity. Migration increased in importance during the colonial period, peaking from the 1940s to 1960s. Young men commonly migrated to Buganda to work on cotton farms. Earnings were considerably higher than could be made in the district and many young men earned money in this way in order to get married and establish a household. More recently, while some migration continues, it is rarely to Buganda. Instead men migrate to nearby trading centres and towns, where there are opportunities of earning money closer to home. Some stay in urban areas for long periods, 'straddling' the rural and urban. While many households receive some remittances from migrants, these rarely form a significant proportion of income, and many households with migrants received no remittances at all. But by enabling young men to establish households, remittances make it possible for them to gain access to resources such as livestock for brideprice and land, without depending on their parents.

Land ownership – so central to people's livelihoods – has always been differentiated, but has become more so – especially at the richer end of the spectrum with the richest people increasing the proportion of the land that they own. While poorer households have not got poorer (in land terms at least) there are more poor than before. The vibrant land market that exists in Kigezi today may have contributed to increased land differentiation, and Kigezi's land market has a long history. Richer households are more involved in the land market, buying and selling land as a normal part of their household cycle. There is also a vibrant market in land rental with about a third of households renting land. Livestock ownership has declined, which is associated with changes in grazing patterns and in the role of livestock in Bakiga society. No longer forming the key component of brideprice payments (which are now largely paid in cash), livestock are not owned by the majority of the population today. But there are livestock owners who have had a major impact on Kigezi's landscape: dairy farmers. These individuals are very often the same individuals who claimed reclaimed swampland, and have established large capital-intensive dairy farms in the former swamps.

People's livelihoods in Kigezi have changed along with the changes to their agricultural system. The picture highlights the multidimensionality of livelihoods, the importance of well-being and the importance of exploring such changes through a historical approach. In the final chapter I place these findings within contemporary development debates.

Notes

[1] Tiffen *et al.*, *More People, Less Erosion.* Murton, 'Population growth and poverty in Machakos'.

[2] See for example D. Booth *et al.*, *Social, Cultural and Economic Change in Contemporary Tanzania: A people-oriented focus*, (Stockholm, 1993). And various works by Bryceson: D. Bryceson, 'Deagrarianization and Rural Employment in sub-Saharan Africa: A Sectoral Perspective', *World Development*, 24 1 (1996) 97–111; D. Bryceson and V. Jamal (eds), *Farewell to Farms: De-agrarianisation and employment in Africa*, (Aldershot, 1997); D. Bryceson, 'African rural labour, income diversification and livelihood approaches: A long-term development perspective', *Review of African Political Economy*, 80 (1999), 171–89; D. Bryceson, *Sub-Saharan Africa Betwixt and Between: Rural Livelihood Practices and Policies*, Africa Studies Centre Working Paper 43 (Leiden, Netherlands, 1999); D. Bryceson, *Rural Africa at the Crossroads: Livelihood Practices and Policies*, ODI Natural Resource Perspectives, 52 (London, 2000).

[3] F. Ellis, 'Household strategies and rural livelihood diversification', *The Journal of Development Studies*, 35 1 (1998), 1–38. F. Ellis, *Rural Livelihoods and Diversity in Developing Countries*, (Oxford, 2000). Bryceson, *Rural Africa at the Crossroads*. T. Reardon, J. Berdegu and G. Escobar (eds), *World Development*, Special Issue on 'Rural nonfarm employment and incomes in Latin America', 29 3 (2001). C.D. Barrett, T. Reardon and P. Webb, 'Non-farm income diversification and household livelihood strategies in rural Africa: Concepts, dynamics, and policy implications' *Food Policy*, 26 4 (2001), 315–331. T. Reardon, 'Using evidence of household income diversification to inform study of rural non-farm labour market in Africa', *World Development*, 25 5 (1997) 735–47; B.L. Turner *et al. Population Growth and Agricultural Change in Africa* (Gainesville, FL, 1993); G. Carswell, 'Livelihood diversification: increasing in importance or increasingly recognised? Evidence from southern Ethiopia', *Journal of International Development* 14 6 (2002), 789–804.

[4] Ellis, *Rural Livelihoods*, 15, 11.

[5] Ellis, 'Household strategies', 7; Ellis, *Rural Livelihoods*.

[6] It is beyond the scope of this chapter to deal with the determinants of diversification or the impact of diversification on income differentiation . See Ellis, 'Household strategies'; S. Dercon and P. Krishnan, 'Income Portfolios in Rural Ethiopia and Tanzania: Choices and Constraints', *The Journal of Development Studies*, 32 6 (1996), 850–75; S. Canagarajah, C. Newman and R. Bhattamishra, 'Non-farm income, gender and inequality: evidence from rural Ghana and Uganda', *Food Policy* 26 (2001), 405–20.

[7] No attempt was made to collect detailed information on the amount of income received from different sources, but simply which of the different sources was most important.

[8] All households were categorised into different wealth groups, based on group discussions with key informants about what constituted wealth, followed by a wealth-ranking exercise. Three groups were initially identified (Rich – *Omugiiga;* Medium – *Omukozi;* Poor – *Aboora).* The largest group was the medium category (23 out of 44), so this was further divided, so that four groups were agreed (with sub-groups within some of the groups), and all households placed into a group. The factors that were raised in discussions of what constituted wealth were whether they had big plantations (the term plantations refers specifically to land under *matoke*, as distinct from simply general land for cultivation), whether or not they have other work (e.g. as a teacher), and whether they do, or use, labour. (Kabirizi Survey, 2000).

[9] *De facto* female-headed households = 36 per cent of Kabirizi survey, while male-headed households made up 64 per cent of the survey. First and second sources of income are combined here.

[10] Bryceson, 'Deagrarianization and Rural Employment'; Bryceson, 'Rural Africa at the crossroads'; Bryceson and Jamal, *Farewell to Farms*.

[11] Bryceson, 'African rural labour, income diversification and livelihood approaches'.

[12] Bryceson, 'Rural Africa at the crossroads'.

[13] It is unclear to what extent the age of informant was taken into account in this calculation. Age and position in the household cycle may be important in determining involvement in diversification activities. Failure to consider the age of the informants would therefore seriously undermine these findings.

[14] Bryceson, *Sub-Saharan Africa Betwixt and Between*, 10.

[15] See Booth *et al.*, *Social, Cultural and Economic Change*. See also E. Francis, *Making a Living: Changing livelihoods in rural Africa* (London, 2000).

[16] Purseglove, 'Kitozho Mutala survey', 5. This survey was conducted in 1939 before attempts were made to restrict and control agricultural sales through colonial marketing regulations – see Chapter 2.

[17] Wright, 'Kitozho Mutala survey' (1938); Kabirizi Survey (2000), Muyebe Survey (2002).

[18] The importance of remoteness to poverty and diversification has been usefully informed by discussions with Kay Sharp, to whom I am grateful. The issue has been explored elsewhere, see for example A. Abdulai and A. CroleRees, 'Determinants of income diversification amongst rural households in southern Mali', *Food Policy*, 26 (2001), 437–52; K. Bird and A. Shepherd, 'Livelihoods and chronic poverty in semi-arid Zimbabwe', *World Development*, 31 3 (2003), 591–610.

[19] While there are obvious difficulties in discussing involvement in the illicit trade with Rwanda, many factors would point to his involvement.

[20] 02/Muy/56.

[21] Rates of pay for labour are generally well known and widely recognised. Today women are paid the same as men, suggesting that they are able to command equal wages as a result of high labour demand.

[22] Lindblade *et al.* 'More People, More Fallow', 48–9.

[23] Lindblade *et al.* 'More People, More Fallow', 49.

[24] A wealth-ranking exercise was conducted in Muyebe. All households were categorised into different wealth groups, based on group discussions with key informants about what constituted wealth, followed by a wealth-ranking exercise. Four groups were initially identified (Rich – *Omugiiga*; Medium– *Omukozi*; Poor – *Aboora*; and Poorest – *Runkunka*). By far the majority of the population were placed in the medium category (49 out of 69), so this was further divided, until eventually seven groups were agreed, and all households placed into a group. The factors that were raised in discussions of what constituted wealth were whether they had a good house, land and livestock and whether their children could go to school. Whether people worked for others, or whether they had formal jobs, were also mentioned. The poorest group, *runkunku* were described as those who, even if they had land, were poor either due to ill-health, laziness or alcoholism: 'they do not even work for others, they just sit on the road and beg, and don't do anything' (Muyebe Survey 2002).

The richest group of 9 households made up 13 per cent of the survey, and 88 per cent of them hired labour. The poorest group of 11 households (this combined *Aboora* and *Runkunka* households) made up 16 per cent of the survey, and 27 per cent of them hired labour (Muyebe Survey 2002). As would be expected, households with more land, those with a migrant member, and those receiving remittances are more likely to hire labour.

[25] 02/Muy/22. For other digging groups where they divide the money each week see 02/Kbz/7. There is no particular Rukiga word for these types of digging groups – they are simply known as *ekiibina kabahiingi*. This literally means 'groups that dig' but does not distinguish whether or not they also function as loaning groups as well (02/Muy/23). Other types of groups include saving groups, brewing groups and 'meat' groups. Saving groups do not always loan money. For example in one Muyebe group each member contributes a fixed sum each month, and they take it in turns to receive the money. (02/Muy/17a). See also 02/Muy/14.

[26] 02/Kbz/10.

[27] He gave the example of digging a pit latrine: A pit latrine is dug to 30 feet. For each foot

he is paid 3000/-, and he can dig between one to one and a half feet per day. In contrast, the standard rate for agricultural labour is 1000/- per day.

[28] 02/Muy/21.

[29] 02/Muy/21.

[30] 02/Kbz/5a, 02/Kbz/5b, 02/Kbz/5c and 02/Kbz/5d.

[31] 02/Kbz/53.

[32] These rates are comparable to those charged by all saving and loaning groups. See 02/Kbz/45 and 02/Kbz/41b and 02/Muy/17a; 02/Muy/17b; 02/Muy/24; 02/Muy/48; 02/Muy/15c; 02/Muy/T60 and 02/Muy/T64.

[33] Purseglove, 'Kitozho mutala survey', 12.

[34] 02/Muy/T30a. Informants frequently state that *okwatira* is using land for free, before going on to explain that the borrower would be expected to work for the land owner.

[35] 02/Muy/T30a and 02/Muy/T34.

[36] Baryayanga was himself employing someone in return for food only, but it was notable that when discussing this man, Baryayanga did not use the term *okucwa encuro*. 02/Kbz/5b.

[37] 02/Muy/53a.

[38] 02/Muy/T34. It was also observed that in practice young women themselves would often end up 'working' their own brideprice – i.e. working for their fathers after marriage in order to payoff the brideprice owed by their husbands.

[39] 02/Muy/36c and 02/Kbz/5d. There was no consensus on the name given to the arrangement of working in return for livestock. The terms *okugabira* and *okugabisa* were used (giving or getting something). Although strictly speaking these terms imply that the thing is given or received for free, in practice there is usually the expectation that something will be done in return, and these terms were also used with reference to working in return for livestock and for land. See 02/Muy/T28; 02/Muy/T34 and 02/Muy/T33.

[40] 02/Muy/T28 and 02/Muy/T34.

[41] Purseglove, 'Kitozho mutala survey'.

[42] 02/Kbz/6 and 02/Kbz/5b; 02/Muy/T33.

[43] 02/Muy/T34 and 02/Muy/T15b.

[44] In 2002 I was told by a number of people in different locations that the recognised daily rate for men and women was 1000/-. In contrast, in 2000 I was told of rates between 500/- and 1000/-. It appeared that the rates were higher closer to Kabale town (800–1500/-). But significantly there also appears to have been a gender dimension. Bujara explained that in the past women worked for less, but more recently they had started refusing lower rates, and as a result sometimes both are paid the same ['now all are paid 1000/- for a working day but … women [were] …working for 800/- but of recent they refused it.' 00/Muy/20a. See also 00/Muy23b.

[45] 00/Kab/T9a. See also 00/Kab/T1b, 00/Kab/T4a and 00/Kab/T7a.

[46] Murton, 'Population growth and poverty', 45. He contrasts this with areas of India where Breman has argued that increasing inequality has arisen 'as a result of exploitation of the poorest farmers by a local bourgeoisie within rural labour markets'. J. Breman, *Of Peasants, Migrants and Paupers: Rural labour circulation and capitalist production in West India* (Delhi, 1985) Breman argues that during the first half of the twentieth century 'terms of employment became increasingly impersonal and more contractual in nature'. He notes therefore that 'given the magnitude of the landless class and the slow growth of the economy in and out of agriculture, the exploitation of labour continued unabated.' (p.300). He also notes that, while the poor have not become poorer, the gap between them and the less poor has increased such that 'prosperity has increased far more strongly than poverty has decreased' (p.332). Also re how the poorest compare their own life standard with visible signs of increasing prosperity that they see around them, especially amongst their employers (p.352). For further discussion about the pros and cons of labour relationships based on patronage see J. Breman, *Beyond Patronage and Exploitation: Changing Agrarian Relations in South Gujarat* (Delhi, 1993).

[47] See for example C. Murray *Families Divided: The Impact of Migrant Labour in Lesotho*

(Cambridge, 1981); Francis, *Making a Living*; A. de Haan and B. Rogaly, *Labour Mobility and Rural Society* (London, 2002).

[48] See for example A. de Haan, K. Brock and N. Coulibaly, 'Migration, Livelihoods and Institutions: Contrasting patterns of migration in Mali' in A. de Haan and B. Rogaly (eds), *Labour Mobility and Rural Society* (London, 2002). For South African studies see Murray, *Families divided* and J. Ferguson, *Expectations of Modernity: Myths and meanings of urban life on the Zambian Copperbelt* (Berkeley, CA, 1999). Other studies from West Africa have found that remittances are low, and rarely invested in agriculture – see R. David, *Changing Places: Women, Resource Management and Migration in the Sahel'* (London, 1995). A recent study of Cameroon found that remittances from young migrants to their elderly parents are less in situations when they do not intend to return to their place of origin and do not expect any sizeable inheritance. See G. Schrieder and B. Knerr, 'Labour migration as a social security mechanism for smallholder households in sub-Saharan Africa: The case of Cameroon', *Oxford Development Studies*, 28 2 (2000), 223–36.

[49] Murton, 'Population growth and poverty in Machakos'.

[50] Wrigley, *Crops and Wealth*, 34–5.

[51] Harsh rural conditions and the demands made on the rural population by chiefs were important in pushing Rwandans to migrate to search for work, while higher earnings than could be got at home were an important pull factor. See Newbury, *The Cohesion of Oppression*, 157. See also Kagame, *Abrégé*, Vol. 2, 205; J.P. Chrétien, 'Des sédentaires devenus migrants: les motifs des départs des Barundi et des Banyarwanda vers l'Uganda (1920–60)', *Cultures et Developpement* 10 1 (1978), 71–101, both cited in Newbury. See also G. Prunier, *The Rwanda Crisis: History of a Genocide* (London, 1995), 35; M. Mamdani, *When Victims Become Killers: Colonialism Nativism and the Genocide in Rwanda* (Princeton, NJ, 2001), 110–11, 162–4.

[52] WPAR, 1923. See also WPARs for 1922 and 1937. P.E. Powesland, 'A history of migration', in Audrey Richards (ed.), *Economic Development and Tribal Change*. 2nd edn. (Nairobi, 1973), 29.

[53] This figure excludes those who were away for five years or more.

[54] Wright, 'Kitozho survey', 25–26.

[55] In 1951 almost as many migrants taking the northern route came from Congo, as came from West Nile. For those on the south-western route just over half were from Ruanda-Urundi, about a quarter were from Kigezi, with the rest from Tanganyika and Ankole. Richards, *Economic Development and Tribal Change*, 63. Labour migrants worked on cotton farms in southern and central Uganda, where demand for labour exceeded supply. See also Wrigley, *Crops and Wealth*.

[56] Annual Report of the Labour Department, 1951. WPAR, 1951 and 1954.

[57] WPAR, 1954, 1956, 1958, 1959. In 1959 it was believed that 40–50 per cent of the total adult male population were absent from Kigezi at any one time. Annual Report of the Labour Department, 1951, WPAR 1954 and 1958.

[58] WPAR, 1952.

[59] For example 00/Kbz/26a, 00/Kbz/30a, 02/Muy/T15e; 02/Muy/T34.

[60] Bosworth, 'Land and Society', 187.

[61] WPAR, 1939–46. See also Powesland, 'History of migration'.

[62] WPAR, 1951.

[63] 1952: 6,700; 1953: 9,697; 1954: 12, 887; 1955: 15,825; 1956: 9,514; 1957: 8,258; 1958: 10,000; 1959: 8,000. Source: WPARs.

[64] WPAR, 1951.

[65] WPAR, 1952, 1953.

[66] WPAR, 1951, 1; WPAR, 1952, para 149.

[67] 02/Muy/T15e, 02/Kbz44b; 00/Kbz/26a and 00/Kbz/30a.

[68] 02/Kbz/44b.

[69] 00/Kbz/26a and 00/Kbz/30a.

[70] Bosworth, 'Land and Society', 103. Furthermore, part of the reason for the decline in migration to Buganda may be because there are fewer opportunities of growing cotton in Buganda today, and it was this that was the real incentive for migration during the

colonial period, rather than just earnings from labouring for Baganda. Others have also suggested that economic downturns have led to significant reductions in labour migration – for Kenya see E. Francis, 'Gender, Migration and Multiple Livelihoods: Cases from Eastern and Southern Africa' in de Haan and Rogaly, *Labour Mobility and Rural Society* and for Zambia see Ferguson, *Expectations of Modernity*.

[71] Cross-border trade has a long history – see Chapter 4. This trade has continued, although periodically (for example from Dec 1990 to late 1994) the border has been closed, and Bosworth argues that this had a seriously detrimental effect on the local economy. (Bosworth, 'Land and Society', 122). Today trade, both legal and illegal, is flourishing.

[72] Lindblade *et al.*, 'More People, More Fallow', 49.

[73] Bosworth, 'Land and Society', 187; Muyebe Survey, 2002.

[74] 48 per cent. Although they were asked whether they had *ever* worked away.

[75] Such straddling often coincides with polygamy, with such migrants having a wife in each of the two locations. This may be because having a wife in the place of origin helps to maintain rights over land. This has also been referred to as bi-locality households or multi-locality households. See S. Wiggins and S. Proctor, 'Migration and the rural non-farm sector' (Reading, 1999). Also see W. Smit, 'The rural linkages of urban households in Durban, South Africa', *Environment and Urbanization*, 10 1 (1998), 77–87; and Francis, 'Gender, migration and multiple livelihoods'.

[76] Bosworth, 'Land and Society', 188.

[77] 13 out of 47 households receive remittances, but only 4 of these classify remittances as their most important source of income (Kabirizi Survey, 2000).

[78] 38 per cent of those receiving remittances are female-headed households, which is equal to female-headed households as a proportion of the total sample. Of the four households for whom remittances were the most important source of income three were *de facto* female-headed households, receiving money from absent husbands or children.

[79] 16 out of 69 households received remittances, but only 8 of these said that remittances were their first or second most important source of income. (Muyebe survey, 2002)

[80] This is confirmed by Bosworth who notes a link between labour migration in the 1950s and 1960s and purchases of land: those who had purchased the most land were usually retired labour migrants, while those who have never migrated have purchased less land. Boworth, 'Land and Society', 191–2.

[81] For example Batuma, Makara, Pison and Otunga all work, or have worked, for the government in various positions, and have all invested heavily in agriculture. Batuma and Makara both have dairy farms on swampland.

[82] None of these were picked up by the 1996, 2000 or 2002 surveys as they do not live at the farms.

[83] International conservation agencies, such as IUCN (World Conservation Union), have expressed concern about the negative impact on biodiversity of the cultivation of swamps, and calls have been made for swamps to be protected. Such concerns that have led to this policy reversal are to a large degree externally driven – see Carswell, 'Continuities in Environmental Narratives'. Paradoxically, these concerns about biodiversity in swamps have largely come too late, as by the time they were being articulated, most of the swamps had already been drained. But legislation that has been put in place in 2000 has been described by the DEO as 'politically explosive' and as a 'wish list' that was impossible to implement.

[84] Murray, *Families Divided*; B. O'Laughlin, 'Missing men? The debate over rural poverty and women-headed households in Southern Africa', *Journal of Peasant Studies*, 25 2 (1998), 1–48, J.C. Plath, D. W. Holland, J. W. Carvalho, 'Labor migration in Southern Africa and agricultural development – some lessons from Lesotho', *Journal of Developing Areas*, 21 2 (1987), 159–76. See also David, 'Changing Places'. See also S. Chant (ed.), *Gender and Migration in Developing Countries* (London, 1992); S. Chant, 'Households, gender and rural–urban migration: reflections on linkages and considerations for policy', *Environment and Urbanization*, 10 1 (1998), 5–21; O. Ruthven and R. David, 'Benefits and

burdens: researching the consequences of migration in the Sahel', *IDS Bulletin*, 26 1 (1995), 47–53; and Francis, 'Gender, migration and multiple livelihoods'.

[85] 00/Kbz/26a and 00/Kbz/30a

[86] See 95/Muy/24a and 95/Muy/30b. Although there are a very few examples of women who cleared land in the swamps – e.g. case of Mrs Kabafunkaki (see 00/Muy/T21a). Chapter 2 has shown that opportunities provided by labour migration were more favourable compared to the growing of cash crops that were being promoted by the colonial state, and this contributed to the failure of these cash crops.

[87] In 1939 all fields were measured. In 2000 this was not possible, so it was necessary to ask people to estimate the amount of land they owned, and the amount they cultivated, and then to explain any difference between these two figures. This led to two difficulties: first, some people were reluctant to give such information, and second, some people found it difficult to make such estimations. Both problems were overcome by cross-checking the data with a number of key informants through a series of interviews and informal discussions in 2000 and 2002. By cross-checking in this way we can have a high degree of confidence in the data.

[88] Without wealth-ranking data for the 1939 survey we cannot draw direct comparisons between these figures and 1939. But land distribution is compared below.

[89] Kabirizi Survey, 2000.

[90] The 1996 survey found that 45.8 per cent of households had rented land in the year prior to the survey. (Lindblade *et al.* 'More People, More Fallow,' 41). The Muyebe 2002 survey found similar patterns of land ownership, but here all wealth groups owned larger areas of land compared to Kabirizi.

[91] Kabirizi Survey, 2000.

[92] *Ibid.*

[93] Wright, 'Kitozho Mutala Survey'; Kabirizi Survey, 2000.

[94] In 1939 the poorest 20 per cent of the population owned 2.3 per cent of the land, and today the poorest 20 per cent of the population own 2.4 per cent of the land. Wright, 'Kitozho Survey', 1939 and Kabirizi Survey, 2000.

[95] Wright, 'Kitozho Survey', 1939 and Kabirizi Survey, 2000.

[96] Lindblade *et al.* 'More People, More Fallow' p 40. Furthermore, this survey selected households along a land transect, and therefore was biased away from smaller land owning households – and completely excluded landless households. Had this sampling method not been used it would undoubtedly have found a more highly differentiated pattern of land ownership.

[97] Murton found that increased land differentiation was driven by differential access to *urban* wages. Literature that deals with the issue of whether increased diversification has an equalising effect on rural incomes or not includes Ellis, *Rural Livelihoods* esp. pp. 89–96; T. Reardon *et al.*, 'Effects of non-farm employment on rural income inequality in developing countries: An investment perspective', *Journal of Agricultural Economics*, 51 2 (2000), 266–288.

[98] Of these 5 households, 4 are female-headed households, and 4 are in the poorest wealth group (out of 4 groups). The only householder not in the poorest wealth group who is landless receives remittances from her son.

[99] Wright, 'Kitozho Mutala Survey'; Kabirizi Survey, 2000.

[100] At first glance it is counter-intuitive that both Figures 7.2 and 7.3 can be correct at the same time (i.e. there can be increases in numbers of landless and near landlessness, without substantial changes to the poor end of the land differentiation chart.) The figures and charts have been checked, and are correct: the sample size increased significantly between 1939 and 2000, which in part explains it.

[101] Purseglove and Wright, 'Kitozho Mutala Survey'.

[102] Kabirizi Survey, 2000.

[103] Further analysis of data collected for Lindblade *et al.*, 'More People, More Fallow'.

[104] Muyebe Survey, 2002.

[105] The percentage owning sheep also fell from 36 to 34 per cent, while the percentage owning chickens was the only one to see a rise: from 41 per cent to 53 per cent. Kabirizi Study, 2000.

[106] 02/Kbz/51 and 02/Kbz/11a.

[107] Lindblade *et al.* 'More People, More Fallow'.

[108] Purseglove, 'Report on the overpopulated areas of Kigezi', para 71.

[109] 51.3 per cent was being used for grazing; 8.5 per cent for cultivation; 39.1 per cent 'currently resting'; and 0.6 per cent for trees. Lindblade *et al.*, 'More People, More Fallow', 33.

[110] Methodological reasons excluded any of the owners of dairy farms from the contemporary surveys, and for this reason these surveys show only a part of the livestock picture. For the Kabirizi (2000) and Muyebe (2002) surveys no dairy farmers were included because the sample was selected based on residence, and none of the dairy farmers actually live in these sites. For the 1996 Lindblade *et al.* survey no dairy farmers were included because of difficulties in tracing them.

[111] 33 per cent of swampland had been purchased. (Lindblade *et al.*, 'More People, More Fallow').

[112] For example livelihoods approaches have been adopted by DfID, SIDA, UNDP, CARE, etc. They have rapidly reached the district level – and were raised in discussions with the District Agricultural Officer, Kabale in 2002.

[113] K. Gardner and D. Lewis, *Anthropology, Development and the Post-modern Challenge* (London, 1996), 112.

[114] For example by 1998 half the completed World Bank poverty assessments included a participatory element. See C. Ruggeri Laderchi *et al.*, 'Does it matter that we do not agree on the definition of poverty? A comparison of four approaches', *Oxford Development Studies* 31 3 (2003) 243–74.

[115] See C. Ashley and D. Carney, *Sustainable Livelihoods: Lessons from early experience* (London, 1999). See also I. Scoones, *Sustainable Rural Livelihoods: A framework for analysis*, IDS Working Paper 72 (Brighton, 1998); D. Carney (ed.), *Sustainable Rural Livelihoods: What contribution can we make?* (London, 1998); DfID, *Sustainable Rural Livelihoods Analysis: Guidance sheets* (London, n.d) [www.livelihoods.org].

[116] See for example R. Chambers, *Whose Reality Counts? Putting the First Last* (London, 1997).

[117] Scoones, *Sustainable Rural Livelihoods* and R. Chambers, 'Responsible well-being – a personal agenda for development', *World Development*, 25 11 (1997), 1743–54. See also DfID Guidance Sheets 2.6.

[118] See IFAD, *Rural Poverty Report 2001: The Challenge of Ending Rural Poverty* (Oxford, 2001).

[119] This was a major exercise across 23 countries to get the views of the poor, carried out as background to the *World Development Report, 2000/2001*. D. Narayan *et al.*, *Voices of the Poor* (Washington, DC, 2000).

[120] A. Sen, *Development as Freedom* (New Delhi, 2000).

[121] 02/Kbz/11c; 00/Kbz/33a. See also 00/Kbz/30b and 00/Kab/T7a.

[122] 00/Kbz/33a. Also see for example 02/Kbz/11c and 00/Kab/T1b.

[123] 02/Kbz/44a.

[124] 00/Kab/T1b.

[125] Breman has written extensively about the transition from patronage-based arrangements to waged labour in the Indian context. He shows that high labour demand is key, as if there is not enough work available (for example, due to mechanisation) then the transition to cash has negative effects. See Breman, *Beyond Patronage and Exploitation*.

Eight

Conclusion

Colonial development policy aimed to transform subsistence producers into market-based producers, linked to world markets. 'Modernisation' was the essential aim of development and the colonial policies that have been explored in this book reflect that desire to modernise Kigezi's agricultural system. Policies to introduce cash crops, maintain productivity, formalise the land market and reclaim swamps were all a part of the modernising project. People's responses to these policies, and the extent to which they were deemed a 'success', varied. Exploring people's responses and the broader outcomes of colonial development policies – both intended and unintended – sheds light on contemporary development issues. While policies were being put into place, there were also changes to the political and social context in Kigezi, and I have highlighted the transformations in agricultural practices over the twentieth century, and the endurance and evolution of agro-ecological practices. I have also discussed how the political economy of land holding and labour relations has been transformed alongside the environmental changes.

Despite the fact that contemporary development is ever more focused on goals and outcomes, there is surprisingly little discussion of the politics around how policies are evaluated. There are, however, some exceptions. White has noted that evaluators have to make 'credible statements' as to whether certain activities being supported by development agencies are making 'a positive contribution toward their stated goals', so that they can 'draw lessons to contribute to more effective development'.[1] There have been changes in the nature of such evaluations. In the immediate post-independence period stand-alone development projects – such as in infrastructure – were evaluated through cost-benefit analysis and this continued into the 1970s. But as there was a shift away from growth as the measure of development, so there was also 'a shift in how effectiveness was evaluated'[2] and by the 1980s more qualitative approaches, that could encompass issues such as gender equality, increasingly came to dominate evaluations.[3] These qualitative measures have included ethnographic and participatory methodologies.

The use of participatory methods of evaluation has been scrutinised by anthropologists. Pottier, for example, examines the use of ethnography in project appraisal. Appraisal is, in Pottier's words, the 'study of the actual implementation process and its social and environmental consequences'. He argues that 'project ethnography, with a focus on understanding participatory processes, must be regarded [as]a major contribution to making planned intervention both more humane and more effective.'[4] In their 1998 study of the organisation and effectiveness of development policy Quarles van Ufford *et al.*, who distinguish between intentions and outcomes, draw attention to the need for a better understanding of problems of effectiveness in development policy.[5]

A number of scholars have risen to this challenge. Crewe and Harrison make use of ethnographic case material to explore how success and failure are judged and the pitfalls involved in evaluating 'success' in development projects. Using evidence from two projects, they highlight the different ways of measuring success, and show how 'one person's failure can be another's success'.[6] In the case of the cooking stove project in Sri Lanka, those concerned with energy and deforestation measure success by changes in fuel consumption, and the impact on forests. Gender analysts judge projects that fail to challenge gender inequalities as 'failures'. But the very same projects might be judged to have succeeded because they generated income and alleviated women's workloads. Similarly, a fish-farming project in Zambia might be judged a 'failure', not having raised incomes. Others might judge them as a success in that they filled seasonal gaps in diet, created assets, and enabled people to lay claim to land and associate themselves with progress. But the projects were not being evaluated on these aspects (although they may have been more important for those for whom the benefits were intended) but instead were being evaluated on aspects judged by others to be important. Crewe and Harrison note that failure 'is far from simple. It means different things to different people, depending on where they locate themselves in relation to what success might be.'[7] It is an obvious – but surprisingly rarely stated – point that a judgement as to whether something is a 'success' depends on what is being evaluated, who decides what is being evaluated and how goals were initially defined.

There is a substantial gender and development literature that explores attempts to measure the 'success' of, for example, microcredit schemes. This has raised questions about what is meant by empowerment (whether related to resources, agency, achievement).[8] Women may gain access to credit, but do they actually control those loans?Goetz and Gupta note that 'donor's interests in seeing the development of financially self-sustaining rural development institutions have resulted in a preoccupation with cost recovery, to the degree that loan repayment rates have become the primary index of success, however much they may obscure the important issue of the quality of loan use.'[9] Kabeer examines a number of evaluations of credit projects that set out to explore the empowerment impact of credit on women and which had contradictory conclusions. She notes that 'the main reasons for these conflicting evaluations lies in the questions asked, and the interpretations given to the answers.'[10]

What about evaluations of agricultural projects?A recent review of 'success stories in African agriculture' notes that 'success is not a word often heard when dealing with contemporary issues in agriculture in sub-Saharan Africa. For 30 years, the overall picture has been one of failure.'[11] This 'failure' is then discussed in terms of decreases in agricultural production per capita, falling share of international trade in agricultural produce and rising levels of food imports. Here, therefore, it is macro indicators that are thus being used to evaluate success. Questions about what defines success have arisen in a number of related arenas. In relation to the debate about collective action and natural resource management, Adger, for example, has noted that the 'key distinction which is overlooked in much of the debate on collective action is whether it is outcome or process that defines success'.[12]

Mosse's 2005 book is an in-depth exploration of evaluations of success in contemporary development. Examining the case of the Indo-British Rainfed Farming Project (IBRFP), he explores the relationship between international development policy and project practice, focusing on 'participatory approaches' that were prominent in the 1990s. Publication of the book proved to be controversial, and key actors who had been involved in the project raised objections to it.[13] Mosse makes a number of arguments; the most relevant to this book is that about project 'success' and 'failure'. He argues that project failure is not the failure to turn designs into reality, but a 'certain disarticulation between practices and their rationalising models'. Failure, he argues, is a 'failure of interpretation'.[14] He explores how policy discourses of 'success' and 'failure' obscure the local social effects of development interventions, which may both perpetuate misleading explanations and conceal positive outcomes. His book does not evaluate a particular project; it is not concerned with whether a project is successful. Rather, it is concerned with how 'success' is socially produced or constructed. He argues that most actors in the development world have very little control over events, but do have control over the interpretation of events.[15] In Mosse's analysis, project success was not just a matter of measurement of achievement and empirical evidence – of yield increases, trees planted, etc. – success was a matter of definition, a question of meaning, of sustaining a particular interpretation of events through the categorisations and causal connections established by the policy model. And while this model was not empirically falsifiable, it was replaceable. And, indeed, when UK aid policy changed in 1997, so the project became, by definition, a failure. The shift towards partnerships with government, and away from projects, meant that IBRFP was in the wrong place. As a project it 'outlived the policy regime that it served', and so a success became a failure, despite the fact that what project staff actually did in terms of project operations and field practices changed little.[16]

Mosse's concern with how success is 'made and managed' thus looks beyond the 'usual monitoring and evaluation concerns, which focus on appropriate definitions of success or measures of progress and achievement'.[17] He argues that development success is not merely a question of measures of performance, but also about how 'particular interpretations are made and sustained socially'. In the case of the IBRFP he argues that success depended on i) establishing a compelling interpretation of events, ii) sustaining this as a key representation (through model building, reporting and field visits), and iii) enrolling a wider network of supporters and their agendas and linking them to the success of the project. There were contradictions with the IBRFP story: on the one hand, there was the high profile and skilfully marketed 'participatory' processes and on the other there was strong vertical control over programme delivery. But Mosse argues that this contradiction was 'easily concealed'.[18]

The case study of Kigezi illustrates that the way success is defined and interpreted has a long history, and the story that Mosse tells is not unique to contemporary development. Rather, policy-makers have always been seeking to present success in particular ways. As would be expected, in colonial Kigezi there was never any claim to being participatory. Strong vertical control was maintained over delivery, for example, of the soil conservation and resettlement programmes. Nonetheless, sustaining the story of success (through field visits by other colonial officials, report writing, etc.) was crucial. Indeed the words 'affirming the project as a replicable model enhanced its appeal'[19] could have been written about Kigezi's soil conservation programme.[20] As well as the numerous reports written 'within' the colonial system, a number of articles were written in both the academic and popular press.[21] Colonial officials from within Uganda and from neighbouring countries made numerous visits to the soil conservation scheme: Kigezi became a 'show piece' for the administration. Purseglove eventually asked the Colonial Office to stop sending him visitors, saying they were getting 'rather embarrassed' by the numbers and it was proving very time-consuming taking people around the district.[22] This can be seen, in Mosse's words, as 'actively recruiting and enrolling a range of supporting actors'.[23]

Discussing contemporary African agriculture, Scoones *et al.* have noted that explaining 'policy failure as a technical problem (be it poor design, faulty implementation or external constraints)', means that it is 'amenable to a technical solution'. Thus 'an inappropriate policy is replaced by a better one.'[24] This perpetuates the legitimacy of further development interventions and projects. But, as this book has shown, the continual justification of further intervention, and the depoliticisation of development through the 'technicalisation' of problems (rendering all problems as technical problems with technical solutions), were as much the case in the colonial period, as they are today. Technicalising development has the effect of depoliticising development, and I have shown that taking politics out of policies – or Ferguson's 'anti-politics machine' – has a long history.

For development organisations, Quarles van Ufford has argued, showing results was not as important as convincing sponsors of 'the need for further action'. Such a need could either be justified because a 'policy is well implemented, or because of grave developmental problems.' [25] In Kigezi both policy success and policy failure justified further intervention. If a policy was a success, as with soil conservation, then obviously it should be replicated, pushed further, or extended to other places. Conversely, if a policy failed, then its very failure meant that another 'improved' intervention should be attempted, thus different cash crops were repeatedly tried. And in Kigezi, shifts in policy meant that what had one day been a failure (in this case to reclaim swampland for subsistence agriculture) became a success (as the *real* aim of policy was to reclaim swampland for 'economic' production.)

While scholars have explored evaluations of success in contemporary development, there remains a dearth of literature on how colonial projects were evaluated,[26] or on the continuities and discontinuities in the ways that colonial and post-colonial development projects have been evaluated.[27] This book, in contrast to Mosse's, does evaluate the success of particular policies, while showing how different people define and interpret that 'success'. It has shown the complexities of evaluating the success of Kigezi's colonial policies: different colonial policies put forward as part of the modernising project in Kigezi had different outcomes. Colonial attempts to establish a cash crop – the essential element of agricultural development in the colonial mind – failed in the long term. As each new crop was introduced some Bakiga did embrace them, but none lasted. There was therefore no fundamental shift to cash crops, and none played a sustained role in Kigezi agriculture in the way that cotton and coffee did in much of the rest of Uganda. However, Bakiga farmers did grow crops for sale, and had been doing this prior to the arrival of Europeans. These were food crops, and sales of food crops as part of a regional trading system had long been a central part of Bakiga livelihoods, although they received little attention from officials. The state failed to recognise the significance of food crops in the exchange economy and this in part explains why 'cash crops' promoted by the colonial state never took off. Women's labour in the production and sale of food crops, and their considerable user rights over land, as well as the restrictive marketing of the new cash crops also made the production of new cash crops unlikely. The importance of how success is defined is highlighted by the case of tobacco, a cash crop that the colonial state deemed a failure in Kigezi. In fact, tobacco did not fail in Kigezi: production continued, and continues to this day. But the colonial state failed to maintain marketing control over tobacco, and for that reason labelled it a failure. Thus while each failure of a cash crop justified further intervention and another cash crop was attempted, in fact it was not *cash crops* that failed in Kigezi, but *cash cropping under the control of the colonial state* that failed.

Similar problems with the evaluation of success or failure can be seen in the context of Kigezi's soil conservation schemes. The story of the 'success' of soil conservation policies in Kigezi is in marked contrast to similar soil conservation schemes across colonial Africa, which were deemed to have failed. Here, colonial efforts to introduce policies of soil conservation were implemented successfully and without opposition. There were good reasons for the successful implementation of these policies. These were related to the labour required to implement the measures; the gradual introduction of the measures; the methods of implementation (the use of education, propaganda, and incentives, and working directly through chiefs); and the absence of both rising nationalism and suspicions about government motives, particularly fears of losing land. But most importantly Kigezi's earliest colonial policies were essentially modifications of the Bakiga agricultural system, and thus could be absorbed into it. Here the policies, although shaped by wider influences, were formulated from within the district itself, and officials on the ground could adapt measures to local conditions and drop those parts of the scheme that proved inappropriate – suggesting greater attention was given to local responses to policies than elsewhere. Those officials could present the scheme as a great success to their superiors – and the scheme became a 'show piece' for the administration, no doubt benefiting the careers of the officials involved. So it was a 'success', but a good part of the reason for this 'success' was that it actually was not that different from what had gone before. Similarly, the successful resettlement scheme was facilitating existing migratory patterns and practices that had a long history. Officials could play down the fact that people would have migrated anyway, or that bunds were being built anyway, and could simply present the schemes as successful colonial projects.

The policy of swamp reclamation similarly demonstrates the difficulty of evaluating 'success'. The policy was successfully implemented in the sense that swamps were indeed reclaimed. But it was a mixed success in terms of its initial aim of increasing land available for food production for people living around the swamps. Different views within the colonial state led to a shift in policy: ultimately it was 'progressive' farmers involved in commercial agriculture who were favoured, and so the policy succeeded on this definition. As a result individuals with access to ample labour, or those with knowledge and information about swamp reclamation (who often had links to the colonial state), used swamp reclamation as an opportunity to significantly increase their ownership of land. Unintended outcomes of swamp reclamation were that swampland ownership has become highly differentiated, and chiefs held onto powers over land, powers that elsewhere were being diminished. Other policies of land reform – including the Land Tenure Pilot Project (LTPP), sporadic titles and the distribution of land at the Kalengyere pyrethrum estate[28] – provided similar opportunities for some individuals to increase their ownership of land or to strengthen their claims over it.

Evaluating the 'success' of colonial land reform policies in Kigezi also demonstrates the ambivalence of outcomes. These policies were to contribute to modernisation by introducing land titles, and it was believed that this would have positive knock-on effects on productivity. While the LTPP was itself successfully implemented, this is entirely unsurprising as the desire for it to succeed led officials to choose an area where it could be implemented with ease. However, while titles were granted, and so the LTPP was deemed to be a 'success', this evaluation is not clear-cut, as few of these titles were ever collected, or used. Did the LTPP really 'succeed' at

Conclusion

anything, apart from the fact that colonial officials could present it as a success?Throughout the rest of the district colonial propaganda failed to stimulate a demand for titling, in large part because of the need to consolidate land prior to titling. Here individualism of tenure was strong, and the region's great agro-ecological variability and Bakiga concerns to minimise risk meant that there were significant advantages in having scattered plots. The implementation of consolidation did fail, by anyone's judgement, in Kigezi. But the reasons for putting a policy of consolidation in place (that fragmented land holdings were believed to hinder the development of a land market) did not apply in Kigezi, for here there was a vibrant land market despite (or because of) the highly fragmented nature of land holdings. This raises questions about the relevance of these policies for Kigezi, and what was driving these policies.

Colonial policies of land reform also had unintended consequences. Colonial propaganda associated with these policies and the language of the courts have encouraged increased recognition of the value of written records for land transfers, both inheritance and sales. These, as well as increased population density and increased value of land, have further increased individualisation of land tenure, as would be expected with the evolutionary theory of land rights. While land tenure has long been highly individualised, the methods of acquiring ownership of land, and gaining access to land, have become increasingly monetarised. Inheritance continues in much the same way (although written statements are increasingly common), but critically many people now acquire land by purchasing it. While there is a long history of land sales in the region, the prevalence of sales has increased and today up to half of all plots are acquired through purchase. Methods of gaining (temporary) access to land have also changed, and are increasingly cash-based. Renting land for cash is now common, and has replaced earlier systems of gaining access to land that were non-cash-based. Cash, however, is not solely important, and personal connections do still matter in the ways that people acquire and gain access to land, and in dispute settlement. But who those key individuals are has changed over time, and this book has shown that local power relations are critical: rulings can be made, and new laws put into place, but these are not necessarily reflected in changes on the ground. The implementation of laws and execution of rulings are areas of research and policy that require further examination.

Unintended outcomes of colonial policies also occurred in relation to Kigezi's soil conservation policies: here the propaganda was so effective that people in Kigezi today are convinced that their agricultural practices are environmentally destructive. This has fed into the narratives about the area, and the view that Kigezi is 'over-populated' and will, should no interventions be made, experience severe environmental damage, is firmly entrenched in the minds of both researchers and Bakiga themselves. Despite this, there is little objective, scientific research to support claims that the environment in the region is severely degraded and none of the envisaged environmental disasters has struck.

This brings me to the second major theme of the book, which has not only been about colonial policies and people's responses to them, but also about the enduring nature of an agricultural system and the changing nature of livelihoods. Research presented here challenges the overwhelming view that population growth in Kigezi has resulted in reduced fallow, which is in turn associated with environmental degradation. The findings suggest that land use changes have occurred that, in conjunction with local farm management practices, have contributed to the lack of severe land degradation in the area. Rather than cultivation techniques being the cause of problems of environmental degradation, these very techniques contribute to the success of the agricultural system. Other positive environmental changes have occurred: tree cover has increased over the past 50 years, and any deforestation that occurred in the district happened long before the beginning of the colonial period. The results demonstrate that common assumptions about population growth and its effects on the environment do not necessarily hold true upon more careful scrutiny.

Thus Kigezi farmers have successfully risen to the challenges faced by their agricultural system. They have, against all predictions, managed their farms in such a way as to maintain production, while they have simultaneously avoided serious environmental degradation. This has occurred through dual processes of agrarian change involving intensification (through increased labour inputs, associated with, for example, increased intercropping) and the extension of agriculture into previously uncultivated land, such as swampland. This is not to say that absolutely no environmental degradation exists, rather that it has not reached the proportions envisaged.

These findings support research from elsewhere that illustrates the dangers of making simple assumptions regarding the impact of population growth on environmental degradation. But it takes this debate further: highlighting, as Murton has done in the Machakos example, the broader effects on livelihoods. The processes of agrarian change have been occurring in a differentiated fashion and there have been broader changes to Bakiga livelihoods, alongside the positive environmental changes in their agricultural system. Changes to patterns of migration have occurred, and there has been an increase in cash-based arrangements around labouring for others. However, this book has shown that this activity has a long and complex history, but, being non-monetarised, was hidden from view. Nowadays most of the earlier non-cash-based arrangements have disappeared as people work for cash. It is striking that, while in the past many people laboured as part of non-cash-based arrangements, today it is only the very poorest who do so.

Kigezi farmers have shown themselves to respond to pressures on their livelihood system and to policies put into place by administrators. They have adapted their agricultural system to increase production in the face of population increase, while sustaining the natural resource base. Environmentally positive practices are not undertaken homogeneously, but by different people and for different reasons. The arrangements through which people labour for others have changed, and for many these changes

Conclusion

have led to improvements in livelihoods in the broadest sense of the term. Such a transition may also have negative effects, which need further investigation. But what is important is that environmental change is only part of the story, and such change needs to be understood in terms of what it means for people. Any analysis of environmental change should, therefore, be undertaken as part of a broader analysis and understanding of changes to livelihoods.

Notes

[1] H. White, *Challenges in Evaluating Development Effectiveness*, IDS Working paper 242 (Brighton, 2005), 1.

[2] *Ibid.*, 1.

[3] White argues that the new focus on results in the context of the Millennium Development Goals demands more than just qualitative studies, and explores how quantitative approaches have re-established themselves in both measuring the performance of particular agencies or donors, and at the level of project interventions. White, 'Challenges in evaluating development effectiveness'.

[4] J. Pottier, 'The role of ethnography in project appraisal', in J. Pottier (ed.) *Practising Development* (London, 1993), 2, 32.

[5] In their exploration of development bureaucracies they speak of these bureaucracies as being 'in between' intentions and outcomes. P. Quarles van Ufford, 'The Hidden Crisis in Development: Development Bureaucracies in between intentions and outcomes', in P. Quarles van Ufford, D. Kruijt and T. Downing (eds), *The Hidden Crisis in Development* (Amsterdam, 1988).

[6] E. Crewe and E. Harrison *Whose Development? An Ethnography of Aid* (London, 1998), 1.

[7] *Ibid.*,146.

[8] See N. Kabeer, 'Resources, Agency, Achievements: Reflections on the Measurement of Women's Empowerment', *Development and Change* 30 3 (1999), 435–64.

[9] A.M. Goetz and R. Sen Gupta, 'Who Takes the Credit? Gender, Power and Control over Loan Use in Rural Credit Programmes in Bangladesh', *World Development* 24 1 (1996), 45–63. See also S. Mahmud, 'Actually how Empowering is Microcredit?', *Development and Change* 34 4 (2003), 577–605.

[10] N. Kabeer, 'Conflicts over credit: re-evaluating the empowerment potential of loans to women in rural Bangladesh', *World Development*, 29 1 (2001), 80.

[11] S. Wiggins, 'Success stories from African agriculture: what are the key elements of success?, *IDS Bulletin*, 36 2 (2005), 17–22.

[12] W.N. Adger, 'Governing Natural Resources: institution adaptation and resilience', in F. Berkhout, M. Leach and I. Scoones (eds), *Negotiating Environmental Change* (Cheltenham, 2003), 199. See N.A. Steins and V.M. Edwards, 'Collective Action in Common-Pool Resource Management: The Contribution of a Social Constructivist Perspective to Existing Theory', *Society and Natural Resources*, 12 6 (1999), 539–57. They note that the definition of successful outcomes in common property management frequently varies among stakeholders for the same set of circumstances.

[13] Lecture given by David Mosse, at the London School of Economics, 2 June 2005.

[14] Mosse, *Cultivating Development*, 182.

[15] *Ibid.*, 8.

[16] *Ibid.*, 184–204.

[17] *Ibid.*, 158.

[18] *Ibid.*, 159–61.

[19] *Ibid.*, 163.

[20] For example, a document entitled 'The Significance of Kigezi District as a Model for Development', by Agricultural Officer A.C.A. Wright (who later worked in Tanganyika)

was sent to Pare District, Tanganyika, and was used when the Pare Development Plan of 1953 was put together. See Maguire, *Towards "Uhuru" in Tanzania*; Kimambo, *Penetration and Protest*, 14–5 and 136–54.

[21] Purseglove wrote many of these in a range of publications: *East African Agricultural Journal, Mass Education Bulletin, Uganda Journal, Journal of African Administration* and *East African Annual*.

[22] Settlement Scheme in Kigezi District, Letter to Rogers (CO) from Steil (Chief Sec's Office, E'be), 5 May 1951, PRO CO 536 40391 ff6.

[23] Mosse, *Cultivating Development*, 168.

[24] Scoones, I., S Devereux and L Haddad, 'Introduction: New directions for African agriculture', *IDS Bulletin* 36 2 (2005), 8.

[25] Quarles van Ufford, 'The Hidden Crisis in Development', 25. See also Mosse, *Cultivating Development*, 180.

[26] Although the failure of the Ground Nut Scheme initiated some discussion of failure of colonial agricultural projects. See J. S. Hogendorn and K.M. Scott, 'Very large-scale agricultural projects; the lessons of the East African groundnut scheme', in R. Rotberg (ed.) *Imperialism, Colonialism and Hunger in East and Central Africa* (Lexington, 1983) ; J. Iliffe, *A Modern History of Tanzania* (Cambridge, 1979); C. Ehrlich, 'Aspects of economic policy in Tanganyika, 1945–60' in D. Low and A. Smith, *History of East Africa* (Oxford, 1976); A. Coulson, 'Agricultural policies in mainland Tanzania, 1946–76', *Review of African Political Economy* 10 (1977): 75–100; Also see F. Samuel, 'The East African Groundnut Scheme', *African Affairs*, 46 (1947), 135–45 and H. Swanzy, 'Quarterly Notes', *African Affairs* 46 and 47 (1947 and 1948), various. These plot the gradual realisation that the scheme was failing.

[27] Continuities between colonial and post-colonial administration have been explored by a number of authors. Cooke, for example, has looked at development's concern with governance and the continuities with indirect rule under colonial administration. B. Cooke, *From Colonial Administration to Development Management*, IDPM Discussion Paper, 63 (London, 2001); B. Cooke, 'A new continuity with colonial administration; Participation in development management', *Third World Quarterly*, 24 1 (2003), 47–61.) Others have looked at institutional linkages (for example, in personnel – see U. Kothari, 'Authority and expertise: The professionalisation of international development and the ordering of dissent', *Antipode*, 37 3 (2005), 425–6. In relation to development and community see J. Grischow and G.H. McKnight, 'Rhyming development: Practising post-development in colonial Ghana and Uganda', *Journal of Historical Sociology*, 16 4 (2003), 517–49.

[28] Also the policy of farm planning. See Carswell, 'African Farmers'.

Appendix

Sources

This book is distinctive for the range of methodologies that it draws upon, combining archival sources, oral history, detailed ethnography, as well as contemporary household surveys. The innovative use of two surveys (conducted fifty years apart) is particularly valuable in the way that it sheds light on land use changes. Comparisons are also made with other areas, to show both the exceptionality and the relevance of Kigezi. The combination of research methods has yielded an extremely rich range of materials that support the arguments of the book.

Existing literature on Kigezi itself is sparse and is dominated by religious issues – both of a contemporary nature (Gingyera-Pinycwa, Turyahikayo-Rugyema, Stanley Smith) and traditional religions – in particular in relation to the cult of the Nyabingi (Vokes, Bessell, Brazier, Feierman, Freedman, Hansen, Hopkins, Rutanga and Turyahikayo-Rugyema). There is also a colonial literature on land issues in the district (Purseglove, Lawrance and Byagagaire and Lawrance), but few works assess the policies of the colonial period, or people's reactions to them (although exceptions include Tindituuza, Kateete, Yeld, and Roth *et al.*) The only major published anthropological study of Kigezi is that by Edel, who conducted fieldwork in 1933, and published her book in 1957. Other works that are referred to include studies carried out from the mid-1950s on, for example, Bakiga chiefs (Baxter), the history of migration (Powesland), land fragmentation (Kagambirwe), land disputes (Obol-Ochola) and a later work on district politics since 1947 (Connor).

With many gaps in the secondary literature, this book necessarily draws very extensively on primary materials. Information on the formulation of broader policy has come from both the Public Record Office and to a lesser extent the Entebbe National Archives. This material is largely in the form of memoranda and correspondence on policy and proposed changes to policy. (For example, discussions around the changes in land tenure legislation and the formulation of the Land Tenure Statement of Policy, were received by the CO and are located in files at the Public Records Office, Kew, e.g. see PRO CO 822/877.) Most documents in the Entebbe National Archives for this period are not catalogued but a small number of useful files were found. The largest source found for both the implementation of different policies and discussion of the existing and changing situation was that of the 'archives' in the Kabale District Offices. This was not an archive as such, but rather a number of storerooms containing piles of files, that had no catalogue or organisation. Different rooms contained files from the District Commissioner's office (Kigezi District Archives, District Commissioner's office KDA DC) and the Department of Agriculture (Kigezi District Archives, Department of Agriculture's office KDA DoA). The DCs files had once been catalogued, but the catalogue could not be located, nor were the files in any order. While this was initially extremely difficult to use, it proved to be an extraordinarily rich source containing a wide variety of exceptionally revealing material. The files mainly contain correspondence and reports that passed both between the District Administration in Kigezi and the colonial administration in Entebbe, and between and within different departments of the District Administration, and in particular between the offices of the District Commissioner (DC) and the District Agricultural Officer (DAO). As such, they revealed information on almost all aspects of colonial administration, and in particular the formulation and implementation of the policies that are relevant to this book. Generally the files had simply been closed and left untouched. They had not been sorted, nor had items been 'weeded' from them. However, confidential files were stored elsewhere and despite strenuous efforts I could not locate them.

The most significant concern about this material was that the 'African voice' would not be heard through these colonial files. But in fact I found that in some areas of the research (for example, related to crop choices, attitudes towards soil conservation and land reform) the voice of Bakiga farmers did come through surprisingly clearly. In other areas the files were remarkably silent – particularly in relation to the views of women. In order to counterbalance this, interviews were conducted in 1995 with 100 elderly men and women. I gathered a wide range of information relating to their experiences of, attitudes to, and understanding of colonial agricultural and land tenure policies. I conducted over 150 further interviews on two return visits to Kigezi in 2000 and 2002, which focused on broader aspects of livelihood change over the period under review (see Map App.1).

In addition to archival research and oral history, further fieldwork was conducted in 1996 that looked specifically at agricultural change over a fifty-year period (Lindblade *et al.*, 1996). This involved undertaking a repeat survey of a transect survey first undertaken in 1945. Two surveys were carried out in the same month, using the same methodology and covering the same territory, and the study thus set up a diachronic comparison that enabled an assessment to be made of land use and agriculture at two points in time over a 51-year period. Finally I conducted two 'livelihood surveys' which collected demographic information, data on settlement history and history of migration, land transfers, livelihood activities and sources of income. The first of these was a survey conducted in 2000 of 48 households living in Kabirizi, which I refer to throughout as the Kabirizi Survey, 2000. (Kabirizi was part of Kitozho *mutala* which had been surveyed in 1939 by two colonial officials, which enabled changes over time to be explored.) The second was a survey conducted in 2002 of 69 households living in Muyebe, which is referred to throughout as the Muyebe Survey, 2002. These livelihood surveys, and in-depth interviews with key informants, enabled me to build up a picture of livelihood change.

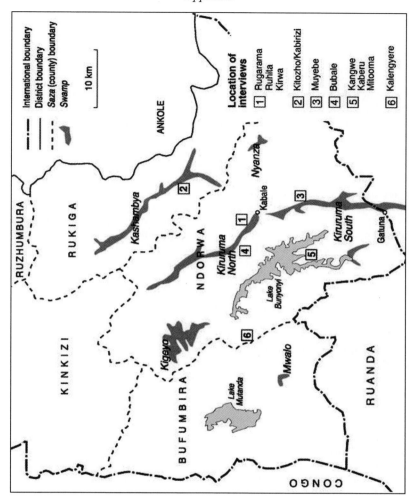

Map App.1
Southern Kigezi,
showing interview sites
in 1996, 2000 and 2002

Oral Sources

1995

I conducted interviews in a number of different areas at varying distances from Kabale town. They were chosen in part to cover all the major issues being examined, in part by accessibility, and in part by contacts with people in the area. Using a loosely structured and open-ended questionnaire elderly men and women were asked a broad set of questions, firstly to uncover the background of the individuals, then their understanding of changes to agriculture and colonial agricultural policies, before moving on to questions related to land ownership. In areas near to swamps questions related to reclamation were also asked, while in the area around Kalengyere the history of the pyrethrum estate was looked into. See Map App.1 for location of interviews. All but three interviews were conducted in Rukiga through an interpreter. They were taped and then fully transcribed and translated.

Rugarama, Kirwa and Ruhita

Rugarama is one of the hills just outside Kabale town on which the CMS established their main mission. Many of the residents living in the area were made to move off their land when the schools and hospital were built. As most had land outside the area defined as church land, they could do so. Kirwa and Ruhita are near to Rugarama, and are down in the valley to the north of Kabale town. People living in this area are living on the edge of the swamp and so were questioned about swamp reclamation. (Interviews number 1–22, 51).

Kitozho

This area was initially chosen as a 1939 *mutala* survey of Kitozho existed. The 1939 survey covered a much larger area than the area that is today known as Kitozho. It is located on the edge of Kashambya swamp, and in this section much of the swamp remains undrained. (Interviews number 52–56, 64–71, 75–82).

Muyebe

This is an area on the edge of Kiruruma South swamp, most of which has been drained. The swamp in this area consists of small plots, land owned by Swamp Societies, and some larger farms. (Interviews number 23–34, 57–63).

Bubale

This area is on the edge of Kiruruma North swamp. It was specifically chosen as it is in the site of some of the large dairy farms on the reclaimed swampland. Individuals who do not own swampland were interviewed, as well as those who do. (Interviews number 91–99).

Bufuka, Kangwe, Kaberu, and other places across Lake Bunyonyi
This area was chosen as it was further from Kabale town, and quite inaccessible, being reached by canoe. It was hoped that this would remove any bias in the selection of areas in terms of more accessible areas being the only ones which had experienced colonial policies. It appears in fact that there was little difference in the experiences of this area in terms of the implementation of colonial policies when compared to elsewhere. (Interviews number 35–50).

Kalengyere
Individuals were selected who lived in the area around Kalengyere Research Station. This enabled questions to be asked specifically on the history of the Kalengyere Pyrethrum Estate. (Interviews number 72–74, 83–90).

Index of 1995 interviews

Interview number	Informant name	Site	Date
95/Kab/1a	Joy Constance (F)	Rugarama, Kabale	6/7/95
95/Kab/1b	Joy Constance (F)	Rugarama, Kabale	2/8/95
95/Kab/2a	Tofus Kigatire (F)	Rugarama, Kabale	6/7/95
95/Kab/2b	Tofus Kigatire (F)	Rugarama, Kabale	9/8/95
95/Kab/3a	William Rutahembya (M)	Rugarama, Kabale	6/7/95
95/Kab/4a	Mary Turyashemererwa (F)	Rugarama, Kabale	6/7/95
95/Kab/5a	Dorothy Mary Katarahweire (F)	Rugarama, Kabale	10/7/95
95/Kab/6a	Esther Ellevaneer Bushoberwa (F)	Rugarama, Kabale	10/7/95
95/Kab/6b	Esther Ellevaneer Bushoberwa (F)	Rugarama, Kabale	2/8/95
95/Kab/7a	Pascal Bisigabusha (M)	Rugarama, Kabale	10/7/95
95/Kab/8a	Paulo Bakinagaga (M)	Rugarama, Kabale	10/7/95
95/Kab/8b	Paulo Bakinagaga (M)	Rugarama, Kabale	2/8/95
95/Kab/9a	Ruth Rukramale (F)	Ruhita, Kabale	13/7/95
95/Kab/10a	Beatrice Birarara (F)	Ruhita, Kabale	13/7/95
95/Kab/11a	Dorcus Koruharo (F)	Ruhita, Kabale	13/7/95
95/Kab/12a	Andrea Nyakarwana (M)	Ruhita, Kabale	13/7/95
95/Kab/13a	Edna Rutindapora (F wife of 14/a)	Ruhita, Kabale	13/7/95
95/Kab/13b	Edna Rutindapora (F wife of 14/a)	Ruhita, Kabale	2/8/95
95/Kab/14a	Sulumani Rutindapora (M husband of 13/a)	Ruhita, Kabale	13/7/95
95/Kab/14b	Sulumani Rutindapora (M husband of 13/a)	Ruhita, Kabale	2/8/95
95/Kab/15a	Edsa Georgna (F)	Ruhita, Kabale	13/7/95
95/Kab/15b	Edsa Georgna (F)	Ruhita, Kabale	2/8/95
95/Kab/16a	Ebriahim Kagangure (M)	Kirwa, Kabale	13/7/95
95/Kab/16b	Ebriahim Kagangure (M)	Kirwa, Kabale	2/8/95
95/Kab/17a	Beatrice Mauda (F wife of 18/a)	Kirwa, Kabale	13/7/95
95/Kab/17b	Beatrice Mauda (F wife of 18/a)	Kirwa, Kabale	2/8/95
95/Kab/18a	Josea Kagarea (M husband of 17/a)	Kirwa, Kabale	13/7/95

95/Kab/19a	John Kijagye (M)	Kirwa, Kabale	13/7/95
95/Kab/20a	Musa Zaram (M husband of 21/a)	Kirwa, Kabale	13/7/95
95/Kab/20b	Musa Zaram (M husband of 21/a)	Kirwa, Kabale	2/8/95
95/Kab/21a	Zipora Zaram (F wife of 20/a)	Kirwa, Kabale	13/7/95
95/Kab/21b	Zipora Zaram (F wife of 20/a)	Kirwa, Kabale	2/8/95
95/Kab/22a	Matia Rutembwe (M)	Kirwa, Kabale	13/7/95
95/Muy/23a	Agnes Kamuchana (F wife of 24/a)	Muyebe	19/7/95
95/Muy/24a	Semu Kamuchana (M husband of 23/a)	Muyebe	19/7/95
95/Muy/24b	Semu Kamuchana (M husband of 23/a)	Muyebe	9/8/95
95/Muy/25a	Esther Mukabazungu (F)	Muyebe	19/7/95
95/Muy/26a	Bahirwa Ntamukiza (F)	Muyebe	19/7/95
95/Muy/27a	Yonia Rutabyama (F)	Muyebe	19/7/95
95/Muy/28a	Alice Torikoko (F)	Muyebe	19/7/95
95/Muy/29a	Dorothy Kihimakazi (F)	Muyebe	19/7/95
95/Muy/30a	Phyllis Rwakari (F)	Muyebe	19/7/95
95/Muy/30b	Phyllis Rwakari (F)	Muyebe	9/8/95
95/Muy/31a	Freda Mary Nyinoburo (F)	Muyebe	19/7/95
95/Muy/32a	Udes Kamyebe (F)	Muyebe	19/7/95
95/Muy/32b	Udes Kamyebe (F)	Muyebe	9/8/95
95/Muy/33a	Audrey Tindimutuma (F)	Muyebe	19/7/95
95/Muy/34a	Sera Zikanga (M)	Muyebe	19/7/95
95/Muy/34b	Sera Zikanga (M)	Muyebe	9/8/95
95/LB/35a	Samuel Mugasha (M)	Bufuka, Bunyonyi,	21/7/95
95/LB/36a	Edreda Kitusi (F)	Katooma, Bunyonyi	21/7/95
95/LB/37a	Zereda Bagabura (F)	Kangwe, Bunyonyi	21/7/95
95/LB/38a	Amoss Tiwange (M)	Kangwe, Bunyonyi	21/7/95
95/LB/39a	Abel Stephen Rwakairu (M)	Kaberu, Bunyonyi	21/7/95
95/LB/40a	Zechera Rutakahweire (M cousin of 39/a)	Kaberu, Bunyonyi	21/7/95
95/LB/41a	Violet Tumwine (F wife of 40/a)	Kaberu, Bunyonyi	21/7/95
95/LB/42a	John Kiyanje (M)	Katooma, Bunyonyi	21/7/95
95/LB/43a	Yoweri Basizoli (M)	Katooma, Bunyonyi	21/7/95
95/LB/44a	Alfred George Rutisire (M)	Bunyonyi	22/7/95
95/LB/45a	Grace Nshemereirwe (F wife of 44/a)	Bunyonyi	22/7/95
95/LB/46a	Daudi Mugisha (M)	Bunyonyi	22/7/95
95/LB/47a	Fredas Tumwine (F wife of 46/a)	Bunyonyi	22/7/95
95/LB/48a	Eria Kanyma (M)	Bunyonyi	22/7/95
95/LB/49a	Kizirooni Sebukingandu (M)	Bunyonyi	22/7/95
95/LB/50a	Shaka Nzarwahabi (M)	Bunyonyi	22/7/95
95/Kab/51a	Ann Joventa (F wife of 16/a)	Kirwa, Kabale	2/8/95
95/Kit/52a	James Katabazi (M) (in English)	Kitozho	8/8/95
95/Kit/53a	ES Kwatiraho (M)	Kitozho	8/8/95
95/Kit/53b	ES Kwatiraho (M)	Kitozho	29/8/95
95/Kit/54a	Harriet Jane Blacka (F)	Kitozho	8/8/95
95/Kit/55a	Christopher Karubogo (M)	Kitozho	8/8/95
95/Kit/56a	Kazlon Ntondogoro (M)	Kitozho	8/8/95
95/Kit/56b	Kazlon Ntondogoro (M)	Kitozho	15/8/95
95/Muy/57a	Wilson Rwambonera (M)	Muyebe	9/8/95

95/Muy/58a	Cosia Rutabyama (M)	Muyebe	9/8/95
95/Muy/59a	David Mashoki (M)	Muyebe	9/8/95
95/Muy/60a	Mr Kamuyebe (M husband of 32)	Muyebe	9/8/95
95/Muy/61a	Nathaniel Rutanga (M)	Muyebe	9/8/95
95/Muy/62a	N Bishisha (M)	Muyebe	9/8/95
95/Muy/63a	John Patrick Rusese (M)	Muyebe	9/8/95
95/Kit/64a	Daniel Bamanya (M)	Kitozho	15/8/95
95/Kit/65a	Stanley Katanzi (M)	Kitozho	15/8/95
95/Kit/66a	Daudi Bujigi (M)	Kitozho	15/8/95
95/Kit/67a	Ida Mary Bagakimu (F wife of 66/a)	Kitozho	15/8/95
95/Kit/68a	George William Mbaguta (M)	Kitozho	15/8/95
95/Kit/69a	Danieli Rwabukye (M)	Kitozho	15/8/95
95/Kit/70a	Patricia Akokyega (F)	Kitozho	15/8/95
95/Kit/71a	John Bahigaine (M)	Kitozho	15/8/95
95/Kal/72a	Pascal Makabore (M)	Kalengyere	16/8/95
95/Kal/73a	Bakihimba Deodanta (M)	Kalengyere	16/8/95
95/Kal/74a	Baraba (M)	Kalengyere	16/8/95
95/Kit/75a	Banyagente Purikeriya (F)	Kitozho	29/8/95
95/Kit/76a	Fredas Worinawe (F)	Kitozho	29/8/95
95/Kit/77a	Misaki Kazimaire (M husband of 78/a)	Kitozho	29/8/95
95/Kit/78a	Mauda Kijarubi (F wife of 77/a)	Kitozho	29/8/95
95/Kit/79a	Elnathan Katahikire (M)	Kitozho	29/8/95
95/Kit/80a	Keziah Kahimakazi (F sister of 79/a)	Kitozho	29/8/95
95/Kit/81a	Elphas Rwakabirigi (M)	Kitozho	29/8/95
95/Kit/82a	Physs Rwakabirigi (F wife of 81)	Kitozho	29/8/95
95/Kal/83a	Michael Zebikire (M)	Kalengyere	30/8/95
95/Kal/84a	Jacob Mwangi (M)	Kalengyere	30/8/95
95/Kal/85a	Matias Rukundo (M)	Kalengyere	30/8/95
95/Kal/86a	Augustine Byarufu (M)	Kalengyere	30/8/95
95/Kal/87a	Nestori Rwakahesi (M)	Kalengyere	30/8/95
95/Kal/88a	Nyasio Bandonde (M)	Kalengyere	30/8/95
95/Kal/89a	Miriano Tibesigwa (M)	Kalengyere	30/8/95
95/Kal/90a	Lissen Birema (M)	Kalengyere	30/8/95
95/Bub/91a	Raphael Kakutu (M)	Bubale	1/9/95
95/Bub/92a	Elisa Kabungurira (M)	Bubale	1/9/95
95/Bub/93a	Nora Nyarufunjo (F)	Bubale	1/9/95
95/Bub/94a	Andrew Makara (M)	Bubale	1/9/95
95/Bub/95a	Andrew Kabonyi (M)	Bubale	1/9/95
95/Bub/96a	Daniel Kayabuki (M)	Bubale	5/9/95
95/Bub/97a	Ishaka Rwantare (M)	Bubale	5/9/95
95/Bub/98a	Lazaro Kamuhire (M)	Bubale	5/9/95
95/Kab/99a	John Batuma (M) (in English)	Kabale	14/9/95
95/Kam/100a	J.M. Byagagaire (M) (in English)	Kampala	21/9/95

Index of 2000 interviews

I conducted interviews in and around Kabale town, as well as in the areas of Muyebe (to the south of Kabale town) and Kabirizi (Kitozho). Some informants who had been interviewed in 1995 were returned to. Some interviews were taped before being transcribed and translated, while others were translated immediately and notes taken. (Taped interviews marked with T below).

Interview number	Informant name	Site	Date
00/Kab/T1a	Vicencio Tibakyenga (M)	Rushaki, Kabale	18/7/00
00/Kab/T1b	Vicencio Tibakyenga (M)	Rushaki, Kabale	31/7/00
00/Kab/T2a	Elizabeth Nyinabebelgi (F)	Rushaki, Kabale	18/7/00
00/Kab/T2b	Elizabeth Nyinabebelgi (F)	Rushaki, Kabale	7/8/00
00/Kab/T2c	Elizabeth Nyinabebelgi (F)	Rushaki, Kabale	9/8/00
00/Kab/T3a	Festo Katambaki (M)	Rushaki, Kabale	31/7/00
00/Kab/T4a	Edna Rutindapora (F)	Ruhita, Kabale	1/8/00
00/Kab/T4b	Edna Rutindapora (F)	Ruhita, Kabale	2/8/00
00/Kab/T5a	Phoebe Birara (F)	Ruhita, Kabale	1/8/00
00/Kab/T5b	Phoebe Birara (F)	Ruhita, Kabale	6/8/00
00/Kab/T6a	Edsa Georgna (F)	Ruhita, Kabale	2/8/00
00/Kab/T6b	Edsa Georgna (F)	Ruhita, Kabale	5/8/00
00/Kab/T6c	Edsa Georgna (F)	Ruhita, Kabale	10/8/00
00/Kab/T7a	Salmi Nytumba (F)	Rushaki, Kabale	2/8/00
00/Kab/T8a	Sarah Batokorora (F)	Nyabikoni, Kabale	4/8/00
00/Kab/T9a	Ebriahim Kagamgure (M)	Ruhita, Kabale	4/8/00
00/Kab/T9b	Ebriahim Kagamgure (M)	Ruhita, Kabale	6/8/00
00/Kab/T9c	Ebriahim Kagamgure (M)	Ruhita, Kabale	9/8/00
00/Kab/T9d	Ebriahim Kagamgure (M)	Ruhita, Kabale	15/8/00
00/Kab/T10a	Kaihari (F)	Nyabikoni, Kabale	4/8/00
00/Kab/T10b	Kaihari (F)	Nyabikoni, Kabale	5/8/00
00/Kab/T11a	Mugarura (M)	Rushaki, Kabale	7/8/00
00/Kab/T12a	Juma Kashumba (M)	Nyabikoni, Kabale	7/8/00
00/Kab/T13a	Francis Ndibeshu (Eng) (M)	Nyabikoni, Kabale	7/8/00
00/Bub/T14a	Elisa Kabungurira (M)	Bubaale	8/8/00
00/Bub/T14b	Elisa Kabungurira (M)	Bubaale	11/8/00
00/Bub/T14c	Elisa Kabungurira (M)	Bubaale	14/8/00
00/Kab/T15a	Dorcus Koruharo (F)	Ruhita, Kabale	10/8/00
00/Muy/T16a	Mrs Kamucaana (F)	Muyebe	10/8/00
00/Muy/T17a	Meraba (F)	Muyebe	10/8/00
00/Muy/T18a	Amos Kahindi (M)	Muyebe	12/8/00
00/Muy/T19a	Kabashagama (M)	Muyebe	12/8/00
00/Muy/T20a	Patric Bujara (M)	Muyebe	12/8/00
00/Muy/T21a	Ezra Batuta (M)	Muyebe	12/8/00
00/Muy/T22a	Keizinoni (M)	Muyebe	12/8/00
00/Muy/23a	Rutabyama (M)	Muyebe	12/8/00
00/Muy/T23b	Rutabyama (M)	Muyebe	14/8/00
00/Muy/T24a	Efuransi Batuta (F)	Muyebe	15/8/00

Appendix

00/Kab/25a	Jackson Mutebi, CARE (M)	Kabale	18/7/00
00/Kbz/26a	Tibwabuse (M)	Kabirizi	19/7/00
00/Kbz/27a	Esau and Ruheeka (M + M)	Kabirizi	20/7/00
00/Kbz/28a	Kashumba (M)	Kabirizi	21/7/00
00/Kbz/29a	Bazaara Nelson (M)	Kabirizi	23/7/00
00/Kbz/30a	Edward Baryayanga (M)	Kabirizi	19/7/00
00/Kbz/30aii	Edward Baryayanga (M)	Kabirizi	24/7/00
00/Kbz/30b	Edward Baryayanga (M)	Kabirizi	26/7/00
00/Kbz/31a	Joy Kibukere (F)	Kabirizi	26/7/00
00/Kbz/32a	Violet Kemishisha (F)	Kabirizi	26/7/00
00/Kbz/33a	Constant & Fumera Rwakira (M + F)	Kabirizi	27/7/00
00/Kbz/34a	Magezi (M)	Kabirizi	27/7/00
00/Kab/35a	Agro-Management Pyrethrum (M)	Kabale	8/8/00
00/Kab/35b	Agro-Management Pyrethrum (M)	Kabale	16/8/00
00/Kab/36a	Nelson, AHI (M)	Kabale	8/8/00
00/Muy/37a	Udes & Matayo Kamueybeje (F + M)	Muyebe	10/8/00
00/Kab/38a	Pascal, AHI (M)	Kabale	11/8/00
00/Muy/39a	Dorothy Rutabyama (F)	Muyebe	12/8/00
00/Muy/40a	Efuransi Batuta (F)	Muyebe	12/8/00
00/Kab/41a	Musca Frank, Agro-Man extension (M)	Kabale	15/8/00
00/Kab/42a	Pyrethrum growers (F)	Kabale	15/8/00
00/Kab/43a	Eric, Agro-Man, Ext. worker (M)	Kabale	15/8/00
00/Kab/44a	Africare employee (M)	Kabale	15/8/00
00/Kab/45a	Benon Biramahira Kabale market (M)	Kabale	16/8/00
00/Kab/46a	Bernard Mafigi, Kabale market (M)	Kabale	16/8/00
00/Kab/47a	Jalence, Kabale market (F)	Kabale	16/8/00
00/Kab/48a	Ebriahim Koyekyeka (M)	Kabale	17/8/00

Index of 2002 Interviews

Interviews were again conducted in three main sites: in and around Kabale town, in the area of Muyebe, and in Kabirizi. Repeat interviews with informants interviewed in 1995 and 2000 were conducted. In addition, a number of group interviews and activities were carried out.

Interview number	Informant name	Site	Date
02/Kab/1	Jackson Mutebi, CARE (M)	Kabale	13/2/02
02/Kab/2	Dr Imelda, CARE (F)	Kabale	13/2/02
02/Kab/3	Sunday Mutabazi, DAO (M)	Kabale	15/2/02
02/Kbz/Venn	Venn Diagram – mixed group of men and women (M + F)	Kabirizi	19/2/02
02/Kbz/4a	Lydia Atuyambe, Catechist (F)	Kabirizi	19/2/02
02/Kbz/4b	Lydia Atuyambe, Catechist (F)	Kabirizi	21/2/02
02/Kbz/5a	Baryayanga (M)	Kabirizi	20/2/02
02/Kbz/5b	Baryayanga (M)	Kabirizi	21/2/02
02/Kbz/ 5c	Baryayanga (M)	Kabirizi	5/03/02
02/Kbz/5d	Baryayanga (M)	Kabirizi	23/3/02
02/Kbz/6	Rwakira Constant (M)	Kabirizi	20/2/02
02/Kbz/7	Gaude Tugumisize (F)	Kabirizi	20/2/02
02/Kbz/8	Lydia Kakuru (F)	Kabirizi	20/2/02
02/Kbz/Obs	Dispute settlement & LC – mixed group of men and women (M + F)	Kabirizi	21/2/02
02/Kbz/Cal	Calendar – mixed group of men and women (M + F)	Kabirizi	21/2/02
02/Kbz/9a	Bruce Natakunda (M)	Kabirizi	21/2/02
02/Kbz/9b	Bruce Natakunda (M)	Kabirizi	22/2/02
02/Kbz/ 9c	Bruce (M)	Kabirizi	5/03/02
02/Kbz/10	Rovince (F)	Kabirizi	21/2/02
02/Kbz/11a	Bazarwa (M)	Kabirizi	22/2/02
02/Kbz/ 11b	Bazarwa (M)	Kabirizi	4/03/02
02/Kbz/11c	Bazarwa (M)	Kabirizi	24/3/02
02/Kbz/11d	Bazarwa (M)	Kabirizi	24/3/02
02/Kbz/12a	Kivebulaya (M)	Kabirizi	22/2/02
02/Kbz/ 12b	Kivebulaya (M)	Kabirizi	3/03/02
02/Muy/Venn	Venn Diagram– mixed group of men and women (M + F)	Muyebe	26/2/02
02/Muy/GAM	'Gender analysis' – group of men (M)	Muyebe	26/2/02
02/Muy/13a	Efuransi Batuta (F)	Muyebe	26/2/02
02/Muy/ T13b	Efuransi Batuta (F)	Muyebe	28/2/02
02/Muy/ 13c	Efuransi Batuta (F)	Muyebe	10/3/02
02/Muy/GAW	'Gender analysis' – group of women (F)	Muyebe	26/2/02
02/Muy/14	Jennina (F)	Muyebe	26/2/02
02/Muy/15	Charles Bisakanwa (M)	Muyebe	27/2/02
02/Muy/T15b	Bisakanwa (M)	Muyebe	28/2/02
02/Muy/15c	Bisakanwa (M)	Muyebe	11/3/02
02/Muy/15d	Bisakanwa (M)	Muyebe	29/3/02

02/Muy/T15e	Bisakanwa (M)	Muyebe	1/4/02
02/Muy/16	William Karuhize (M)	Muyebe	27/2/02
02/Muy/17a	Bright Bakesiga (M)	Muyebe	27/2/02
02/Muy/17b	Bright (M)	Muyebe	30/3/02
02/Muy/18	John (LC C'man) (M)	Muyebe	27/2/02
02/Muy/19	Moscow (M)	Muyebe	27/2/02
02/Muy/20a	Kiribata (M)	Muyebe	27/2/02
02/Muy/20b	Kiribata (M)	Muyebe	30/3/02
02/Muy/21	Muchore (M)	Muyebe	28/2/02
02/Muy/22	Tumuhimbise (F)	Muyebe	28/2/02
02/Muy/23	Margaret Tunmeswigye (F)	Muyebe	28/2/02
02/Muy/24	Georgina (F)	Muyebe	28/2/02
02/Muy/25	Sunday (M)	Muyebe	28/2/02
02/Muy/26	Georgina and 2 brickmakers (F + M)	Muyebe	28/2/02
02/Muy/27	Margaret (F) & Richard (M)	Muyebe	28/2/02
02/Muy/ T28	Rutagira (F)	Muyebe	26/2/02
02/Muy/T28b	Rutagira (F)	Muyebe	11/3/02
02/Muy/28c	Rutagira (F)	Muyebe	29/3/02
02/Muy/ T29	Joseline (F)	Muyebe	26/2/02
02/Muy/T29b	Joseline (F)	Muyebe	11/3/02
02/Muy/ T30a	Kazeene (M)	Muyebe	27/2/02
02/Muy/T30b	Kazeene (M)	Muyebe	11/3/02
02/Muy/30c	Kazeene (M)	Muyebe	11/3/02
02/Muy/30d	Kazeene (M)	Muyebe	30/3/02
02/Muy/ T31a	Ephraim Bamiza (M)	Muyebe	27/2/02
02/Muy/31b	Bamiza (M)	Muyebe	30/3/02
02/Muy/T31c	Bamiza (M)	Muyebe	1/4/02
02/Muy/ T32	Ezra Batuta (M)	Muyebe	27/2/02
02/Muy/ T33	Eric (M)	Muyebe	28/2/02
02/Muy/ T34	Cosia (M)	Muyebe	28/2/02
02/Muy/ T36a	Zakayo a.k.a. Rukabire (M)	Muyebe	28/2/02
02/Muy/ 36b	Rukabire (M)	Muyebe	10/3/02
02/Muy/36c	Rukabire (M)	Muyebe	30/3/02
02/Muy/ T37	Charles Kagirite (M)	Muyebe	28/2/02
02/Muy/ T38	Semu Baryahabara (M)	Muyebe	28/2/02
02/Muy/ T39	Buhiire (M)	Muyebe	28/2/02
02/Kbz/ 40	Fidel Biryatwita (M)	Kabirizi	3/03/02
02/Kbz/ 41a	Rubizira (M)	Kabirizi	3/03/02
02/Kbz/ 41b	Rubizira (M)	Kabirizi	5/03/02
02/Kbz/ GAW	'Gender analysis'– group of women (F)	Kabirizi	3/03/02
02/Kbz/ 42a	Joy Kibukere (F)	Kabirizi	3/03/02
02/Kbz/42b	Joy Kibukere (F)	Kabirizi	24/3/02
02/Kbz/ 43	Kellen (F)	Kabirizi	4/03/02
02/Kbz/ 44a	Daniel Ruheeka (M) & Hope Felestance (F)	Kabirizi	4/03/02
02/Kbz/44b	Ruheeka (M)	Kabirizi	22/3/02
02/Kbz/ 45	Enid Kanyesigye (F)	Kabirizi	4/03/02
02/Kbz/ 46	LC3 hearing (M + F)	Kabirizi	4/03/02
02/Kbz/ 47a	Milka (F)	Kabirizi	5/03/02
02/Kbz/47b	Milka (F)	Kabirizi	24/3/02

02/Muy/Q1-69	Questionnaires (M + F)	Muyebe	7/03/02+
02/Muy/48	Aida Kabongoya (F)	Muyebe	10/3/02
02/Muy/49	Kellen Turyagenda Isaaya (F)	Muyebe	11/3/02
02/Muy/50	Joyce (F)	Muyebe	13/3/02
02/Muy/WR	Wealth rank – mixed group of men and women (M + F)	Muyebe	14/3/02
02/Kbz/51	Bamera (M)	Kabirizi	22/3/02
02/Kbz/GAM	'Gender analysis' – group of men (M)	Kabirizi	23/3/02
02/Kbz/52	Bazarwa's son; Mukabazungu Fangera (M)	Kabirizi	24/3/02
02/Kbz/53	Apollo Byauruhanga (M)	Kabirizi	24/3/02
02/Kab/T54	Eseza Bisagavu (F)	Ruhita, Kabale	27/3/02
02/Muy/55	Richard Musca (M)	Muyebe	29/3/02
02/Muy/56	Habaasa (M)	Muyebe	29/3/02
02/Muy/57	Kyinuubi (M)	Muyebe	29/3/02
02/Muy/58	Allen Bariyo (F)	Muyebe	30/3/02
02/Muy/59	Topher Kwikiriza (M)	Muyebe	30/3/02
02/Muy/T60	Damson Byarabahe (M)	Muyebe	31/3/02
02/Muy/T61	Mary Bagenda (F)	Muyebe	31/3/02
02/Muy/T62	Moses Twijnkye (M)	Muyebe	31/3/02
02/Muy/T63	Generous Ntamukyiza (F)	Muyebe	31/3/02
02/Muy/T64	Enos Turigye (M)	Muyebe	31/3/02
02/Muy/T65	Janet Namara (F)	Muyebe	1/4/02
02/Kab/66	Jenn Kalikumutima, Kabneto offices (F)	Kabale	27/3/02

Bibliography

Archival sources

PUBLIC RECORD OFFICE, KEW

This contained correspondence and reports that were sent between the Colonial Office in London and the Ugandan Administration in Entebbe (and occasionally Kigezi District). The most significant classes were:

CO 536 – Uganda, Original Correspondence. This class contains correspondence and memoranda relating specifically to Uganda from the earliest colonial period to 1951. From this date correspondence was either placed in the Regional classes (East Africa, CO 822) or into subject files (eg Economic, CO 852). CO 536 is used in conjunction with the Registries of Correspondence (CO 682).

CO 822 – East Africa, Original Correspondence. This class contains material on the whole of East Africa. It increases dramatically in importance from 1951 when the Country classes ceased to be used.

CO 537 – Supplementary Correspondence. This contains material that was withheld from the subject files, and is material of a secret, or more confidential, nature.

CO 892 – East Africa Royal Commission. This class proved to be an incredibly rich source. It contains an enormous amount of material collected by the Royal Commission, including memoranda submitted by district officials and members of the public.

ENTEBBE NATIONAL ARCHIVES, UGANDA (ENA)

I hoped that the Entebbe National Archives would contain a wide range of relevant material, particularly correspondence and memoranda between the central and district administrations. However, the inadequacy of the catalogue for the period, and in particular the latter part of the colonial period, meant that only a relatively small amount of information was gleaned from this source.

KIGEZI DISTRICT ARCHIVES, KABALE (KDA)

The Kigezi District Archives is not an archive as such, but rather a collection of storerooms, attic rooms and cupboards in which are stored closed files of the district administration. Despite the difficulties encountered in working in this archive, the rewards were enormous. Some of the files of the District Commissioner's office had once been sorted, renumbered and a catalogue presumably made, but this was never located. At least three file numbering systems appear to have been used at different times, but explanations could not be found for any of them. Given this complex and chaotic situation, it was decided that the original file reference would be used. Where there was no reference number a shortened version of the file title was used (eg TEAM-MIN for District Team Minutes). There was no apparent relationship between the filing systems of the District Commissioner's office (eg DEV4 and MP68) and the Department of Agriculture's office (eg 11/A/1 and 16).

OTHER ARCHIVAL COLLECTIONS

The Rhodes House library contained a number of collections of papers of individuals who had worked or visited Kigezi, which proved to be of value. These included the diary of J.R.McD. Elliot, (MSS Afr s 1384) who was a district officer in Kigezi in the early 1920s; papers of Snowden, including Report to Director of Agriculture on Tour of Kigezi District, 16 November 1929 (MSS Afr s 921); and the papers of D.W. Malcolm, (Secretary to Lord Hailey 1935–36) (MSS Afr s 1445), who visited Uganda from 22 December 1935 to 19 January 1936.

The Church Missionary Society Archives in the Special Collection of the University of Birmingham Library was used but little material of direct relevance was found, with the exception of the photograph reproduced in Chapter 6.

PRIVATE PAPERS of J.W. Purseglove, J.C.D. Lawrance and G.B. Masefield
The first mentioned papers were particularly rich, containing the Kitozho Mutala Survey (parts by both Purseglove and Wright), and the 'Report on the Overpopulated areas of Kigezi' by Purseglove, as well as numerous photographs, cuttings and papers related to Purseglove's time in Kigezi.

Government published reports

UK GOVERNMENT, PARLIAMENTARY PAPERS & COLONIAL REPORTS

East African Royal Commission (EARC), *Report of the East African Royal Commission, 1953-55* (London, Cmd 9475, 1955).

Bibliography

Governors of Kenya, Uganda and Tanzania, *Commentary on the Despatches from the Governors of Kenya, Uganda and Tanzania and the Administrator, East African High Commission, on the East African Royal Commission 1953-55 Report* (London, Cmd 9804, 1956).

Governors of Kenya, Uganda and Tanzania, *Despatches from the Governors of Kenya, Uganda and Tanzania and the Administrator, East African High Commission, on the East African Royal Commission 1953-55 Report* (London, Cmd 9801, 1956).

VARIOUS ANNUAL REPORTS
Kigezi District Annual Reports (KDAR)
Western Province Annual Reports (WPAR)
Department of Agriculture Annual Reports (DoAAR)

UGANDA GOVERNMENT PUBLICATIONS
1923   *Laws of Uganda*
1935   *Laws of Uganda*
1937   *Report on soil erosion and water supplies in Uganda* (E.J. Wayland and N.V. Brasnett)
1938   *Report on nineteen surveys done in small agricultural areas in Uganda with a view to ascertaining the position with regard to soil deterioration* (J.D. Tothill)
1938   *Report of the Committee of Enquiry into the Labour Situation in the Uganda Protectorate* (Elliot)
1939   *Agricultural Survey Committee: Nutrition Report No. 3 – Unskilled Labour. The Effect of Dietary and Other Supplements on the Health and Working Capacity of Banyaruanda Labourers* (L.J.A. Loewenthal)
1940   *Report of the Committee of Enquiry into the Labour Situation in the Uganda Protectorate: Statement of Conclusions by Government*
1943   *Laws of Uganda*
1943   *Second Report of the Labour Advisory Committee* (Earl Hutt Report)
1947   *A Development Plan for Uganda* (E.B. Worthington)
1948   *Population Census*
1949   *African Local Government Ordinance*
1953   *Report of Inquiry into African Local Government in Protectorate of Uganda* (C.A.G. Wallis)
1954   *Report of the Agricultural Productivity Committee: Supplement to the Report of the Development Council entitled 'A Five Year Capital Development Plan 1955-1960'*
1955   *Land Tenure Proposals*
1956   *Water Resources Survey in Uganda 1954–55* (Sir Alexander Gibb and Partners, Africa)
1957   *Effect of Customs of Inheritance on Sub-Division and Fragmentation of Land in South Kigezi* (J.M. Byagagaire and J.C.D. Lawrance)
1961   *Report of the Commissioner appointed to Inquire into the Operation of the Land Tenure Scheme in Ankole*
1963   *Fragmentation of Agricultural Land in Uganda* (J.C.D. Lawrance)

1964   *Laws of Uganda*
1991   *Population Census*
1992   *Report on Uganda National Census of Agriculture and Livestock (1990–1991)* (Ministry of Agriculture, Entebbe)
1994   *State of the Environment Report for Uganda* (Ministry of National Resources, National Environment Information Centre)
1995   *Kabale District Environment Profile* (National Environment Information Centre, Kampala)
1998   *State of the Environment Report for Uganda* (Ministry of National Resources, National Environment Information Centre)
2002   *Population and Housing Census – provisional results* (Kampala, 2002)
n.d.   *Kabale Environment Profile* (Department of Environment, Kabale)

Bibliography

Abbott, G. C., 'A re-examination of the 1929 Colonial Act', *Economic History Review*, 24 1 (1971), 68–81.
Abdulai, A. and A. CroleRees, 'Determinants of income diversification amongst rural households in southern Mali', *Food Policy*, 26 (2001), 437–52.
Acland, J.D., *East African Crops* (London, 1971).
Adams, W.M., 'Green Development Theory?', in J. Crush, *Power of Development* (London, 1995).
Adger, W.N., 'Governing Natural Resources: institution adaptation and resilience', in F. Berkhout, M. Leach and I. Scoones, *Negotiating Environmental Change* (Cheltenham, 2003).
Adoko, J. and S. Levine, 'A Land Market for Poverty Eradication? A case study of the impact of Uganda's Land Acts on policy hopes for development and poverty eradication' (Land and Equity Movement in Uganda, Kampala, 2005) (mimeo).
AFRENA, 'Agroforestry Research Networks for Africa Uganda National Taskforce. Agroforestry potentials for the land-use systems in the bimodal highlands of eastern Africa: Uganda', *AFRENA Report* 4 (1988).
African Highlands Initiative (AHI) C and D Uganda Team, 'Natural resource management constraints and prospects in Kabale District', (Kampala, 1998).
African Studies Branch (CO), 'A survey of local government in Uganda since 1947', *Journal of African Administration*, IV (1952).
African Studies Branch (CO), 'The EARC and African land tenure', *Journal of African Administration*, 8 2, (April 1956), 69–74.
Africare, 'Baseline Survey', (Kabale, 1997) mimeo.
Africare, 'The Status of Uganda Food Security Initiative (UFSI)', (Kabale, mimeo, 2000).
Allan, W., *The African Husbandman* (Edinburgh, 1965).
Anderson, D.M., 'Depression, dust bowl, demography and drought: The colonial state and soil conservation in East Africa during the 1930s', *African*

Bibliography

Affairs, 83 (1984), 321-43.

Anderson, D. M. and D.H. Johnson (eds), *Revealing Prophets: Prophecy in Eastern African history* (London, 1995).

Anderson, G.W., 'Agriculture and land tenure in Uganda', in W.T.W. Morgan (ed.), *East Africa: Its people and resources* (Nairobi, 1969), 199-207.

Andersson, J.A., 'Potato cultivation in the Uporoto Mountains, Tanzania', *African Affairs*, 95, 378 (1996), 85–106.

Apthorpe, R. (ed.) *Land Settlement and Rural Development in Eastern Africa* (Kampala, 1968).

Ashley, C. and D. Carney, *Sustainable Livelihoods: Lessons from early experience* (London, 1999).

Atwood, D.A., 'Land registration in Africa: The impact on agricultural production', *World Development*, 18 5 (1990), 659–71.

Bagoora, F.D.K., 'Soil erosion and mass wasting risk in the highland areas of Uganda', *Mountain Research and Development*, 8 (1988), 173-82.

Baker, C., *Seeds of Trouble: Government Policy and Land Rights in Nyasaland, 1946-64* (London, 1993).

Bamwerinde, W.M., S.B. Dickens, J. Musiime, and T. Raussen, 'Sharing local knowledge: farmers from Kabale (Uganda) study tree pruning systems and agroforesty in Embu (Kenya)' (Kabale, 1999).

Bananuka-Rukara, F., 'Rukiga resistance and adaptation to British rule', in D.J.W. Denoon (ed.), *A History of Kigezi in South West Uganda* (Kampala, 1972).

Barkan, J.D., (ed.), *Uganda District Government and Politics, 1947-1967* (Madison, WI, 1977).

Barrett, C.D., T. Reardon and P. Webb, 'Non-farm income diversification and household livelihood strategies in rural Africa: concepts, dynamics, and policy implications', *Food Policy*, 26 4 (2001), 315–31.

Barrows, R. and M. Roth, 'Land tenure and investment in African agriculture: Theory and evidence', *Journal of Modern African Studies*, 28 2 (1990), 265–97.

Bassett, T.J. and D.E. Crummey, *Land in African Agrarian Systems* (Madison, WI, 1993).

Bates, R., *Essays on the Political Economy of Rural Africa* (Cambridge, 1983).

Bates, R.H., *Beyond the Miracle of the Market: The Political Economy of Agrarian Development in Kenya* (Cambridge, 1990).

Baxter, P.T.W., 'The Kiga', in A.I. Richards, *East African Chiefs: A Study of Political Development in some Uganda and Tanganyika Tribes* (London, 1960), 278-310.

Bazaara, N., 'Civil society and the struggle for land rights for marginalized groups: the contribution of the Uganda Land Alliance to the Land Act 1998' (draft mimeo, no date. Produced for Civil Society and Governance Project, IDS and Ford Foundation.)

Beinart, W., 'Soil erosion, conservationism and ideas about development: A Southern African exploration, 1900-1960', *Journal of Southern African Studies*, 11 1 (1984), 52–83.

Beinart, W., 'Introduction: The politics of colonial conservation', *Journal of*

Southern African Studies, 15 2 (1989), 143–62.

Beinart, W., 'African history and environmental history', *African Affairs*, 99 (2000), 269–302.

Beinart, W., *The Rise of Conservation in South Africa* (Oxford, 2003).

Beinart, W. and C. Bundy, *Hidden Struggles in Rural South Africa: Politics and Popular Movements in Transkei and Eastern Cape* (London, 1987).

Beinart, W. and J. McGregor (eds), *Social History and African Environments* (Oxford, 2003).

Belshaw, D.G.R., 'Outline of resettlement policy in Uganda: 1945-63', in Raymond Apthorpe, *Land Settlement and Rural Development in Eastern Africa* (Kampala, 1968).

Berman, B. and J. Lonsdale, *Unhappy Valley – Conflict in Kenya and Africa: State and Class* (Book 1) (London, 1992).

Berman, B. and J. Lonsdale, *Unhappy Valley – Conflict in Kenya and Africa: Violence and Ethnicity* (Book 2) (London, 1992).

Bernstein, H. and P. Woodhouse, 'Telling environmental change like it is? Reflections on a study of Sub-Saharan Africa', *Journal of Agrarian Change*, 1 2 (2001), 283–324.

Berry, S., *Cocoa, Custom and Socio-economic Change in Rural Western Nigeria* (Oxford, 1975).

Berry, S., 'The food crisis and agrarian change in Africa', *African Studies Review*, 27 2 (1984), 59–112.

Berry, S., *No Condition is Permanent: The Social Dynamics of Agrarian Change in Sub Saharan Africa* (Madison, WI, 1993).

Bessell, M.J., 'Nyabingi', *Uganda Journal*, 6 (1938), 73-86.

Biebuyok, D., *African Agrarian Systems* (Cambridge, 1963).

Bilsborrow, R.E. and H.W.O. Okoth Ogenda, 'Population-driven changes in land use in developing countries', *Ambio*, 21 (1992), 37-45.

Bird, K. and A. Shepherd, 'Livelihoods and chronic poverty in semi-arid Zimbabwe', *World Development*, 31 3 (2003), 591–610.

Bisamunya, E.N., 'Buganda agency 1911–24', in D.J.W. Denoon (ed.), *A History of Kigezi in South West Uganda* (Kampala, 1972).

Biteete-Tukahiirwe, J. M., 'Measurement, Predictions and Social Ecology of Accelerated Soil Erosion in Kabale District, South-West Uganda' (PhD, Department of Geography, Makerere University, Kampala, 1995).

Black, R. and H. White (eds), *Targeting Development: Critical Perspectives on the Millennium Development Goals* (London, 2004).

Blaikie, P., *The Political Economy of Soil Erosion in Developing Countries* (London, 1985).

Bohannan, P., '"Land", "Tenure" and "Land Tenure"', in D. Biebuyck (ed.), *African Agrarian Systems*, (London, 1963).

Booth, D., *et al.*, *Social, Cultural and Economic Change in Contemporary Tanzania: A people-oriented focus* (Stockholm, 1993).

Boserup, E., *The Conditions of Agricultural Growth: the economics of agrarian change under population pressure* (London, 1965).

Boserup, E., *Population and Technological Change* (Chicago, 1981).

Bosworth, J., 'Land and Society in South Kigezi, Uganda' (DPhil, University of Oxford, 1995).

Bosworth, J., 'Uganda Case Study' (Paper presented at Regional Workshop on Land Issues in Africa, Kampala, 2002).

Brasnett, N.V., 'Soil erosion', *Uganda Journal*, 4 (1936), 156–61.

Brazier, F.S., 'The incident at Nyakishenyi, 1917', *Uganda Journal*, 32 (1968), 17-27.

Brazier, F.S., 'The Nyabingi cult: Religion and political scale in Kigezi, 1900-1930' (EAISR Conference, 1968).

Breman, J., *Of Peasants, Migrants and Paupers: Rural labour circulation and capitalist production in West India* (Delhi, 1985).

Breman, J., *Beyond Patronage and Exploitation: Changing agrarian relations in South Gujarat* (Delhi, 1993).

Brett, E.A., *Colonialism and Underdevelopment in East Africa: The Politics of Economic Change 1919-1939* (London, 1973).

Brock, B., 'Customary land tenure, individualisation and agricultural development in Uganda', *East African Journal of Rural Development*, 2 (1969), 1-27.

Brock, B., 'Land tenure and social change in Bugisu', in Peter Rigby, *Society and Social Change in Eastern Africa* (Kampala, 1969).

Brown, D. and P. Allen, *An Introduction to the Law of Uganda* (London, 1968).

Brown, I., *The Economies of Africa and Asia in the Interwar Depression* (London, 1989).

Brown, L.R., *The State of the World* (New York, 1992).

Bruce, J.W. and S.E. Migot-Adholla (eds), *Searching for Land Security in Africa* (Washington, DC, 1994).

Bryceson, D., 'Peasant cash cropping versus self-sufficiency in Tanzania: A historical perspective', *IDS Bulletin* 192 (1988), 37–46.

Bryceson, D.F., *Liberalizing Tanzania's food trade: public and private faces of urban marketing policy 1939–1988.* (London, 1993).

Bryceson, D., 'Deagrarianization and Rural Employment in sub-Saharan Africa: A Sectoral Perspective', *World Development*, 24 1 (1996), 97–111.

Bryceson, D., 'African rural labour, income diversification and livelihood approaches: A long-term development perspective', *Review of African Political Economy*, 80 (1999), 171–89.

Bryceson, D., *Sub-Saharan Africa Betwixt and Between: Rural livelihood practices and policies.* Africa Studies Centre Working Paper 43 (Leiden, 1999).

Bryceson, D., *Rural Africa at the Crossroads: Livelihood practices and policies*, ODI Natural Resource Perspectives, 52 (London, 2000).

Bryceson, D. and V. Jamal (eds), *Farewell to Farms: De-agrarianisation and employment in Africa* (Aldershot, 1997).

Bunker, S., *Peasants Against the State: The Politics of Market Control in Bugisu, Uganda 1900–1983* (Chicago, 1987).

Burke, F.G., 'The new role of the chief in Uganda', *Journal of African Administration*, 10 (1958), 153-60.

Burke, F.G., *Local Government and Politics in Uganda* (Syracuse, NY, 1964).

Busingye, H., 'Customary Land Tenure Reform in Uganda; Lessons for South Africa', in *International Symposium on Communal Tenure Reform* (Johannesburg, 2002).

Byagagaire, J.M. and J.J.D. Lawrance, *Effects of Customs of Inheritance on Sub-Division and Fragmentation of Land in South Kigezi, Uganda* (Entebbe, 1957).

Canagarajah, S., C. Newman and R. Bhattamishra, 'Non-farm income, gender and inequality: evidence from rural Ghana and Uganda', *Food Policy* 26 (2001), 405–20.

CARE, 'Development Through Conservation project proposal, 1992–1993 A proposal to USAID' (Kabale, 1992).

Carney, D. (ed.), *Sustainable Rural Livelihoods: What contribution can we make?* (London, 1998).

Carruthers, J., 'Africa: Histories, Ecologies and Societies', *Environment and History*, 10 (2004), 379–406.

Carswell, G. 'African Farmers in colonial Kigezi, Uganda, 1930–1962: Opportunity, Constraint and Sustainability' (PhD, SOAS, 1996).

Carswell, G., 'Continuities in environmental narratives: the case of Kabale, Uganda, 1930–2000', *Environment and History*, 9 1 (2003), 3–29.

Carswell, G., 'Livelihood diversification: increasing in importance or increasingly recognised? Evidence from southern Ethiopia', *Journal of International Development*, 14 6 (2002), 789–804.

Carswell, G. *et al.* 'Sustainable livelihoods in Southern Ethiopia', *IDS Research Report*, 44 (Brighton, 2000).

Chambers, R., 'Participatory rural appraisal (PRA): analysis of experience', *World Development*, 22 9 (1994), 1253–68.

Chambers, R., 'Participatory rural appraisal (PRA): challenges potentials and paradigm', *World Development*, 22 10 (1994), 1437–54.

Chambers, R., 'The origins and practice of participatory rural appraisal', *World Development*, 22 7 (1994), 953–69.

Chambers, R., 'Responsible well-being – a personal agenda for development', *World Development*, 25 11, (1997), 1743–54.

Chambers, R., *Whose Reality Counts? Putting the first last* (London, 1997).

Chanock, M., *Law, Custom and Social Order – the Colonial Experience in Malawi and Zambia* (Cambridge, 1985).

Chanock, M., 'Paradigms, policies, and property: A review of the customary law of land tenure', in K. Mann and R. Roberts, *Law in Colonial Africa* (London, 1991).

Chant, S. (ed.), *Gender and Migration in Developing Countries* (London, 1992).

Chant, S., 'Households, gender and rural–urban migration: reflections on linkages and considerations for policy', *Environment and Urbanization*, 10 1, (1998), 5–21.

Chrétien, J.P., 'Des sédentaires devenus migrants: les motifs des départs des Barundi et des Banyarwanda vers l'Uganda (1920–60)', *Cultures et Développement*, 10 1 (1978), 71–101.

Chrétien, J.P., *The Great Lakes of Africa: Two Thousand Years of History* (New York, 2003).

Church, Dr J.E., *Quest for the Highest: An Autobiographical Account of the East African Revival* (Exeter, 1981).

Clayton, E., *Purseglove: A Pioneer of Rural Development* (Wye, 1993).

Bibliography

Cleaver, K., and G. Schreiber, *Reversing the Spiral: The population, agriculture and environment nexus in sub Saharan Africa*. Directions in Development Series (Washington, DC, 1994).

Cliffe, L., 'Nationalism and the reaction to enforced agricultural change in Tanganyika during the colonial period', in L. Cliffe and J. Saul (eds), *Socialism in Tanganyika* (Vol. 1) (Nairobi, [1964] 1972).

Cline Cole, R.A., H. A. C. Main and J. E. Nichol, 'On Fuelwood consumption, population dynamics and deforestation in Africa', *World Development* 18 4 (1990), 513–527.

Cohen, D.W., 'Food production and food exchange in pre-colonial lakes plateau region', in R.I. Rotberg, (ed.), *Imperialism, Colonialism and Hunger: East and Central Africa* (Lexington, MA, 1983).

Coldham, S., 'Land reform and customary rights: The case of Uganda', *Journal of African Law*, 44 (2000) 65–77.

Collinson, M.P., *The Economic Characteristics of the Sukuma Farming System* (Dar es Salaam, 1972).

Colson, E., 'The impact of the colonial period on the definition of land rights' in V. Turner (ed.), *'Profiles of Change: African Society and Colonial Rule'*, Vol. 3 of L. Gann and P. Duignan, *Colonialism in Africa* (Cambridge, 1971).

Connor, K.T., 'Kigezi', in J.D. Barkan, *et al.*, (eds), *Uganda District Government and Politics, 1947-1967* (Madison, WI, 1977).

Constantine, S., *The Making of British Colonial Development Policy, 1914–1940* (London, 1984).

Cooke, B., *From Colonial Administration to Development Management*. Institute for Development Policy and Management Discussion Paper, 63 (Manchester, 2001).

Cooke, B., 'A new continuity with colonial administration; Participation in development management', *Third World Quarterly*, 24 1 (2003), 47–61.

Coote, J.M. (with postscript by H.B. Thomas), 'The Kivu Mission, 1909-1910', *Uganda Journal*, 20 (1956), 105-12.

Cornet, A., 'Histoire d'une Famine: Rwanda 1927–30. Crise Alimentaire entre Tradition et Modernité' (Louvain-La-Neuve, 1996).

Cornwall. A., I. Guijt and A. Welbourn, 'Acknowledging process: methodological challenges for agricultural research and extension', in I. Scoones and J. Thompson (eds), *Beyond Farmer First* (London, 1994).

Cotran, E., 'The place and future of customary law in East Africa', *East African Law Today* 5 (1966), 72–92.

Coulson, A., 'Agricultural policies in mainland Tanzania, 1946–76', *Review of African Political Economy*, 10 (1977), 75–100.

Coulson, A., 'Agricultural policies in mainland Tanzania', in J. Heyer (ed.), *Rural Development in Tropical Africa* (London, 1981), 52–89.

Cowen, M., 'Capital and household production: the case of wattle in Kenya's Central Province, 1903–64' (PhD, Cambridge University, 1979).

Crewe, E. and E. Harrison, *Whose Development? An Ethnography of Aid* (London, 1998).

Crummey, D. (ed.), *Banditry, Rebellion and Social Protest in Africa* (London, 1986).

Crush, J., *Power of Development* (London, 1995).

Cunningham, A.B., 'People, park and plant use: Research and recommendations for multiple-use zones and development alternatives around Bwindi-Impenetrable National Park, Uganda' (Report prepared for CARE-International, Kabale, 1992).

Czekanowski, J., *Forschungen im Nil-Kongo-Zwischengebeit. Vol. 1., Ethnographie Zwischenseegebiet Mpororo-Ruanda* (Leipzig, 1917).

Czekanowski, J., *Forschungen im Nil-Kongo-Zwischengebeit. Vol. 3., Ethnographische-Anthropologischer Atlas Zwischenseen-Bantu, Pygmäen und Pygmoiden, Urwaldstämme* (Leipzig, 1911).

David, R. *et al.*, *Changing Places: Women, Resource Management and Migration in the Sahel* (London, 1995).

Ddungu, E., *A Review of the MISR – Wisconsin Land Tenure Center study on land tenure and agriculture development in Uganda*. CBR Working Paper 11 (Kampala, 1991).

de Haan, A. and B. Rogaly (eds), *Labour Mobility and Rural Society* (London, 2002).

de Haan, A., K. Brock and N. Coulibaly, 'Migration, Livelihoods and institutions: Contrasting patterns of migration in Mali' in A. de Haan and B. Rogaly, *Labour Mobility and Rural Society* (London, 2002).

de Wilde, J.C., *Experiences with Agricultural Development in Tropical Africa* (2 Vols) (Baltimore, MD, 1967).

Denoon, D.J.W., 'Agents of colonial rule, Kigezi, 1908-1930' (EAISR Conference, 1968).

Denoon, D.J.W. (ed.), *A History of Kigezi in South West Uganda* (Kampala, 1972).

Denoon, D.J.W., 'The allocation of official posts in Kigezi, 1908–1930', in D.J.W. Denoon (ed.), *A History of Kigezi in South West Uganda* (Kampala, 1972).

Department for International Development, *Sustainable Rural Livelihoods Analysis: Guidance sheets* (London, n.d) [www.livelihoods.org].

Dercon, S., and P. Krishnan, 'Income Portfolios in Rural Ethiopia and Tanzania: Choices and Constraints', *The Journal of Development Studies*, 32 6 (1996), 850–75.

des Forges, A., 'The drum is greater than the shout: The 1912 rebellion in Northern Rwanda', in D. Crummey (ed.), *Banditry, Rebellion and Social Protest in Africa* (London, 1986).

Downs, R.E. and S.P. Reyna (eds), *Land and Society in Contemporary Africa* (Hanover, NH, 1988).

Drinkwater, M., 'Technical development and peasant impoverishment: Land use policy in Zimbabwe's Midlands Province', *Journal of Southern African Studies*, 15 2 (1989), 287–305.

Driver, T., 'Soil conservation in Mokhotlong, Lesotho 1945–55: A success in non-implementation' (Paper presented at African History Seminar, SOAS, 1996).

Ecaat, J. and A. Rutasikwa, 'Report of the wetlands component, Kabale District' (The Environment Management Capacity Building Project, May 1994).

Bibliography

Edel, M.M., 'The Bachiga of East Africa', in M. Mead (ed.), *Cooperation and Competition among Primitive Peoples* (New York, 1937), 127-52.

Edel, M.M., 'Property among the Chiga in Uganda', *Africa*, 11 (1938), 325-41.

Edel, M.M., *The Chiga of Western Uganda* (Oxford, 1957).

Edel, M.M., *The Chiga of Western Uganda*, 2nd edition (New Brunswick, NJ, 1996).

Ehrlich, C., 'Some social and economic implications of paternalism in Uganda', *Journal of African History*, iv 2 (1963), 275–85.

Ehrlich, C., 'The Uganda economy 1903-1945', in V. Harlow and E.M. Chilver (eds), *History of East Africa* (Vol. 2) (Oxford, 1965), 395-475.

Ehrlich, C., 'Aspects of economic policy in Tanganyika, 1945–60' in D. Low and A. Smith, *History of East Africa* (Oxford, 1976).

Ehrlich, P., *The Population Bomb* (London, 1972).

Ehrlich, P.R., *The Population Explosion* (New York, 1990).

Ehrlich, P. and A. Ehrlich, *Population, Resources and Environment* (New York, 1970).

Elkan, W., 'Review of East Africa Royal Commission, 1953-55 Report', *Uganda Journal*, 20 (1956), 100-1.

Elkan, W., *An African Labour Force: Two Case Studies in East African Factory Employment* (Kampala, 1956).

Ellis, F., *Peasant Economics: Farm households and agrarian development* (Cambridge, 1993), 2nd edition.

Ellis, F., 'Household strategies and rural livelihood diversification', *The Journal of Development Studies*, 35 1 (1998), 1–38.

Ellis, F., *Rural Livelihoods and Diversity in Developing Countries* (Oxford, 2000).

Fairhead, J., *Food Security in North and South Kivu (Zaire), 1989*. Final consultancy report for Oxfam. Part 1, Section 2 (London, 1989).

Fairhead, J.R., 'Fields of struggle: towards a social history of farming knowledge and practice in a Bwisha community, Kivu, Zaire' (PhD, SOAS, 1990).

Fairhead, J. and M. Leach, 'Contested forests: Modern conservation and historical land use in Guinea's Ziama Reserve', *African Affairs*, 93 (1994), 481-512.

Fairhead, J. and M. Leach, *Misreading the African Landscape* (Cambridge, 1996).

Fairhead, J. and M. Leach, *Reframing Deforestation: Global Analyses and Local Realities: Studies in West Africa* (London, 1998).

Fairhead, J. and M. Leach, *Science, Society and Power: Environmental knowledge and policy in West Africa and the Caribbean* (Cambridge, 2003).

Fallers, L., *Law Without Precedent: Legal Ideas in Action in the Courts of Colonial Busoga* (Chicago, 1969).

Farley, C. 'Local knowledge and soil resource management in the highlands of southwest Uganda' (IDRC Workshop of Sustainable Mountain Agriculture, Nairobi, 1993).

Farley, C., 'Smallholder knowledge, soil resource management and land use change in the highlands of southwest Uganda' (PhD, University of Florida, Gainesville, 1996).

Feder, G. T. Onchan, Y. Chalamwong and C. Hongladarom, *Land Policies and Farm Productivity in Thailand* (Baltimore, MD, 1988).

Feierman, S., 'Healing as social criticism in the time of colonial conquest', *African Studies*, 54 1 (1995), 73–88.

Feierman, S., *Peasant Intellectuals: Anthropology and History in Tanzania* (Madison, 1990).

Fennell, G.A., 'Flax', in J.D. Jameson, *Agriculture in Uganda*. 2nd edition (London, 1970).

Ferguson, J., *The Anti-Politics Machine: 'Development', Depoliticization and Bureaucratic Power in Lesotho* (Cambridge, 1990).

Ferguson, J., *Expectations of Modernity: Myths and meanings of urban life on the Zambian Copperbelt* (Berkeley, CA, 1999).

Fiennes, R.N.T.W., 'Soil erosion and agricultural planning', *Uganda Journal*, 6 (1939), 137–47.

Ford, J., *The Role of Trypanosomiasis in African Ecology: a Study of the Tsetse Fly Problem* (London, 1971).

Francis, E., 'Migration and changing divisions of labour: Gender relations and economic change in Koguta, Western Kenya', *Africa*, 65 2 (1995), 197–216.

Francis, E., *Making a Living: Changing livelihoods in rural Africa* (London, 2000).

Francis, E., 'Gender, Migration and Multiple Livelihoods: Cases from Eastern and Southern Africa' in A. de Haan and B. Rogaly, *Labour Mobility and Rural Society* (London, 2002).

Francis, E., 'Gender, migration and multiple livelihoods: Cases from eastern and southern Africa', *Journal of Development Studies* 38 5 (2002), 167–90.

Freedman, J., *Nyabingi: The Social History of an African Divinity* (Butare, 1984).

Gardner, K. and D. Lewis, *Anthropology, Development and the Post-modern Challenge*, (London, 1996).

Geertz, C., *Agricultural Involution: The process of ecological change in Indonesia* (Berkeley and Los Angeles, CA, 1963).

Geraud, F., 'The settlement of the Bakiga', in D.J.W. Denoon (ed.), *A History of Kigezi in south-west Uganda* (Kampala, 1972).

Gershenberg, I. 'Customary land tenure as a constraint on agricultural development: A revaluation', *East African Journal of Rural Development*, 4 (1971), 51-62.

Gertzel, C., 'Kingdoms, districts and the unitary state: Uganda 1945-62', in D.A. Low and A. Smith, *History of East Africa* (Vol. 3) (Oxford, 1976).

Giblin, J.L., *The Politics of Environmental Control in North Eastern Tanzania 1840–1940* (Philadelphia, 1992)

Gingyera-Pinycwa, A.G.G., *Issues in Pre-Independence Politics in Uganda: A Case Study on the Contribution of Religion to Political Debate in Uganda in the Decade 1952-62* (Kampala, 1976).

Goetz, A.M. and R. Sen Gupta, 'Who takes the credit? Gender, power and control over loan use in rural credit programmes in Bangladesh', *World Development*, 24 1 (1996), 45–63.

Good, C.M., *Rural Markets and Trade in East Africa: A study of the functions and development of exchange institutions in Ankole, Uganda* (Chicago, 1970).

Good, C.M., 'Salt, trade and disease: Aspects of development in Africa's northern great lakes region', *International Journal of African Historical Studies*, Vol. 4 (1972), 543–86.

Gray, R. and D. Birmingham, *Pre-Colonial African Trade – Essays on Trade in Central and Eastern Africa before 1900* (London, 1970).

Green, E.D., *Ethnic Politics and Land Tenure Reform in Central Uganda*. LSE DESTIN Working Paper, 05-58 (London, 2005).

Griffiths, T. and L. Robin, *Ecology and Empire: environmental history of settler societies* (Edinburgh, 1997).

Grischow, J. and G.H. McKnight, 'Rhyming development: Practising post-development in colonial Ghana and Uganda', *Journal of Historical Sociology*, 16 4 (2003), 517–49.

Grisley, W. and David Mwesigwa, 'Socio-Economic determinants of seasonal cropland fallowing decisions: Smallholders in south-western Uganda', *Journal of Environmental Management*, 42 (1994), 81-9.

Grogan, E. and A. Sharp, *From the Cape to Cairo: The First Traverse of Africa from South to North* (London, 1900).

Grove, R., 'Scottish missionaries, evangelical discourses and the origins of conservation thinking in Southern Africa 1820–1900', *Journal of Southern African Studies*, 15 2 (1989), 163–187.

Grove, R., *Green Imperialism: colonial expansion, tropical island edens and the origins of environmentalism, 1600–1860* (Cambridge, 1996).

Grove, R., 'Editorial', *Environment and History*, 6 2 (2000), 127.

Hailey, Lord, *An African Survey: A Study of Problems arising in Africa South of the Sahara* (London, 1938) (2nd edn., 1957).

Hailey, Lord, *Native Administration in British African Territories*, Part 1 'East Africa' (London, 1950).

Hamilton, A., 'The vegetation of South West Kigezi', *Uganda Journal*, 33 (1969), 175-200.

Hamilton, A., D. Taylor and J.C. Vogel, 'Early forest clearance and environmental degradation in South West Uganda,' *Nature*, 320 (1986), 164–7.

Hansen, H.B., 'The colonial control of spirit movements in Uganda', in D.M. Anderson and D.H. Johnson (eds), *Revealing Prophets* (London, 1995), 143–63.

Hansen, H.B. and M. Twaddle (eds), *Changing Uganda: the dilemmas of structural adjustment and revolutionary change* (London, 1991).

Hansen, H.B. and M. Twaddle (eds), *Developing Uganda* (Oxford, 1998).

Harlow, V., E.M. Chilver and A. Smith (eds), *History of East Africa* (Vol. 2) (Oxford, 1965).

Havinden, M. and D. Meredith, *Colonialism and Development, Britain and its Tropical Colonies, 1850–1960* (London, 1993).

Heyer, J., 'Agricultural development policy in Kenya from colonial period to 1975', in J. Heyer, P. Roberts and G. Williams (eds), *Rural Development in Tropical Africa* (London, 1981), 90–120.

Heyer, J., D. Ireri and J. Morris, *Rural Development in Kenya* (Nairobi, 1971).

Heyer, J. (ed.), *Agricultural Development in Kenya* (Nairobi, 1976).
Heyer, J., D. Ireri and J. Morris, *Rural Development in Tropical Africa* (London, 1981).
Hill, D.S. and J.M. Waller, *Pests and Diseases of Tropical Crops* (Vol. 1) (London, 1982).
Hill, P., *Migrant Cocoa Farmers of Southern Ghana* (Cambridge, 1972).
Hogan, D.J., 'The impact of population growth on the physical environment', *European Journal of Population*, 8 (1992), 109–23.
Hogendorn, J. S. and K.M. Scott, 'Very large scale agricultural projects; the lessons of the East African groundnut scheme', in R. Rotberg (ed.) *Imperialism, Colonialism and Hunger in East and Central Africa* (Lexington, MA, 1983).
Holmgren, P., E.J. Masakha and H. Sjoholm, 'Not all African land is being degraded: A recent survey of trees on farms in Kenya reveals rapidly increasing forest resources', *Ambio*, 23 7 (1994), 390–5.
Hopkins, A.G., *Economic History in West Africa* (London, 1973).
Hopkins, E., 'The Nyabingi cult of southwestern Uganda', in R. Rotberg and A. Mazrui, *Protest and Power in Black Africa* (New York, 1970), 258-336.
Huggins, C. and J. Clover (eds), *From the Ground Up: Land rights, conflict and peace in Sub-Saharan Africa* (Pretoria, 2005).
Humphrey, N., *The Kikuyu Lands: The Relation of Population to the Land in South Nyeri* (Nairobi, 1945).
Hunt, D., 'Unintended Consequences of Land Rights Reform: The case of the 1998 Uganda Land Act', *Development Policy Review*, 22 2 (2004), 173-91.
ICRAF (International Centre for Research in Agroforestry), 'The African highlands initiative: A conceptual framework. Integrated natural resource management research for enhancing land productivity in the highlands of eastern and central Africa' (Nairobi, 1994).
IFAD, *Rural Poverty Report 2001: the challenge of ending rural poverty* (Oxford, 2001).
Iliffe, J., *A Modern History of Tanganyika* (Cambridge, 1979).
Ingham, K., *The Making of Modern Uganda* (London, 1958).
International Bank for Reconstruction and Development, *Economic Development of Uganda: A Report of the Mission Organised by the IBRD at the Request of the Government of Uganda* (Washington, DC, 1962).
Jack, Capt. E.M., 'The Mufumbiro mountains' (Lecture to Royal Geographical Society, 14 April 1913) *Geographical Journal*, VI (June 1913), 532–50.
Jacks, Major E.M., *On the Congo Frontier: Exploration and Sport* (London, 1914).
Jameson, J.D., *Agriculture in Uganda* (2nd edn) (London, 1970).
Jolly, C.L., 'Four theories of population change and the environment', *Population and Environment*, 6 1 (1994), 61–90.
Jones, S. and G. Carswell (eds), *An Earthscan Reader in Environment, Development and Rural Livelihoods* (London, 2004).
Jorgensen, J.J., *Uganda: A Modern History* (London, 1981).
Kabananukye, K. and D. Musakwe, 'Kitanga demonstration site: Socio economic survey' (Kampala, 1994).

Bibliography

Kabeer, N., 'Resources, Agency, Achievements: Reflections on the Measurement of Women's Empowerment', *Development and Change*, 30 3 (1999), 435–64.

Kabeer, N., 'Conflicts over credit: re-evaluating the empowerment potential of loans to women in rural Bangladesh', *World Development*, 29 1 (2001), 63–84.

Kagambirwe, E.R., *Causes and Consequences of Land Shortage in Kigezi* (Makerere, Department of Geography, Occasional Paper 23, 1973).

Kagame, A., *Un Abrégé de l'ethno-histoire du Rwanda* Vol. 2 (Butare, 1975).

Kalinga, O.J.M., 'The Master Farmers' Scheme in Nyasaland, 1950–62: A study of a failed attempt to create a 'Yeoman' Class', *African Affairs*, 92 (1993), 367–87.

Karugire, S.R., *A Political History of Uganda* (Nairobi, 1980).

Kateete, B.M., 'Land tenure and land use in Humurwa parish, Ikumba sub-county, Rubanda County, Kigezi District' in R. Tindituuza and B.M. Kateete, *Essays on Land Fragmentation in Kigezi District* (Makerere, Dept. of Geography, Occasional Paper 22, 1971).

Kato, L.L. and J. Obol-Ochola, *Land Law Reform in East Africa* (Kampala, 1970).

Keeley, J. and I. Scoones, *Environmental Policy Processes: Cases from Africa* (London, 2003).

Kevane, M. and L.C. Gray, 'A woman's field is made at night: Gendered land rights and norms in Burkina Faso', *Feminist Economics*, 5 1 (1999), 1–26.

Khadiagala, L.S., 'The failure of popular justice in Uganda: Local councils and women's property rights', *Development and Change*, 32 (2001) 55–76.

Khadiagala, L. S., 'Justice and power in the adjudication of women's property rights in Uganda', *Africa Today*, 49 2 (2002) 101–121.

Khadiagala, L. S., 'Negotiating law and custom: Judicial doctrine and women's property rights in Uganda', *Journal of African Law*, 46 1 (2002), 1–13.

Kidd, A., *Extension, Poverty and Vulnerability in Uganda: Country Study for the Neuchâtel Initiative*. ODI Working Paper 151 (London, 2001).

Kigula, J., 'Land disputes in Uganda: An overview of the types of land disputes and the dispute settlement fora' (Kampala, 1993).

Kimambo, I.N., *Penetration and Protest in Tanzania: the Impact of the World Economy on the Pare 1860-1960* (London, 1991).

Kisamba-Mugerwa, W., 'Institutional dimensions of land tenure reform' in H.B. Hansen and M. Twaddle, *Changing Uganda* (London, 1991).

Kitching, G., *Class and Economic Change in Kenya: The Making of an African Petite Bourgeoisie 1905–70* (New Haven, CT, 1980).

Kjekshus, H., *Ecology Control and Economic Development in East African History: The Case of Tanganyika, 1850-1950* (London, 1977).

Kothari, U., 'Authority and expertise: The professionalisation of international development and the ordering of dissent', *Antipode*, 37 3 (2005), 425–46.

Kururagire, A.R., 'Land fragmentation in Rugarama, Kigezi', *Uganda Journal*, 33 (1969), 59-64.

Langlands, B.W., *A Population Geography of Kigezi District* (Makerere, Department of Geography, Occasional Paper 26, 1971).

Langlands, B.W., *Notes of the Geography of Ethnicity in Uganda* (Makerere, Department of Geography, Occasional Paper 62, 1975).

Langlands, B.W., *Geographical Notes on Land Tenure in Uganda* (Makerere, Department of Geography, Occasional Paper 55, 1976).

Langlands, B.W. and G. Namirembe, *Studies in the Geography of Religion in Uganda* (Makerere, Department of Geography, Occasional Paper 4, 1967).

Lawrance, J.C.D., 'A pilot scheme for grant of land titles in Uganda', *Journal of African Administration*, 12 (1960), 135–42.

Lawrance, J.C.D., 'The position of chiefs in local government in Uganda', *Journal of African Administration*, 8 (1956), 186-92.

Leach, M. and J. Fairhead, 'The forest islands of Kissidougou: social dynamics of environmental change in West Africa's forest savanna mosaic' (Report for the ODA, 1994).

Leach, M. and R. Mearns (eds), *The Lie of the Land: Challenging Received Wisdom on the African Environment* (London, 1996).

Lee, J.M., *Colonial Development and Good Government* (Oxford,1967).

Lee, J.M. and M. Petter, *The Colonial Office, War and Development Policy: Organisation and the Planning of a Metropolitan Initiative 1939–45* (London, 1982).

Lee, R.D., W.B. Arthur, A.C. Kelley, G. Rodgers and T.N. Srinivasan (eds), *Population, Food and Rural Development* (Oxford, 1988).

Leys, C., *Politicians and Policies: An Essay on Politics in Acholi, Uganda, 1962–65* (Nairobi, 1967).

Lindblade, K., G. Carswell and J.K. Tumahairwe, 'Mitigating the relationship between population growth and land degradation: Land-use change and farm management in southwestern Uganda', *Ambio*, 27 7 (1998), 565–71.

Lindblade, K., J.K. Tumahairwe, G. Carswell, C. Nkwiine and D. Bwamiki, 'More People, More Fallow – Environmentally favorable land-use changes in southwestern Uganda' (Report prepared for the Rockefeller Foundation, 1996).

Lindblade, K.A., E.D. Walker, A.W. Onapa, J. Katungu, and M.L. Wilson, 'Land use change alters malaria transmission parameters by modifying temperature in a highland area of Uganda', *Tropical Medicine & International Health*, 5 4 (2000), 263–274.

Louis, W.R., 'The diary of the Kivu Mission', *Uganda Journal*, 27 (1963), 187-93.

Louis, W.R., *Ruanda-Urundi 1884-1919* (Oxford, 1963).

Low, D. and J. Lonsdale, 'Introduction: Towards a new order 1945–63', in D. Low and A. Smith (eds), *History of East Africa* (Vol. 3) (Oxford, 1976).

Low, D. and A. Smith, *History of East Africa* (Vol. 3) (Oxford, 1976).

Lugan, B., 'Causes et effets de la famine 'Rumanura' au Rwanda, 1916–18', *Canadian Journal of African Studies*, X 2 (1976), 347–56.

Lugard, Lord F.J.D., *The Dual Mandate in British Tropical Africa* (Edinburgh, 1922).

Lury, D.A., 'Dayspring Mishandled? The Uganda economy 1945-60' in D.A. Low and A. Smith, *History of East Africa* (Vol. 3) (Oxford, 1976).

Lwanga, M., 'Social and cultural values of wetlands' (Masters thesis, Makerere University, 1991).

Maack, P.A., 'We Don't Want Terraces!' Protest and identity under the Uluguru

Land Usage Scheme', in G. Maddox *et al.* (eds), *Custodians of the Land: Ecology and Culture in the History of Tanzania* (London, 1996), 152-69.

Mackenzie, F., '"A piece of land never shrinks": Reconceptualising land tenure in a smallholding district, Kenya', in T.J. Bassett and D.E. Crummey (eds), *Land in African Agrarian Systems*, (Madison, WI, 1993), 194–221.

Mackenzie, F., 'Selective silence: A feminist encounter with environmental discourse in colonial Africa', in J. Crush, *Power of Development* (London, 1995).

Mackenzie, F., *Land, Ecology and Resistance in Kenya, 1880–1952* (Edinburgh, 1998).

Mackenzie, F., 'Land tenure and biodiversity: An exploration of the political ecology of Murang'a district, Kenya', *Human Organization*, 62 3 (2003), 255–66.

Mackenzie, J. (ed.), *Imperialism and the Natural World* (Manchester, 1990).

Mackenzie, J., 'Empire and the ecological apocalypse: the historiography of the imperial environment', in T. Griffiths and L. Robin, *Ecology and Empire: environmental history of settler societies* (Edinburgh, 1997).

Macmillan, H., 'The East African Royal Commission' in D.A. Low and A. Smith, *History of East Africa* (Vol. 3) (Oxford, 1976).

Maddox, G., J.L. Giblin and I. Kimambo (eds), *Custodians of the Land: Ecology and Culture in the History of Tanzania* (London, 1996).

Maguire, G.A., *Towards "Uhuru" in Tanzania: The Politics of Participation* (London, 1969).

Magunda, M. K., 'Influence of some physico-chemical properties on soil strength, stability of crusts and soil erosion', (PhD, University of Minnesota, 1992).

Mahmud, S., 'Actually How Empowering is Microcredit?', *Development and Change*, 34 4 (2003), 577–605.

Malcolm, D.W., *Sukumaland: An African People and their Country, a Study of Land Use in Tanganyika* (London, 1953).

Malthus, T.R. *An Essay on the Principle of Population* (London, 1798).

Mamdani, M., *When Victims Become Killers: Colonialism Nativism and the Genocide in Rwanda* (Princeton, NJ, 2001).

Mandala, E.C., *Work and Control in a Peasant Economy* (Madison, 1990).

Manji, A., 'Land reform in the shadow of the State: the implementation of new land laws in sub-Saharan Africa', *Third World Quarterly*, 22 3 (2001), 327–42.

Mann, K. and R. Roberts, *Law in Colonial Africa* (London, 1991).

Marquardt, M. and A. Sebina-Zziwa, 'Land reform in the making' in H.B. Hansen and M. Twaddle (eds), *Developing Uganda* (London, 1998).

Martin, W.S., 'Soil structure', *The East African Agricultural Journal* (1944), 189–95.

Masefield, G.B., *A Handbook of Tropical Agriculture* (Oxford, 1949).

Masefield, G.B., *A Short History of Agriculture in the British Colonies* (Oxford, 1950).

Masefield, G.B., *A History of the Colonial Agricultural Service* (Oxford, 1972).

McAuslan, P., 'Supporting local rights: will the centre let go? Reflections from Uganda and Tanzania', Workshop Report: *Securing customary land tenure in Africa: alternative approaches to the local recording and registration of land rights.* (London, 2000).

McAuslan, P., *Bringing the Law Back In: Essays in Land, Law and Development* (Aldershot, 2003).

McCann, J., 'Review Article: Agriculture and African history', *Journal of African History*, 32 (1991), 507-13.

McLoughlin, P.F.M., 'Sukumaland', in J.C. de Wilde, *Experiences with Agricultural Development in Tropical Africa* (Vol. 2) (Baltimore, MD, 1967).

McNeill, J., 'Observations on the nature and culture of environmental history', *History and Environment*, 42 (2003), 5–43.

Mead, M., *Cooperation and Competition among Primitive Peoples* (New York, 1937), 127–52.

Meadows, D.H., D.I. Meadows, J. Randers and W.W. Behrens, *The Limits of Growth* (New York, 1972).

Meek, C.K., *Land Law and Custom in the Colonies* (London, 1968) (1st edn 1946).

Meillassoux, C. (ed.), *The Development of Indigenous Trade and Markets in West Africa* (London, 1971).

Mifsud, F.M., *Customary Land Law in Africa* (Rome, 1967).

Migot-Adholla, S., P. Hazell, B. Blarel and F. Place, 'Indigenous land rights systems in Sub Saharan Africa – A constraint on development?', *World Bank Economic Review*, 5 11 (1991), 155–75.

Miiro D. *et al.*, 'Participatory Rural Appraisal Report, Bubaale Sub-county, Kabale District' Indigenous Soil and Water Conservation Project (Kabale, 1998).

Ministry of National Resources, National Environment Information Centre, *State of the Environment Report for Uganda* (Kampala, 1994).

MISR and Land Tenure Center, University of Wisconsin, 'The Rujumbura pilot land registration scheme – Kigezi (Rukungiri District). The impact of titling on agricultural development' (Madison, WI, 1988).

MISR and Land Tenure Center, University of Wisconsin, *Land Tenure and Agricultural Development in Uganda* (Madison, WI, 1989).

Moore, H.L. and M. Vaughan, *Cutting Down Trees: Gender, nutrition and agricultural change in the northern province of Zambia, 1890–1990* (London, 1994).

Moore, S.F., *Social Facts and Fabrications: "Customary" Law on Kilimanjaro 1880-1980* (Cambridge, 1986).

Morgan, D.J., *The Official History of Colonial Development* (5 vols) (London, 1980).

Mosse, D., *Cultivating Development: An ethnography of aid policy and practice*, (London, 2005).

Mugisha, R., *Emergent Changes and Trends in Land Tenure and Land Use in Kabale and Kisoro Districts*. CBR Working Paper 26 (Kampala, 1992).

Munro, J.F., *Colonial Rule and the Kamba: Social Change in Kenya Highlands 1889–1939* (Oxford, 1979).

Murray, C., *Families Divided: The Impact of Migrant Labour in Lesotho* (Cambridge, 1981).

Murton, J., 'Population growth and poverty in Machakos, Kenya', *Geographical Journal*, 165 1 (1999), 37–46.

Musahara, H. and C. Huggins, 'Land reform, land scarcity and post-conflict reconstruction: A case study of Rwanda', in C. Huggins and J. Clover (eds), *From the Ground Up: Land rights, conflict and peace in Sub-Saharan Africa* (Pretoria, 2005).

Mushanga, M.T., 'Polygyny in Kigezi', *Uganda Journal*, 34 (1970), 201-10.

Mushanga, M.T., 'Violent deaths in western Uganda', *East African Law Journal*, 8 (1972), 182-7.

Mutombo, R., 'Marchés et circuits commerciaux de la région des Masangano à la fin de l'époque pré coloniale', *Etudes Rwandaises* 11 Numero Special Mars (1978), 33-45.

Mwebaza, R., *How to Integrate Statutory and Customary Tenure: The Uganda case.* IIED Drylands Programme Issue paper 83 (London, 1999).

Narayan, D., with R. Patel, K. Schafft, A. Rademacher and S. Koch-Schulte, *Voices of the Poor* (Washington, DC, 2000).

Nash, R., *Wilderness and the American Mind* (New Haven, CT, 1969).

National Environmental Management Authority (NEMA), *The National Soils Policy for Uganda* (Kampala, 1998).

National Environment Management Authority (NEMA), *State of the Environment Report for Uganda 1998* (Kampala, 1999).

Neimeijer, D., 'The dynamics of African agricultural history: is it time for a new development paradigm?', *Development and Change*, 27 3 (1996), 87-110.

Newbury, C., *The Cohesion of Oppression: clientship and ethnicity in Rwanda, 1860-1960* (New York, 1988).

Newbury, D.S., 'Lake Kivu regional trade in the nineteenth century', *Journal des Africanistes*, 50 2 (1980), 6-30.

Newbury, D.S., *Kings and Clans: Ijwi Island and Lake Kivu Rift 1780-1840* (Madison, 1992).

Ngologoza, P., *Kigezi and Its People* (Kampala, 1969).

Nkambo Mugerwa, P.J., 'Land tenure in East Africa – some contrasts', *East African Law Today* 5 (1966), 101-14.

Nsamba-Gayiiya, E., *Implementing Land Tenure Reform in Uganda: A Complex Task Ahead.* IIED Drylands Programme Issue Paper 84 (London, 1999).

Nyambara, P.S., 'Colonial policy and peasant cotton agriculture in Southern Rhodesia, 1904-1953', *International Journal of African Historical Studies*, 33 1 (2000), 81-111.

O'Laughlin, B., 'Missing men? The debate over rural poverty and women-headed households in Southern Africa', *Journal of Peasant Studies*, 25 2 (1998), 1-48.

Obol-Ochola, J., 'Ideology and tradition in African land tenure', *East African Journal*, 6 (1969), 35-41.

Obol-Ochola, J., *Land Law Reform in East Africa* (Kampala, 1969).

Obol-Ochola, J.Y., *Customary Land Law and the Economic Development of Uganda* (Dar-es-Salaam, 1971).

Okoth Ogendo, H.W.O., 'African land tenure reform', in J. Heyer (ed.), *Agricultural Development in Kenya* (Nairobi, 1976), 152-85.

Okoth Ogendo, H.W.O., 'Some issues in the study of land tenure relations in African agriculture', *Africa*, 59 1 (1989), 6-17.

Palmer, R., *Oxfam GB's land advocacy work in Tanzania and Uganda: the end of an era* (Oxford, 1998).

Pearce, R.D., *The Turning Point in Africa: British Colonial Policy 1938–48* (London, 1982).

Peters, P., 'Inequality and social conflict over land in Africa', *Journal of Agrarian Change*, 3 1/2 (2004), 269–314.

Pingali, P. and H.P. Binswanger, 'Population density and farming systems: the changing locus of innovations and technical change', in R.D. Lee *et al.* (eds), *Population, Food and Rural Development* (Oxford, 1988).

Pingali, P., Y. Bigot and H.P. Binswanger, *Agricultural Mechanisation and Evolution of Farming Systems in Sub-Saharan Africa* (Baltimore, MD, 1987).

Pingali, P.L., 'Institutional and environmental constraints to agricultural intensification', *Population and Development Review*, 15 suppl, (1990), 243–60.

Place, F. and Hazell, P., 'Productivity effects of indigenous land tenure systems in sub-Saharan Africa', *American Journal of Agricultural Economics*, 75 (1993), 16–19.

Plath, J.C., D. W. Holland, and J. W. Carvalho, 'Labor migration in Southern Africa and agricultural development – some lessons from Lesotho', *Journal of Developing Areas*, 21 2 (1987), 159–76.

Platteau, J.P., *Formalization and Privatization of Land Rights in Sub-Saharan Africa: a Critique of Current Orthodoxies and Structural Adjustment Programmes* (London, 1991).

Platteau, J.P., 'The evolutionary theory of land rights as applied to Sub-Saharan Africa: A critical assessment', *Development and Change*, 27 (1996), 29-86.

Platteau, J.P, 'Does Africa need land reform?', in C. Toulmin and J. Quan (eds), *Evolving Land Rights, Policy and Tenure in Africa* (London, 2000).

Pottier, J., 'The politics of famine prevention: Ecology, regional production and food complementarity in Western Rwanda', *African Affairs*, 85 (1986), 207–37.

Pottier, J., 'The role of ethnography in project appraisal', in J. Pottier (ed.), *Practising Development* (London, 1993).

Pottier, J., *Re-Imagining Rwanda: Conflict, Survival and Disinformation in the Late Twentieth Century* (Cambridge, 2002).

Pottier, J., 'Customary land tenure', in Sub-Saharan Africa today: meanings and contexts', in C. Huggins and J. Clover (eds), *From the Ground Up: Land rights, conflict and peace in Sub-Saharan Africa* (Pretoria, 2005)

Pottier, J. and J. Fairhead, 'Post famine recovery in highland Bwisha, Zaire: 1984 in its context', *Africa*, 61 (1991), 437-70.

Powesland, P.G., *Economic Policy and Labour: A Study of Uganda's Economic History* (Kampala, 1957).

Powesland, P.G., 'History of migration', in Audrey Richards (ed.), *Economic Development and Tribal Change: A Study of Immigrant Labour in Buganda* (2nd edition) (Nairobi, 1973).

Pratt, R.C., 'Administration and Politics in Uganda, 1919–45', in V.T. Harlow, E.M. Chilver and A. Smith, *History of East Africa* (Vol. 2) (Oxford, 1965).

Prunier, G., *The Rwanda Crisis: History of a Genocide* (London, 1995).

Purseglove, J.W., 'Kitozho Mutala Survey' (1940).

Purseglove, J.W., 'Report on the overpopulated areas of Kigezi district' (1945).

Purseglove, J.W., 'Land Use in the overpopulated areas of Kigezi District, Uganda', *East African Agricultural Journal,* 12 1 (1946), 3–10.

Purseglove, J.W., 'Community development on the Uganda–Congo border', *Mass Education Bulletin,* 3 (1950), 46–50.

Purseglove, J.W., 'Kigezi resettlement', *Uganda Journal,* 14 (1950), 139-52.

Purseglove, J.W., 'Uganda's pearl reclaimed: The pioneer Kigezi scheme', *East African Annual* (1950–51), 47-52.

Purseglove, J.W., 'Resettlement in Kigezi, Uganda', *Journal of African Administration,* 3 (1951), 13-21.

Quarles van Ufford, P., 'The hidden crisis in development: Development bureaucracies in between intentions and outcomes', in P. Quarles van Ufford, D. Kruijt and T. Downing (eds), *The Hidden Crisis in Development* (Amsterdam, 1988).

Ranger, T., 'Whose heritage? The case of the Matobo National Park', *Journal of Southern African Studies,* 15 2 (1989), 217–49.

Ranger, T., *Voices from the Rocks* (Oxford, 1999).

Reardon, T., 'Using evidence of household income diversification to inform study of rural non-farm labour market in Africa', *World Development,* 25 5 (1997) 735–47;

Reardon, T., J. Berdegué and G. Escobar (eds), *World Development,* Special Issue on 'Rural nonfarm employment and incomes in Latin America', 29 3 (2001).

Reardon, T., J.E. Taylor, K. Stamoulis, P. Lanjouw and A. Balisacan, 'Effects of non-farm employment on rural income inequality in developing countries: An investment perspective', *Journal of Agricultural Economics,* 51 2 (2000), 266–88.

Richards, A.I., *East African Chiefs: A Study of Political Development in some Uganda and Tanganyika Tribes* (London, 1960).

Richards, A.I., *Economic Development and Tribal Change: A Study of Immigrant Labour in Buganda* (2nd edition) (Nairobi, 1973).

Richards, A.I., F. Sturrock and J.M. Fortt, *From Subsistence to Commercial Farming in Buganda* (Cambridge, 1973).

Richards, P., 'Ecological change and the politics of African land use', *African Studies Review,* 26 2 (1983), 1–72.

Roberts, A., 'The sub-imperialism of the Baganda', *Journal of African History,* 3 (1962), 435-50.

Robertshaw, P. and D. Taylor, 'Climate change and the rise of political complexity in western Uganda', *Journal of African History,* 41 1, (2000) 1–28.

Roe, E.M., 'Except Africa: Postscript to a special section on development narratives', *World Development,* 23 6, (1995), 1065–9.

Roscoe, J., *The Soul of Central Africa: A General Account of the Mackie Ethnological Expedition* (London, 1922).

Roscoe, J., *The Bagesu and Other Tribes of the Uganda Protectorate. The Third Part of the Report of the Mackie Ethnological Expedition of Central Africa* (Cambridge, 1924).

Rotberg, R.I., *Imperialism, Colonialism and Hunger in East and Central Africa* (Lexington, MA, 1983).

Rotberg, R.I. and A.A. Mazrui, *Protest and Power in Black Africa* (New York, 1970).
Roth, M., J. Cochrane and W, Kisamba-Mugerwa, *Tenure Security, Credit Use, and Farm Investment in the Rujumbura Pilot Land Registration Scheme, Rukungiri District, Uganda.* University of Wisconsin, Land Tenure Center Research Paper 112 (Madison, WI, 1993).
Roth, M., J. Cochrane and W. Kisamba-Mugerwa, 'Tenure security, credit use and farm investment in Rujhumbura Pilot land registration scheme, Uganda', in J.W. Bruce and S.E. Migot-Adholla (eds), *Searching for Land Security in Africa* (Washington, DC, 1994).
Ruggeri Laderchi, C., R. Saith and F. Stewart, 'Does it matter that we do not agree on the definition of poverty? A comparison of four approaches', *Oxford Development Studies* 31 3 (2003), 243–74.
Rutabajuka, S., *Conditions of migrant labour in Masaka District, 1900-1962: The case of coffee shamba labourers* (Kampala, 1989).
Rutanga, M., *Conditions of labour on commercial dairy farms in Kabale District* (Kampala, 1991).
Rutanga, M., *Nyabingi movement: People's anti-colonial struggles in Kigezi, 1910-1936* (Kampala, 1993).
Ruthenberg, H., *Agricultural Development in Tanganyika* (Berlin, 1964).
Ruthenberg, H., *Farming Systems in the Tropics*, 3rd edition (Oxford, 1980).
Ruthven, O. and R. David, 'Benefits and burdens: researching the consequences of migration in the Sahel', *IDS Bulletin* 26 1 (1995), 47–53.
Samuel, F., 'The East African Groundnut Scheme', *African Affairs*, 46 (1947), 135–45.
Sathyamurty, T.V., 'Central–local relationships in the district headquarters' (EAISR Conference, 1966).
Sathyamurthy, T.V., 'Central government - district administration relations: the case of Uganda', *Africa Quarterly*, 22 (1982), 5-44.
Scherer, F., *The Development of Small Holder Vegetable Production in Kigezi, Uganda: Data, Observations and Experiences* (Munich, 1969).
Schoenbrun, D.L., 'The contours of vegetation change and human agency in Eastern Africa's Great Lakes region: ca 2000 BC to ca AD 1000', *History in Africa*, 21 (1994), 269–302.
Schrieder, G. and B. Knerr, 'Labour migration as a social security mechanism for smallholder households in sub-Saharan Africa: The case of Cameroon', *Oxford Development Studies*, 28 2 (2000) 223–36.
Scoones, I., *Sustainable Rural Livelihoods: A Framework for Analysis*. IDS Working Paper 72 (Brighton, 1998).
Scoones, I. and J. Thompson (eds), *Beyond Farmer First: Rural people's knowledge, agricultural research and extension practice* (London, 1994).
Scoones, I., S. Devereux and L. Haddad, 'Introduction: New directions for African agriculture', *IDS Bulletin*, 36 2 (2005), 1–12.
Sen, A., *Resources, Values and Development* (Oxford, 1984).
Sen, A., *Commodities and Capabilities* (Amsterdam, 1987).
Sen, A., *Development as Freedom* (New Delhi, 2000).
Shepherd, A., *Sustainable Rural Development*, (Basingstoke, 1998).

Sheridan, M.J., 'The environmental consequences of independence and socialism in North Pare, Tanzania, 1961–88', *Journal of African History*, 45 1 (2004), 81–102.

Shipton, P., 'Strips and patches: A demographic dimension in some African land-holding and political systems', *Man N.S.*, 19 (1984), 613-34.

Shipton, P., 'Debts and Trespasses: Land, mortgages and the ancestors in Western Kenya', *Africa*, 62 (1992), 357-88.

Shipton, P. and M. Goheen, 'Introduction – Understanding African land-holding: power, wealth and meaning', *Africa*, 62 (1992), 307-26.

Showers, K., *Imperial Gullies: Soil erosion and conservation in Lesotho* (Athens, OH, 2005).

Showers, K., 'Soil erosion in the Kingdom of Lesotho: Origins and colonial response, 1830s-1950s', *Journal of Southern African Studies*, 15 2 (1989), 263–86.

Showers, K., 'Oral evidence in historical environmental impact assessment: Soil conservation in Lesotho in the 1930s and 1940s', *Journal of Southern African Studies*, 18 (1992), 276-96.

Smit, W., 'The rural linkages of urban households in Durban, South Africa', *Environment and Urbanization*, 10 1 (1998), 77–87.

Smyth, R., 'British Colonial Film Policy 1927–1939', *Journal of African History*, 20 3 (1979), 437–50.

Sorensen, P., 'Commercialization of food crops in Busoga, Uganda, and the renegotiation of gender', *Gender & Society*, 10 5 (1996), 608–28.

Sorrenson, M.P.K., 'The official mind and Kikuyu land tenure 1895-1939' (EAISR Conference, 1963).

Sorrenson, M.P.K., *Land Reform in the Kikuyu Country – A study in Government Policy* (Nairobi, 1967).

Ssebalijja, Y., 'A history of Rukiga and other places' (Manuscript in MISR, Kampala, translation by William Mukasa) (n.d.).

Stanley Smith, A.C., *Road to Revival* (London, 1946).

Steins, N.A. and V.M. Edwards, 'Collective Action in Common-Pool Resource Management: The Contribution of a Social Constructivist Perspective to Existing Theory', *Society and Natural Resources*, 12 6 (1999), 539–57.

Stockdale, F., 'Soil erosion in the colonial empire', *Empire Journal of Experimental Agriculture*, V 20, (1937).

Stocking, M., 'Soil conservation policy in colonial Africa', *Agricultural History*, 59 (1985), 148-61.

Sutton, J., 'Towards a history of cultivating the fields', *Azania*, Special Issue on 'History of African agricultural technology and field systems', 24 (1989), 98–122.

Swanzy, H., 'Quarterly Notes', *African Affairs*, 46 and 47 (1947 and 1948).

Taylor, B.K., *The Western Lacustrine Bantu: Nyoro, Toro, Nyankore, Kiga, Haya and Zinza* (London, 1962).

Taylor, D., 'Late quaternary pollen records from two Uganda mires: Evidence for environmental change in the Rukiga highlands of southwest Uganda', *Palaeogeography, Palaeobotany and Palynology*, 80 (1990), 283–300.

Taylor, D. and R. Marchant, 'Human impact in the Interlacustrine region: long-term pollen records from the Rukiga Highlands', *Azania*, xxix-xxx (1994–95), 283–95.

Taylor, D., P. Robertshaw and R.A. Marchant, 'Environmental change and political-economic upheaval in precolonial western Uganda', *The Holocene*, 10 4 (2000), 527–36.

Thomas, H.B., 'Kigezi operations 1914-17', *Uganda Journal*, 30 (1966), 165–73.

Throup, D., 'The Origins of Mau Mau', *African Affairs*, 84 (1985), 399–433.

Throup, D., *The Economic and Social Origins of Mau Mau 1945-53* (London, 1987).

Tibenderana, P.K., 'Supernatural sanctions and peacekeeping among the Bakiga of western Uganda during the 19th century', *Journal of African Studies*, 7 (1986), 144-51.

Tiffen, M., 'Land and Capital: Blind spots in the study of the 'resource-poor' farmer', in M. Leach and R. Mearns (eds), *Lie of the Land: Challenging Received Wisdom on the African Environment* (London, 1996).

Tiffen, M., M. Mortimore and F. Gichuki, *More People, Less Erosion: Environmental Recovery in Kenya* (Chichester, 1994).

Tilley, H., 'African environments and environmental sciences', in W. Beinart and J. McGregor (eds), *Social History and African Environments* (Oxford, 2003), 109–30.

Tindituuza, R.J., 'Study on land tenure at Nyarurambi parish', in R. Tindituuza and B.M. Kateete, *Essays on Land Fragmentation in Kigezi District* (Makerere, Geography Dept, Occasional Paper 22, 1971).

Tosh, J., 'The cash crop revolution in tropical Africa: An agricultural reappraisal', *African Affairs*, 79 (1980), 79–94.

Tosh, J., *Clan Leaders and Colonial chiefs in Lango: The Political History of an East African Stateless Society*, *c1800-1939* (Oxford, 1978).

Tosh, J., 'Lango agriculture during early colonial period: Land and labour in a cash crop economy', *Journal of African History*, 19 (1978), 415–39.

Tothill, J.D., *Agriculture in Uganda* 1st edition (London, 1940).

Toulmin, C. and J. Quan (eds), *Evolving Land Rights, Policy and Tenure in Africa* (London, 2000).

Tripp, A., 'Women's movements, customary law, and land rights in Africa: the case of Uganda', *African Studies Quarterly*, 7 4 (2004) [online].

Tukahirwa E.M., (ed.), *Environmental and Natural Resource Management Policy and Law: Issues and Options, Summary* (Washington, DC, 1992).

Tukahirwa, E.M., *Soil Erosion Research: The Uganda experience - A review* (Kampala, 1994).

Tukahirwa, E.M. and P. Veit, *Public Policy and Legislation in Environmental Management: Terracing in Nyarurembo, Uganda* (Nairobi, 1992).

Tukahirwa, J.M., 'Soil resources in the highlands of Uganda: Prospects and sensitivities', *Mountain Research and Development*, 8 (1988), 165–72.

Turner, B.L., K. Kates and G. Hyden, *Population Growth and Agrarian Change in Africa* (Gainesville, FL, 1993).

Turyagenda, J.D., 'Overpopulation and its effects in the gombolola of Buhara, Kigezi', *Uganda Journal*, 28 (1964), 127–33.

Turyahikayo-Rugyema, B., 'A history of the Bakiga in south western Uganda and northern Rwanda c1500–1930' (PhD, University of Michigan, 1974).

Turyahikayo-Rugyema, B., 'The origins and development of the Nyabingi cult in southern Uganda and Northern Rwanda', *Makerere Historical Journal*, 2 (1976), 145–66.

Turyahikayo-Rugyema, B., 'Bakiga institutions of government', *Uganda Journal*, 40 (1982), 14–27.

Turyahikayo-Rugyema, B., 'The British imposition of colonial rule on Uganda: The Buganda agents in Kigezi, 1908-30', *Transafrican Journal of History*, 5 (1976), 111–33.

Turyahikayo-Rugyema, B., 'The introduction of Christianity on East African societies - A case study of the Bakiga of SW Uganda', *Makerere Historical Journal*, 2 (1976), 57–72.

Turyahikayo-Rugyema, B., *Philosophy and Traditional Religion of the Bakiga in South West Uganda* (Nairobi, 1983).

Vail, D.J., *A History of Agricultural Innovation and Development in Teso District, Uganda* (Syracuse, NY, 1972).

Van Zwanenberg, R.M.A. with A. King, *An Economic History of Kenya and Uganda, 1800-1970* (London, 1975).

Vincent, J., 'Colonial chiefs and the making of a class: A case study from Teso, eastern Uganda', *Africa*, 47 (1977), 140–59.

Vincent, J., *Teso in Transformation: The Political Economy of Peasant and Class in Eastern Africa* (Berkeley, CA, 1982).

Vokes, R., 'The Kanungu Fire: Transformations of the Nyabingi Spirit Cult' Paper presented at 'Qualities of Time', ASA Conference 2002, Arusha.

Vokes, R., 'The Kanungu Fire: Power, patronage and exchange in south western Uganda' (PhD, University of Oxford, 2003).

Wallman, S., *Take Out Hunger: Two Case Studies of Rural Development in Basutoland* (London, 1969).

Were, J.M., 'Population pressure, land use changes and consequences on the environment in Kabale District.' (Makerere University Department of Geography, Kampala, 1992) (mimeo).

West, H.W., *Mailo Policy in Buganda: A Preliminary Case Study in African Land Tenure* (Entebbe, 1964).

West, H.W., *Land Policy in Buganda* (Cambridge, 1972).

Weyel, V., 'Land ownership in Nyakinengo, Ruzhumbura.' (EAISR Conference, 1972).

White, H., 'Challenges in evaluating development effectiveness', *IDS Working paper*, 242, (2005).

White, L., 'Blood brotherhood revisited: kinship, relationship, and the body in East and Central Africa', *Africa*, 64 3 (1994), 359–72.

Whitehead, A., 'Continuities and discontinuities in political constructions of the working man in rural sub-Saharan Africa: The 'lazy man' in African agriculture', *European Journal of Development Research*, 12 2 (2000), 23–52.

Whitehead, A. and D. Tsikata, 'Policy Discourses on Women's Land Rights in sub-Saharan Africa: The implications of the return to the customary'

Journal of Agrarian Change, 3 1 (2003), 67–112.

Wiggins, S., 'Success stories from African agriculture: what are the key elements of success?', *IDS Bulletin*, 36 2 (2005), 17–22.

Wiggins, S. and S. Proctor, 'Migration and the rural non-farm sector', (Reading, *mimeo*, 1999).

Williams, G., 'Modernizing Malthus: The World Bank, population control and the African environment', in J. Crush, *Power of Development* (London, 1995).

Willis, J., 'Clan and History in Western Uganda: A new perspective on the origins of pastoral dominance', *International Journal of African Historical Studies*, 30 3 (1997), 583–600.

World Bank, *Land Reform* (Washington, 1974).

World Bank, *Population Growth and Policies in Sub-Saharan Africa* (Washington, DC, 1986).

World Bank, *Sub-Saharan Africa: from crisis to sustainable growth* (Washington, DC, 1989).

Worster, D., *The Ends of the Earth* (New York, 1988).

Worster, D. and A.W. Crosby, *Studies in Environment and History* (Cambridge, 1995).

Worthington, E.B., *Science in Africa* (London, 1938).

Wright, A.C.A., 'Kitozho Mutala Survey' (1938).

Wrigley, C.C., *Crops and Wealth in Uganda: A Short Agrarian History* (Kampala, 1959).

Xavier, N., *Land Privatisation, Security of Tenure and Agricultural Production: The Ugandan Experience*. Institute of Social Studies Working Paper (The Hague, 1997), 263.

Yeld, R.E., 'Continuity and change in Kiga patterns of marriage: An analysis of structural change in Kigezi marriage in 1930s and 60s' (EAISR Conference, 1967).

Yeld, R., 'Land hunger in Kigezi, southwest Uganda', in Raymond Apthorpe, (ed.), *Land Settlement and Rural Development in Eastern Africa* (Kampala, 1968), 24–8.

Yeld, R.E., 'The family and social change: A study among the Kiga of Kigezi, south west Uganda' (PhD, Makerere, 1969).

Yngstrom, I., 'Representations of custom, social identity and environmental relations in Tanzania 1926–1950', in W. Beinart and J. McGregor (eds), *Social History and African Environments* (Oxford, 2003).

Yngstrom, I., 'Women, wives and land rights in Africa: Situating gender beyond the household in the debate over land policy and changing tenure systems', *Oxford Development Studies*, 30 1 (2002), 21–40.

Young, R. and H. Fosbrooke, *Smoke in the Hills: Land and Politics among the Luguru of Tanganyika* (London, 1960).

Zake, J. Y. K., *Report of the Soil Fertility Survey of South Western Region Kabale and Rukungiri*. South-west Regional Agricultural Rehabilitation Project (Mbarara, 1991).

Index